Moodle 3 Administration
Third Edition

An administrator's guide to configuring, securing, customizing, and extending Moodle

Alex Büchner

BIRMINGHAM - MUMBAI

Moodle 3 Administration
Third Edition

First published: September 2008

Second Edition: October 2011

Third Edition: February 2016

Production reference: 1240216

Published by Packt Publishing Ltd.
Livery Place
35 Livery Street
Birmingham B3 2PB, UK.

ISBN 978-1-78328-971-4

www.packtpub.com

Credits

Author
Alex Büchner

Reviewers
Chad Outten

Ian Rifkin

Shashikant Vaishnav

Acquisition Editors
Reshma Raman

Rebecca Youe

Content Development Editor
Rashmi Suvarna

Technical Editor
Shivani Kiran Mistry

Copy Editor
Sonia Cheema

Project Coordinator
Suzanne Coutinho

Proofreader
Safis Editing

Indexer
Tejal Daruwale Soni

Production Coordinator
Nilesh Mohite

Cover Work
Nilesh Mohite

About the Author

Alex Büchner is the co-founder and technical director of the Platinum Totara, Moodle, and Mahara partner, Synergy Learning. He has been involved in system and database administration for more than two decades and has been administering virtual learning environments of all shapes and sizes since their advent on the educational landscape.

Alex holds a PhD in computer science and an MSc in software engineering. He has authored over 50 international publications, including two books, and is a frequent speaker on Totara, Moodle, Mahara, and related open source technologies. His first two books on Moodle Administration by Packt Publishing have become the de facto standard on the topic.

The best learning experience in Moodle is provided when communication and collaboration is utilized. The same has been applied in writing this book, which would not have been possible without the support of the Packt editorial team.

I would like to thank the reviewers for their constructive feedback provided during the reviewing process. This book would not be the same without your comments and suggestions.

Special thanks must go to all my colleagues at Synergy Learning. No matter how tricky the Moodle problem, somebody will always be there to come up with a rock solid solution.

I have to thank all our customers. Without you, we wouldn't be aware of all the Moodle hitches and glitches that are out there. Keep them coming!

Last but not least, I have to thank AB + ab for their support and patience while I have been hiding away writing yet another book. I will make up for it. Promise!

About the Reviewers

Chad Outten is a qualified educator and technologist with more than 15 years of experience in the education and ICT sectors. He is the Managing Director at My Learning Space, an Australian e-learning company, and has worked closely with high-profile organizations such as eBay, Shell, Ricoh, iiNet, Rip Curl, and Queensland Health, among a diverse range of clients to help them improve staff performance and business outcomes through better learning, training, and compliance programs.

Chad is a Moodle certified teacher and has acted as a mentor and assessor for the internationally recognized Moodle Teacher Certification program. He is a proud member of the esteemed Particularly Helpful Moodlers and Quality Assurance Testers groups at `moodle.org`, and in 2008, he organized the Australian Moodle Moot. Chad is passionate about e-learning, admires educators, and understands the value of a good learning management system to address the challenges of 21st century education.

Ian Rifkin has experience with servers and applications (purchased, open source, and custom), and acts as a release engineer for his institution. He has in-depth knowledge of web application development and middleware integrations, including identity management systems. He is a developer and manager who has intimate knowledge of command-line Unix environments.

He has worked with Moodle as a student, faculty member, and administrator. Currently, he is employed as the software systems manager at Brandeis University, where he manages a small web team. He also holds a part-time adjunct instructor role for the Graduate Professional Studies division at Brandeis University, where he teaches web content management and web application development.

Ian holds an M.Sc. degree in information technology management and a BA degree in anthropology (with a minor in Internet studies). In his spare time, he enjoys computer games, genealogy research, baking, gardening, and spending time with his wife, Valerie, and son, Caleb.

Shashikant Vaishnav was born and brought up in Jodhpur, a desert town in Rajasthan, India. He's involved with a London-based Seedcamp-supported start-up, Shoprocket. It's an e-commerce system delivered over the cloud and integrates seamlessly into any application with a single line of code.

He is been involved with Moodle for quite a long time as a student. While an undergraduate, he participated in Google's Summer of Code program and integrated Apache Solr with Moodle. He also participated as a mentor in Google's Code-in program for the Sugar Labs organization.

He finished his graduation from the Government Engineering college Bikaner with a bachelor's of engineering and technology degree in computer science in 2013. His focus on academics aside, he harbors a deep interest in music and sports.

He loves to blog about his experiences with open source technology, travel, and life. He reads spiritual books, indulges in photography, and hacks around with open source projects.

He previously collaborated with Packt Publishing as a technical reviewer of *Git Version Control Cookbook* and *Moodle 3 Administration, Third Edition*.

www.PacktPub.com

eBooks, discount offers, and more

Did you know that Packt offers eBook versions of every book published, with PDF and ePub files available? You can upgrade to the eBook version at www.PacktPub.com and as a print book customer, you are entitled to a discount on the eBook copy. Get in touch with us at customercare@packtpub.com for more details.

At www.PacktPub.com, you can also read a collection of free technical articles, sign up for a range of free newsletters and receive exclusive discounts and offers on Packt books and eBooks.

https://www2.packtpub.com/books/subscription/packtlib

Do you need instant solutions to your IT questions? PacktLib is Packt's online digital book library. Here, you can search, access, and read Packt's entire library of books.

Why subscribe?

- Fully searchable across every book published by Packt
- Copy and paste, print, and bookmark content
- On demand and accessible via a web browser

Table of Contents

Preface

Since its launch in 2002, Moodle has become the benchmark that every learning management system is measured against. It has won a wide range of international accolades and established itself as an ecosystem for a large number of educational tools and services.

Moodle 3 Administration, Third Edition is a complete, practical guide for administering Moodle sites. It covers setting up Moodle, configuration, and day-to-day administrative tasks as well as advanced options to customize and extend Moodle.

The author, who has been at the cutting edge of Moodle administration since its advent, has adopted a problem-solution approach to bring the content in line with your day-to-day operations. The practical examples will help you to set up Moodle for large organizations and small courses alike.

This is a one-stop reference for tasks that you will come across when administering a Moodle site of any shape or size. It not only covers core Moodle functionality, but also third-party tools and add-ons that will increase your flexibility and efficiency even further when dealing with administrative duties.

Why another book on Moodle administration? Since the second edition of the title in 2011, the system has been modified and extended significantly to cover all the relevant new functionality in Moodle 3.

What this book covers

Moodle has grown into a mature, sophisticated, and complex software system. As a result, Moodle Administration covers a wide range of topics. A fun way to demonstrate the various subjects is in the form of a tube/subway/metro/underground map (under the Creative Commons license by Synergy Learning):

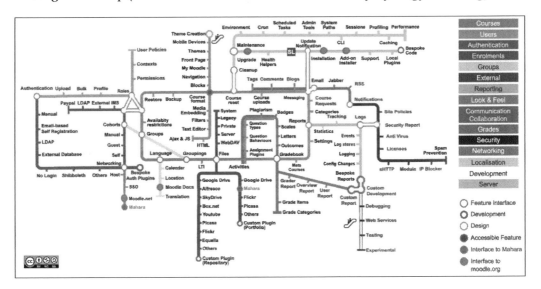

Chapter 1, Moodle Installation, tells you about the most suitable Moodle setup for your organization, including software and hardware requirements. You will learn how to install Moodle in three environments, namely, LAMP/Unix, Windows, and Mac OS, before Moodle updates options are covered in detail. Throughout the chapter, you will also learn how to perform some of the described operations using the Moodle Command-line Interface (CLI), Git, and Moodle Shell (Moosh).

Chapter 2, The Moodle System, covers the building blocks of the learning platform. First, we cover the Moodle architecture, that is, the main Moodle components and where its data and code is stored. We then provide you with the skills to find your way a round in Moodle via its intuitive user and administration interface. Finally, we deal with the management of files, which includes Moodle's standard file management, web host file management, and file management via the file system repository.

Chapter 3, Courses, Users, and Roles, gives you an overview of Moodle courses, users, and roles. It covers the basics of the three key concepts and demonstrates how the three core elements are inherently intertwined.

Chapter 4, Course Management, shows you how to set up new courses (also in bulk) and organize them in categories. The remainder of the chapter deals with an array of enrolment options, covering Moodle's internal enrolment (manual, self, and guest), cohort enrolment and synchronization, database-driven enrolment, for instance, via LDAP, meta courses, and payment-driven enrolments.

Chapter 5, User Management, explains how to manage users on your system. We first cover what user profiles look like and how they can be extended before presenting (manual and bulk) standard user actions. We then explain how to add users to Moodle manually, that is, one-by-one, and via batch upload before dealing with cohorts. Then, you will learn about a plethora of authentication mechanisms that Moodle equips us with. Finally, we discuss the best practices of user naming schemes.

Chapter 6, Managing Permissions – Roles and Capabilities, guides you through permission management. It applies roles and capabilities to users in different contexts. We will cover the assignment of roles, modification of existing roles, and creation of new roles before we deal with any administrative role-related settings.

Chapter 7, Moodle Look and Feel, tells you how to adapt your Moodle system to bring it in line with the corporate branding of your organization. We will cover the customization of the front page, basic creation of Moodle themes, and support for mobile devices via responsive themes. You will also learn how to configure the Moodle editor and support users with accessibility requirements.

Chapter 8, Moodle Plugins, explains in detail how to extend your Moodle system via third-party add-ons. You will be able to distinguish between good add-ons and not-so-good add-ons before we cover extensions that are popular with other users. We will then cover how to install, configure, and uninstall third-party add-ons. Plugins that are covered are activities, blocks and filters, repositories, portfolios, text editors, licenses, question types and behaviors, plagiarism prevention, licenses, and availability restrictions.

Chapter 9, Moodle Configuration, deals with the educational and technical configuration of your Moodle system. Pedagogical topics that are covered are badges, collaboration (blogs, comments and tags), LTI, localization, grades and gradebook settings, and a number of miscellaneous parameters. Technical subjects that are dealt with include synchronous communication (instant messaging and video conferencing), asynchronous communication (inbound and messaging as well as RSS feeds), and a number of experimental settings.

Chapter 10, *Moodle Logging and Reporting*, equips you with the tools that you require in order to interpret and analyze the vast amount of usage data that Moodle is collecting. You will learn about the logging framework and monitoring facilities provided by Moodle that include activity reporting, user tracking, and some basic statistics. Then, we will take a look at third-party tools that cover learning analytics, report generation, web log analyzers, and live data trackers such as Google Analytics and Piwik.

Chapter 11, *Moodle Security and Privacy*, focuses on ensuring that the data in your Moodle system is protected from any misuse. You will learn about security notifications, user security, data and content security, and system security. We will conclude the chapter with information on privacy and data protection concerns.

Chapter 12, *Moodle Performance and Optimization*, makes sure that your Moodle system runs to its full potential. We will cover configuring, monitoring, and fine-tuning your virtual learning environment for maximum speed. You will learn how to optimize Moodle content before we focus on system parameters, namely, caching via the Moodle Universal Cache (MUC), session handling, cron management, scheduled tasks, module settings, and miscellaneous settings. We also present some basic performance profiling and monitoring tools.

Chapter 13, *Backup and Restore*, focuses on ensuring that your data would not be lost in the event of a disaster. We will cover course backups, site backups, system backups, and restoring data from the taken data archives.

Chapter 14, *Moodle Admin Tools*, covers Moodle admin tools that assist you with certain specific administrative tasks. These include web-based helpers such as upgrade and database tools as well as CLI scripts. We will also be looking at some add-ons, especially the powerful Moodle Shell, Moosh.

Chapter 15, *Moodle Integration*, looks at ways to integrate Moodle with other systems via web services. We will provide information about the basic concepts of Moodle web services before you learn how to set up external systems and users controlling Moodle. This also covers the support for the official mobile app.

Chapter 16, *Moodle Networking*, tells you how to connect disparate Moodle and Totara systems either in a peer-to-peer setup or via a Moodle hub. You will also be able to apply the learned networking techniques to connect the popular open source e-portfolio system, Mahara, and the social learning tool, Totara Social, to Moodle. We will further show you how to connect to Moodle.net and set up your own community hub.

Appendix, *Configuration Settings*, provides you with a list of parameters that can be modified in Moodle's configuration file and the impact that each of these values will have. The areas covered are Administration Settings and System Settings.

What you need for this book

For Moodle, you must have the following components up and running on your server (at the time of writing for version 3.0):

- **Database**: MySQL (version 5.5.31 or later with the InnoDB storage engine activated), PostgreSQL (9.1 or later), Microsoft SQL Server (2008 or later), Oracle (10.2 or later), or Maria DB (5.5.31 or later)
- **Web server**: Apache is the preferred web server, but Microsoft IIS is also possible
- PHP 5.4.4 or later is required to run Moodle (PHP 7 is supported as well)

PHP extensions: Moodle makes use of a number of PHP extensions—most of which are compiled in PHP by default.

Depending on your specific setup, additional software and hardware might be required.

Who this book is for

This book is written for technicians and systems administrators as well as academic staff, that is, basically for anyone who has to administer a Moodle system. Whether you are dealing with a small-scale local Moodle system or a large-scale multi-site Virtual Learning Environment (VLE), this book will assist you with any administrative tasks. Some basic Moodle knowledge is helpful, but not essential.

VLE job functions

A Moodle administrator is basically a VLE administrator who manages a Moodle system. A quick search through recruitment agencies specializing in the educational sector reveals a growing number of dedicated job titles that are closely related to VLE administration. A few examples are as follows:

- VLE administrator (or LMS administrator or MLE administrator)
- VLE support officer
- VLE architect
- VLE engineer
- VLE coordinator

The list does not include functions that regularly act in an administrative capacity, such as IT support. It also does not include roles that are situated in the pedagogical field, but often take on the work of a VLE administrator, such as learning technologists or e-learning coordinators.

A VLE administrator usually works very closely with the staff who has the responsibility for the administration of IT systems, databases, and networks. It has been proven beneficial to have some basic skills in these areas. Additionally, links are likely in larger organizations where content management systems, student information management systems, and other related infrastructure is present.

Given this growing number of VLE administration-related roles, let's look at some key obligations of the job functions and what skills are essential and desirable.

Obligations and skill sets of a VLE administrator

The responsibilities of a VLE administrator differ from organization to organization. However, there are some obligations that are common across installations and setups:

- User management (learners, teachers, and others)
- Course management (prospectus mapping)
- Module management (functionality provided to users)
- Look and feel of the VLE (often carried out by a web designer)
- Year-end maintenance (if applicable)
- Beginning-of-year setup (if applicable)
- Support teaching staff and learners

In addition to these VLE-specific features, you are required to make sure that the virtual learning environment is secure and stable and performs well. Backups have to be in place, monitoring has to be set up, reports about usage have to be produced, and regular system maintenance has to be carried out.

If you host your own system, you will be responsible for all of the listed tasks and many more. If your VLE is hosted in a managed environment, some of the tasks closer to system level will be carried out by the hosting provider. So, it is important that they have a good understanding of Moodle. Either way, you will be the first person to be contacted by staff and learners if anything goes wrong, if they require new functionality, or if some administrative task has to be carried out.

 With great power comes great responsibility!

While a range of e-learning-related activities are now taught as part of some academic and vocational qualifications (for instance, instructional design or e-moderation), VLE administration per se is not. Most VLE administrators have a technical background and often have some system or database administration knowledge. Again, it entirely depends on whether you host your VLE locally or externally. The administration skills of a remotely hosted system can be learned by anybody with some technical knowledge. However, for an internally hosted system, you will require a good working knowledge of the operating system on which the VLE is installed, the underlying database that is used, the network in which the VLE has to operate, and any further components that have to work with the learning system.

Conventions

In this book, you will find a number of text styles that distinguish between different kinds of information. Here are some examples of these styles and an explanation of their meaning.

Code words in text are shown as follows:

If the `cron.php` script is invoked over HTTP (either using `wget` or `curl`), more memory is used than calling directly via the `php -f` command.

Any command-line input and output is written as follows:

There are two ways you can create a so-called database dump from a MySQL database, either via command line or via Moodle's optional database interface.

The simplest syntax for the command line tool is:

```
mysqldump -u <user> -p <database> > backup.sql
```

New terms and **important words** are introduced in a bold-type font. Words that you see on the screen, in menus or dialog boxes for example, appear in our text like this:

Clicking on the **Enabled protocols** link in the overview table will guide you to **Plugins | Web services | Manage protocols** screen.

Warnings or important notes appear in a box like this.

Tips and tricks appear like this.

Reader feedback

Feedback from our readers is always welcome. Let us know what you think about this book—what you liked or disliked. Reader feedback is important for us as it helps us develop titles that you will really get the most out of.

To send us general feedback, simply e-mail feedback@packtpub.com, and mention the book's title in the subject of your message.

If there is a topic that you have expertise in and you are interested in either writing or contributing to a book, see our author guide at www.packtpub.com/authors.

Customer support

Now that you are the proud owner of a Packt book, we have a number of things to help you to get the most from your purchase.

Downloading the color images of this book

We also provide you with a PDF file that has color images of the screenshots/diagrams used in this book. The color images will help you better understand the changes in the output. You can download this file from http://www.packtpub.com/sites/default/files/downloads/Moodle3AdministrationThirdEdition_ColorImages.pdf.

Errata

Although we have taken every care to ensure the accuracy of our content, mistakes do happen. If you find a mistake in one of our books—maybe a mistake in the text or the code—we would be grateful if you could report this to us. By doing so, you can save other readers from frustration and help us improve subsequent versions of this book. If you find any errata, please report them by visiting http://www.packtpub.com/submit-errata, selecting your book, clicking on the **Errata Submission Form** link, and entering the details of your errata. Once your errata are verified, your submission will be accepted and the errata will be uploaded to our website or added to any list of existing errata under the Errata section of that title.

To view the previously submitted errata, go to https://www.packtpub.com/books/content/support and enter the name of the book in the search field. The required information will appear under the **Errata** section.

Piracy

Piracy of copyrighted material on the Internet is an ongoing problem across all media. At Packt, we take the protection of our copyright and licenses very seriously. If you come across any illegal copies of our works in any form on the Internet, please provide us with the location address or website name immediately so that we can pursue a remedy.

Please contact us at copyright@packtpub.com with a link to the suspected pirated material.

We appreciate your help in protecting our authors and our ability to bring you valuable content.

Questions

If you have a problem with any aspect of this book, you can contact us at questions@packtpub.com, and we will do our best to address the problem.

1
Moodle Installation

Let's get started by installing Moodle.

After providing an overview that describes which setup is most suitable, software as well as hardware requirements are outlined.

We will then cover the following installations:

- Installing Moodle in a LAMP/Unix environment
- Installing Moodle in a Windows environment
- Installing Moodle in a Mac OS X environment
- Installing Moodle via the Command Line Interface (CLI)
- Upgrading Moodle manually and via CLI and Git

You will only need to study the section(s) of the operating system(s) you are planning to use. Moodle can be scaled from a single instructor to an entire institution. We will only be able to cover the most *common* installations and present solutions to some common problems. We also have to assume that you are familiar with basic system administration of the operating system on which you will be installing Moodle.

Moodle installation – an overview

Before we start installing Moodle, you have to decide which setup is right for your organization. Once you have come to a conclusion, there are a number of prerequisites that you have to provide before we can get started.

Choosing the best setup

There are a number of different environments in which you can set up Moodle. The three main criteria that should dictate the choice of the correct setup are:

- **Flexibility**: If you want to have full control over your system, be able to tweak system settings, and make frequent changes to the setup, you are best suited to host your own server. However, if your preferred choice is to only administer Moodle while somebody else is looking after the operating system, the web server, and backups, it is better to opt for a professionally-hosted setup, and particularly, the offerings provided by the authorized Moodle Partners.

- **Scalability**: This is entirely driven by the number of concurrent users, that is, the number of active learners and teachers logged in to Moodle at the same time. A Moodle on a single-processor desktop computer will not be able to cope with hundreds of simultaneously logged-in users. A load-balanced cluster, on the other hand, would be overkill for a small institution with a handful of learners. The following table provides some indicative setups for different types of educational organizations, and is by no means complete:

Max number of concurrent users	Recommended setup
1 (to experiment locally)	Desktop, laptop, memory stick
20 (single class)	Public server or https://moodlecloud.com/en/
100 (small school / company)	Shared server
250 (large school / company)	Dedicated server
500 (medium-to-large college)	Dedicated application and database servers
+500 (university/corporate)	Load-balanced cluster

Please bear in mind that these are only indicative numbers, which are not written in stone, and also depend on the other factors mentioned here. The mentioned hosting option on https://moodlecloud.com/en/ offers free Moodle hosting by Moodle HQ with a number of limitations: maximum number of users is set to 50, storage capacity is limited to 200 MB, there is no ability to install plugins, and there is advertisement displayed throughout the site. This is a good way to try out Moodle, but not intended for production sites.

Organizations require a server (either dedicated or shared) that is either hosted in-house or externally. If you decide to go down the hosted route, it is highly recommended to avoid a cheap hosting package as their systems are not optimized for Moodle usage. This will have a significant impact on the performance of the system, especially with an increasing number of users.

- **Cost**: Budgetary constraints will certainly play an important role in your setup. Unless you already have the appropriate infrastructure in place, it is likely to be more cost-effective to host your Moodle system externally as it saves you from having to purchase servers and provide a 24/7 data connection that caters to your learners' needs. Licensing cost is significantly higher if you use commercial operating systems, web servers, and database systems, instead of an open source solution. Either way, Moodle is designed to support a wide range of possible infrastructures suitable to your organization's IT policy.

In addition to these three key criteria that usually influence the decision about the underlying infrastructure, there are other factors that will have an impact on your decision, such as *in-house expertise*, *compatibility with other systems*, *personal preference*, and *existing resources*.

We will cover the three most popular operating systems for hosting Moodle—Linux, Windows, and Mac OS. For other setups such as on a memory stick, in a virtualized environment, or a larger multi-server cluster, please consult your local Moodle Partner (https://moodle.com/). Some hosting companies offer quick one-click installations (often via the Fantastico installer, which usually doesn't contain the latest version). While the resulting Moodle system is sufficient for experimental sites, it is certainly unsuitable for production environments.

Moodle prerequisites

There are a number of hardware and software requirements that have to be satisfied before we can start installing Moodle.

Hardware requirements

These requirements apply if you host Moodle yourself or if it is hosted on an external server (shared, virtual, dedicated, or clustered). On cheaper hosting packages, the hardware configuration is often insufficient to run Moodle efficiently:

- **Disk space**: Moodle takes up between 150 MB and 200 MB of disk space. However, this only provides you with an empty system and does not take into account the space you require for any learning resources. The faster the disks, the better. RAIDed disks are recommended, but are not essential on smaller installations.

- **Memory**: The (absolute) minimum requirement is 256 MB for a single-user instance, but more is necessary in a multiuser setup. A good rule of thumb is to have 1 GB of RAM for every 10-15 concurrent users. You have to double this calculation on Windows-based systems due to the higher overhead of the operating system.

[🔆 The more RAM the better; the faster the RAM the better.]

- **CPU:** Processor type and speed is important too, but not as important as RAM. As always, the faster the CPU the better, and the more cores a CPU has, the more powerful it will be.

- **Network**: While Moodle can run on a standalone machine, its full potential is in a networked environment. A fast network card is essential, as is good upload and download speed if the LMS is accessed over the Internet.

Software requirements

While it is recommend to have the latest version installed, for Moodle 3, you must have the following components up and running on your server (release specific notes can be found at `https://docs.moodle.org/dev/Releases`):

- **Database**: Moodle officially supports four database systems: MySQL (version 5.5.31 or later utilizing the ACID-compliant InnoDB storage engine), PostgreSQL (version 9.1+), MariaDB (version 5.5.31+) Microsoft SQL Server (version 2008+), and Oracle (version 10.2+).

- **Web server**: Apache is the preferred web server option, but Moodle works well with any other web server that supports PHP such as Microsoft IIS.

- **PHP**: PHP 5.4.4 is the minimum PHP version to run Moodle 3. PHP 7 is also supported. There are a number of PHP settings, which you might have to change in the `php.ini` or `.htaccess` file (see `https://docs.moodle.org/en/ Installing_Moodle` for more details).

- **PHP extensions**: Moodle makes use of a number of extensions, most of which are compiled into PHP, by default. They are as follows:

  - **Compulsory extensions**: `curl`, `ctype`, `dom`, `gd`, `hash`, `iconv`, `json`, `pcre`, `simplexml`, `spl`, `xml`, `zip`, and `zlib`

  - **Recommended extensions**: `intl`, `mbstring`, `openssl`, `tokenizer`, `soap`, and `xmlrpc`

  - **Conditional extensions**: `mysql`, `odbc`, `pgsql`, (depending on database) and `ldap`, `ntlm`, and so on (depending on authentication mechanism used)

Depending on your specific setup, additional software and hardware might be required. It is assumed that the database, web server, PHP, and its extensions have been installed correctly as this is not a VLE administrator task. Once this is the case, we are ready to go.

 Internet Explorer 8 is not supported by Moodle. A modern web browser (Internet Explorer 9+, Firefox 25+, Google Chrome 30+, or Safari 6+) is required to access Moodle.

Installation in a LAMP environment

Moodle is developed in Linux using Apache, MySQL, and PHP (known as the **LAMP platform**). If you have a choice, this is the preferred environment to use. There is ongoing debate whether PostgreSQL is the more suitable database option, but we will stick with MySQL as this is the system most administrators are familiar with. Also, some organizations are bound to Microsoft SQL or Oracle. If this is the case, please refer to the respective installation guide as this is beyond the scope of this book.

Downloading Moodle

Go to `https://download.moodle.org/` and select **Latest release** in the **Standard Moodle** section:

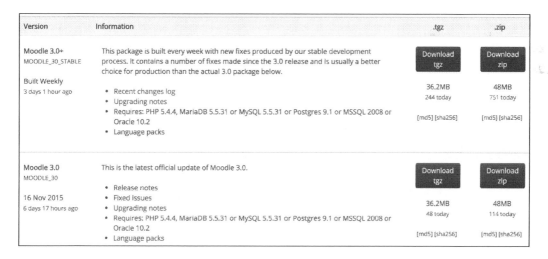

Version	Information	.tgz	.zip
Moodle 3.0+ MOODLE_30_STABLE Built Weekly 3 days 1 hour ago	This package is built every week with new fixes produced by our stable development process. It contains a number of fixes made since the 3.0 release and is usually a better choice for production than the actual 3.0 package below. • Recent changes log • Upgrading notes • Requires: PHP 5.4.4, MariaDB 5.5.31 or MySQL 5.5.31 or Postgres 9.1 or MSSQL 2008 or Oracle 10.2 • Language packs	Download tgz 36.2MB 244 today [md5] [sha256]	Download zip 48MB 751 today [md5] [sha256]
Moodle 3.0 MOODLE_30 16 Nov 2015 6 days 17 hours ago	This is the latest official update of Moodle 3.0. • Release notes • Fixed issues • Upgrading notes • Requires: PHP 5.4.4, MariaDB 5.5.31 or MySQL 5.5.31 or Postgres 9.1 or MSSQL 2008 or Oracle 10.2 • Language packs	Download tgz 36.2MB 48 today [md5] [sha256]	Download zip 48MB 114 today [md5] [sha256]

By the time of reading, a newer version is likely to be available. If you wish to go with the 3.0 version this book has been written for, select **Other supported releases** on the right; otherwise, feel free to go with the latest stable build; most content in this book will still be applicable.

There are five types of builds available on Moodle's download site:

- **Latest release**: For the current version of Moodle, there are two releases — the latest stable build and the latest official release. The latest stable version is created weekly (every Wednesday) and is the best choice for a new server. The latest official release contains the stable build as well as new fixes, but the version will not have gone through the weekly code review and might contain unresolved issues.

- **Other supported releases**: Older versions than the current one are maintained by the Moodle development team and bug fixes are back-ported for 12 months after release. Sometimes, the newly-added functionality is back-ported. Version 3.1 will be a long-term support release and will be supported for 3 years.

- **Security-only-supported releases**: For one further release, critical fixes that will impact on security or data loss will be provided, but no other bug fixes will be back-ported.

- **Legacy releases**: For older versions, the last build is made available. However, these are not maintained any further.

- **Development release**: Moodle also offers you the option to download beta releases of the software (if available) and also the latest development release. These should only be downloaded for testing or development purposes, never in production environments!

Each version is made available in the two compressed formats: TGZ (use the `tar` command to uncompress) and ZIP (requires `unzip`). You can either download them by clicking on the respective link or, if you have (secure) shell access, retrieve the file directly by using the `wget` command:

```
wget http://download.moodle.org/moodle/moodle-latest.zip
```

 The location where you install Moodle is referred to as `dirroot`.

If you make use of **Moodle Shell** (**MOOSH**), which is described in more detail in *Chapter 14*, *Moodle Admin Tools*, you can use the following command to download the latest stable branch of Moodle:

```
moosh download-moodle
```

Once you have moved the file to the location where you want to install it on your web server (`dirroot`), extract the file using the `unzip` command (or `tar xvfz` if you downloaded the TGZ version). In a hosted environment, you might have to use the uncompressing method provided by the web administration interface (cPanel, Plesk, or any bespoke system):

```
unzip moodle-latest.zip
```
```
tar xvfz moodle-latest.tgz
```

If you place the entire folder in your web server documents directory, the site will be located at `www.yourwebserver.com/moodle`. To access your site from `www.yourwebserver.com`, copy the contents directly into the main web server's documents directory.

 The URL via which Moodle is accessed is referred to as `wwwroot`.

Once this has been successfully done, you have to create the database that Moodle uses to store its data.

Creating the Moodle database and the data directory

Moodle requires a database where it can store its information. While it is possible to share an existing database, it is highly recommended to create a separate database for Moodle. This can either be done via a web interface, as provided for hosted servers, or via the Unix command line.

Using a hosted server

Most hosting providers provide a dedicated web interface to carry out basic database operations. Alternatively, you can use phpMyAdmin, an open source software that allows you to manage MySQL databases over the Web. It is part of most Linux distributions and many control panels, such as CPanel or Plesk. (phpMyAdmin is often configured not to allow new databases to be created. If this is the case, you have to create the database from the database manager in your control panel.)

Once you have started phpMyAdmin, go to the **Databases** section and create a new database using the UTF collation (utf8_general_ci collation). You don't need to create any tables; Moodle will be populating the database during the installation process.

While you can use an existing database user account, it is good practice to create a dedicated user for the Moodle database. This step is carried out in the **Privileges** section.

 Do not use the MySQL root account for your Moodle database!

phpMyAdmin allows you to perform both steps—creating a database and adding a new user—in a single action, as shown in the following screenshot. We will create a user, book, and also check the **Create database with same name and grant all privileges** option:

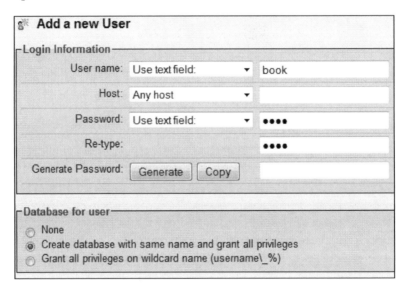

Using the command line

If you don't have access to a web interface to create MySQL databases and user accounts or if you prefer to use a Linux shell, you can perform these steps via the command line:

1. Start the database command line tool by entering mysql -root -p and enter the password at the prompt.

2. Create a database here (called moodle) by entering CREATE DATABASE moodle; (all MySQL commands have to be completed with a semicolon).

3. Set the default character and collation order to UTF8 by entering ALTER DATABASE moodle DEFAULT CHARACTER SET utf8 COLLATE utf8_ unicode_ ci;.

4. Create a user and password (here user@localhost and password, respectively) and grant database access permissions by entering GRANT SELEC T, INSERT, UPDATE, DELETE, CREATE, CREATE TEMPORARY TABLES, DROP, INDEX, ALTER ON moodle.* TO user@localhost IDENTIFIED BY 'password';.

5. Exit the MySQL command tool by entering QUIT.

It is necessary to reload the grant tables using the following command line:

```
mysqladmin -u root -p reload
```

You have now completed the database setup. All we have to do now is to create Moodle's data directory before we are ready to start the installation of Moodle itself.

Creating the Moodle data directory

Moodle stores most of its information in the database you have just created. However, any uploaded files such as assignments or pictures are stored in a separate directory. This data directory in Moodle is usually referred to as moodledata.

 The location which holds your Moodle data files is referred to as dataroot.

Later on, the Moodle installer will attempt to create this directory but, in some setups, this is not possible due to security restrictions. To be on the safe side, it is better to create moodledata manually or via a web-based file manager, as provided by some systems:

 It is crucial to create moodledata on your server where it cannot be accessed publicly, that is, outside your web directory.

1. Create the directory by entering mkdir moodledata. This is where all the uploaded files by course authors and learners will be stored, so make sure this is dimensioned properly. You might also consider to create this in a separate partition.

2. Change permissions recursively by entering chmod -R 0770 moodledata (if you use 0777, then everybody on the server will have access to the files).

3. Change the user and group of the directory to that of your web server (usually `apache` or `www-data` and `nobody` or `www-data`, respectively) by entering `chown -R apache:nobody moodledata`.

If you don't have permission to create the data directory in a secure location, create the `.htaccess` file in your home directory containing the following two lines:

```
order deny,allow
deny from all
```

This will prevent files from being accessed without the user having permissions to do so.

Running the installer script

The installer script performs two main actions—populating the database and creating the configuration file, `config.php`. The Moodle installer is initiated by entering the URL of `wwwroot` (the location where you copied Moodle) into your web browser; Moodle will recognize that it hasn't been installed yet and start the process automatically.

The Moodle installer has to set a session cookie. If your browser has been configured to trigger a warning, make sure you accept that cookie.

The first screen lets you choose the language to be used during installation. This is not the locale used for Moodle, only the language for the installation:

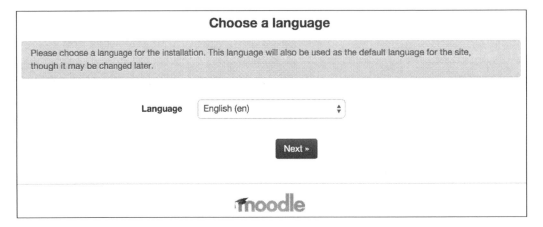

The following screenshot displays the expected values for **Web address** of the site (wwwroot), **Moodle directory** (dirroot) and **Data directory** (dataroot); you might have to modify the data directory entry if the location of your moodledata differs:

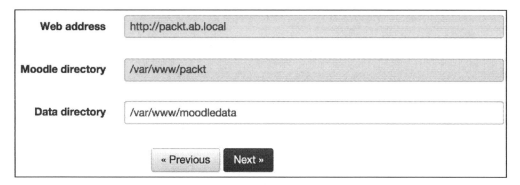

If dataroot cannot be located or does not have the correct permissions, an error message with details will be displayed. The same applies if dataroot is accessible directly via the Web and is hence, not secure.

In the following screenshot, you have to select which database you wish to use. On my system, only the drivers for MySQL, MariaDB, and PostgresSQL are installed. To use other database systems such as Oracle or MS SQL Server, the respective driver has to be installed first.

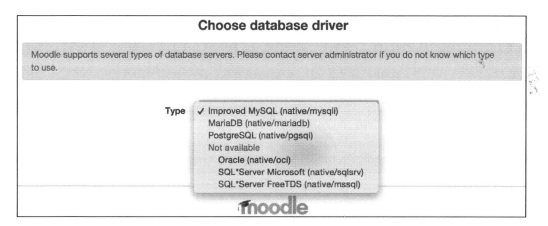

This interface is using the configuration details previously established. The following screenshot will look slightly different if you have chosen a different database driver to the native MySQL:

Improved MySQL (native/mysqli)

The database is where most of the Moodle settings and data are stored and must be configured here.

The database name, username, and password are required fields; table prefix is optional.

If the database currently does not exist, and the user you specify has permission, Moodle will attempt to create a new database with the correct permissions and settings.

Database host	localhost
Database name	packt
Database user	packt
Database password	password
Tables prefix	mdl_

Setting	Description
Database host	The default is localhost ($127.0.0.1$), which is correct if the database is located on the same server as the web server. If it is located on a separate server, specify the IP address (preferably unresolved, to improve performance).
Database name Database user Database password	This is the database name, user name, and password you enter when you run the mysql command.
Tables prefix	All the tables the Moodle installer is going to create will be prefixed with mdl_. This should only be changed if you run multiple Moodle installations using the same database.
Database port	This is the port of the database in your setup. It is usually empty or 3306.
Unix socket	If selected, the connection takes place through the file system as opposed to TCP/IP. A Unix socket file connection is marginally faster than TCP/IP, but it can only be used when connecting to a server on the same computer.

Once you see the following screen, you will know the Moodle configuration file, `config.php`, has been successfully created. If the creation of the configuration file fails (usually because of incorrect permissions), the installer will display the content of the configuration file. You will have to copy the text from the screen and paste it to `config.php` in your `dirroot`.

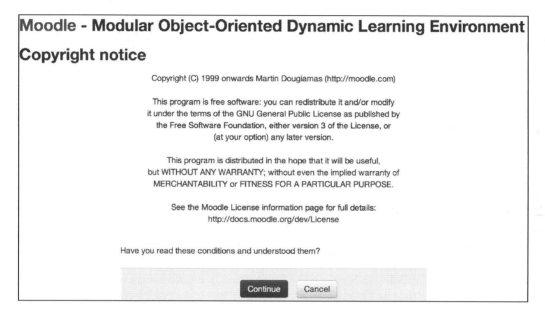

Before Moodle can proceed with the installation, you have to agree to the GPL license agreement. You find the full license text at `https://docs.moodle.org/dev/License`.

Once you have accepted the license agreement, the Moodle installer checks to see whether certain components are installed. Not all the modules are compulsory—see the *Moodle prerequisites* section in this chapter and notice on screen. The installer also verifies the key PHP settings. If any of the tests are not passed, it is important that you go back to the *Software requirements* section to resolve any problems and restart the installation process after the issues have been fixed. Otherwise, some features may not work or the installer will not continue, depending on the importance of the module.

Two common issues that arise when using MySQL are the prerequisite to use the InnoDB Barracuda file format and file-per-table mode. In both cases entries have to be added to the [mysqld] section in /etc/mysql/my.cnf (innodb_file_format=Barracuda and innodb_file_per_table, respectively).

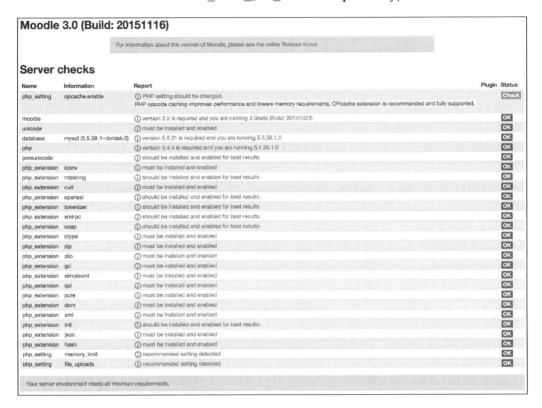

Once this screen has been confirmed, the Moodle installer will create all the tables in the database. This process might take a few minutes.

Once the table creation and population has been concluded, you will see the screen to set up the administrator account. The default **Username** is `admin`, which should be changed for security reasons. The self-explanatory fields you have to fill in are **New password**, **First name**, **Surname**, **Email address**, **City/town**, and **Select a country**. All other fields are explained in great detail in *Chapter 5, User Management*.

Installation

On this page you should configure your main administrator account which will have complete control over the site. Make sure you give it a secure username and password as well as a valid email address. You can create more admin accounts later on.

▶ Expand all

General

Username*	admin
Choose an authentication method ⑦	Manual accounts
	The password must have at least 8 characters, at least 1 digit(s), at least 1 lower case letter(s), at least 1 upper case letter(s), at least 1 non-alphanumeric character(s)
New password* ⑦	·········· ▢ Unmask
Force password change ⑦	▢
First name*	Alex
Surname*	Büchner
Email address*	··························
Email display	Allow everyone to see my email address ⬍

The last screen of the installation script asks you to enter some front page settings, namely, the **Full site name**, **Short name for site** and **Front page description**. These front page settings can be modified later (see *Chapter 7, Moodle Look and Feel*). Additionally, the installer allows you to turn on **Self registration**. Leave this disabled for now, until you have covered *Chapter 5, User Management*.

Once this information has been entered and the screen has been confirmed, you are ready to start using Moodle. However, it is recommended to finalize the installation and to set up the execution of the Moodle maintenance script.

Finalizing the installation

To make sure that Moodle is running without problems, go to **Notifications** in the **Site administration** menu in the **Settings** block:

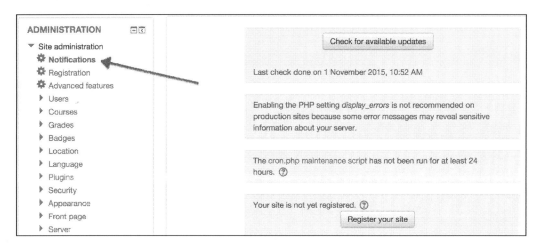

In the case of my installation, there are two issues—a PHP setting has a value that is not recommended (I have to change this in the php.ini file) and the so-called **cron** maintenance script has not run for at least 24 hours. We will solve that mystery after we have registered our site. Other messages might appear in the **Notifications** area, and you should resolve them in due course.

Moodle provides some statistics about its usage on https://moodle.net/ stats/. To be included in these figures, you have to register your Moodle site. **Registration**(below the **Notification** link) with https://moodle.org/ (MOOCH) is optional and free, and you decide what information will be made public. Even if you opt out of providing any usage patterns for your site, it is still highly recommended to register, as you will get occasional notices, for example, advanced security alerts:

The settings for the registration screen are as follows:

Field	Description
Name	The name of your site, as you just specified in the front page settings.
Privacy	You have these options: • **Please do not publish this site(default)** • **Publish the site name only** • **Publish the site name with a link**
Description	This is a short narrative describing your site.
Language	This is the language your site is published in.
Postal address/Country	Enter your address and select the country in which your organization is located.
Geolocation	This is the latitude and longitude of your location.
Administrator	Enter your name.
Phone/Email address	Enter your contact phone number and e-mail address.
Contact form	By default, Moodle creates a form for other Moodle users to contact you—this can be turned off.
Email notifications	By default, Moodle e-mails you important information, such as upgrades and security issues.
Site Url, **Moodle version**, **Moodle release** and **More information**	This is the data sent to `https://moodle.org/` on a regular basis. This information will not be displayed to the public and will only be used for statistical purposes.

Setting up the cron process

Moodle has to perform a number of background tasks on a regular basis. The script that performs these tasks is known as a cron script, and is executed by the cron process. An entire page has been dedicated to this in the Moodle documentation; you can find it at `https://docs.moodle.org/en/Cron`. It is important that you set up the cron process; otherwise, any timed Moodle features, such as scheduled backups, sending forum notifications, statistics processing, and so on, will not work.

The script, `cron.php`, is located in the `admin` directory and can be triggered manually through a web browser (unless your security settings have been changed). Once executed, the output from the script (`http://yoursite/admin/cron.php`) is shown on screen and you have to navigate back to your Moodle system manually.

Most control panels allow you to set up scheduled tasks via a cron job management tool. Bear in mind that this is not part of Moodle but a part of your hosting package. The following screenshot is from the widely used Plesk system, which executes the script every five minutes:

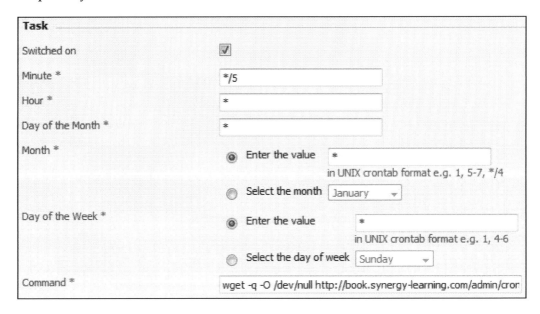

There are a number of ways to call the cron script. The most popular option in a Linux environment is wget -q -O /dev/null http://<yoursite>/admin/cron. php (see **Command** in the preceding screenshot). However, if this does not suit your setup, check out https://docs.moodle.org/en/Cron for alternatives.

The interface shown earlier creates an entry in crontab, a file located in the /etc directory that contains all the system-wide cron entries. This file can also be edited manually using crontab -e, but be careful to get the syntax right!

 On larger sites, it is recommended to run the cron process every minute!

This concludes the installation process for Moodle in a LAMP environment. If you have come across any problems that have not been covered in these instructions or if your setup differs from the one described, go to https://docs.moodle.org/en/ Installing_Moodle, where more installation details are provided and exceptions are covered in great detail.

Installation in a Windows environment

XAMPP is a free Apache distribution that contains MySQL and PHP (as well as Perl) and exists for a number of operating systems. The Moodle distribution for Windows makes full use of XAMPP and is located at `https://download.moodle.org/windows`. The installation works on all the latest Windows PCs and server variants.

The XAMPP-based Moodle distribution is only suitable for servers with a small number of users. For larger Windows installations, you have to install Moodle manually. This involves installing a database server (MS SQL or any other support system), a web server (Microsoft IIS or Apache), and PHP, separately. You can find details about this process at `https://docs.moodle.org/en/Windows_installation`.

Once downloaded, follow these ensuring steps:

1. Copy the distribution to a folder on your PC and unzip the archive in your folder of choice.
2. Make sure any software that uses port 80 (such as Skype) is not running, or change its settings to point it to an alternative port.
3. Double-click on `StartMoodle.exe`.
4. If you have a firewall installed, allow any shown services to be executed.
5. The XAMPP service will run in the Windows background.
6. Go to your web browser and enter `http://localhost` to your address bar.
7. You will see the same installer being launched as the one described for the LAMP environment. All values have already been populated; all you have to do is navigate through all the screens until you see the familiar **Setup administrator account**. This process will take a few minutes.
8. Enter the administrator details and select **Update profile**.
9. Enter the **Front Page settings** for your site.
10. Check that no warnings are displayed in the **Notifications** section of the **Site administration** area in the **Settings** block.

That's it! Your Moodle system is now up and running and you are now able to use Moodle locally or from a web browser on another machine as long as your IP address is accessible via the network you are on.

To stop using Moodle, double-click on `StopMoodle.exe`. If you have a firewall installed, you might have to allow the program to be executed.

Instead of starting and stopping Moodle manually, you can start Apache and MySQL automatically as Windows services. In the server directory of your Moodle system, you find an executable called `service.exe`, which you have to run with the `-install` parameter as administrator, as in the following example:

```
C:/moodle/server/service.exe -install
```

Installation in a Mac OS X environment

MAMP is a free distribution that contains Apache (and Nginx), MySQL, and PHP for Mac OS X. Like its Windows counterpart, the Moodle distributions for Mac OS X (10.4 or higher) are only intended for local installations and not for production environments. There is also a link on the download site for Mac server installation.

Moodle4Mac is available as universal binaries using MAMP, which is located at `https://download.moodle.org/macosx`. Once downloaded, follow these steps:

1. Double-click on the downloaded DMG file to start the installation. This will open a screen as follows, which explains the remainder of the installation process:

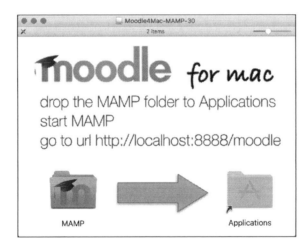

2. Drag the MAMP folder on this screen onto the **Applications** icon, which will copy the Moodle system and its required components.

3. Open the MAMP folder in **Applications**, where you will find the following relevant icons:

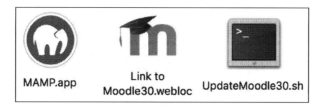

4. Double-click on the **MAMP.app** icon and start servers (Apache and MySQL). You can configure MAMP to automatically start the two servers in the preferences:

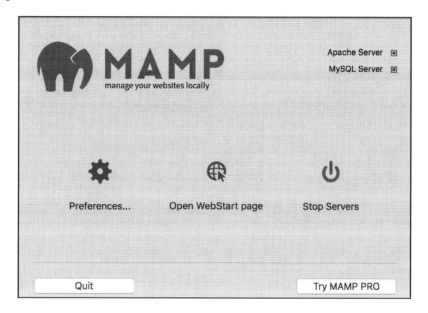

5. Double-click on the **LinktoMoodle30** icon, which opens your Moodle instance on your localhost in your default web browser.

And that's it! An installation cannot be easier than that! You don't even have to go through the installation process. Moodle is already preconfigured, and you are ready to go.

The default password for the admin account is 12345, which you should change in the user profile.

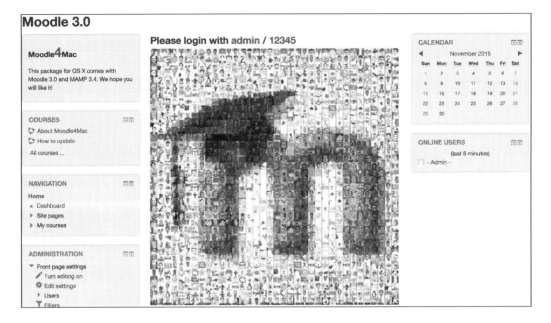

The MAMP folder also includes a shell script called UpdateMoodle30.sh (this requires Git to be installed—see the *Updating Moodle* section discussed later). When you double-click on the file, the script will be executed to download the latest version of Moodle and install it on your Mac. On all other operating systems, you will have to go through a more cumbersome update process, which is described further.

Installation via the Command Line Interface

Moodle provides a **Command Line Interface (CLI)**, which lets you perform a number of administrative tasks from the Unix shell prompt. There is no CLI for Windows-based systems. CLI-based installations are useful if you need to automate setups, for example, in an environment where you have to host multiple Moodle instances.

The CLI is not for the faint-hearted, so be careful when using it. You have to execute the installation script as the same user used for the web server, usually www-data or apache. You can run the installation script, install.php, in interactive mode (you will have to enter any parameters by hand) or in non-interactive mode where the script will run silently.

From your `dirroot`, you can initiate the interactive script as follows:

```
sudo -u www-data /usr/bin/php admin/cli/install.php
```

More interesting is the non-interactive mode as this can be used for scripting and automation purposes. The list of all the available parameters is displayed using the `--help` command:

```
sudo -u www-data /usr/bin/php admin/cli/install.php --help
```

```
Options:
--chmod=OCTAL-MODE     Permissions of new directories created within dataroot.
                       Default is 2777. You may want to change it to 2770
                       or 2750 or 750. See chmod man page for details.
--lang=CODE            Installation and default site language.
--wwwroot=URL          Web address for the Moodle site,
                       required in non-interactive mode.
--dataroot=DIR         Location of the moodle data folder,
                       must not be web accessible. Default is moodledata
                       in the parent directory.
--dbtype=TYPE          Database type. Default is mysqli
--dbhost=HOST          Database host. Default is localhost
--dbname=NAME          Database name. Default is moodle
--dbuser=USERNAME      Database user. Default is root
--dbpass=PASSWORD      Database password. Default is blank
--dbport=NUMBER        Use database port.
--dbsocket=PATH        Use database socket, 1 means default. Available for some databases only.
--prefix=STRING        Table prefix for above database tables. Default is mdl_
--fullname=STRING      The fullname of the site
--shortname=STRING     The shortname of the site
--summary=STRING       The summary to be displayed on the front page
--adminuser=USERNAME   Username for the moodle admin account. Default is admin
--adminpass=PASSWORD   Password for the moodle admin account,
                       required in non-interactive mode.
--adminemail=STRING    Email address for the moodle admin account.
--upgradekey=STRING    The upgrade key to be set in the config.php, leave empty to not set it.
--non-interactive      No interactive questions, installation fails if any
                       problem encountered.
--agree-license        Indicates agreement with software license,
                       required in non-interactive mode.
--allow-unstable       Install even if the version is not marked as stable yet,
                       required in non-interactive mode.
--skip-database        Stop the installation before installing the database.
-h, --help             Print out this help

Example:
$sudo -u www-data /usr/bin/php admin/cli/install.php --lang=cs
```

An example command line would look similar to the following, where you will have to adjust the parameters to your local setup:

```
sudo -u www-data /usr/bin/php admin/cli/install.php
--wwwroot=http://123.54.67.89/moodle --dataroot=/var/moodledata/
--dbtype=mysqli --dbhost=localhost --dbname=moodle --dbuser=moodle
--dbpass=Password123! --fullname=moodle2 --shortname=moodle2
--adminpass=Password123! --non-interactive --agree-license
```

There are more Moodle tasks that can be administered via the CLI, for example, resetting passwords or putting Moodle in maintenance mode. We will show the relevant syntax at the appropriate places throughout the book.

 If your installer crashes, you might have to increase your PHP `memory_limit` and `post_max_size` settings in `php.ini`.

Updating Moodle

Moodle is being updated constantly, which is common practice in open source development environments. A new version containing resolved bug fixes is created every night and, as mentioned earlier, a fully-tested version is released on a weekly basis. There is usually no need to install updates every week; however, there are a number of scenarios when you should upgrade your Moodle system:

- Security patches have been issued
- New features have been added
- Bugs have been fixed that affect your setup
- A new version is released

There are principally two ways Moodle systems can be updated. You can either run updates manually (using the web interface or the CLI) or stay up to date using Git commands. Both procedures are described in this section.

Either way, before you start, make sure you put Moodle in maintenance mode to ensure that no other user is logged in during the update. Go to **Server** | **Maintenance mode**, **Enable** the **Maintenance mode**, and enter a maintenance message:

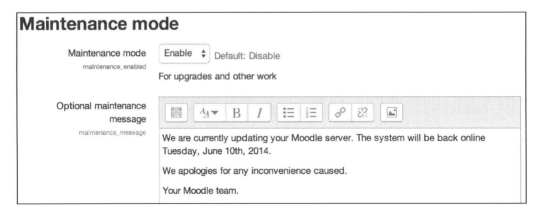

You can also put Moodle in maintenance mode using its CLI as follows:

```
sudo -u www-data /usr/bin/php admin/cli/maintenance.php --enable
```

Using the `--enablelater=MINUTES` flag you can specify the time period before entering CLI maintenance mode. This is useful when you run an automatic update.

To change back to normal mode, use the `--disable` parameter instead of `--enable` as follows:

```
sudo -u www-data /usr/bin/php admin/cli/maintenance.php --disable
```

Manual update

The high-level process for updating a Moodle system manually is as follows:

1. Creating a backup.
2. Creating a new Moodle system.
3. Installing the update.

If you are updating from a previous version of Moodle, the process is the same. However, double-check the **Upgrading** document at https://docs.moodle.org/en/Upgrading for any version-specific issues.

> You have to be at least on version 2.2 to update directly to the current version of Moodle.

If you are still on version 1.9 or on a dinosaur release that is even older, you will need to get to version 2.0 first, before upgrading to 2.2, and then to the latest version.

> Updating from Moodle 1.x to Moodle 3 is a big version jump that has some serious implications. For example, some theme elements will have to be recreated, custom code will need adjusting and, most importantly, your support and faculty staff is likely to require training before the new version is put in production.
>
> Moving from Moodle 1.x to Moodle 3 is more a migration from one system to another than an update. Setting up a separate test system to test the migration process has proven valuable. You will have to plan and have a budget for this.

Creating a backup

Before you install a new update, it is highly recommended that you run a backup of your Moodle system. While most updates will run smoothly, the backup will be required if you have to revert the system to the pre-update version. There are three parts that have to be backed up:

- **Database**: There are two ways you can create a so-called database dump from a MySQL database, either via command line or via Moodle's optional database interface.

   The simplest syntax for the command line tool is:

   ```
   mysqldump -u <user> -p <database> > backup.sql
   ```

   To restore the database you need to use the `mysql` command line tool as follows:

   ```
   mysql -u <user> -p <database> < backup.sql
   ```

   The interface for the database tool is accessed via **Server | Moodle Adminer**. This is an optional module and has to be installed separately refer to *Chapter 8, Moodle Plugins*, for more details).

   Click on the **Dump** link on the front page, select the database to export, and click on **Export**, as shown in the following screenshot. The output of the command will be displayed on screen.

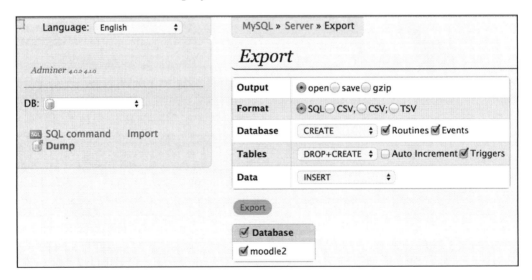

- **Data directory**: This is the `moodledata` directory. Create a copy of this elsewhere on the server (using `cp -R`) or create an archive using the `tar` command (`tar -cvf moodledata`).

- **Moodle**: This is the Moodle software itself. Create a copy of the directory elsewhere on the server. While only some parts of this backup are required (`config.php`, added themes, modified language packs, and so on), it is good practice to create a backup of the entire software. Finally, rename your Moodle system from `moodle` to, say, `moodle.old` (`mv moodle moodle.old`).

 For more information on backups, check out *Chapter 13, Backup and Restore.*

Creating your new Moodle system

Once you have created a backup, it is time to download the new version of Moodle. This is done in the same way as described earlier, during the installation process.

First, create a new `moodle` directory (`dirroot`) and copy the new version to that location (using the same `unzip` or `tar` command as during the installation). Also make sure the permissions as well as user and group are correct.

Now, copy the following files and directories from your `moodle.old` directory to your new `dirroot`. The existing files and directories will have to be overwritten:

- `config.php`
- `.htaccess` (only if present)
- Any theme folders that have been created
- Any modified language packs
- The content of the `local` directory
- Any third-party modules and custom code that is not located in `local`

That's it! The next time you start Moodle, the update script will kick in. We'll go through that next.

Once you are more confident with the update process, you can copy the new version straight on top of the current version after you have created backups. This will save you the last steps of manually copying files from the old to the new versions.

Running the update script

Once you go to the location of your Moodle site and log in as administrator, the system will recognize that a new version is available and kick off the installer automatically.

The first screen displays the build of the new version (here, 3.0) and asks you to confirm that you wish to go ahead with the upgrade:

Next, a screen is displayed that provides a link to the release notes and performs the same server check as the one described during the installation.

Moodle plugins, whether core (**Standard**) or third-party (**Additional**), sometimes cause problems when upgrading Moodle. The **Status** column highlights any actions required or problems found. You should resolve any issues that have arisen. Refer to *Chapter 8, Moodle Plugins*, for more details.

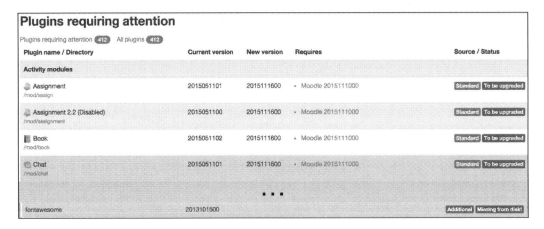

Once this screen has been confirmed, the actual installation starts, during which new database fields are created and data is modified if and when necessary. Any new system settings that have been added to Moodle are shown and can be changed straightaway. For example, in the following screenshot, a new **Always send email from the no-reply address** parameter has been added:

Once the upgrade process has been completed, make sure you check the **Notifications** page as earlier. Also, don't forget to turn off the **Maintenance mode**!

Updating Moodle via CLI

As you would expect, Moodle updates can also be run using the already-discussed CLI. Once you have backed up your data and updated to the latest version, all you need to do is run the following script:

```
sudo -u www-data /usr/bin/php admin/cli/upgrade.php --non-interactive
```

Updating Moodle via CLI is even more powerful when combined with the Git checkout of the Moodle source code. That is what we look at next.

An alternative approach exists to keep a current version up-to-date. It uses an open source versioning system which is supported by Moodle, namely Git. All checked-in Moodle code is made available via this method, which allows you to update only the modules that have actually changed.

Setting up Git is a cumbersome process, which is beyond the scope of this book. You can find details at https://docs.moodle.org/en/Git_for_Administrators. However, once set up, Git is a very streamlined system to use, particularly, in conjunction with the CLI we discussed earlier. The following is a sample script which gets the latest version of the source code, puts Moodle in maintenance mode, merges the old code with the new, runs the upgrade script, and disables the maintenance mode:

```
git fetch
sudo -u www-data /usr/bin/php admin/cli/maintenance.php
--enable
git merge origin/cvshead
sudo -u www-data/usr/bin/php admin/cli/upgrade.php
sudo -u www-data/usr/bin/php admin/cli/maintenance.php
--disable
```

```
root@debian:/var/www/moodle2# git fetch
remote: Counting objects: 1541, done.
remote: Compressing objects: 100% (229/229), done.
remote: Total 1001 (delta 788), reused 973 (delta 764)
Receiving objects: 100% (1001/1001), 162.68 KiB, done.
Resolving deltas: 100% (788/788), completed with 194 local objects.
From git://git.moodle.org/moodle
   25b43f7..19a4491  MOODLE_26_STABLE -> origin/MOODLE_26_STABLE
   3caea82..146c80d  MOODLE_27_STABLE -> origin/MOODLE_27_STABLE
   edbcfbd..da0ef2e  master      -> origin/master
 * [new tag]         v2.6.7       -> v2.6.7
From git://git.moodle.org/moodle
 * [new tag]         v2.7.4       -> v2.7.4
```

If you have changed any core code, potential conflicts might arise and will have to be resolved (Git will prompt you to do so).

You might also come across some conflicting advice on whether to use Git for production sites or not. The advantage is that your system is always up to date and that the updates are carried out automatically. The disadvantage is that the update process might require intervention to resolve any conflicts or it might fail, especially when a lot of third-party add-ons have been employed.

Update notifications

Moodle can notify you about a newly available version. In order to support this feature, you will need to change the **Enable updates deployment** settings in **Server | Update notifications** as follows:

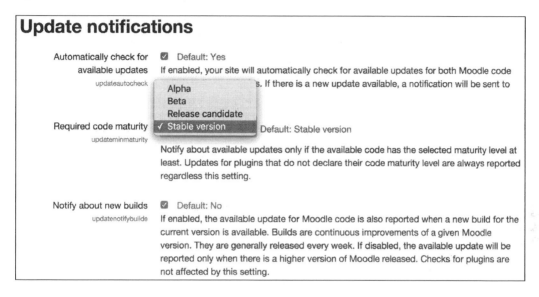

Once this has been changed, you will be notified of any updates (system as well as plugins), and options will be shown in **Notifications**:

Summary

In this chapter, you learned how to install Moodle on the most popular operating systems and upgrade the LMS. You also learned how to use the powerful command-line interface.

The fact that Moodle uses a portable software architecture and facilitates standard open source components allows the installation on multiple platforms. However, this also means that different idiosyncrasies have to be considered in different environments.

Now that your system is up and running, let's have a look at the components of Moodle, which will provide you with a better understanding of the system and how to administer it.

2
The Moodle System

Now that your Moodle system is up and running, we will be looking at the components that make up the learning platform. Think of these as the foundation on which Moodle is built. The subjects we will cover are:

- **Moodle architecture**: In this section, you will learn what the main components of Moodle core are and where its data is stored.

- **Finding your way around in Moodle**: Moodle has an intuitive user interface that takes a little time to get used to. You will learn the main navigation and also where to find help if it is required.

- **File management**: Dealing with files in web-based applications is not always straightforward. You will learn the different options available to deal with this, which will cover:
  - Moodle's file management
  - Web host file management
  - File management via the File system repository

Moodle architecture

We will first look at the overall architecture on which Moodle is based, before we cover the internal components of the VLE application layer.

The LAMP architecture

Moodle has been developed on the open source LAMP framework consisting of Linux (operating system), Apache (web server), MySQL (database), and PHP (programming language). While Moodle runs on other technology stacks, we will focus on LAMP since it has proven to be the most popular setup among Moodle administrators. Due to the portability of these components and the modularity of Moodle itself (that's what the M stands for), it can support a wide range of operating systems, database systems, and web servers. The following diagram shows a simple overview of the overall architecture:

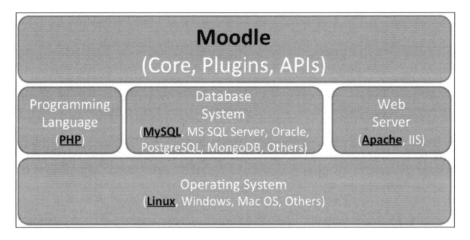

The lowest level is the operating system. While Linux is the preferred platform, other Unix derivatives such as Solaris and AIX are supported, along with Windows and Mac OS X (preferably the server variants for production sites). Certain libraries will have to be installed; refer to *Chapter 1, Moodle Installation*.

PHP is the programming language in which Moodle is written (accompanied by HTML, JavaScript, and CSS files). It is the only component that cannot be replaced with any other counterpart.

MySQL is the database of choice for most open source applications, but other database systems such as Microsoft SQL Server, Oracle, PostgreSQL, and MongoDB are fully supported. Some details have been provided in the previous chapter but, as mentioned before, the focus in this book will be on MySQL.

Apache has become the de facto standard for large-scale web applications, closely followed by Microsoft IIS. Both web servers are supported like any others offering PHP support. In this book, we will focus on Apache as it is the most popular option for Moodle setups.

The following diagram shows the interaction of the elements in the Moodle architecture:

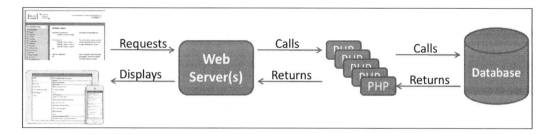

The user makes requests via the web browser interface or a mobile Moodle application (for example, to display a learning resource). The web browser passes the request on to the web server(s), which calls the PHP module that is responsible for the call. The PHP module calls the database with an action (query, update, insert, or delete operation) that returns the requested data. Based on this information, the PHP module returns data (usually in the form of HTML or JavaScript code) to the web server(s), which passes the information to be displayed back to the user's browser or application.

The Moodle layer

Now, let's look at the Moodle layer in more detail. Moodle's main building blocks are shown in the following diagram:

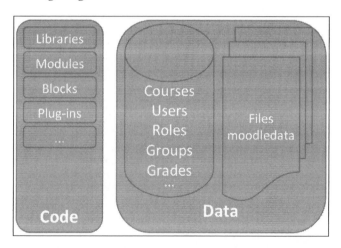

Moodle distinguishes between code (mostly written in PHP, HTML, and CSS) and data (mostly value added via the Moodle interface).

Moodle libraries, modules (such as resources and activities), blocks, plugins, and other entities are represented in code. It is always stored in the file system in a Moodle directory referred to as `dirroot`, which has been specified during the installation process in the previous chapter. The code includes all the elements that deal with the backend (server) and frontend (user interface) operations.

Moodle courses, users, roles, groups, grades, and other data such as learning resources added by teachers, forum posts added by students, and system settings added by the administrator are mostly stored in the Moodle database. However, files such as user pictures or uploaded assignments are stored in another Moodle directory, known as `moodledata`, which is located in a directory called `dataroot`. Information about files (metadata such as the name, location, last modification, license, and size) is stored in the database, which references the respective files.

 Moodle manages its files internally, and it is important to stress that interfering with any files in `moodledata` will break the application.

Even copying a file from one folder to another or adding a file manually will break the consistency of your system and further behavior cannot be predicted. Internally, Moodle uses a mechanism called **SHA1 hashing**. Moodle fully supports Unicode file names and also avoids redundant storage when the same file is used twice (even by different users). Again, you must not modify any Moodle files at system level!

Now let's have a closer look how the Moodle files area—the directory structure—is organized.

Code and data locations

Though Moodle takes care of the organization, of its code and data, it is usually good to know where a file is located in your learning system, for example, when installing add-ons or applying patches.

System files—files that are required to run Moodle—are located in a number of directories under `dirroot` (the root directory of your Moodle installation):

Directory	Functionality	Chapter number
`admin`	Moodle administration and some unsupported scripts	All
`auth`	User authentication plugins	5
`availability`	Management of availability restrictions	-
`backup`	Backup and restore operations	13

Directory	Functionality	Chapter number
badges	Management of badges	9
blocks	Blocks placed in courses and the front page	7
blog	Internal and external blogging functionality	9
cache	Cache stores and performance scripts	12
calendar	Calendar and event management	9
cohort	Handling of site-wide groups (cohorts)	4
comment	Comments used in courses	9
completion	Course completion criteria and aggregation methods	-
course	Management of courses and categories plus course formats	4
enrol	User enrolment plugins	4
error	Error handling; mostly used by developers	-
files	File management	2
filter	Moodle filters applied to text authored in the editor	7
grade	Grade and grade book management as well as reports	9
group	Groups and groupings handling	4 and 5
install	Moodle installation and update scripts	1
iplookup	Look up of IP addresses	-
lang	Localization strings; one directory per language	9
lib	Libraries of core Moodle code	2
local	Recommended directory for local customizations	14
login	Login handling and account creation	5
message	Messaging tool supporting multiple channels	9
mnet	Peer-to-peer and hub networking	16
mod	Core Moodle course modules	9
my	Users' personal dashboards, known as MyMoodle	7
notes	Handling of notes in user profiles	11
pix	Generic site graphics	-
plagiarism	Plagiarism detection plugins	8
portfolio	Portfolio plugins allowing users to export data	8
question	Question and question bank handling plus question types	9
rating	Ratings used in forums, glossaries, and databases	-
report	Report plugins and events list	10
repository	Repository plugins allowing users to import and load data	8
rss	RSS feeds	9

Directory	Functionality	Chapter number
`tag`	Tagging	9
`theme`	Themes to change branding of site	7
`user`	User management	5
`userpix`	Displays thumbnails of all user profile pictures	5
`webservice`	Web services functionality	15

The `moodledata` directory (`dataroot`) is organized as follows:

`cache`	Caching data
`filedir`	That is the actual user content — files that have been uploaded
`filter`	Caching of filtered data
`lang`	Locally used language packs and customizations
`localcache`	Caching data of plugins
`lock`	Locked files
`muc`	Moodle Universal Cache files
`repository`	External location accessible from within Moodle (see the *File management via the file system repository* section)
`sessions`	Session information
`temp`	Temporary files
`trashdir`	Deleted files

If problems occur before carrying out an update, it is sometimes necessary to delete caching data and any temporary information Moodle has created. This data is located in the respective directories in the structure shown in the preceding table. In other words, once everybody has logged out, you can safely delete any files in the directories named `cache`, `filter`, `localcache`, `lock`, `muc`, `sessions`, `temp`, and `trashdir`. This can either be done manually or, better, via **Development | Purge all caches** in the Moodle interface, which we will cover next.

Finding your way around in Moodle

As an administrator, you will be performing most tasks from the **Site administration** section in the **ADMINISTRATION** block, which you will see once you log in to Moodle. We will cover all the aspects of the menus and submenus throughout the remainder of the book:

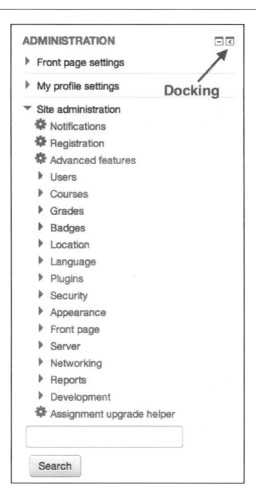

The items displayed in the preceding screenshot will change, depending upon where in Moodle it is shown. For example, inside a course, an additional **Course administration** section will be displayed. As administrator, you will always see the **Site administration** section; other users with lesser rights will only see the menu items they have access to.

You can dock the **Settings** block (like any other block) to the left to save space by clicking on the **Dock administration block** icon in the top-right corner of the block. Once you hover over the docked block, it will pop out.

The Navigation bar

Moodle uses the so-called **breadcrumb trail interface** for its navigation. Once you select a menu or submenu item, Moodle displays the respective crumbs in your navigation bar. These crumbs can be used to jump back to any previous menus. In the following menu, the trail consists of five crumbs:

The first crumb is always the name of the site and represents your Moodle front page (here, called **Home**). That is, if you ever get lost, click on the first crumb, and you will be back in familiar territory. Throughout the book, we will be referring to the location of menu items in the **Site administration** section via a consistent notation, for instance, go to **Plugins** | **Repositories** | **File system** for the trail shown in the preceding screenshot.

In **Appearance** | **Navigation,** it is possible to change the way the navigation bar behaves. More on this in *Chapter 7, Moodle Look and Feel*.

The administrator search facility

To simplify the identification of any setting in the administration section, a search facility is provided, which is located below the hierarchical **Site administration** menu.

When searching for any term, Moodle displays the results in an expanded form that allows you to change settings immediately. For example, when searching for calendar, numerous sections appear as a result, which can be changed in each section straightaway, rather than navigating to each separate section to make changes.

The search facility is also highly beneficial when upgrading from older versions of Moodle where configuration settings have been re-organized and their location is difficult to trace.

Moodle bookmarks

Bookmarks are shown in the **ADMIN BOOKMARKS** block, which has to be added by clicking on **Turn editing on** and selecting the block from the **Add a block** pull-down list. They allow bookmarking any admin menu for easy access to the pages that you require regularly. Select **Bookmark this page** to add a bookmark and **Unbookmark this page** to delete it. Moodle automatically displays the latter option, when you are on the bookmarked page:

In the preceding screenshot, two pages have already been bookmarked (**Browse list of users** and **File system**) and the mentioned link is provided to add more bookmarks.

Moodle Docs and Help

The entire Moodle documentation is online at `https://docs.moodle.org/en/Main_page`. If you wish to provide your own documentation, modify the **Moodle Docs document root** setting in **Appearance | Moodle Docs**. On this screen, you can also select **Language for docs** that will be used in links for the documentation pages and enable the **Open in new window** option. A link at the bottom of each page provides a reference to the relevant page in Moodle Docs. In addition to the actual online documentation, some features provide inline help, which is indicated by a question mark symbol. When it is clicked, a help window will appear, providing assistance relevant to the respective topic.

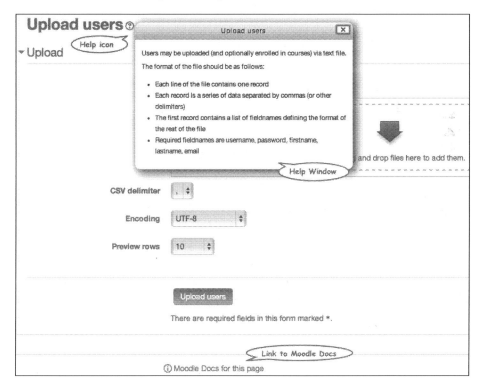

For instance, when clicking on the **Moodle Docs for this page** link in the **Upload users** section, the following article will be opened:

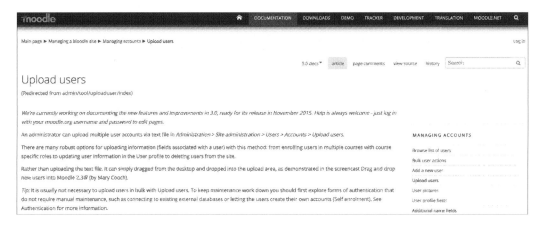

For each version of Moodle, separate Moodle Docs are published. The preceding screenshot is from version 3.0.

The Moodle community is growing continuously and, at the time of writing, had well over 1 million registered users (yes, that's 1 million!), of which, over 5% are active. If you cannot find a solution to any of your Moodle problems in Moodle Docs, use the **Search moodle.org** functionality at the top of the screen at `moodle.org`. In order of priority, the search brings forth the already mentioned Moodle Docs, the most active user forums, and the **Moodle Tracker**, which keeps track of all the issues and feature requests (`https://tracker.moodle.org/secure/Dashboard.jspa`). A search in the Moodle forums can often result in a large number of links. To narrow down the search space, use **Advanced search** in the **Search forums** block. If you still cannot find the solution to your problem, which is relatively rare, post a question on the relevant forum, and somebody is likely to assist you further.

File management

Dealing with files in web-based applications is not always straightforward. While Moodle provides a user interface to perform this task, it is sometimes necessary that, as the administrator, you will have to bypass this mechanism and use other means. First though, let's look at the built-in file handling that is also the one used by students and teachers.

The Moodle file management interface

Moodle offers a basic file management interface, which lets you upload, move, delete, and rename files and directories. It is also possible to copy or link to files from third-party services such as Dropbox; on the same token, Moodle isn't a content management system.

We already talked about how Moodle stores files at system level—the ones we are not to touch! At application level, it arranges files according to Moodle's structure.

[In Moodle, a file is always connected to the particular bit of Moodle that uses it.]

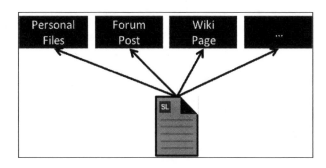

Files are organized in a tree-like structure, which has three types of main branches:

- Categories, courses, activities, and resources
- Users (private files and personal backups)
- Front Page (Moodle's home page)

We will be dealing with all those concepts at later stages so, for now, let's just take them for granted. Courses are arranged in categories (and sub-categories) and consist of activities and resources. There are usually further subdirectories inside activities and resources.

There are multiple users on your system, each with a dedicated file area that can be accessed from anywhere in Moodle, but there is only a single **Front Page**. Remember, a file is always connected to the particular bit of Moodle content that uses it, which is reflected by the directory-like structure:

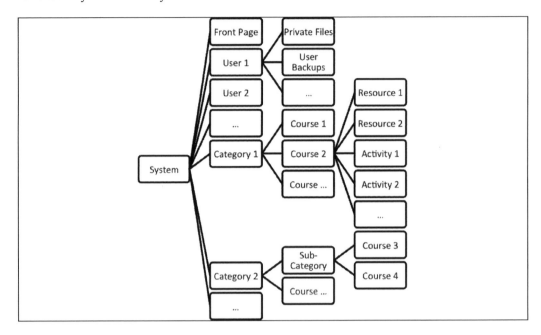

Uploading files

Uploading files usually takes place via drag and drop.

 Drag and drop works in Firefox 25+, Chrome 30+, Safari 6+ and Internet Explorer 10+. Older versions of IE are not supported.

Adding single or multiple files via drag and drop is straightforward. Simply select the files in your Explorer (Windows) or Finder (Mac) and drag them onto the provided area inside the dotted lines:

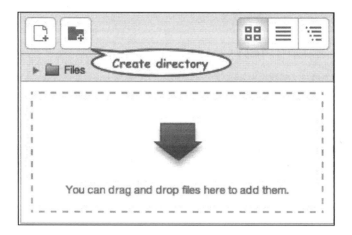

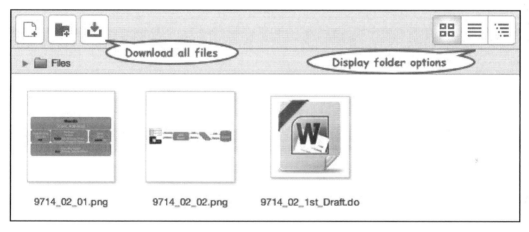

When you click on a file once it has been uploaded, you have the option to **Download** or **Delete** the file. If multiple files are allowed (as is in the preceding example), you also have the option to set the selected document as the main file. If the selected file is a compressed archive, you have the **Unzip** option. This file will then appear on the view page. Additionally, meta information about the file (name, author, license, icon, last modified, created, and size) is displayed.

For some file operations, it is necessary to use the **File picker**, which is a tool that is utilized whenever files have to be added to a particular object in Moodle. A user can choose from multiple file sources, known as repositories (see the screenshot in the *File system repository* section further down). We will be dealing with them in *Chapter 8, Moodle Plugins*. The **File picker** can be accessed using the **Add...** button at the top-left on the files area.

Private files

Every user has an area where personal files can be stored and managed. These are only visible to the user the private files belong to. Any item stored in this protected area can be used throughout the site, that is, across courses. Private files can be accessed via the File picker, the **Private files** block, or directly via **Home | My profile | My private files**.

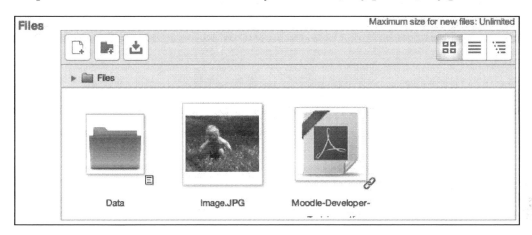

The handling of files and directories is identical to any other file areas. However, you might have spotted the **Link** icon in the PDF file in the preceding screenshot.

To link or to copy?

By default, files in Moodle are copied. That is, when you add a file from a source (for instance, your computer or your private files), it will be copied. This means that the source and the resulting file will be logically separated. For example, if you have stored an image in your private files and you use it in three different courses, there are three logical copies. If you change the source in your private files, the three images will not be affected.

Moodle also supports linking of files. Let us stick to the same example, but this time round, the three images are linked. If the source is changed, the three files in the courses will also have changed. Beware that there are some access restrictions with linked files, for example, instructor A might not be able to make a link with instructor B's file.

When you select a file from a source (repository) that supports linking, a **Create an alias/shortcut to the file** option is provided:

Moodle keeps track of linked files and guarantees that inconsistencies cannot occur:

- When deleting a linked file, copies of the file will be created for each link
- When a linked file is overwritten, all the links are updated
- When a link is overwritten by a file, the files are separated

File types

Moodle itself does not restrict which types of files can be uploaded by users, for instance, an assignment in a course. For most popular file types, Moodle comes with predefined values in terms of the icon that is displayed as well as the program that will be opened, for example, PDF files or PowerPoint documents. However, you have the ability to add new file types and view, modify, and delete the existing file types by navigating to **Site administration** | **Server** | **File types**.

File types

Extension		Type	MIME type	Type groups	Description
3gp	⚙ ✕	Standard	video/quicktime	video	
7z	⚙ ✕	Standard	application/x-7z-compressed	archive	Archive (7Z)
aac	⚙ ✕	Standard	audio/aac	audio	Audio file (AAC)
accdb	⚙ ✕	Standard	application/msaccess		
ai	⚙ ✕	Standard	application/postscript	image	Image (POSTSCRIPT)

When you add a new file type via the button at the bottom of the screen, you will need to provide the file **Extension** and its **MIME type**. Furthermore, you have the option to select a **File icon, type groups** (such as image or document), a **description type, custom description** (if **description type** is **Custom description specified in this form**), **Alternative language string** (if selected in **description type**), and **Default icon for MIME type**.

The upload limit

Your site has a file upload limit, which is set to 2 MB, by default. If you need to support files larger than the 2 MB threshold, you will have to increase the limit as follows:

- In your `php.ini` file, modify the following two lines; `<value>` represents the maximum limit (multiple input formats are supported, for example, 20M or 20971520):

```
upload_max_filesize = <value>
post_max_size = <value>
```

- If you don't have access to the `php.ini` file, create a `.htaccess` file in your main Moodle directory and add the following two lines:

```
php_value upload_max_filesize = <value>
php_value post_max_size = <value>
```

On some systems, you will also have to increase the `LimitRequestBody` parameter, which is usually found in the Apache configuration file, `httpd.conf`. You may also need to modify your database configuration, such as the `max_allowed_packet` size.

Once these changes have been applied, make sure **Maximum upload file size** in **Security | Site policies** is set to **Site upload limit**. Underneath this parameter, you can also change **User quota** for private files. When changing these two values, bear in mind that they potentially will have an impact on bandwidth and disk space, respectively.

Alternatively, you can use other file management operations, which we will cover next.

Web host file management

Most web hosts offer a web interface that provides a file management facility, for example, cPanel and Plesk. Unless your browser does not support drag and drop or you need to bypass the set upload limit, there is usually no need to use such a facility.

It has to be stressed again that you should only modify files in `dirroot`, for instance, to install third-party add-ons. Unless you know SHA1, do not change any files in `moodledata`. If you do, Moodle will not function correctly afterward.

For very large files, such as high-quality learning resources, it would be useful to be able to upload the content via (secure) FTP and then use the built-in unzip functionality in the File picker. However, it is not possible to upload files directly via FTP. Instead, you have to make use of the file system repository, which is discussed in the following section.

File management via the file system repository

The objective is to make the files appear in the File picker in a separate section; Moodle calls them repositories. To achieve this, we have to go to **Plugins | Repositories | Manage repositories**. Activate the **File system** plugin via **Enabled and visible**. Click on **Settings** and check the first box to allow access from courses before saving the settings (to grant access from users' personal files as well, check the second box).

Manage repositories

Name	Active?	Order	Settings
File system	✓ Enabled and visible	↓	Settings
	Enabled but hidden		
	Disabled		2 Site-wide common instance(s)
			1 Course-wide common instance(s)
			1 User private instance(s)

You might have spotted the `repository` directory when we looked at the data locations in the Moodle layer earlier. Any subdirectories in `dataroot/repository` can be read from within Moodle. First, create a subdirectory in that folder and copy or transfer (using FTP) some data into it.

Now go to a course where you wish to allow access to the folder, select the **Repositories** link in the **Course administration** section, and click on **Create "File system" instance**. Give the new repository a name and select a folder in case you have created more than one (we have created two). To support relative files (see the preceding screenshot), select the last option on the screen:

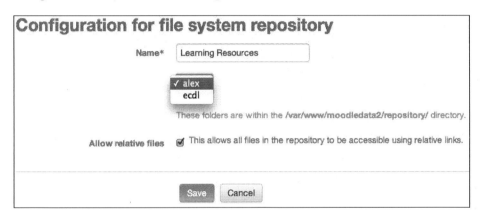

From now on, any user with access to the File picker in that particular course has read-only access to the material. How cool is that! You can also grant access to directories at user level. Go to a user's profile settings where you will see the same **Repositories** link as in courses:

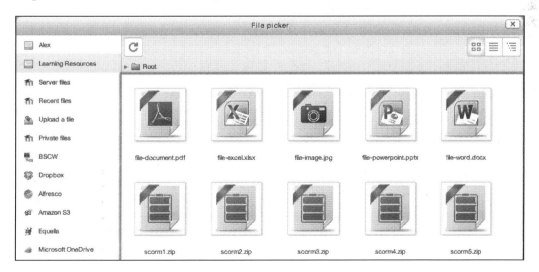

We will be dealing with repositories in more detail in *Chapter 8, Moodle Plugins*, and have only focused on the files-related ones for now. For more detail on the file system repository, visit `docs.moodle.org/en/File_system_repository_configuration`.

Summary

In this chapter, we learned what the building blocks of Moodle core look similar to and where they are located. Furthermore, we dealt with a number of options for managing files, including the basics of some file repositories.

As we found out in the previous chapter, Moodle can be installed on multiple operating systems, supports a wide range of database systems, and can be used with different web servers. Due to the openness of Moodle, it should have come across in this chapter that all its components can be accessed without any restrictions. This allows the management of files via a number of channels that we have covered, such as Moodle's file management, web host file management, and file management via the file system repository for FTP access.

Now that your system is up and running and you know what its insides look similar to, it's time to deal with courses, users, and roles.

3

Courses, Users, and Roles

The objective of this chapter is to give an overview of Moodle courses, users, and roles. The three concepts are inherently intertwined and any one of these cannot be used without the other two. We will deal with the basics of the three core elements and show how they work together. Let's see what they are:

- **Moodle courses**: Courses are central to Moodle as this is where learning takes place. Teachers upload their learning resources, create activities, assist in learning and grade work, monitor progress, and so on. Students, on the other hand, read, listen to or watch learning resources, participate in activities, submit work, collaborate with others, and so on.

- **Moodle users**: These are individuals accessing our Moodle system. Typical users are students and teachers/trainers, but also there are others such as teaching assistants, managers, parents, assessors, examiners, or guests. Oh, and the administrator, of course!

- **Moodle roles**: Roles are effectively permissions that specify which features users are allowed to access and, also, where and when (in Moodle) they can access them.

Bear in mind that this chapter only covers the basic concepts of these three core elements. The dedicated chapters — *Chapter 4, Course Management*; *Chapter 5, User Management*; and *Chapter 6, Managing Permissions – Roles and Capabilities* — will then deal with the three concepts in greater detail.

A high-level overview

To give you an overview of courses, users, and roles, let's have a look at the following diagram. It shows nicely how central the three concepts are and also how other features are related to them. Again, all of their intricacies will be dealt with in due course, so for now, just start getting familiar with some Moodle terminology.

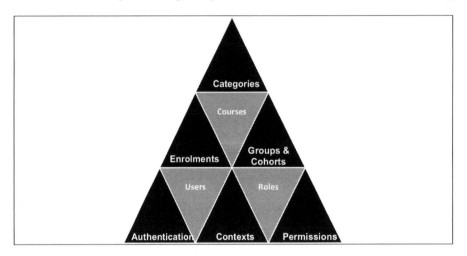

Let's start at the bottom-left and cycle through the pyramid clockwise. Users have to go through an **Authentication** process to get access to Moodle. They then have to go through the **Enrolments** step to be able to participate in **Courses**, which themselves are organized into **Categories**. **Groups & Cohorts** are different ways to group users at course level or site-wide. Users are granted **Roles** in particular **Contexts**. Which role is allowed to do what and which isn't, depends entirely on the **Permissions** set within that role.

The diagram also demonstrates a catch-22 situation. If we start with users, we have no courses to enroll them in to (except the front page); if we start with courses, we have no users who can participate in them. Not to worry though. Moodle lets us go back and forth between any administrative areas and, often, perform multiple tasks at once.

Moodle courses

Moodle manages activities and stores resources in courses, and this is where learning and collaboration takes place. Courses themselves belong to categories, which are organized hierarchically, similar to folders on our local hard drive. Moodle comes with a default category called **Miscellaneous**, which is sufficient to show the basics of courses. We will deal with categories in more detail in *Chapter 4, Course Management*.

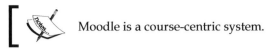

Moodle is a course-centric system.

To begin with, let's create the first course. To do so, go to **Courses | Manage courses and categories**. Here, select the **Miscellaneous** category. Then, select the **Create new course** link, and you will be directed to the screen where course details have to be entered. For now, let's focus on the two compulsory fields, namely **Course fullname** and **Course shortname**. The former is displayed at various places in Moodle, whereas the latter is, by default, used to identify the course and is also shown in the breadcrumb trail.

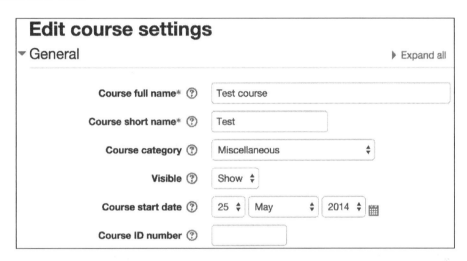

For now, we leave all other fields empty or at their default values and save the course by clicking on the **Save changes** button at the bottom.

The screen displayed after clicking on **Save changes** shows enrolled users, if any. Since we just created the course, there are no users present in the course yet. In fact, except the administrator account we are currently using, there are no users at all on our Moodle system. So, we leave the course without users for now and add some users to our LMS before we come back to this screen (select the **Home** link in the breadcrumb).

Moodle users

Moodle users, or rather their user accounts, are dealt within **Users | Accounts**. Before we start, it is important to understand the difference between authentication and enrolment.

Moodle users have to be authenticated in order to log in to the system. Authentication grants users access to the system through login where a username and password have to be given (this also applies to guest accounts where a username is allotted internally). Moodle supports a significant number of authentication mechanisms, which are discussed later in detail.

Enrolment happens at course level. However, a user has to be authenticated to the system before enrolment to a course can take place. So, a typical workflow is as follows (there are exceptions as always, but we will deal with them when we get there):

1. Create your users.
2. Create your courses (and categories).
3. Associate users to courses and assign roles.

Again, this sequence demonstrates nicely how intertwined courses, users, and roles are in Moodle. Another way of looking at the difference between authentication and enrolment is how a user will get access to a course. Please bear in mind that this is a very simplistic view and it ignores the supported features such as external authentication, guest access, and self-enrolment.

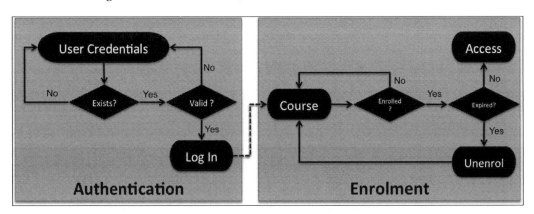

During the authentication phase, a user enters his credentials (username and password) or they are entered automatically via single sign-on. If the account exists locally, that is within Moodle, and the password is valid, he/she is granted access. The next phase is enrolment. If the user is enrolled and the enrolment hasn't expired, he/she is granted access to the course. You will come across a more detailed version of these graphics later on, but for now, it hopefully demonstrates the difference between authentication and enrolment.

To add a user account manually, go to **Users | Accounts | Add a new user**. As with courses, we will only focus on the mandatory fields, which should be self-explanatory:

- **Username** (has to be unique)
- **New password** (if a password policy has been set, certain rules might apply)
- **Firstname**
- **Surname**
- **Email address**

Make sure you save the account information by selecting **Create user** at the bottom of the page. If any entered information is invalid, Moodle will display error messages right above the field.

I have created a few more accounts; to see who has access to your Moodle system, go to **Users | Accounts | Browse list of users**, where you will see all users. Actually, I did this via batch upload, which will be dealt within *Chapter 5, User Management*.

First name / Surname	Email address	City/town	Country	Last access	Edit		
Alex Büchner	alex.buchner@synergy-learning.com	Heidelberg	Germany	28 secs	✿		
Participant One	participant01@myschool.edu	Heidelberg	Germany	Never	✕	👁	✿
Participant Two	participant02@myschool.edu	Heidelberg	Germany	Never	✕	👁	✿
Participant Three	participant03@myschool.edu	Heidelberg	Germany	Never	✕	👁	✿
Participant Four	participant04@myschool.edu	Heidelberg	Germany	Never	✕	👁	✿
Participant Five	participant05@myschool.edu	Heidelberg	Germany	Never	✕	👁	✿
Participant Six	participant06@myschool.edu	Heidelberg	Germany	Never	✕	👁	✿
Participant Seven	participant07@myschool.edu	Heidelberg	Germany	Never	✕	👁	✿
Participant Eight	participant08@myschool.edu	Heidelberg	Germany	Never	✕	👁	✿
Participant Nine	participant09@myschool.edu	Heidelberg	Germany	Never	✕	👁	✿
Participant Ten	participant10@myschool.edu	Heidelberg	Germany	Never	✕	👁	✿
Tommy Teacher	tommy@myschool.edu	Heidelberg	Germany	Never	✕	👁	✿

Now that we have a few users on our system, let's go back to the course we created a minute ago and manually enroll new participants to it. To achieve this, go back to **Courses | Manage courses and categories**, select the **Miscellaneous** category again, and select the created demo course. Underneath the listed demo course, course details will be displayed alongside a number of options (on large screens, details are shown to the right). Here, select **Enrolled users**.

As expected, the list of enrolled users is still empty. Click on the `Enrolled users` button to change this. To grant users access to the course, select the **Enrol** button beside them and close the window. In the following screenshot, three users, `participant01` to `participant03` have already been enrolled to the course. Two more users, `participant04` and `participant05`, have been selected for enrolment.

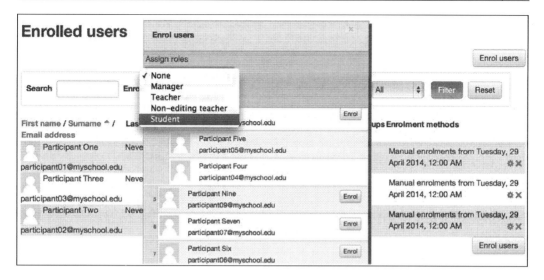

You have probably spotted the **Assign roles** dropdown at the top of the pop-up window. This is where you select what role the selected user has, once he/she is enrolled in the course. For example, to give Tommy Teacher appropriate access to the course, we have to select the **Teacher** role first, before enrolling him to the course.

This leads nicely to the third part of the pyramid, namely, roles.

Moodle roles

Roles define what users can or cannot see and do in your Moodle system. Moodle comes with a number of predefined roles—we already saw **Student** and **Teacher**—but it also allows us to create our own roles, for instance, for parents or external assessors.

Each role has a certain scope (called **context**), which is defined by a set of permissions (expressed as **capabilities**). For example, a teacher is allowed to grade an assignment, whereas a student isn't. Or, a student is allowed to submit an assignment, whereas a teacher isn't.

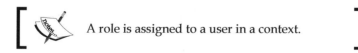

A role is assigned to a user in a context.

Okay, so what is a context? A context is a ring-fenced area in Moodle where roles can be assigned to users. A user can be assigned different roles in different contexts, where the context can be a course, a category, an activity module, a user, a block, the front page, or Moodle itself. For instance, you are assigned the **Administrator** role for the entire system, but additionally, you might be assigned the **Teacher** role in any courses you are responsible for; or, a learner will be given the **Student** role in a course, but might have been granted the **Teacher** role in a forum to act as a moderator.

To give you a feel of how a role is defined, let's go to **Users | Permissions**, where roles are managed, and select **Define roles**. Click on the **Teacher** role and, after some general settings, you will see a (very) long list of capabilities:

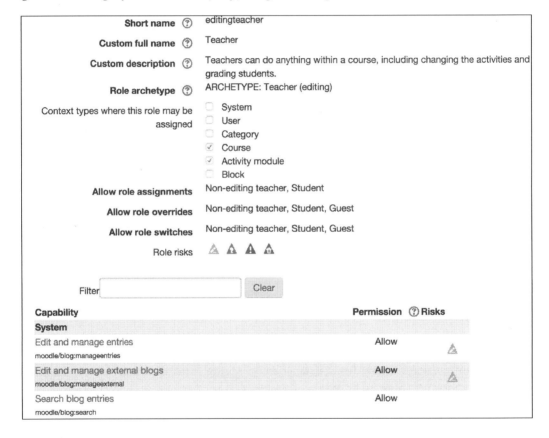

We will deal with all this in greater detail in *Chapter 6, Managing Permissions – Roles and Capabilities*, so don't panic!

For now, we only want to stick with the example we used throughout the chapter. Now that we know what roles are, we can slightly rephrase what we have done. Instead of saying, "We have enrolled the user `participant01` in the demo course as a student", we would say, "We have assigned the student role to the user `participant01` in the context of the demo course."

In fact, the term enrolment is a little bit of a legacy and goes back to the times when Moodle didn't have the customizable, finely-grained architecture of roles and permissions that it does now. One can speculate whether there are linguistic connotations between the terms role and enrolment.

Summary

In this chapter, we very briefly introduced the concepts of Moodle courses, users, and roles. We also saw how central they are to Moodle and how they are linked together. Any one of these concepts simply cannot exist without the other two, and this is something you should bear in mind throughout. Well, theoretically they can, but it would be rather impractical when you try to model your learning environment.

If you haven't fully understood any of the three areas, don't worry. The intention was only to provide you with a high-level overview of the three core components and to touch upon the basics.

There are chapters, dedicated to each concept, which will hopefully clarify any outstanding issues and will also go significantly into them in more detail. As we did earlier, let's start with courses.

4
Course Management

Moodle stores learning resources and activities in courses, which belong to categories. In the first part of this chapter, you will learn to:

- Organize courses in categories and sub-categories
- Create and manage courses
- Deal with course requests
- Manage courses in bulk

In the second part of the chapter, we will cover different ways of enrolling users to courses. The enrolment mechanisms that will be covered are:

- Internal enrolment (manual, self, and guest)
- Cohort enrolment and synchronization
- Database-driven enrolment (LDAP, external databases, flat files, and IMS Enterprise files)
- Meta courses
- Payment-driven enrolment (PayPal)

Course categories

The role of the Moodle administrator is to manage categories and courses. It is possible to delegate these tasks to non-administrators, and we will deal with this in *Chapter 6, Managing Permissions – Roles and Capabilities*. Here, let's start with an overview of course categories.

Course categories – an overview

Categories act as containers for courses. They can have subcategories, which can have sub-subcategories, and so on. The arrangement is similar to that of files and folders on a disk drive, where courses are like files and categories are like folders. This hierarchical structure can be visualized as follows:

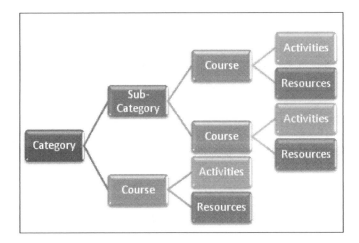

A course always belongs to a single category. It cannot belong to multiple categories and also cannot be without a category. There is one exception to this rule, namely, the front page (*course id* = 1). Internally, the front page is treated as a course that neither belongs to a category, nor can be deleted.

There are different ways of organizing course and category hierarchies, for instance, by department, subject area, semester, and so on. The following figure shows the positioning of the same course hierarchies, of two different categories representing the same organization:

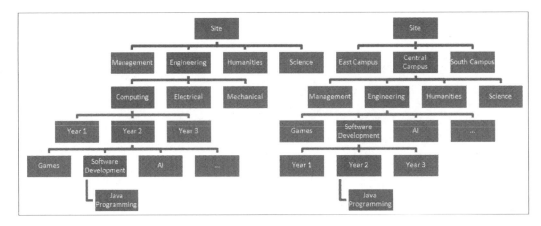

As you can see, each hierarchy represents the same information, but in different forms. There is no right or wrong way when it comes to organizing your courses. The structure depends on the following parameters:

- The size of your organization
- The number of courses you offer
- The type of courses you run
- The frequency of course commencement (once a term, once a year, roll-on/roll-off, and so on)

It is highly advisable to get the structure right the first time around, as changing it is time consuming and potentially confusing for the users. Also, try to plan ahead, thinking about whether the structure will work in the future, for example, when changing from one academic year to another (see also *Chapter 13, Backup and Restore,* when we look at year-end procedures).

As mentioned before, different organizations apply different categorization approaches. Some examples of the category levels are:

- **Campus | Department/School | Year | Subject**
- **Year of Entry | Topic | Subject**
- **Customer | Subject | Proficiency Level**
- **Trainer | Module**

Sometimes, deep levels of categories can be off-putting as their management is cumbersome. However, bear in mind that only you, as the administrator, will see the entire category structure. The students and teachers will usually only see the courses they are enrolled or assigned to, unless they browse the full course index.

Managing course categories

Once you have planned your category hierarchy structure, it is time to represent the organization in Moodle. Categories are administered in **Courses | Manage courses and categories**, as shown in the following screenshot:

Initially, Moodle comes with a single category called **Miscellaneous**. In the previous screenshot, you can see that two courses have already been created in that category in our system.

Adding course categories

To add a new category, click on the **Create new category** option or go directly to **Courses** | **Add a category** and enter a new name in the **Category name** field. The **Parent category** drop-down menu indicates where in the hierarchy the course is located. We will leave this at **Top** and come back to it shortly. It is good practice to provide the optional **Category ID number** and **Description**; the former is used when automating certain tasks such as user uploads, while the latter is for example shown in the course index. You can force a theme that will be applied to all the courses in the category. This option will only appear at the bottom of the screen when category themes are enabled in **Appearance** | **Themes** | **Theme settings** (refer to *Chapter 7, Moodle Look and Feel*).

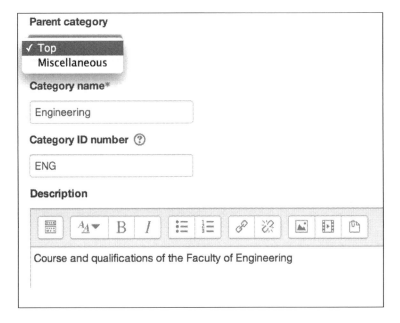

Course sub-categories

As mentioned earlier, to improve the organization of courses, Moodle allows the creation of sub-categories. You can create a sub-category by choosing an existing category and then selecting **Create new sub-category** from the drop-down menu in the options or adding a new category (as shown in the preceding screenshot) and then moving it into a parent category using the drop-down menus on the **Course categories** page. For example, to create sub-categories called **Computing-Year 1**, **Computing-Year 2**, and **Computing-Year 3** in **Computing**, first create the sub-categories and then move them into **Computing** using the drop-down menu. Alternatively, you can select the correct parent category when you create the sub-category, as shown in the following screenshot:

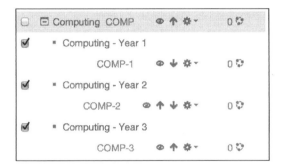

Deleting course categories

When deleting a course category using the respective option in the drop-down menu, you have to decide what to do with courses and sub-categories if any exist:

- Move courses and sub-categories to another category. You will need to select one from the **Move into** option.

- Delete all courses and sub-categories permanently. This step cannot be undone!

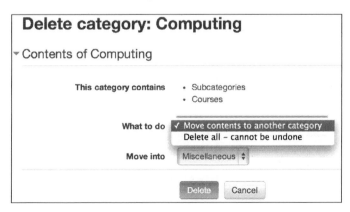

Organizing courses and categories

Use the up and down arrows to change the position of a course category. You have various options to sort and move the selected categories:

- You can either order all categories, the selected ones, or the current one (with **This category** option).

- Categories can be sorted in ascending or descending order by their **name** or **ID number**. They can also be unsorted (that is, you can put them in the original order when they were created).

- Once you have selected your option, press the **Sort** button. Alternatively, you can expedite this process by selecting a sorting option from the pull-down menu for each parent category.

- Moving categories requires you to select a new location. This feature is useful if you need to merge a number of categories into one. When you move a parent category, all the child categories will move with it.

You can hide categories using the eye icon (like **Miscellaneous** in our case). This is usually done when courses within a category are undergoing development or if you want to create an experimental area (sandpit) that is not to be seen by anybody without permission to see hidden courses.

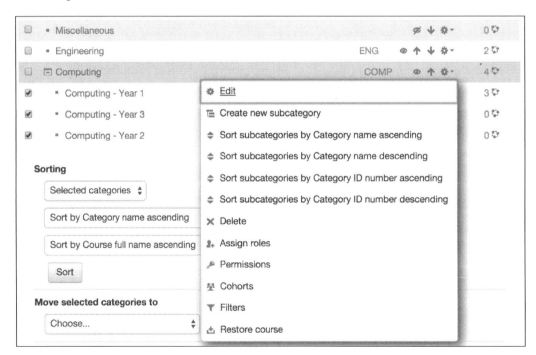

From the options menu, there are a number of actions that can be triggered. They are as follows in the table:

Option	Description
Edit	Modify category details
Create new subcategory	It does exactly what it says on the tin
Sort...	Refer to the preceding image
Delete	Remove category after choosing some options
Assign roles	Assign category roles (see *Chapter 6, Managing Permissions – Roles and Capabilities*)
Permissions	Manage permissions in category (see *Chapter 6, Managing Permissions – Roles and Capabilities*)
Cohorts	Manage category cohorts (see *Chapter 5, User Management*)
Filters	Link to course filters (see *Chapter 8, Moodle Plugins*)
Restore	Restore a course in this category (see *Chapter 13, Backup and Restore*)

Once you select a category, it shows all its courses in a separate area, and depending on your device and screen size, this can be to its right or underneath the categories area.

While you can use the up and down arrows to reorganize courses, you can use the crossbar at the left and drag each course to its new location—a very handy feature, indeed. Courses can be sorted in ascending as well as descending order by their full name, short name, ID number, and course time created, and you also have an option to modify the number of courses that are shown per page. Deleting and hiding courses works in the same way as it does for categories. The same holds for moving the selected courses to another course category.

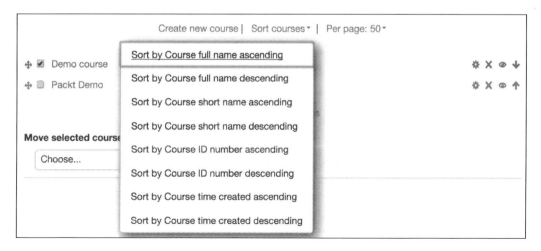

The one feature that is missing from the preceding list is creating a new course, which we are going to deal with in the next section.

Creating courses

Once the **Create a new course** link has been selected from the **Course categories** screen, Moodle directs you to the page where course details have to be entered. We already came across this screen in *Chapter 3, Courses, Users, and Roles* when we introduced the concepts of users, courses, and roles, respectively.

The following settings are available in the **General** and **Description** sections:

Setting	Description
Course full name	This is the full name of the course (displayed at the top of the screen and in the course listings). This is required.
Course short name	Many organizations have a short form for referring to a course. The field is compulsory as it is used in several places where the full name is inappropriate (such as in the breadcrumb trail or when uploading users in batch files). This field is required.
Course category	This is the category to which the course belongs.
Visible	If it is set to **Yes**, the course is hidden. Other than the course teachers and administrators, no one will be able to view it in any course listings.
Course start date	This refers to the starting date of the course.
Course ID Number	This is the course code (often used in conjunction with external systems).
Course summary	It is recommended to write a concise paragraph that explains what the course is about. The summary is displayed when a user clicks on the information icon, and when the course appears in a list.
Course summary files	You have the option to upload an image, which will be shown in the course listing. This is highly recommended to make the course catalogue a bit more visually attractive.

The fields, **Course full name**, **Course short name** and **Course ID Number**, can be modified by a teacher, by default. You can disallow this by changing the appropriate permissions for the **Teacher** role by navigating to **Users | Permissions | Define roles** (search for capabilities starting with moodle/course:change, using the **Filter** box). We are going to deal with this in *Chapter 6, Managing Permissions – Roles and Capabilities*.

The following section in the course settings lets you choose a so-called **course format**. A course format dictates the way course content will be presented to the learner. Moodle ships with four formats, but more can be installed (see *Installing third-party add-ons* section in *Chapter 8, Moodle Plugins*). Once you have selected a course format, the screen has to refresh in order to load the respective course format settings:

- **Single-activity format**: This shows only the selected activity in a course, for instance, a **Sharable Content Object Reference Model (SCORM)** package, assignment, forum, quiz, and so on

- **Social format**: This is one main (social) forum, which is listed on the main course page, for example, a notice board

- **Topics format**: This is similar to the weekly format, except that each week is called a topic and no time restriction applies

- **Weekly format**: In this format, a course is organized week-by-week, with a start and a finish date

The remaining options in the **Appearance, Files and uploads, Completion tracking, Guest access,** and **Groups** sections are as follows:

Setting	Description
Force theme	A theme that is to be used for this course is forcibly applied through this option. This requires course themes to be enabled in **Appearance	Themes	Theme Settings** (see *Chapter 7, Look and Feel*).
Force language	If this is set, the selected language is used throughout the course and cannot be changed.
News items to show	This determines how many recent items appear on your course home page in the news section (if any). Set this to 0 if the default news forum shown in a course should not be created automatically once it has been deleted!
Show gradebook to students	This determines whether students are shown the **Grades** link in their **Settings** block. You can set this to No and still grade your activities.
Show activity reports	This determines whether students can see their own activity reports (see *Chapter 10, Moodle Logging and Reporting*) via their profile page.
Maximum upload size	This setting limits the size of a file a user can upload into this course.
Enable completion tracking	Once completion tracking is enabled sitewide (**Advanced features**), it has to be activated at course level.

Setting	Description
Group mode	This sets the group mode of the course to: • **No groups**: There are no subgroups. Everyone is part of one big community or class • **Separate groups**: Users can only see their own group, while other groups are invisible • **Visible groups**: Users work in their own group, but can also see other groups
Force group mode	If this is set, the selected group mode is used for every activity, and group settings in individual activities are ignored. This is useful when the same course is run multiple times with separate batches of students. Also, if group mode is forced and set to **No groups**, the **Groups** link will not be shown in the course administration menu.
Default grouping	If grouping is enabled and used within the course, the one that is to be used as default can be selected.

Once a course has been created, you can assign users to various roles in the course (such as, enrolling students and assigning teachers); we have briefly covered this in *Chapter 3, Courses, Users, and Roles* and have dedicated the entire *Roles management* section in *Chapter 6, Managing Permissions – Roles and Capabilities* to roles, and will therefore be ignoring the **Role renaming** part, for now. The same holds for an optional **Tags** section, which is dealt with in *Chapter 9, Moodle Configuration*.

For most parameters, you can specify the course default settings when creating new courses; you can find these in **Courses | Course default settings**. The fields and values are identical to the ones we have described in the preceding screenshots.

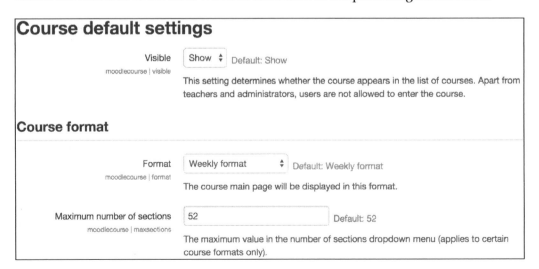

Course requests – enabling teachers to ask for new courses

Only the administrators or course creators (or any other role with course creation rights) are allowed to create new courses. In order to streamline the procedure for requesting courses, especially in larger organizations, Moodle offers a course requesting facility. This has to be enabled by going to **Courses | Course request**.

You have to specify **Default category for course requests**, which is where the courses created upon request will be placed. You can also enable **Enable category selection**, if your users are familiar with the course category structure. As the courses have to be approved, you can specify who will receive **Course request notification**:

Course request

Enable course requests enablecourserequests	☑ Default: No This will allow any user to request a course be created.
Default category for course requests defaultrequestcategory	Miscellaneous ▲▼ Default: Miscellaneous Courses requested by users will be automatically placed in this category.
Enable category selection requestcategoryselection	☐ Default: No Allow the selection of a category when requesting a course.
Course request notification courserequestnotify	Nobody Everyone who can 'Approve course creation' Alex Büchner Default: Nobody Users who will be notified when a course is requested. Only users who can approve course requests are listed here.

As soon as the feature is enabled, each teacher has the ability to request new courses (via the **Request a course** button at **Home | Courses**). The information that has to be provided is:

- Course full name
- Course short name
- Course category (if selected above)
- Summary
- Reasons for course request

A new item, **Courses | Pending requests**, appears in the **Site administration** section. On selection, a list of requested courses is shown, which you can then **Approve** or **Reject** by selecting the appropriate button.

Courses pending approval

The user requesting this course will be automatically enrolled and assigned the role of Teacher.

Course short name	Course full name	Requested by	Summary	Category	Reason for course request	Action
Bootstrap	Bootstrap design	Tommy Teacher	Understanding the bootstrap framework and creating web content for mobile devices.	Computing	New element in MSc. Instruction Design	Approve Reject...

Back to course listing

When you approve a course, the familiar course settings screen appears. This screen already contains the provided values of the course as well as the default or provided category specified in the system settings. Furthermore, the user who has requested the course will be automatically enrolled to the course and, by default, he/she will be assigned the teacher role. If you reject a course, a reason has to be given, which is then e-mailed to the requester.

Managing courses in bulk

So far, all the operations in this chapter have been carried out manually. However, in an organization with a large number of courses and categories, this process should be automated. In **Courses | Upload courses**, Moodle provides us with a powerful tool to manage courses in bulk. This not only lets us create new courses, it also caters for updating and deleting courses as well as restoring courses from backups and course templates.

In order to create courses in batch mode, you will need to create a CSV file, which contains the following fields (the full list can be found at `https://docs.moodle. org/en/Upload_courses`):

- **Course information fields:** These are identical to the fields on the course settings page, for example, short name, full name, and ID number.

  In order to specify the category in which the course has to be placed, you have three options (in order of precedence):

  ```
  category (internal ID)category_idnumber (ID number)category_path (
  [category]<space>/<space>[subcategory]…).
  ```

  The following is a sample file demonstrating all the three options:

  ```
  shortname,fullname,category,category_idnumber,category_path
  course1,Course One,4,,
  course2,Course Two,,COMP-1,
  course3,Course Three,,,Computing / Computing - Year 1
  ```

   Categories cannot be created in batch mode; they MUST exist! Alternatively, make use of MOOSH, a Moodle Shell, which will be explained in more detail in *Chapter 14, Moodle Admin Tools*.

- **Enrolment fields**: These let you enable and configure enrolment plugins. We will be dealing with enrolments further down in this section, so here is a sample to configure self-enrolment:

  ```
  shortname,fullname,category,enrolment_1,enrolment_1_startdate
  course1,Course One,4,self,06/10/14
  course2,Course Two,4,self,06/10/14
  course3,Course Three,4,self,06/10/14
  ```

  At the time of writing, only the enrolment methods manual and self are supported by course uploads. To monitor progress on this missing subfeature, monitor MDL-43127 in the bug tracker database.

- **Role renaming**: This provides a means to rename standard roles. We will be dealing with roles in *Chapter 5, User Management*.

In addition to these three types of fields, so-called course action fields can be specified in order to perform an action other than creating courses:

- **delete**: 1 to delete a course.
- **rename**: new shortname.
- **backup file**: absolute path of a backup file (`.mbz`), which will be used as a source. This can potentially lead to performance problems (check out `$CFG-> keeptempdirectoriesonbackup` in the *Appendix, Configuration Settings*).
- **template course**: shortname of an existing course which will be used as a source.
- **reset**: 1 to reset the course, that is to remove any user data.

Once a file has been uploaded, you will have to change the file format settings **CSV delimiter** and **Encoding** if they are incorrect. You can further specify the number of **Preview rows**. Then, the following import options can be configured:

Option	Description
Upload mode	There are four self-explanatory options whether courses will be created or updated: • Create new courses only, skip existing ones • Create all, increment if needed (see templates further down) • Create new courses, or update the existing ones • Only update the existing ones If any of the latter two options are selected, the following settings will become available.
Update mode	The modes specifies what data source will be used for updating fields: • No changes • Update with CSV data only • Update with CSV data only and defaults • Fill in missing items from CSV and defaults
Allow deletes	Determines whether the **delete** field will be accepted or not
Allow renames	Determines whether the **rename** field will be accepted or not
Allow resets	Determines whether the **reset** field will be accepted or not

General

File* ⑦	Choose a file...

courses.csv

CSV delimiter ⑦	, ⬍
Encoding ⑦	UTF-8 ⬍
Preview rows ⑦	10 ⬍

Import options

Upload mode ⑦	✓ Create new courses only, skip existing ones
	Create all, increment shortname if needed
	Create new courses, or update existing ones
Update mode ⑦	Only update existing courses ⬍
Allow deletes ⑦	No ⬍
Allow renames ⑦	No ⬍
Allow resets ⑦	No ⬍

Preview

When in preview mode, you will see these import options again as well as the **Course process** settings and **Default course values**. The latter are the values used if not provided in the CSV file and an update mode is chosen that supports defaults. The course process supports two types of templates, which require some more explanation:

- **Course name templates**: If the CSV file does not contain a **shortname** column, you have the option to use template syntax to set the name, depending on either the **idnumber (%i)** or the **fullname (%f)**. For instance, **Template to generate a shortname** is **Test %i** with **Upload mode** set to **Create all, increment shortname if needed** would result in the three courses Test_1, Test_2, and Test_3 with our previously used input file.

- **Course content templates**: You can either specify the absolute path of a Moodle backup file or the shortname of an existing course as a content template for the newly-created course. We will be dealing with backup in *Chapter 13, Backup and Restore*, so for now, let's assume that they have a suffix, .mbz. If either option is chosen, you need to select the **Reset course after upload** option to remove any user data that has been added in the source course:

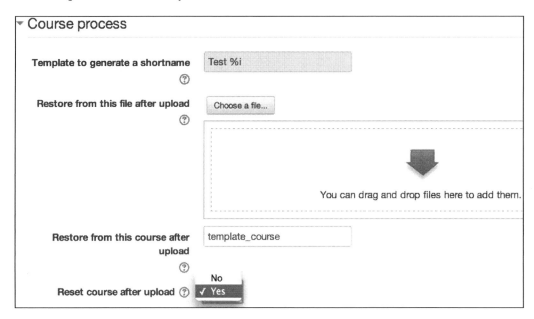

Once courses have been uploaded, you will see the summary of results, which is shown in the next screenshot:

Upload courses results

Line	Result	ID	Short name	Full name	ID number	Status
1	✓	17	course1	Course One		Course created
2	✗		course2	Course Two		Could not resolve category by ID number
3	✓	18	course3	Course Three		Course created
4	✓	16	dummy			Course deleted
5	✗		test	Test course		Could not resolve category by ID

- Courses total: 5
- Courses created: 2
- Courses updated: 0
- Courses deleted: 1
- Courses errors: 2

There is also a CLI tool to perform course uploads from the command line. You can find it in `admin/tool/uploadcourse/cli/uploadcourse.php`. You will see all the supported parameters by calling the help mode:

```
sudo /usr/bin/php admin/tool/uploadcourse/cli/uploadcourse.php --help
```

Here is an example of its usage:

```
sudo /usr/bin/php admin/tool/uploadcourse/cli/uploadcourse.php
--mode=createall --updatemode=dataordefaults --file=./courses.csv --
delimiter=comma
```

Forms of enrolment

We have already touched upon enrolment in the introductory chapter, *Chapter 3, Courses, Users, and Roles*. Now, we will go into more detail and look at the different mechanisms that can be set up to grant users access to courses. You may recall the basic enrolment workflow presented in the earlier chapter. Let's have a look at a more detailed version:

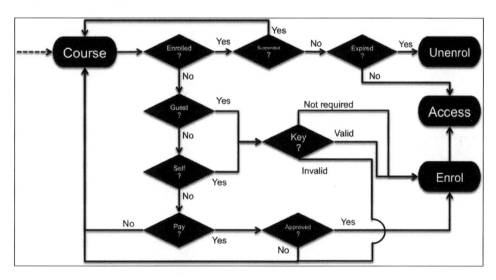

Let's start from the top-left, where the user attempts to access a course. If he/she is already enrolled and the enrolment has not expired yet, he will be granted access. If he/she is suspended, access will be denied. If he/she is not enrolled, Moodle checks whether guest or self enrolment access is allowed. If either is the case, the enrolment key will be checked. If the key is correct or not required, enrolment will take place and access will be granted. Lastly, it is checked if payment is accepted and, if approved, the user will be enrolled to the courses. You might come back to this diagram when we deal with a specific enrolment mechanism.

Students need to be given access to a course before they are allowed to use it. Or, in Moodle-speak, users need to be assigned a role in the course context. They can be assigned the role automatically via cohorts or external enrolment facilities, by self-enrolling, or manually via **Users | Enrolled users** in the **Course administration** section in a course.

Granting access is performed via an enrolment mechanism. Moodle supports a wide range of enrolment options, which are discussed in the remainder of the chapter.

The actual enrolment of students does not require administrator rights, and is a task that can be performed by teachers. The role of the administrator is to set up the enrolment mechanisms available site wide.

You can access the course enrolments configuration page via **Plugins | Enrolments | Manage enrolment plugins**. Each supported enrolment mechanism is represented by an enrolment plugin that can be enabled and configured separately.

Available course enrolment plugins

Name	Instances / enrolments	Version	Enable	Up/Down	Settings	Test settings	Uninstall
Manual enrolments	7 / 5	2013110500	👁	↓	Settings		
Guest access	7 / 0	2013110500	👁	↑ ↓	Settings		Uninstall
Self enrolment	7 / 0	2013112100	👁	↑ ↓	Settings		Uninstall
Cohort sync	0 / 0	2013110500	👁	↑ ↓	Settings		Uninstall
LDAP enrolments	0 / 0	2013110500	👁	↑ ↓	Settings		Uninstall
External database	0 / 0	2013110500	👁	↑	Settings	Test settings	Uninstall
Category enrolments	0 / 0	2013110500	🚫		Settings		Uninstall
Flat file (CSV)	0 / 0	2013110500	🚫		Settings		Uninstall
IMS Enterprise file	0 / 0	2013110500	🚫		Settings		Uninstall
Course meta link	0 / 0	2013110500	🚫		Settings		Uninstall
MNet remote enrolments	0 / 0	2013110500	🚫		Settings		Uninstall
PayPal	0 / 0	2013110500	🚫		Settings		Uninstall

For every plugin, the number of instances and enrolments are shown. Each plugin can be enabled or disabled separately, and multiple plugins can be enabled simultaneously (multi-enrolment). The arrangement of plugins determines in which order user enrolments are checked when a user attempts to enter a course. It is recommended to give the plugins, that are used by the majority of users, higher priority over the ones that are only used sporadically as this will benefit system performance.

All the plugins have to be configured; we will deal with these settings when we cover the individual enrolment mechanisms. While it is possible to uninstall plugins, it is not recommended. If they are required at a later stage, they will have to be re-installed. The preference is to simply leave them disabled.

 Users need to have a user account before they can be enrolled in a course.

Each enrolment type is now covered in some detail except MNet remote enrolments (Moodle Networking), which is covered in *Chapter 16, Moodle Networking* and category enrolments, which is a legacy solution and has been replaced by cohort synchronization. The type of enrolment mechanism you choose depends entirely on the infrastructure you have in place, that is, where and in what format learners' data is stored.

Once an enrolment form has been set up, it has to be configured inside the course in which it will be used. Go to **Users | Enrolment methods** in **Course administration**, where you will see a list of all the enrolment plugins that are active (shown) and not active (hidden). Each enrolment method comes with a number of settings (except **Guest access**), which we will cover as part of the plugin itself.

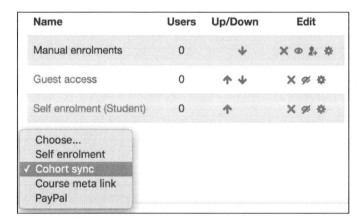

Any non-database enrolment method that has been enabled and configured at site level can be added via the **Add method** drop-down menu. Whether a plugin automatically appears in the list of new courses depends on the **Add instance to new courses** parameter. Some plugins, for example, **Self enrolment** or **PayPal**, can be added multiple times in the same course, which is useful if you need to support multiple roles.

Internal enrolment

Moodle supports three types of internal enrolments:

- Manual enrolment
- Self enrolment
- Guest access

Manual enrolment

Manual enrolment is the default enrolment mechanism when Moodle is installed. The sitewide settings are set at **Plugins | Enrolments | Manual enrolments**:

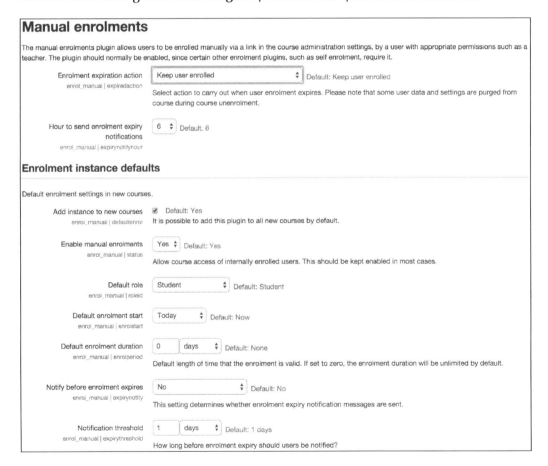

Option	Description
Enrolment expiration action	This is the action to be taken when a user enrolment expires.
Hour to send enrolment expiry notifications	This is the time when the enrolment expiry notification will be sent out to the user.
Add instance to new course	Every newly-created course will contain this plugin, by default.
Enable manual enrolments	The plugin is enabled by default.
Default role	This is the role that manually enrolled users will have by default.
Default enrolment start	The three options when the enrolment is to commence are **Course start**, **Today** (default), and **Now**.
Default enrolment duration	This is the default time for how long users are enrolled in a course.
Notify before enrolment expires	You can opt to notify only the enroller or the enrolled user and also the effected user.
Notification threshold	This is the time before expiration a user will be notified.

Once the plugin has been set up, you will see a very similar-looking screen under **Users** | **Enrolment methods** | **Manual enrolments** | **Edit**, in the **Course administration** section:

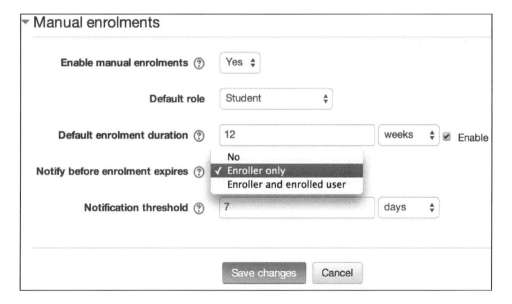

The actual enrolment of users takes place in **Users | Enrolled users** as we have already covered this in the previous chapter. What we haven't covered yet are suspension and expiry of enrolments. You can change these via the edit symbol in the **Enrolment methods** column of your enrolled course users:

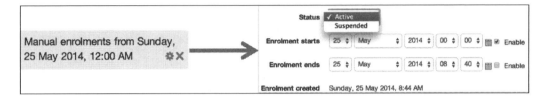

A teacher can carry out all of these steps, but you might decide that these tasks should be carried out centrally for reasons of consistency and also to simplify their workflows. If this is the case, their role has to be modified so that only administrators or dedicated users can deal with enrolments.

If you need to unenrol multiple users from a course, select the **Enrol users** icon in the **Edit** column of **Enrolment methods** where you can select multiple users and remove them from the course.

Self enrolment

The concept of self enrolment is relatively simple. Users choose which courses they want to participate in. A course can contain a password, known as the enrolment key. Anyone who knows this key is able to add themselves to a course. An opened-door icon is shown besides courses that allow guest access without a password; a closed-door icon is shown otherwise.

The enrolment key is set at course level. The teacher has to inform the students about the key and ideally limit the enrolment period to an appropriate time frame to avoid any misuse.

Once the enrolment key has been set, learners will have to enter it when they try to access the course for the first time. If the key is entered correctly, access will be granted, otherwise, it will be denied.

 Self enrolment requires manual enrolment to be enabled.

Self enrolment

The self enrolment plugin allows users to choose which courses they want to participate in. The courses may be protected by an enrolment key. Internally the enrolment is done via the manual enrolment plugin which has to be enabled in the same course.

Require enrolment key enrol_self | requirepassword	☐ Default: No Require enrolment key in new courses and prevent removing of enrolment key from existing courses.
Use password policy enrol_self | usepasswordpolicy	☐ Default: No Use standard password policy for enrolment keys.
Show hint enrol_self | showhint	☐ Default: No Show first letter of the guest access key.
Enrolment expiration action enrol_self | expiredaction	Keep user enrolled ▲▼ Default: Keep user enrolled Select action to carry out when user enrolment expires. Please note that some user data and settings are purged from course during course unenrolment.
Hour to send enrolment expiry notifications enrol_self | expirynotifyhour	6 ▲▼ Default: 6

Enrolment instance defaults

Default enrolment settings in new courses.

Add instance to new courses enrol_self | defaultenrol	☑ Default: Yes It is possible to add this plugin to all new courses by default.
Enable existing enrolments enrol_self | status	No ▲▼ Default: No

The site-wide settings for self enrolments that are found in **Plugins | Enrolments | Self enrolment**, are as follows:

Setting	Description
Require enrolment key	If set, new courses must have an enrolment key. Enrolment keys set in the existing courses cannot be removed, but can be modified.
Use password policy	If set, the password policy (see *Chapter 11, Security and Privacy*) will be applied to enrolment keys.
Show hint	If set, the first letter of the enrolment key is shown.
Enrolment expiration action	This is the action to be taken when a user enrolment expires.

Setting	Description
Hour to send enrolment expiry notifications	This is the time when the enrolment expiry notification will be sent out to the user.
Add instance to new courses	Every newly-created course will contain this plugin, by default.
Enable existing enrolments	If set, all the existing enrolments will be suspended and new users cannot enrol.
Allow new enrolments	If set, new users can enroll to the course.
Use group enrolment keys	If set, users can self-enrol via a group enrolment key and this also makes them a member in that group.
Default role assignment	This is the role self-enrolled users will have, by default.
Enrolment duration	This is the default time for how long users are enrolled in a course.
Notify before enrolment expires	You can opt to notify only the enroller or the enroller and also the effected user.
Notification threshold	This is the time before expiration a user will be notified.
Unenrol inactive after	This is the number of days after users will be unenrolled after they have been logged in to the course.
Max enrolled users	This is the maximum number of users who can enrol in the course (0 means no limit).
Send course welcome message	If set, a welcome message will be sent to the user by e-mail.

Once the plugin has been set up, you will be able to instantiate it at **Users | Enrolment methods | Self enrolment** inside a course:

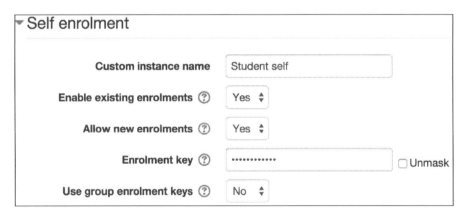

You can create multiple instances of the self enrolment method inside a course, which is why you have to assign **Custom instance name**. This is useful if you need to give different user roles access to the same course, for instance, students and teachers. In addition to the sitewide default settings, you can specify a course **Start date** and **End date** as well as **Custom welcome message**, which will be sent out to newly-enrolled users by e-mail.

Guest access

Guest access can be seen as temporary enrolment. Users, whether authenticated on the system or not, will be granted controlled (read-only) access to a course. Non-authenticated users will get there via the **Login as a guest** button on the login screen. Internally, they are being allocated a temporary user ID, which will be disposed of afterward. The guest icon is shown beside courses that allow guest access.

The sitewide settings for guest access are found in **Plugins | Enrolments | Guest access**:

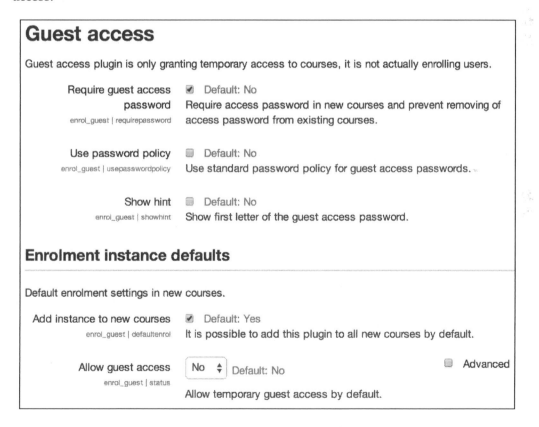

It is possible to specify a password in the course settings for guest access. If you wish to make this compulsory, select **Require guest access password**. For newly-created courses, a random password will be generated (unmask the password in the course settings to view it). It will not be possible to remove guest access passwords from courses, but they can be changed.

The **Enrolment instance defaults** settings are the same as the first two of the manual and self enrolment methods.

The guest access enrolment method can only be allowed or disallowed inside a course. This is done via the **Guest access** enrolment method where you have to set **Allow guest access** to **Yes** and also specify the **Password**.

Cohort enrolment and synchronization

Cohorts are sitewide or global groups. Once cohorts have been created and members have been allocated, it is possible to enrol an entire cohort to a course or to synchronize the membership of a cohort with that of a course.

For example, in a school, you might have a class called 7c with 24 students. The same class has to be enrolled in eight different courses, where each course represents a subject. We only have to create the cohort 7c once and then we can enroll all members of that cohort to each course one-by-one. Alternatively, we can activate cohort synchronization with the eight courses, and Moodle will take care of the rest. Also, if a new pupil joins the class, we only have to add his account to the cohort, and the enrolment will be done automatically. Similarly, if a cohort member is removed, the pupil will be unenrolled.

Cohorts are also great for organizations where groups move together between classes, like an elementary school. Instead of moving individual users from one year to the next, you will be dealing with cohorts of users, which is less time-consuming and more fault-tolerant. Cohorts will be covered in detail in *Chapter 5, User Management*.

The **Cohort sync** plugin (**Plugins | Enrolments | Cohort sync**) only contains two parameters—the **Default role** value that is given to users when they are enrolled and what action to take when users are removed from an external enrolment source, example LDAP:

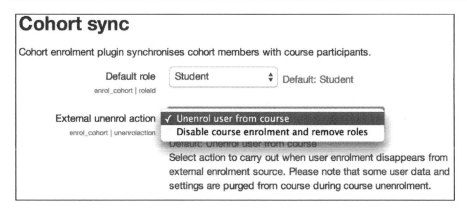

To see cohort synchronization in action, we have to create a cohort and assign some members to it. Go to **Users | Accounts | Cohorts** and add a cohort by clicking on the **Add new cohort** tab. Give the cohort **Name** (in our case, **7c**) and, from the **Context** drop-down menu, select the category in which all the courses belong to class **7c**. Select **System,** if that doesn't apply. The **Cohort ID** and **Description** are optional fields; make sure **Visible** is checked. Once saved, you have to assign members to the cohort by selecting the Assign icon beside it.

Once this has been successful, we can enrol the cohort (that is, all users of the cohort) to our first course. Inside a course, go to **Users | Enrolled users**, click on the **Enrol users** button and select **Browse cohorts**:

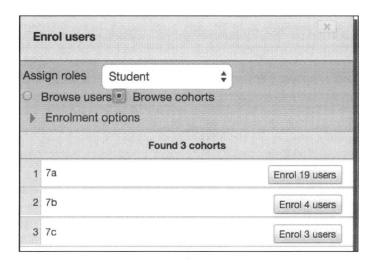

If we select **Enrol n users**, all *n* users of the cohort will be enrolled to the course in a way similar to manual enrolment. However, no further synchronization is carried out. It is effectively the same as manually enrolling all 10 users, but in a single step.

An alternative to this one-off exercise is a permanent arrangement where we set up an enrolment method instance via the familiar **Enrolment methods** link in the course administration section and then add **Cohort Sync**:

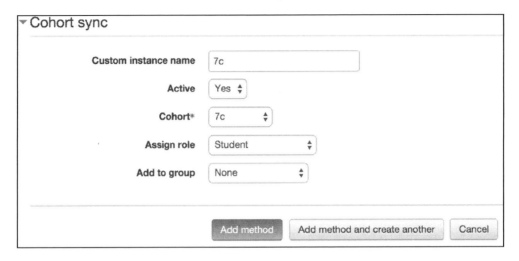

Once added, all users of the cohort will be enrolled and synchronized. Moodle will automatically keep track of the cohort going forward—if a user is added to the cohort, it will also be enrolled to the courses; if a user is removed from the cohort, it will be unenrolled. As with self enrolment, cohort sync allows multiple instances inside a course.

Cohort synchronization is a great way to organize your users if you have groups that have to be enrolled in multiple courses. Whether to use one-off or permanent synchronization depends on the turnover of group members and whether courses have to be kept in sync with those groups.

Database-driven enrolment

In larger organizations, it is common to store certain user-related information on a separate database or directory. If this information contains course-related information, it should be utilized for enrolment. In doing so, you minimize the effort that is necessary when using manual enrolment.

 Unlike internal enrolment methods, database-driven enrolment cannot be configured at course level. They are applied across the site once set up.

LDAP

Lightweight Directory Access Protocol (LDAP) is an application standard for querying and modifying directory services. It is used by many organizations to store learner details and is therefore, well-suited as an enrolment source for Moodle.

It is necessary that the PHP LDAP extension is installed on the server for the enrolment to work. If it is not installed, Moodle will display an error message. The module supports Microsoft's implementation of LDAP, called **Active Directory**, as well as OpenLDAP, an open source implementation of the authentication mechanism. It is common for sites that use LDAP enrolment also to use LDAP for authentication, which is discussed in great detail in *Chapter 5, User Management*.

The principle of the enrolment method is rather simple, but effective. The information stored in the data source about students, teachers, and courses is mapped to the Moodle counterparts. Enrolments are updated when a user logs in. All we have to provide are the mappings.

Moodle makes a number of assumptions when working with LDAP enrolment:

- Your LDAP tree contains groups that map to courses
- Each group has multiple membership entries to map to students
- Users have a valid **ID number** field

The LDAP settings are located at **Plugins | Enrolments | LDAP enrolments**. They have been annotated with detailed explanations, hence I will not repeat them; instead, I will provide additional information where applicable. If you are not sure where to locate some of the required information, contact your system administrator.

There are seven sections of parameters that have to be provided:

- The **LDAP server settings** establish the connection to the directory. LDAP servers with TSL encryption are also supported.

- The **Bind settings** specify details about the credentials to access the LDAP server, that is, the provided username and password.

- The **Role mappings** specify how user-related information is stored in the LDAP server. The roles have to be set which contain a context (usually the same as the one in the server settings) and the member attribute (user IDs). It is important to set **Search subcontexts** correctly. If it is set to **No**, subcontexts will not be searched, but the search is potentially faster and vice versa. Also make sure that the **User type** is set to the type of server you use, for example, **MS Active Directory**.

- The **Course enrolment settings** specify how course and module information is stored on the LDAP server. It also provides options for different forms of unenrolment.

- The **Automatic course creation** is a potentially time-saving feature. A course is created for each entry on the LDAP server in the category specified. To expedite the process and to guarantee consistency among courses, you should create a course with the preferred settings and use it (its course ID) as a template for all the newly-created courses.

- The **Automatic course update settings** lets you specify which fields to update when the CLI script, `enrol/ldap/cli/sync.php`, is run.

- The **Nested groups settings** lets you configure support for groups of groups inside your LDAP server.

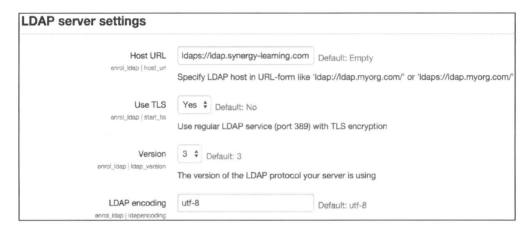

Working with LDAP enrolments often requires a degree of trial and error. It is recommended to create a number of sample courses and enrolments in a playpen, before applying the mechanism to your production server.

If you need to access multiple LDAP systems with different settings, you will need to duplicate the enrolment plugin at system level and modify the source code accordingly. This task has to be carried out by a programmer as source code changes are required in the copied module.

External databases

A lot of organizations use a **Management Information System (MIS)**, either proprietary or developed in-house, that holds information about staff and/or learners and the courses they are enrolled in. It makes perfect sense to utilize this data for enrolment to Moodle. As all the information systems use a database at their core, all we have to do is to get access to the relevant data.

The bad news is that there is a plethora of database systems out there that need to be supported, from the big players such as Oracle and Microsoft SQL Server to the lesser-known systems such as Informix or Sybase. The good news is that there exists a layer called ActiveX Data Objects (ADO), the successor to Open Database Connectivity (ODBC), which does all of the hard work for us. We only have to talk to the ADO layer, and its internals will deal with the rest, no matter what database it is talking to.

The database has to contain course ID and user ID fields. These two fields are compared with fields that you choose in the local course and user tables.

 Get your database administrator to set up a read-only view to the relevant data and provide you with the details. That way, your enrolment mechanism is nicely decoupled from the database itself.

To configure database-driven enrolment, go to **Plugins | Enrolments | External database**:

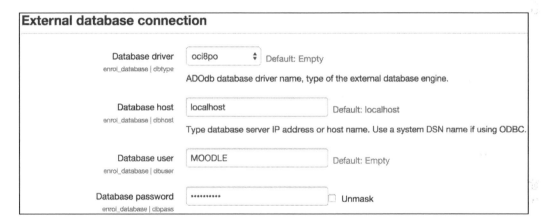

The database connection settings have been annotated on the screen with good explanations, which we are not going to repeat here. If you are not sure where to locate some of the required information, contact your database administrator.

 Some databases, such as Oracle, are case-sensitive, that is, field names have to be provided with the correct casing for the database link to work properly.

For an external database, it is possible to test your settings via the respective link at **Plugins | Enrolments | Manage enrolment plugins**. The thrown error messages will help you to debug your settings until a valid connection has been established.

Flat files

Moodle provides a flat file enrolment mechanism that is configured at **Plugins | Enrolments | Flat file (CSV)**. The method will repeatedly (via the Moodle cron process) check for and process a specially-formatted **Comma Separated Value (CSV)** file in the location that you specify. The format of the file is as follows:

Field	Description
operation	add (to add an enrolment) or del (to remove it).
role	See **Flat file mapping** in the lower part of the same screen, for example, student or editing teacher.
idnumber (user)	This is the ID number of the user to be enrolled. It is optional.
idnumber (course)	This is the ID number of course in which the user is to be enrolled. It is optional
start time/end time	This is the start/end time in seconds since epoch (January 1, 1970). It is optional.

The following is a sample file snippet:

```
add, teacher, 5, Psychology1
add, student, 12, Psychology1
del, student, 17, English2
add, student, 29, English, 1207008000, 1227916800
```

The start time and end time have to be provided together. To generate the numbers since epoch, it is best to use an online converter.

In the text file settings at **Plugins | Enrolments | Flat file (CSV)**, you have to provide the absolute file location on the server. Moodle has to be able to read the file and delete it once it has been processed!

You can choose to send a log file to the administrator and a notification to the user responsible for enrolments and students. **External unenrol action** specifies what happens when a user has been removed from the source file. Similarly, **Enrolment expiration action** specifies what happens to users once their enrolment has expired. The default roles (**Flat file** having role as **mapping**) can be overridden with other values, if required:

| File location | /packt.ab.local/tempdata/enrol.txt | Default: Empty |
| enrol_flatfile \| location | | |

Specify full path to the enrolment file. The file is automatically deleted after processing.

| File encoding | UTF-8 ⬍ | Default: UTF-8 |
| enrol_flatfile \| encoding | | |

| Notify enrolled users | ☐ Default: No |
| enrol_flatfile \| mailstudents | |

| Notify user responsible for enrolments | ☐ Default: No |
| enrol_flatfile \| mailteachers | |

| Notify administrator | ☑ Default: No |
| enrol_flatfile \| mailadmins | |

| External unenrol action | Disable course enrolment and remove roles ⬍ |
| enrol_flatfile \| unenrolaction | |

Default: Disable course enrolment and remove roles
Select action to carry out when user enrolment disappears from external enrolment source. Please note that some user data and settings are purged from course during course unenrolment.

Keep user enrolled
✓ Disable course enrolment and remove roles
Unenrol user from course

| Enrolment expiration action | |
| enrol_flatfile \| expiredaction | |

Default: Disable course enrolment and remove roles
Select action to carry out when user enrolment expires. Please note that some user data and settings are purged from course during course unenrolment.

The IMS Enterprise file

The IMS Global Learning Consortium has specified an XML file format that represents student and course information. Moodle is capable of using any file that conforms to the format as its enrolment source. Like the flat file format, Moodle checks regularly for its presence and, if found, it will process the file and delete it. You can find details of the basic structure of the format at `https://docs.moodle.org/en/IMS_Enterprise`.

The plugin is also able to create user accounts if they aren't yet created, or change user details if requested. Furthermore, new courses can also be created if they are not found on Moodle.

All other fields, including role mappings, are self-explanatory. They can be found at **Plugins | Enrolments | IMS Enterprise file**.

Meta courses – sharing enrolment across courses

Meta courses are courses that take their enrolment from other courses. They populate many courses from one enrolment, or one course from many enrolments. There are two main scenarios when this is useful, which are as follows:

- Multiple courses want to share information or resources (meta course)
- A course is part of a qualification where students have to be enrolled in a number of courses; each course is set up as a meta course

Both scenarios are depicted in the following diagram:

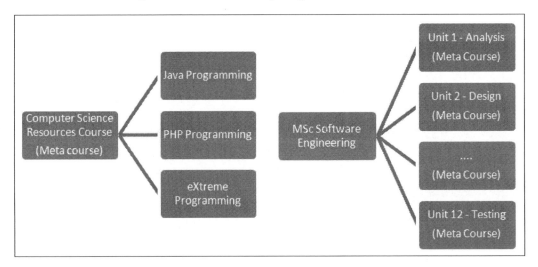

Go to **Plugins | Enrolments | Course meta link**. The list contains any roles that are not synchronized, that is, users with those roles in child courses will also be given access to their parent courses. **Synchronise all enrolled users** means that users will also be enrolled if they do not have a role in any parent courses. **External unenrol action** specifies what happens when a user has been removed from the external enrolment source, for instance, a CSV file or LDAP. The parameter, **Sort course list,** determines whether courses are being ordered as specified at **Courses | Manage courses and categories (Sort order)** or by one of the selected sort criteria.

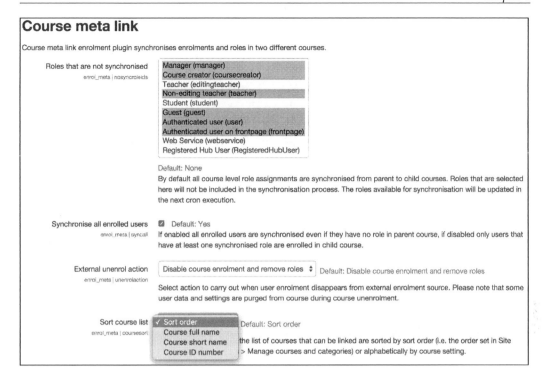

Course meta link

Course meta link enrolment plugin synchronises enrolments and roles in two different courses.

Roles that are not synchronised enrol_meta | nosyncroleids	Manager (manager) Course creator (coursecreator) Teacher (editingteacher) Non-editing teacher (teacher) Student (student) Guest (guest) Authenticated user (user) Authenticated user on frontpage (frontpage) Web Service (webservice) Registered Hub User (RegisteredHubUser)

Default: None

By default all course level role assignments are synchronised from parent to child courses. Roles that are selected here will not be included in the synchronisation process. The roles available for synchronisation will be updated in the next cron execution.

Synchronise all enrolled users
enrol_meta | syncall

☑ Default: Yes

If enabled all enrolled users are synchronised even if they have no role in parent course, if disabled only users that have at least one synchronised role are enrolled in child course.

External unenrol action
enrol_meta | unenrolaction

Disable course enrolment and remove roles ⬍ Default: Disable course enrolment and remove roles

Select action to carry out when user enrolment disappears from external enrolment source. Please note that some user data and settings are purged from course during course unenrolment.

Sort course list
enrol_meta | coursesort

✓ Sort order
Course full name
Course short name
Course ID number

Default: Sort order

the list of courses that can be linked are sorted by sort order (i.e. the order set in Site > Manage courses and categories) or alphabetically by course setting.

Teachers have the right to set up meta courses and to manage its dependents via **Course meta link** under **Enrolment method** in the **Users** section of a course. While it is the role of the teacher to manage meta courses, experience has shown that the administrator is frequently asked to set these up on behalf of others.

 A child course gives its enrolments to the parent course. Create a link from the parent course to the child course.

To set up the first scenario, as shown in the earlier diagram, where the meta course holds shared resources, you have to create all the four courses first and create three separate course meta link instances from within the **Computer Science Resources Course**. Each instance has to link to a separate child course.

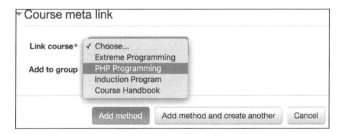

To model the second scenario, you will have to create all 13 courses (one course for MSc Software Engineering and a course for each unit) and add a course meta link method in each of the 12 parent courses to the MSc Software Engineering course.

Meta courses are a great way to synchronize users across courses. There are scenarios where you can achieve the same with cohorts and cohort synchronization. If this is the case, it is usually the preferred option to work with cohorts as they are easier to manage, especially on larger sites.

Enrolment with payment

Moodle comes with a single enrolment plugin that enables you to set up paid courses. There exist other third-party plugins fulfilling the same purpose, but they have not been incorporated into the core Moodle system. Popular examples are Course Merchant (a fully-featured e-commerce service, dedicated to e-learning applications) and `Authorize.net` (a payment gateway which supports credit card and electronic check payments).

PayPal

Moodle supports payments for courses, a feature that has been implemented as an enrolment plugin. Simply put, once the payment has been successful, the user will be enrolled in the course.

You have to specify the default cost and currency at site level (**Plugins | Enrolments | PayPal**).This amount can be overridden in the course. If a course is free of cost, students are not asked to pay for entry. If you enter an enrolment key in the course settings, then students will also have the option to enroll using a key. This is useful if you have a mixture of paying and non-paying learners.

You require a valid PayPal account that can be set up at no cost at `https://www.`
`paypal.com/in/webapps/mpp/home` (PayPal does take a small percentage of each
transaction, though). The notification parameters indicate who is going to be sent an
e-mail once a user has enrolled via a PayPal payment. The language encoding has to
be set to UTF-8/Unicode in the **More Options** area of your PayPal account.

PayPal

The PayPal module allows you to set up paid courses. If the cost for any course is zero, then students are not asked to pay for entry. There is a site-wide cost that you set here as a default for the whole site and then a course setting that you can set for each course individually. The course cost overrides the site cost.

PayPal business email enrol_paypal	paypalbusiness	youremail@paypal.com Default: Empty The email address of your business PayPal account
Notify students enrol_paypal	mailstudents	☑ Default: No
Notify teachers enrol_paypal	mailteachers	☑ Default: No
Notify admin enrol_paypal	mailadmins	☐ Default: No
Enrolment expiration action enrol_paypal	expiredaction	Disable course enrolment and remove roles ⬍ Default: Disable course enrolment and remove roles Select action to carry out when user enrolment expires. Please note that some user data and settings are purged from course during course unenrolment.

Enrolment instance defaults

Default enrolment settings in new courses.

Allow PayPal enrolments enrol_paypal	status	Yes ⬍ Default: No Allow users to use PayPal to enrol into a course by default.
Enrol cost enrol_paypal	cost	199 Default: 0
Currency enrol_paypal	currency	Euro ⬍ Default: US Dollar
Default role assignment enrol_paypal	roleid	Student ⬍ Default: Student Select role which should be assigned to users during PayPal enrolments
Enrolment duration enrol_paypal	enrolperiod	0 days ⬍ Default: None Default length of time that the enrolment is valid. If set to zero, the enrolment duration will be unlimited by default.

Inside a course, you can create multiple instances of PayPal enrolment methods. This allows you to charge different amounts to different user groups/roles or in different currencies.

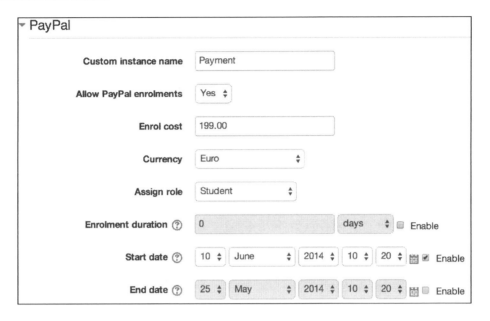

Moodle has the ability to test the PayPal enrolment mechanism using the PayPal developer sandbox. You will have to add `$CFG->usepaypalsandbox` to your `config.php` file (see *Appendix, Configuration Settings* for details).

Summary

In this chapter, you learned everything about courses and categories. As we have discovered, courses are key to Moodle as they contain all the learning activities and content prepared by teachers and used by students. Even Moodle's front page is a course, but we will deal with this later when we customize the look and feel of your VLE.

Closely related to courses is the enrolment of users. It is important that you understand the difference between enrolment, which we covered in this chapter, and authentication, which we will discuss in great detail in the following chapter.

5
User Management

In this chapter, you will learn how to manage users in your Moodle system. We will first look at what information is stored for each user and how we can extend their profiles. We will then perform a number of standard user actions before dealing with cohorts. Finally, we will deal with a wide range of user authentication mechanisms before concluding the chapter with a best practice section. We will cover the following topics:

- User profiles
- Standard user actions (manual and bulk)
- Manual accounts (including a batch upload)
- Cohorts (including a batch upload)
- User authentication
- Usernames—best practice

This is a lot to take in, so we'd better get going!

User profiles

Other than guests, each user has a profile that contains information about them. We will first deal with the information that is stored for each user and how it is organized in Moodle.

You can view your own profile by selecting the **Preferences** item in the drop-down menu beside your name at the top of the screen. Click on the **Edit profile** link in the **User account** section to change your profile details. To modify the profiles of other users, click on the **Edit** icon beside their name by navigating to **Users | Accounts | Browse list of users**.

Profile fields

Moodle user profiles are divided into a number of categories, of which the first five cannot be changed via the Moodle user interface:

- **General**: Standard user fields
- **User picture**: Image of the user
- **Additional names**: Phonetic names, middle name, and alternate name
- **Interests**: Tags for social networking activities
- **Optional**: Additional user information
- **User-defined**: Newly created fields

General category

The following screenshot shows the profile fields of the **General** category:

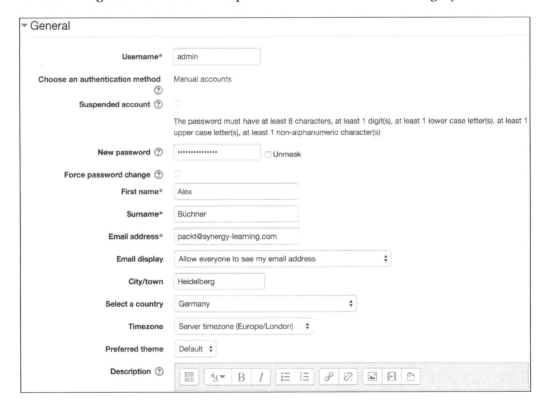

Most of these items are self-explanatory, but there are a few things you need to know about each of them. Here is a brief description of each profile element, along with tips to use them effectively:

- **Username**: A unique username has to be provided. *By default*, only alphanumeric lowercase characters, underscores (_), hyphens (-), periods (.), or the at symbol (@) *are allowed*. If you also want to use other characters in usernames, such as umlauts(¨), you will have to enable these by turning on the **Allow extended characters in usernames** and going to **Security | Site Policies**. It is important to remember that you ought to have administrator rights to change the username.

- **Choose an authentication method**: This menu allows changes to the authentication method for the user. While useful for testing and development purposes, it is highly recommended that you do not select any disabled option from this menu. You cannot change the `auth` method of the main admin account. We'll take a look at authentication methods in detail in the second half of this chapter.

 Selecting the incorrect authentication method will prevent users from logging in or even deleting their account completely!

- **Suspended account**: If you wish to prevent a user from logging in, select this option. This is useful as a disciplinary measure or in case of a longer absence, for instance, a sabbatical term. There is no expiry date on the suspension, so you need to change this back manually.

 Note that this is not the same as changing a user's enrolment to suspended, which only affects an individual course enrolment.

- **New password**: A password has be provided for security reasons when creating manual accounts. If the user ought to change the given (default) password on their first login, the **Force password change** option has to be selected. You can unmask (show) your own password but not that of other users. However, administrators can override the existing password of a user.

  If **Password policy** is enabled (go to **Security | Site policies**), the password has to adhere to this policy.

 For more details on password policy, refer to *Chapter 11, Moodle Security and Privacy*.

- **First name** and **Surname**: These are compulsory fields for users, for which diacritical marks (ä, â, à, á, ...) are fully supported.

- **Email address**: This is a compulsory field and has to be unique in Moodle. It is important that the address is correct, since Moodle makes regular use of it, for example, to notify when a user has forgotten their username or password.

- **Email display**: Choices can be made as to who exactly can see the user's e-mail address. The choices are: **Hide my email address from everyone**, **Allow every one to see my email address**, and **Allow only other course members to see my email address** (default). Administrators and teachers (with editing rights) will always be able to see e-mail addresses even if they are hidden.

- **City/town** and **Select a country**: These are used to further identify users by their geographical location.

- **Timezone**: This is is used to convert time-related messages on the system (such as assignment deadlines) from the local time (typically, the server time) to the correct time in whichever zone the user has selected. It is necessary as your users may be geographically spread across a number of time zones. The default city, country, and time zone can be specified by navigating to **Location | Location settings**.

Additionally, a **Description** field is shown, which is used to provide additional information about the user. As an administrator, you can leave the field empty. However, when a user logs in to their profile, populating the field is compulsory.

A number of additional options might appear in the user's profile, for example, **Preferred theme** or **Email charset**, but this requires the settings to be changed elsewhere. We will mention these when the respective topics are being dealt with.

User picture category

The second category is called **User picture** and, as the name suggests, it deals with the image attached to a user's profile.

To upload a new picture, simply drag it to the **New picture** pane or select the image from the file picker. The image cannot be larger than the maximum size that's listed (here, it's 2 MB) or it will not be uploaded. If your image is too large, it is recommended that you reduce its size to a minimum of 100 x 100 pixels. The formats that are supported are JPG and PNG; however, be careful with transparent backgrounds as they are not supported by older browsers.

The **Picture description** field is used as an alt tag, a description of the image, which is used for nonvisual browsers; it is in conformance with accessibility guidelines.

Once a picture has been assigned, it will be shown in place of the **None** label. To remove the picture, check the **Delete** checkbox, and the picture will be removed when the profile information is updated.

Moodle will automatically crop the image to a square and resize it to 100 x 100 pixels for the larger view and 35 x 35 pixels for the smaller, thumbnail view.

Both of these images are created automatically during the upload process, which also reduces the file size to approximately 4 KB. All the uploaded user pictures can be viewed by a logged-in administrator via the `<moodleurl>/userpix` URL.

If you suspect that your learners are likely to misuse this feature by uploading unsuitable pictures, you can disable the functionality. Go to **Security | Site policies** and check the **Disable user profile images** checkbox. Bear in mind that once this feature is disabled, pictures cannot be assigned to any users (except the administrator), nor will it be possible for teachers to represent groups in courses with images.

Additional names

This section comprises the following fields:

- **First name – phonetic and Surname – phonetic**: The main use case for the field pair is in Far East languages where users have an original and a Romanized version (for example, Japanese) or a phonetic name is being displayed (for instance, Pinyin).

- **Middle name**: In some cultures, it is common to have three or more names that are displayed.

- **Alternate name**: This can either be a nickname, handle, or an alias that is being used in certain pedagogical settings, for example, in a gamification or role playing scenario.

Interests category

Interests, such as hobbies or professional activities, can be entered one by one. To remove a tag, select its label; to recover it again, select it from the pull-down menu. The given **List of interests** represents tags, which are used by Moodle activities, such as the Flickr, YouTube blocks, and for tagging blog entries. You can find more information on tagging at `https://docs.moodle.org/en/Tags` and in *Chapter 9, Moodle Configuration.*

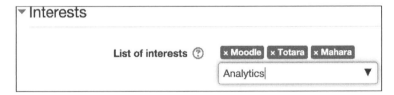

Optional category

More personal details are grouped under the **Optional** category:

▼ Optional	
Web page	www.synergy-learning.com
ICQ number	
Skype ID	synergy-learning
AIM ID	
Yahoo ID	
MSN ID	
ID number	
Institution	
Department	
Phone	+44 (0)28 9042 2000
Mobile phone	
Address	Holywood House, 1 Innis Cou

- **Web page**: This is the URL of the user's web or home page.

- **Messenger information**: Moodle supports a range of popular messenger services. These are ICQ, Skype, AOL Instant Messenger (AIM), Yahoo Messenger, and Microsoft's MSN. When entering any of the services' IDs, Moodle will make use of their functionalities, if possible (for instance, displaying the user's Skype status information in their profile).

- **ID number, Institution, and Department**: This contains IDs of students or staff and information on a school and department. The **ID number** is used by some synchronization tools with HR systems, for instance, Totara's HR Import facility.

- **Contact details**: It has the user's phone numbers and postal address.

Some organizations rename some of these fields to ones that are required in their setup. For more information on how to do this, refer to the *Localization* section in *Chapter 9, Moodle Configuration*.

Creating user-defined profile fields

Moodle allows new arbitrary fields to be added to the user profile. This feature can be found by navigating to **Users | Accounts | User profile fields**.

Profile categories

The profile fields are organized into categories (**General, User picture, Interests,** and **Optional**). Additional categories can be created and user-defined fields can then be placed within these new categories. A default category, called **Other fields**, is already present, which can be deleted or renamed via the standard Moodle icons. To create a new category, click on the **Create a new profile category** button:

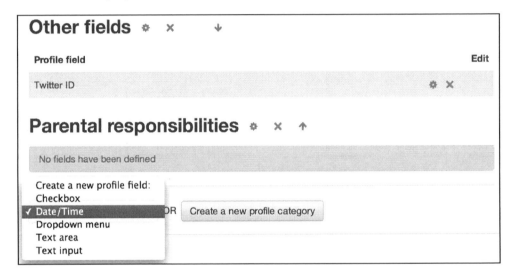

You are asked to provide a unique category name. The category will be displayed at the bottom of the user profile once profile fields have been added to the category.

Profile fields

Once a category has been created, five types of profile fields can be added to Moodle via the **Create a new profile field** pull-down menu:

- **Checkbox** (here, the values are true or false)
- **Date/Time** (this contains the date and an optional time field)
- **Dropdown menu** (selection of a single value from a predefined list)
- **Text area** (multiline formatted text)
- **Text input** (a single line of text or a number)

Once you have chosen your field type, you are taken to a settings screen for that field. It has two sections — **Common settings** deal with parameters that apply to all fields, and **Specific settings** contains parameters that apply only to the chosen field type.

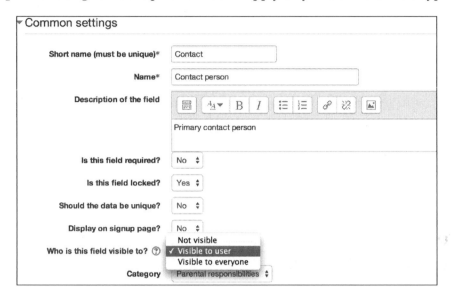

- The **Short name** is a unique identifier of the field that is accompanied by the actual **Name**, which is the label displayed in the profile. An optional **Description** of the field can be given, which is for reference only.

- If the field is to be made obligatory, the **Is this field required?** option has to be set to **Yes**. The field can be locked, that is, the user can be prevented from modifying it. If the value entered needs to be unique, the **Should the data be unique?** field must be changed accordingly.

- When self-registration is enabled, a number of default fields have to be provided at signup. If the new field should also be displayed on the signup page, the **Display on signup page?** option has to be set to **Yes**. This can be very useful in a commercial training setting when additional information, such as the address of the learner or previous qualifications, is required.

The custom field can be given one of the following three visibility settings:

- The **Not visible** setting is typically set by an administrator who wants to hold private data on the users.

- The **Visible to user** setting is normally selected for fields that hold sensitive information.

- The **Visible to everyone** setting is used for any other type of information. This is the default setting.

A **Category** has to be chosen from the list of added entries before the specific settings are shown for each field type. It is only possible to select newly created categories; default categories cannot, unfortunately, be selected. For example, if you wish to extend the existing address field with a ZIP code, you will have to do this in a separate category.

In addition to the common field settings, specific settings have to be provided for each profile field type:

- **Checkbox**: This type has only a single setting. It specifies whether the checkbox will be **Checked by default** in new user profiles or not.

- **Date/time**: The **Start year** (by default, the current year) and **End year** value (by default, the current year + 30) have to be specified. Additionally, an optional time field can be included by checking the **Include time?** option.

- **Drop-down menu**: For this type, a list of **Menu options (one per line)** and an optional **Default value** have to be provided. The list consists of a single item per line. In the following screenshot, three options (Father, Mother, and Carer) have been entered, with Mother being the default value:

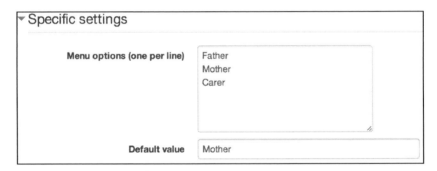

If you wish to allow empty values, leave the first entry empty:

- **Text Area**: This type allows users to define **Default value** in a free-form textbox.

- **Text Input**: For this type, **Default value**, **Display size** (the size of the textbox), and **Maximum length** have to be provided. Additionally, it has to be specified whether the field is a password field, which will lead to masking being turned on, if enabled.

The **Link** field lets you create dynamic links, where $$ represents the parameter that will be replaced with the entered text. In the following screenshot, we have specified `http://twitter.com/$$`. The transformed link will be shown in the user profile. **Link target** specifies where this link will be opened once it's selected:

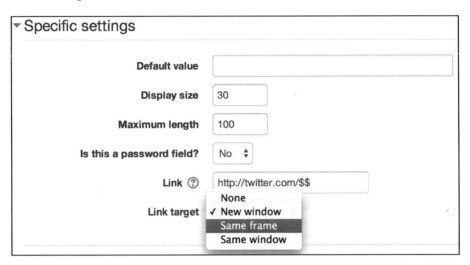

Once all the required fields have been added, the order in which they will be displayed in the user profile can be changed by using the up and down arrows, as shown in the following screenshot:

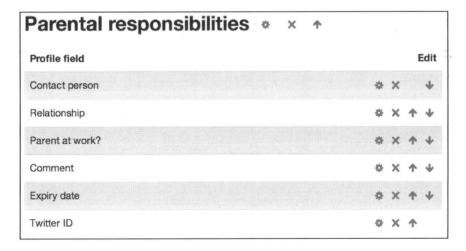

These fields will now be shown in the user profile in the same way as the generic Moodle fields:

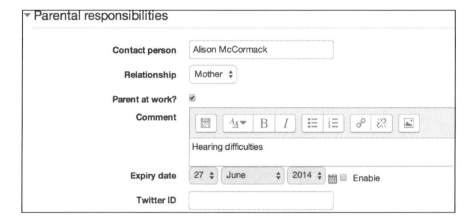

User preferences

There are some more fields that technically belong to the user profile, but they have recently been moved to the **User preferences** section, which can be accessed via the drop-down menu besides the user icon in the toolbar. The reason why this has been done is that you can disallow users from editing their profile altogether (via the `moodle/user:editownprofile` capability) and let them specify certain preferences via dedicated forms:

- **Preferred language**: The default language of the system is shown and can be changed to the preferred language of the user. We will deal with localization in *Chapter 9, Moodle Configuration*.

- **Forum preferences**: There are three forum-related entries:

Preferences	Description
E-mail digest type	This setting determines how a user receives posts from forums to which a subscription exists. There are three possible choices, which are No digest (single e-mail per forum post) — which is the default, Complete (daily email with full posts), or Subjects (daily email with subjects only).
Forum auto-subscribe	This setting dictates whether a user is automatically subscribed to forums to which they post.
Forum tracking	If enabled, posts that have not yet been read will be highlighted, which improves forum usability.

- **Editor preferences**: This option determines which of the configured editors should be used when entering information in text areas. Unless the user has special requirements or preferences, this should be left as the **Default editor** option. You'll learn more about editors in *Chapter 7, Moodle Look and Feel*.

  The default preferences of some settings (e-mail and forums) can be specified by navigating to **Users | Accounts | User profile fields**.

Standard user actions

So far, you have learned what type of user information Moodle holds and how to extend the information that is stored in each profile. Now, it is time to work with existing users on your system.

Browsing users

The quickest way to get access to your Moodle users is by navigating to **Users | Accounts | Browse list of users**. Initially, a list of users is displayed, ordered by **First name**. Thirty users are shown at a time and, if applicable, you can navigate via the **(Next)** and **(Previous)** links or jump directly to another page by selecting a number. Each column can be sorted in ascending or descending order by clicking on the column header.

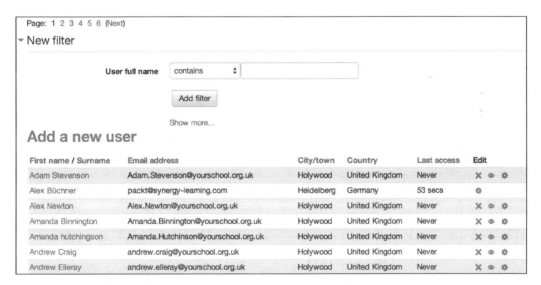

You can view an individual's profile information by clicking on a user's name in the first column. Here, you are looking at your own (admin) profile and not the profile of another user:

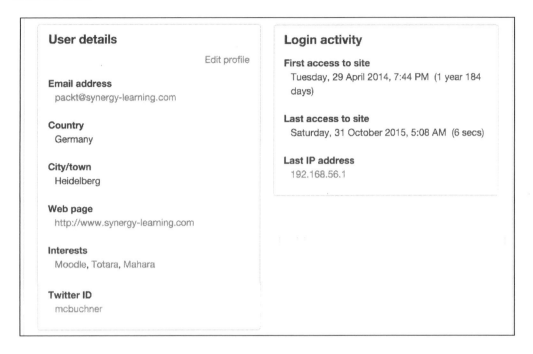

The profile provides detailed information on the user. Hyperlinks are provided to e-mail, web pages, and some messaging services. For instance, in the preceding screenshot, a link is provided to launch Skype, indicating that the user is currently unavailable. Additionally, you can see information about **First access to site**, **Last access to site**, and **Last IP address** took place from.

You can specify which identity information (ID number, e-mail, phone, cell/mobile phone, department, or institution) about the users is shown in this list as well as other places. Go to **Users | Permissions | User policies** and select the fields that should be shown in the **Show user identity** list. This only applies to users who have the `moodle/site:viewuseridentity` capability roles.

When you look at the profile of another user account, you will see a **Login as** link in the **Administration** pane, which lets you masquerade as another user. This is useful when tracking down issues, which you cannot locate as an administrator. To view all the user profile fields of a user or modify any of them, as discussed earlier, click on the **Edit profile** link. To modify any of the user's preference, select the respective link.

To delete a user, go back to the user list and click on the **Delete** icon in the right-most column. A confirmation screen has to be answered before the user is irreversibly removed. Actually, the user is *irreversibly removed* only from Moodle's user interface. Internally, the user is still retained in the database with the *deleted* flag turned on. This is necessary so that certain contributions of this user don't disappear, for instance, forum posts. Technically, a user can be reinstated by changing the delete flag manually in the database; the Moodle distribution Totara makes use of this functionality that offers a recycling function. Totara also supports the full deletion of users, which is very useful indeed.

Filtering users

Very often, we may be required to search for a particular user or for a number of users. Moodle provides a very powerful and flexible filtering mechanism to narrow down the list of displayed users. In the basic mode, you can filter by the full name of a user, that is, the first name and last name combined. The following filter operations are available, all of which are case-insensitive:

Filter operation	Description
contains	The provided text has to be contained in the field
doesn't contain	This is the opposite of contains
is equal to	The provided text has to be the same as the value of the field
starts with	The field has to begin with the provided text
ends with	The field has to end with the provided text
is empty	The field has to be empty

For example, when adding a filter, such as **First name starts with "chr"**, all users whose first name begins with chr are displayed. Take a look at the following screenshot:

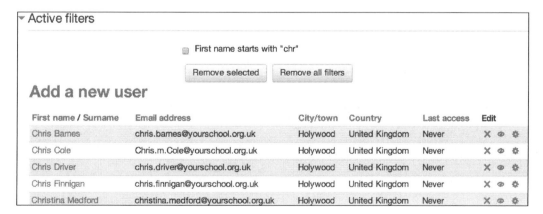

You can see that the added filter is now active at the top of the menu. This becomes more useful once multiple filters have been added, which is done in the advanced mode (via the **Show more...** link). Now, we have the ability to apply filters to a wide range of fields:

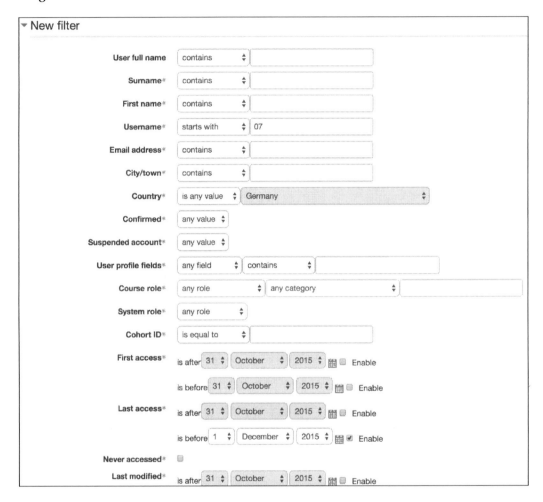

For instance, in the preceding screenshot, we look for all users whose username starts with 07 (our naming scheme starts with the year of entry) and who haven't accessed the system before December 2015. Using this mechanism, it is possible to add as many filters as required.

Every time a filter is added, it will be shown in the **Active filters** frame and be applied to the user data in Moodle.

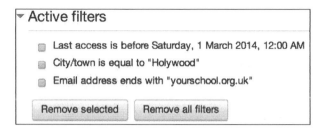

Here, three self-explanatory filters have been added. It is now possible to either delete individual filters (check the filter and click on the **Remove selected** button) or **Remove all filters**.

The filter criteria for text fields has been described earlier in this section. Depending on the field type, there are a number of additional operations that can be used, as listed in the following table:

Filter operation	Field type	Description
is any value	Lists	All values are acceptable; the filter is disabled
is equal to	Lists	The list value has to be the same as the one that's been selected
isn't equal to	Lists	This is the opposite of is equal to
any value	Yes/no	The value can be either Yes or No; the filter is disabled
Yes	Yes/no	The value has to be Yes
No	Yes/no	The value has to be No
is defined	Profile fields	The field has to be defined for the user
isn't defined	Profile fields	This is the opposite of is defined
is after	Date	This contains all dates after the specified day, month, and year
is before	Date	This contains all dates before the specified day, month, and year

The **Authentication** criterion offers a selection of all the authentication methods that are supported. We will deal with these later in the chapter. **MNet ID provider** will be dealt with in *Chapter 16, Moodle Networking*.

If user profile fields have been specified, an additional **User profile fields** criterion is shown, offering a choice of all the user-defined fields (as specified earlier).

The current filter settings are saved and can be used the next time you log in. Not only that, they are also saved for bulk uploading, which is covered in the next section.

Bulk user actions

There are several actions that Moodle allows, which include taking on many users at a time; for example, forcing a password to change or simply sending a message. As an administrator, you can apply these operations, which Moodle calls bulk user actions. They are accessed by going to **Users** | **Accounts** | **Bulk user actions**.

The screen contains two main parts. The first part is the familiar filter and is identical to the one in the **Browse list of users** submenu. Interestingly, filters that are already created will also show up in this screen since they have been saved.

The second part displays the users that match the specified filter criteria in the **Available** list. Before you can do anything with the users, you have to move them to the **Selected** list using the **Add to selection** button. In the preceding screenshot, all five users have been moved across. To move them back to the **Available** list, select the users and click on the **Remove from selection** button. Two shortcut buttons exist, which allow you to **Add all** users from the **Available** list to the **Selected** list and **Remove all** users (move them in the opposite direction).

The advantage of this approach is that you can apply a number of filters in succession and select the respective users. For example, in our setting, if we wish to select all the users from two entry years, we can create a **User full name starts with 07** filter for all usernames that start with 07 and select all the users that show up in the results. You can then delete the filter and create another one for all usernames that start with 08.

When the **Go** button for the **With selected users...** drop-down menu is clicked on, the operation selected will be performed on the users from the **Selected** list. The available operations are shown in the following table:

Action	Description
Confirm	After a confirmation screen, pending user accounts will be confirmed. This is only applicable to e-mail-based self-registrations.
Send a message	You are asked to write a message body, which will be sent to the selected users.
Delete	After a confirmation screen, users will be irreversibly removed from the system (refer to the information on user deletion in the *Browsing users* section, as discussed earlier).
Display on page	The user information is shown on the screen. By default, the fields displayed are **Full name**, **Email address**, **City/town**, **Country**, and **Last access** (take a look at the **Show user identity** setting by going to **Users | Permissions | User policies** for more details).
Download	You can choose between three download formats: • **Text**: Comma-separated text file • **ODS**: Open Document Format • **Excel**: Microsoft Excel The fields that are included are (Moodle's internal user) **id**, **username**, **email**, **first name**, **last name**, **id number**, **city**, and **country**.
Force password change	Users will have to change their password the next time they log in to Moodle.
Add to cohort	Select a cohort that users will be added to. Cohorts will be dealt with in detail in the next section.

Now that we know how to deal with existing users, let's have a look how they are added to the system.

Manual accounts

There are two ways for users to manually (that is, via the internal Moodle authentication mechanism) get access to your system and its courses:

- Adding individual users
- Uploading users in bulk

You will learn how to perform and support each type in the two sections that follow.

Adding individual users

To add user accounts manually, go to **Users | Accounts | Add a new user**. You will see the same screen here that you saw earlier when you edited the user's profile.

You should avoid adding individual users manually as much as possible, as it is a very time-consuming, cumbersome, and potentially error-prone procedure. However, there are situations when you cannot avoid it, for example, when a student joins a school halfway through the term.

If you have more than one user to add, use Moodle's batch uploading facility, which we will look at next.

Bulk uploading and updating of users and their pictures

Uploading users in bulk allows the importing of multiple user accounts from a text file or the updating of user accounts that already exist in your system.

Student information is often available in existing applications, such as the internal student management information system, which can export data to an Excel spreadsheet or directly to a text file.

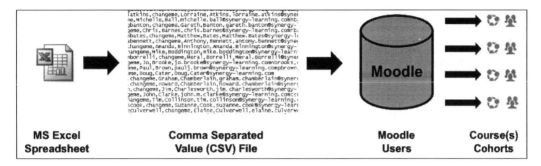

| MS Excel Spreadsheet | Comma Separated Value (CSV) File | Moodle Users | Course(s) Cohorts |

You will find good and detailed documentation on uploading and updating users in the batch mode at https://docs.moodle.org/en/Upload_users.

The text file format

Before uploading users, you have to generate a text file that has to conform to a certain format. Its general format is that of a **Comma Separated Value(CSV)** file, which is a flat text file format. You can create such a CSV file in Excel or any other spreadsheet application. Use the first row to provide the field names, and then fill in each cell with the required data. Then, save the file as CSV, making sure that you specify that the top row contains field names.

The format of a text file is as follows:

- Each line of the file must contain a single record
- Each record must be a series of data that is separated by commas or other delimiters
- The first record of the file must contain the list of field names that will define the format of the rest of the file

An example of a valid input file is as follows:

```
username, password, firstname, lastname, email
galmond, pwd, Graham, Almond, graham.almond@yourschool.ac.uk
earmstrong, pwd, Eleanor, Armstrong, eleanor. armstrong@yourschool.
ac.uk
jarnold, pwd, Joanne, Arnold, joanne.arnold@yourschool.ac.uk
```

The first line contains the list of fields that are provided, while the remaining three lines represent individual users to be uploaded.

Moodle's upload function supports five types of data fields:

- **Required**: Compulsory fields that have to be included
- **Password**: A password field
- **Optional**: If no value is provided, specified default values will be used
- **Custom**: User-defined profile fields
- **Enrolment**: This deals with courses, roles, and groups
- **System**: Assigning and unassigning system roles to and from users
- **Special**: This is used to change or remove users

Required fields

When adding new users, only `firstname` and `lastname` are compulsory. When updating records, only `username` is required. You might recall that the user profile has a few more compulsory fields such as the e-mail address. If these fields are not provided, a default value has to be specified via a template. We will deal with this a little later.

The sample file is an example of a valid input file containing five fields, including the required `firstname` and `lastname`.

Password

The `password` value is required unless **Create password if needed** has been enabled (take a look at the following information). If this is the case, an e-mail will be sent out to the respective user the next time the cron process runs.

If you set `password` to `changeme`, the user will be forced to change the password when they log in for the first time. This only works if the password policy has been deactivated. A better way to do this is using **Force password change** in **Bulk user actions**.

If no password is set, Moodle will, by default, generate one and send out a welcome e-mail.

Optional fields

Optional fields do not have to be specified—if they are not included in the text file, default values are taken, if present. These optional fields are listed as follows:

Field	Values
address	Text
auth	Text (from an existing list)
autosubscribe	0: No and 1: Yes
city	Text
country	Text (from an existing list); the two-letter code must be in capitals
department	Text
description	Text
htmleditor	0: standard web forms and 1: HTML Editor
icq	Text
idnumber	Text
institution	Text
lang	Text (from an existing list)
maildisplay	0: Hide, 1: Allow everyone, and 2: Allow course members
mailformat	0: Pretty and 1: Plain
phone1, phone2	Text
timezone	Text (from an existing list)
url	Text

Let's assume that the default city has been set to Birmingham. In order to override the field for the users who are not living in the default town, the following sample file can be used:

```
username, password, firstname, lastname, city, email
galmond, changeme, Graham, Almond, London, graham.almond@yourschool.
ac.uk
earmstrong, changeme, Eleanor, Armstrong, , eleanor.armstrong@
yourschool.ac.uk
jarnold, changeme, Joanne, Arnold, York, joanne.arnold@yourschool.
ac.uk
```

In the preceding sample file, a city field has been added. After uploading the file, city for Graham Almond is set to London and that for Joanne Arnold is set to York. The city value for Eleanor Armstrong has been left empty and will be set to the default value of Birmingham.

It is important to include empty fields in the data when the default setting has to be used. These must be left empty even if it includes the last field in each record. An empty field is represented by two consecutive commas (as shown in the sample file).

In fields that have numeric values, the options are numbered in the same order as they appear in the Moodle interface—the numbering starts with 0. For instance, **Email display** allows the following settings:

- **Hide my email address from everyone**
- **Allow everyone to see my email address**
- **Allow only other course members to see my email address**

For Boolean fields, such as **Forum auto-subscribe**, use 1 for Yes and 0 for No.

If any fields in your upload file contain commas (for example, in **Description**), you have to encode them as , the upload function will automatically convert these back to commas.

Custom profile fields

Any user-defined fields that you specify (in our case, the ones for parental responsibilities) can also be used as part of the batch upload process. Each field has to be preceded by `profile_field_`; for instance, the field representing the Twitter ID would be called `profile_field_twitter`.

Custom fields are treated in the same way as optional fields. If they are specified, the values are taken; otherwise, default values will be used, if present.

Enrolment fields

Enrolment fields allow you to assign roles to users, that is, you can enroll them to courses and also groups. Groups are created by teachers in courses. Roles will be covered in greater detail in *Chapter 6, Managing Permissions – Roles and Capabilities*.

Each course has to be specified separately by `course1`, `course2`, `course3`, and so on. The course name is the short name of the course. Each corresponding type, role, group, enrolment period, and enrolment status has to have the same postfix, that is, `type1`, `role1`, `group1`, `enrolperiod1`, and `enrolstatus1` have to correspond to `course1`.

It is further possible to set the role of a user in a course. Each role has a role short name and a role ID, either of which can be specified. If the type is left blank, or if no course is specified, the user will be enrolled as a student. The enrolment period sets the enrolment duration in terms of days; the enrolment status suspends a user from a course when it's set to 1.

If you want to assign users to groups in a course (group1 in course1, group2 in course2, and so on), you have to specify the group name or ID. If a specified group does not exist, it will be created automatically.

The following example demonstrates some of the enrolment features:

```
username, course1, role1, course2
galmond, Advanced, editingteacher, Staff
earmstrong, Advanced, examiner, Staff
jarnold, Basic, 3, Staff
```

As explained earlier, the first line specifies the fields in the file. The course1 field and its corresponding role2 as well as course2 are optional enrolment fields. Graham Almond will be assigned the editingteacher role in the Advanced course and a student role in the Staff course (no role has been specified, and hence the default is set). Eva Armstrong will be assigned the examiner role and also a student role in the Staff course. Jonny Arnold will be editingteacher (the role ID is 3) in the Basic course and student in the course labeled Staff.

Cohort fields

Cohort fields allow you to add users as members to cohorts. Like enrolments and groups in courses, the field name has to be cohort1, cohort2, and so on. An example file snippet is as follows:

```
username, firstname, lastname, cohort1
pupil1, Pupil, One, 7a
pupil2, Pupil, Two, 7a
```

Users can be added to system cohorts as well as context cohorts. Cohorts will be dealt with after this main section.

System role

If you need to assign users a system role, you need to specify this via sysrole1, sysrole2, and other similar fields. The value of the field has to be shortname of the role, for instance, manager or coursecreator.

You can also unassign a system role from a user by preceding the role name with the minus symbol, for example, -manager or -coursecreator.

Special fields

The following special fields are supported:

- `oldusername`: When changing a username, you will have to provide the current value

- `deleted`: When removing a user, you will set `deleted` to `1`

- `suspended`: When suspending a user, you will set `suspended` to `1`; to activate, set `suspended` to `0`.

Uploading users

In order to upload or update users in the batch mode, go to **Users | Accounts | Upload users**.

The following settings are available:

Setting	Description
File	The name of the text file.
CSV delimiter	Specify whether the delimiter is a comma (default), semicolon, colon, or tab. In most European locales, for instance, German, French, and Dutch, the default delimiter is a semicolon!
Encoding	The encoding scheme of your uploaded file, which specifies the locale in which it has been saved (the default is UTF-8).
Preview rows	The number of rows that will be displayed on the preview screen.

Once this screen has been confirmed, you will see the following four sections:

- A preview of the specified number of rows that will be uploaded. Records that are to be skipped will not be shown.

- **Settings** will also be included, which will depend on the selected upload type.

- All the user fields for which default values can be set.

- Any user-defined fields that are grouped by category, if present.

Bear in mind that not all settings exist for all upload types; they will remain grayed out if they are not applicable. The following settings have to be applied:

Setting	Description
Upload type	There are four self-explanatory upload types: • **Add new only, skip existing users** • **Add all, append number to usernames if needed** • **Add new and update existing users** • **Update existing users only**
New user password	Moodle requires either a password to be in the file (**Field required in file**) or the cron process will generate a password automatically if none is specified (**Create password if needed**). This one-off password will be sent out to the user by e-mail.

Existing user details	Specifies what is done with the existing user details when an account is updated. The options are: • **No changes** • **Override with file** • **Override with file and defaults** • **Fill in missing[fields] from file and defaults**
Existing user password	Specifies what is done with users' passwords when the user details are updated. The password can either be left unchanged (**No changes**) or be overridden (**Update**).
Allow renames	Specifies whether the changing of usernames is allowed. This only applies to the special `oldusername` field.
Allow deletes	Specifies whether the removing of users is allowed. This only applies to the special `deleted` field.
Allow suspending or activating of accounts	Specifies whether the suspending or activating of users is allowed. This only applies to the special `suspended` field.
Standardise usernames	Removes any invalid characters from usernames (extended characters, unless allowed, as well as spaces) and ensures that all characters are lowercase.
Select for bulk user operations	You can specify whether **New users**, **Updated users**, or **All users** should be selected for bulk operations. You will see the respective names in the **Selected list for Bulk user actions**.

Setting default values and templates

As mentioned earlier, the Moodle batch upload function supports default values that are used instead of optional fields if no value has been set. This includes all the values in the user profile that can be uploaded and also any user-defined custom fields.

Each text-based field can be populated using a template. This is useful for some fields, for instance, the URL of students' websites, and is compulsory for required fields if they're not specified in the CSV file, for example, `username` and `email`. Moodle will warn you if the latter is the case. For example, in the following screenshot, **Username template** has not been provided, which is indicated by the red warning message:

Username template＊

Required. You may use template syntax here (%l = lastname, %f = firstname, %u = username). See help for details and examples.

Email display

Allow only other course members to see my email address ‡

The template (or pattern) will create a value that's based on the values of other fields and the standard characters you specify. For example, if the username should be the first name of a user, followed by a period, and then the surname, the template you have to specify would look like `%f.%l`.

Four replacement values can be used:

- `%f` will be replaced by `firstname`
- `%l` will be replaced by `lastname`
- `%u` will be replaced by `username`
- `%%` will be replaced by `%` (this is required if you need a percentage sign in the generated text)

Between the `%` sign and any of the three code letters (`l`, `f`, and `u`), the following four modifiers are allowed:

- `-`: This value will be converted to lowercase
- `+`: This value will be converted to uppercase
- `~`: This value will be converted to title case
- `#`: This value will be truncated to that many characters (where the hash represents a decimal number)

For instance, if `firstname(%f)` is `Aileen` and `lastname(%l)` is `Bittner`, the following values will be generated:

Pattern	Value
`%f%l`	`AileenBittner`
`%l%f`	`BittnerAileen`
`%l%2f`	`BittnerAi`
`%-f_%-l`	`aileen_bittner`
`http://www.youruni.edu/~%-1f%-l/`	`http://www.youruni.edu/~abittner/`

The last template is an example of embedding the replacement values inside other text; in this case, it is a URL that represents a user's home page.

Loading of data

Once all the settings have been specified, the default values have been provided, and the **Upload users** button has been clicked, Moodle will finally start the actual importing process.

 It is recommended that you create a test file with a smaller number of dummy records first so as to ensure that the syntax is correct.

Moodle displays a large table that contains all the user fields that have been added and/or changed. It also displays a status for each field, including any problems or errors that have occurred.

At the end of the user upload process, a message is displayed, summarizing the upload process. It contains the number of users that were created, updated, the ones who have a weak password (according the password policy), and the number of errors that occurred. Take a look at the following screenshot:

Status	CSV line	ID	Username	First name	Surname	Email address	Password	Authentication	Enrolments	Suspended account	Delete
User not added - already registered	2	158	galmond	Graham	Almond	graham.almond@yourschool.org.uk		manual			
User not added - error	3		sworthington	Steve	Worthington	Invalid email address	xxx	manual		No	
New user	4	312	jwatts	John	Watts	John.Watts@yourschool.org.uk	1234567 Invalid password policy	manual		No	
New user	5	313	dwilliams	David	Williams	David.Williams@yourschool.org.uk	Abcd$ef12	manual		No	
User not added - already registered	6	298	pkennedy	Peter	Kennedy	Peter.Kennedy@yourschool.org.uk	Abcd$ef12	manual			
New user	7	314	pwilliams	Paul	Williams	paul.williams@yourschool.org.uk	Abcd$ef12	manual		No	
New user	8	315	nwilson	Nigel	Wilson	Nigel.Wilson@yourschool.org.uk	Abcd$ef12	manual		No	
New user	9	316	awright	Andrew	Wright	Andrew.w.wright@yourschool.org.uk	changeme Invalid password policy	manual		No	

Users created: 5
Users skipped: 2
Users having a weak password: 2
Errors: 1

It is recommended that you identify the respective users immediately and modify their user settings manually.

Uploading user pictures

The process to upload users, as described so far, does not support their profile pictures. These have to be uploaded separately by going to **Users | Accounts | Upload user pictures**.

The images to be uploaded have to be archived in a ZIP file. Each image filename has to conform to the `user-attribute.extension` format. The **User attribute to use to match picture** field is set to any one of these values: **username**, **idnumber**, or **id** of the user. This attribute is used to match the picture to an existing user, and you have to select the attribute in the respective pull-down menu. The extension is the filename extension (`.jpg` or `.png`). The image filenames are not case-sensitive.

For example, if the username consists of an initial name and a surname (`%1f%1`, if expressed in the template style), the valid filenames are `psmith.png`, `lcohen.png`, and `mstripe.png`. If the users exist, the pictures will be added to their profile. If a picture already exists for a user, it will only be replaced if you have enabled the **Overwrite existing user pictures?** option.

Manual account settings

There are two types of settings for all accounts that are created manually or by batch creation: password expiry and the locking of user fields. These can be changed by navigating to **Plugins | Authentication | Manual accounts**.

Password expiry lets you choose how long a password is valid for via the **Password duration** setting before it has to be changed by a user. **Notification threshold** lets you specify when a user is being notified of the password rotation.

You have the ability to lock fields for accounts that are manually created or uploaded via batch files. This is useful whenever you do not want users to be able to change certain data in their user profiles—young students may misuse the **Description** field, **idnumber** may be used by Moodle to link to other systems, **Email address** might have been provided by the company, and so on.

If a field is **Locked**, the user will not be able to change its value. If you lock any compulsory fields, you either have to make sure that they are populated correctly or you set its lock state to **Unlocked if empty**. This will force the user to enter the value and then it will be locked. In the following screenshot, this has been done for the **Email address** field. If a required field is locked and not populated, Moodle will not operate correctly.

Unfortunately, the locking mechanism is only available for a number of user fields.

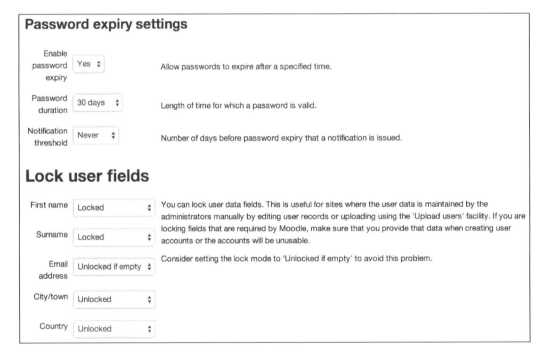

Cohorts

Cohorts are category, site-wide, or global groups that are used to logically cluster related users. We have already come across cohorts in *Chapter 4, Course Management*, when we dealt with enrolments to courses. Now, we are going to have a closer look at how to create and manage cohorts. To do this, navigate to **Users** | **Accounts** | **Cohorts**.

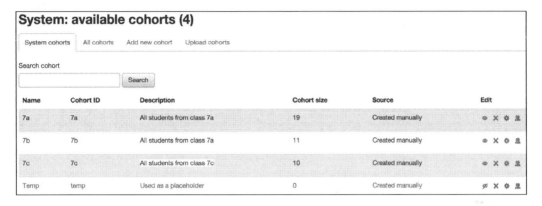

The details of each cohort, as displayed, and its actions (hide, delete, edit and assign) are provided. In the **All cohorts** tab, an almost identical view is provided, displaying system as well as category cohorts.

To create a cohort, select **Add new cohort tab**. A cohort comprises **Name**, **Context**, and **Cohort ID** whether the context is **Visible** and an optional **Description**. Here, the context is equal to the course category in which the cohort can be used. The **Cohort ID** is optional, but it is a good practice to set this as it will be used in a number of operations, for example, when adding users in bulk.

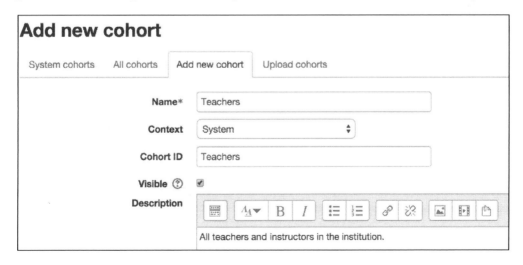

Once you have added the cohort, you will return to the list of all the cohorts. Now, you should add members to it by selecting the assign icon in the list of cohorts. This will display the familiar user selection screen.

Instead of adding cohorts manually, you have the ability to perform this task in a batch via the **Upload cohorts** link. The principle is the same as adding users in the batch mode, as described in the previous section. Here is a sample file representing the cohorts used earlier:

```
name, contextid, idnumber, description, visible
7a, 7a, All students from class 7a, 1
7b, 7b, All students from class 7b, 1
7c, 7c, All students from class 7c, 1
Temp, temp, Used as a placeholder, 0
```

You can find details on uploading cohorts, including all the optional and additional fields, at `https://docs.moodle.org/en/Upload_cohorts`.

User authentication

Now that you know everything about users and the information that is stored about them, let's look at how to authenticate them with Moodle. So far, we have only dealt with manual accounts, which are activated by default after the installation of Moodle.

Moodle supports a significant number of authentication types. Furthermore, Moodle supports **multi-authentication**, that is, concurrent authentication from different authentication sources. For example, your organization might use an LDAP server containing user information for all your full-time students and staff, but it wishes to manage part-time users manually.

Remember the basic authentication workflow we looked at in *Chapter 3, Courses, Users, and Roles*. Now, we can have a look at a more complete picture, as shown in the following diagram:

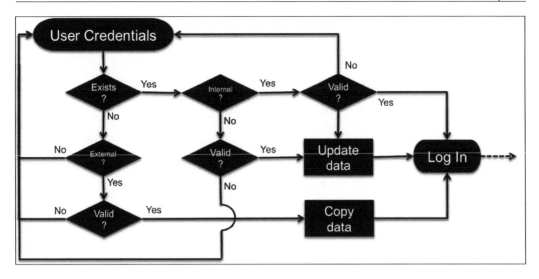

Let's start at the top where the user enters their user credentials, that is, username and password. Bear in mind that this could take place automatically, for example, in a single sign-on setup. Moodle checks whether a profile exists for the user. If it does and the account is authenticated via an internal mechanism, Moodle only has to check whether the password is valid.

If it doesn't exist, which is the case the first time a user attempts to log in, Moodle checks for any enabled and configured external authentication mechanisms. If there is a valid entry, an account will be created, and any existing data for which a mapping exists will be copied to the local user profile and access will be granted.

Once the profile exists and authentication is external, Moodle checks whether the credentials are valid for the set authentication method. If this is the case, any modified data in the source will be updated and access will be granted.

To access all the authentication plugins, go to **Plugins | Authentication | Manage authentication**. You will see a list of **Available authentication plugins**. Each plugin can be activated by clicking on the closed eye icon. If you click on the open eye icon, it will be deactivated again. The settings for each type, which are discussed in this section, are accessed by their respective links or directly through the **Site administration** block once the settings are active.

You can also change the order in which Moodle attempts to authenticate users via the up and down arrows. The order in which authentication plugins are applied will have an impact on how long it takes for users to login, so make sure that the main ones are at the top. The **Users** column gives you an indication about the number of users for each authentication mechanism. Alternatively, you can arrange them in order of fail through if any of your authentication mechanisms might be disconnected, which would prevent other users from logging in, too.

Name	Users	Enable	Up/Down	Settings	Test settings	Uninstall
Manual accounts	155			Settings		
No login	1			Settings		
LDAP server	3	👁	↓	Settings		
Email-based self-registration	2	👁	↑ ↓	Settings		
MNet authentication	0	👁	↑	Settings		
CAS server (SSO)	0	⌀		Settings		Uninstall
External database	0	⌀		Settings	Test settings	Uninstall
FirstClass server	0	⌀		Settings		Uninstall
IMAP server	0	⌀		Settings		Uninstall
NNTP server	0	⌀		Settings		Uninstall
No authentication	0	⌀		Settings		Uninstall
PAM (Pluggable Authentication Modules)	0	⌀		Settings		Uninstall
POP3 server	0	⌀		Settings		Uninstall
RADIUS server	0	⌀		Settings		Uninstall
Shibboleth	0	⌀		Settings		Uninstall
Web services authentication	0	⌀		Settings		

Additional authentication methods are supported by external plugins on `https://moodle.org/`, for example, OAuth and SAML. Once installed (refer to *Installing third-party add-ons* section in *Chapter 8, Moodle Plugins*), they will appear in the list alongside all the core mechanisms. It is not recommended that you remove plugins via the provided **Uninstall** option—delete them at system level instead.

Common authentication settings

First of all, let's have a look at the common authentication settings, which you will see under the list of available plugins. Whatever your preferred authentication system(s) are, there are a number of common settings that apply across all mechanisms.

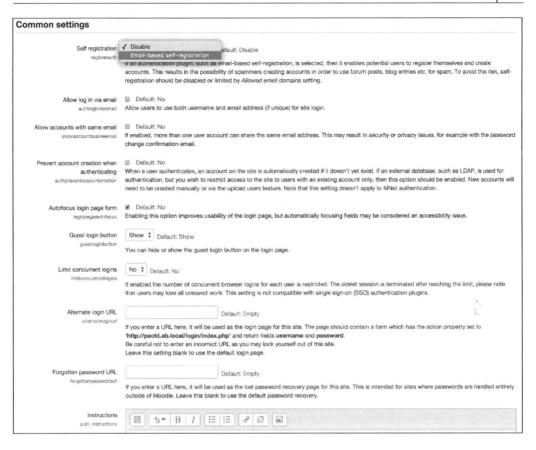

Setting	Description
Self registration	Here, you specify which plugin is used for self-registration (refer to the next section for details).
Allow login via email	Users can either log in via their username or e-mail address as long as the latter is unique.
Allow accounts with same email	In some settings, users will have to share the same e-mail address. If enabled, be aware of the fact that user-specific messages will be potentially read by multiple persons, for instance, the password change confirmation e-mail.
Prevent account creation when authenticating	Some authentication mechanisms, for instance, LDAP, support the creation of new accounts if they're not present. If this is prevented, you will need to ensure that the accounts are created by other means.
Auto focus login page form	When enabled, the cursor on the login page will always jump directly to the username input field if empty, or to the password field otherwise.

Setting	Description
Guest login button	By default, guest access to your Moodle system is allowed. If you disable this, which is recommended for most educational and commercial sites, the guest login button will not be shown on the login screen.
Limit concurrent logins	You can specify the number of simultaneous browser logins. Once the number has been exceeded, the oldest session will be terminated. This is useful in exam scenarios where you might want to allow only a single concurrent login.
Alternate login URL	By default, users have to log on to Moodle via the standard login screen. However, to change the source of the login credentials (username and password), enter the correct URL here. This is necessary if you wish to have a login block on a separate web page, such as your home page. Details of this mechanism are shown in *Chapter 7, Moodle Look and Feel*.
Forgotten password URL	Moodle has a built-in mechanism to deal with lost or forgotten passwords. If you use an authentication method that has its own system to do this, you have to enter its URL here.
Instructions	It is good practice to provide information on how to sign up for the system and what format the username should have (this only applies to self-registration). There are default instructions if it's left blank.
Allowed email domains	You can restrict the e-mail domains for self-registration that are allowed on your system when new user accounts are created, for example, `yourschool.ac.uk` or `.edu`.
Denied email domains	Similarly, you can specify which e-mail domains are not allowed on your system.
Restrict domains when changing email	If enabled, the two e-mail domain settings, mentioned earlier in the table, will be applied when an e-mail address is changed.
ReCAPTCHA public key	This is the key to display the **reCAPTCHA** element on the signup form (refer to the *Email-based self-registration* section).
ReCAPTCHA private key	This is the key to communicate with the reCAPTCHA server (refer to the *Email-based self-registration* section).

Email-based self-registration

If enabled by the administrator, Moodle supports a mechanism that allows users to create an account without any intervention or knowledge of the administrator. When a new user signs up with Moodle via the **Create new account** button on the login screen, they can choose their own new username and password. Once this step has been completed, a confirmation mail is sent to the user's e-mail address, containing a secure link to a page where the user has to confirm the account. The signup screen looks like this:

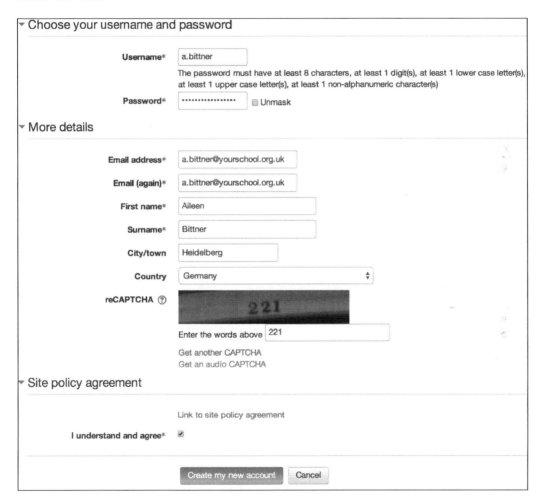

When dealing with user-defined profile fields, we saw how to add more items to the signup screen (the **Display on signup page** option) in the *Profile fields* section. This is often invaluable in commercial training settings when additional data, such as the address of the learner or a customer number, has to be gathered.

Moodle supports a **reCAPTCHA** mechanism that has been activated on the preceding signup screen. The facility is used to avoid automated signups by bots.
In order to activate this facility, you will have to sign up for a free account at `http:// www.google.com/recaptcha/intro/index.html`, add the public and private key provided in **Common settings** in the **Manage Authentication** area, and enable the **reCAPTCHA** element, as shown in the *Common authentication settings* section.

 The PHP cURL extension has to be installed for reCAPTCHA to work.

The same locking settings can be set for self-registration as for manual accounts (go to **Plugins | Authentication | Email-based self-registration**). Also, the same restrictions apply as described earlier. Additionally, you have the option to **Enable reCAPTCHA element**.

If a site policy has been specified when you navigate to **Security | Site policies**, a link to the agreement with the confirmation checkbox, **I understand and agree**, is shown on the signup screen.

The LDAP server

We have already seen a basic introduction to LDAP in the previous chapter when we dealt with enrolments. Now, let's look at how it can be utilized for authentication. We will only cover the basic LDAP settings and exclude advanced setups, such as multiple LDAP servers and the secure LDAP. These are discussed in greater detail in the Moodle Docs at `https://docs.moodle.org/en/LDAP_authentication`.

The principle of the authentication method is rather simple but effective—if the entered username and password are valid, Moodle creates a new user account in its database if it doesn't already exist. Once it does exist, that is, from the second login onwards, the credentials are checked against LDAP for validity.

 It is necessary for the PHP LDAP extension to be installed on the server for the authentication to work.

Go to **Plugins | Authentication | LDAP server** to see the settings, which also cover Active Directory (Microsoft's implementation of LDAP). There are a significant number of parameters that you have to set to communicate with an LDAP server. The settings have been amended with detailed explanations (which I will not repeat). Instead, additional information is provided wherever applicable. If you are not sure where to locate some of the required information, contact your system administrator.

There are two types of parameters that have to be populated to make Moodle work in your LDAP setup, namely, settings and mappings, which are discussed in the sections that follow.

The LDAP server settings

There are nine sections of LDAP settings that have to be provided:

- **LDAP server settings**: These establish the connection to the directory. LDAP servers with the SSL encryption are also supported.

- **Bind settings**: These specify details about the credentials needed to access the LDAP server. If you have multiple bases, it is recommended that you put them in order of importance as Moodle stops searching once it has found an entry. For example, if you have ou=Students and ou=Staff and your students make up 90% of the logins, it is recommended that you put them before their lecturers unless the staff is given priority.

- **Don't cache passwords**: This specifies whether passwords are being stored in the Moodle database or not. This is useful because your LDAP server might not always be accessible, which would prevent users from logging in.

- **User lookup settings**: These describe how and where a user is stored on your LDAP directory. Make sure you select the correct **User type**. For multiple contexts, the same applies as for the distinguished name in the bind settings. It is important to set **Search subcontexts** correctly. If it is set to **No**, subcontexts will not be searched, but the search is potentially faster and vice versa.

- **Force change password**: This specifies whether and how passwords have to be changed by users when they first access Moodle.

- **LDAP password expiration settings**: These are concerned with password lapsing and how this is being dealt with.

- **Enable user creation**: Lets you activate a mechanism that's similar to self-registration, but in addition to this, an account is created with the values from your LDAP.

- **Course creator**: This specifies which LDAP user groups will have course creator permissions in Moodle.

- **Cron synchronization script**: This setting specifies what Moodle should do with local user accounts when these have been deleted on the LDAP server.

- **NTLM SSO**: This describes how in a Windows-based environment with MSAD active, NTLM, if configured correctly, supports single sign-on. That is, users logged in via the Windows domain do not have to reenter their credentials when accessing Moodle. Check out https://docs.moodle. org/en/NTLM_authentication for details.

Data mapping

It is common for user profile information to be stored in the LDAP server. In order to connect the two, user profile fields and Active Directory, a mapping has to be provided where a counterpart in the directory has to be provided for each field in Moodle (including user-defined profile fields). All the fields are optional. Default values are used if you leave any of the fields blank:

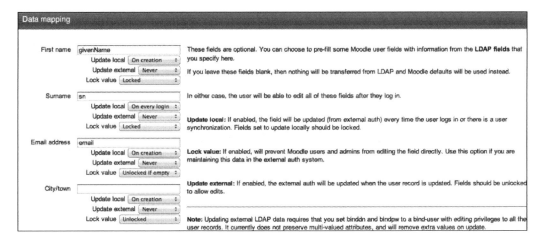

If you provide the field information, you will have to set four parameters for each data field, as follows:

Setting	Description
Field name	This is the field name in the external database representing the value in Moodle.
Update local	For each external user, information is stored locally. You can update this information **on creation** (this is faster but potentially not up to date) or **every login** (this a bit slower but it's always up to date).
Update external	If a user updates the value of the data field in Moodle, you can decide whether you want to write this information back to the external database (**on update**) or not (**never**). Often, the external database is a read-only view, which will prevent Moodle from updating data in it.
Lock value	You can specify whether the value can be modified by the user. The setting is identical to the lock field, which was explained earlier.

If you use Microsoft's Active Directory, check out the Data Mapping section in `https://docs.moodle.org/en/LDAP_authentication` for details.

When using LDAP, you might come across a situation where you wish to assign courses to users before they have logged in to the system for the first time. This scenario regularly applies before the start of the academic year. The problem is that the local user accounts do not exist yet, and you cannot access this information as it is only stored in the external directory. A way around this is to create the user accounts via batch files and set the `auth` field to `ldap`. You can effectively mimic the initial logging in of each user.

The same applies to all external authentication mechanisms, including external databases, which are covered next.

External databases

Most large organizations use a student or some form of **management information system**—either open source, proprietary, or developed in-house—which holds information about staff and learners. It makes perfect sense to utilize this data for authorization to Moodle. Since all information systems use a database at their core, all we have to do is to get access to the relevant data.

IT departments are usually not too keen for external systems to connect to their database. A mechanism that has proven valuable is the read-only view. This has a number of advantages:

- A view can be prepared for Moodle usage, that is, only required fields are shown in the required format
- There's no write access to the database
- If the database schema of the information system ever changes, only the view has to be adapted, not Moodle

The external database authentication method contains two types of parameters that you have to provide by going to **Plugins** | **Authentication** | **External database**, namely, connection settings and data field mappings.

Connection settings

The database connection settings have been amended with good explanations. If you are not sure where to locate some of the required information, contact your database administrator.

Some databases, such as Oracle, are case-sensitive, that is, field names have to be provided with the correct casing for the database link to work properly.

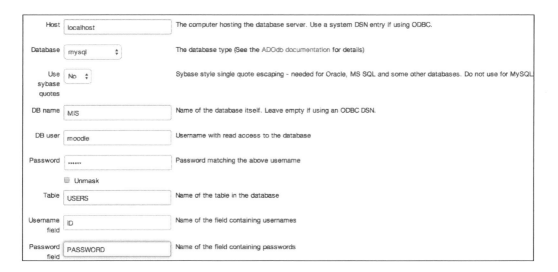

Host	localhost	The computer hosting the database server. Use a system DSN entry if using ODBC.
Database	mysql	The database type (See the ADOdb documentation for details)
Use sybase quotes	No	Sybase style single quote escaping - needed for Oracle, MS SQL and some other databases. Do not use for MySQL
DB name	MIS	Name of the database itself. Leave empty if using an ODBC DSN.
DB user	moodle	Username with read access to the database
Password	......	Password matching the above username
	Unmask	
Table	USERS	Name of the table in the database
Username field	ID	Name of the field containing usernames
Password field	PASSWORD	Name of the field containing passwords

If you experience problems establishing a connection between Moodle and the external database, you can run a test against the database via the **Test settings** option in the table of available authentication plugins. More detailed error messages will be displayed, which will help you identify the connection issue.

Data mapping

User profile information is stored in the external database. In order to connect the two—the user profile fields and the database—a mapping has to be provided where a counterpart in the external store has to be provided for each field in Moodle, including user-defined profile fields. All the fields are optional. Default values are used if you leave any of the fields blank.

This mechanism is identical to the one for the mapping of data in the LDAP setup, which we covered prior to this section.

Other authentication mechanisms

In addition to the popular authentication mechanisms that we have dealt with so far, Moodle supports a number of additional external authentication methods as well as some internal ones, which we will cover in the following sections.

External Moodle authentication methods

Due to the fact that these external authentication methods are not utilized as often as LDAP and external databases, we will only cover them in brief. Some pointers to websites for further information are as follows:

- **CAS Server(SSO)**: Central Authentication Service (CAS) is an open source authentication server that's based on Tomcat and supports single sign-on in a web environment. CAS is gaining in popularity, particularly in environments that comprise multiple authentication sources and consumers. It utilizes LDAP and, therefore, requires the PHP LDAP modules to be installed.

- **First Class Server**: By Open Text Corporation is a commercial client/server groupware, e-mail, online conferencing, voice/fax service, and a bulletin board system for Windows, Macintosh, and Linux. The product is used for the authentication of pupil accounts. In addition to some First Class-specific settings, user fields can be locked in the same way as described earlier.

- **IMAP Server**: Internet Message Access Protocol (IMAP) is a standard used by many e-mail servers such as Microsoft Exchange. The user contact information in the server is used for Moodle authentication. In addition to some IMAP-specific settings, user fields can be locked in the same way as described earlier.

- **NNTP Server**: Network News Transfer Protocol (NNTP) is mainly used to transfer articles and Usenet messages between news servers. Its user details are used for Moodle authentication.

- **PAM**: Pluggable Authentication Modules (PAM) is yet another authentication scheme that maps user information onto a higher-level application interface. PAM is open source and has been adopted as the authentication framework of the Common Desktop Environment. It is currently supported by all the main Linux derivatives. The PHP PAM Authentication module has to be installed on the Moodle server.

- **POP3 Server**: Post Office Protocol version3 (POP3) is a standard used by many e-mail servers. The user contact information on the server is used for the Moodle authentication. In addition to some POP3-specific settings, user fields can be locked in the same way as described earlier.

- **RADIUS Server**: Remote Authentication Dial In User Service (RADIUS) is a protocol to control access to various network resources. It supports authentication, authorization, and accounting and is used by Internet Service Providers.

  It is necessary for the `Auth_RADIUS` module to be installed on the server.

- **Shibboleth**: Shibboleth is a SAML-based open source middleware that provides Internet single sign-on across organizational boundaries. Privacy and security as well as its flexibility in terms of multi-setups, are at the heart of Shibboleth, which is the main reason for its growing popularity. However, the price to pay is a complicated setup process that has been detailed in the readme file at `https://moodle.org/auth/shibboleth/README.txt` of your Moodle site.

  More information on Shibboleth can be found at `http://www.internet2.edu/products-services/trust-identity-middleware/shibboleth/`.

- **Web services authentication**: This plugin is for users who are authenticated via external clients communicating with Moodle via web services (take a look at *Chapter 16, Moodle Networking* for details). The authentication plugin has no settings.

  Other external authentication modules are available as contributed third-party modules, for instance, OAuth and SAML. These can be found in the **Downloads** section on `https://moodle.org/`. More details on third-party add-ons will be covered in *Installing third-party add-ons* section in *Chapter 8, Moodle Plugins*.

Internal Moodle authentication methods

Moodle provides three authentication methods, which are used by a range of internal operations:

- **No login**: This plugin has no settings and cannot be disabled. Its purpose is to suspend a user from logging in to your Moodle system. This is done in the user's profile where you have to select the authentication method in the **Choose an authentication method** drop-down list.

- **No authentication**: When this method is enabled, users can create accounts without any kind of authentication or e-mail-based confirmation. It is highly recommended that you do not use this method since it creates a very insecure Moodle site, and should only be used for testing or development purposes.

  Only user fields can be locked in the same way as described earlier.

- **Moodle Network authentication**: Moodle networking allows the connection of multiple Moodle sites in a peer-to-peer or hub style. *Chapter 16, Moodle Networking* has been dedicated to the details of this powerful feature.

Usernames – best practice

User management in an organization is a critical subject for a variety of reasons:

- Once implemented, it is difficult to change

- A system that is too simple is potentially unsafe and not future-proof

- A system that is too complicated is unlikely to be accepted by users and is likely to cause administrative difficulties

There is no ideal user management scheme since the preference in every organization is different. However, there are a number of issues that are considered to be best practice.

Usernames have to be unique. The simplest way to implement this is to give each user a unique number, which is never reused even after students have finished a course. However, such a number-based system will be very difficult for learners to remember, especially younger learners. It is, therefore, necessary to come up with a more user-friendly scheme considering the following potential issues:

- `firstname.lastname`: This causes difficulties when the same name exists twice

- `class.firstname.lastname`: This causes difficulties when the same name exists twice in a class or group. Also, when learners transfer from one class/group to another, there is scope for a potential conflict.

- `startyear.firstname.lastname`: This causes difficulties when the same name exists more than once a year. Furthermore, students who have to repeat a class or join a school at a later stage will be out of sync with the rest of the pupils in the same class. The same holds true for the `endyear.firstname.lastname` naming scheme.

A system-compliant naming scheme would, therefore, be `startyear.firstname.lastname`, with an optional number added in case there is an overlap. Students who repeat or join the school at a later stage would then be changed manually so as to be in sync with the rest of their peers in the year. Some examples of this are `12.michael.stipe`, `13.leonard.cohen.1`, `13.patti.smith.2`, and `14.bob.dylan`.

For smaller learning organizations, a system that uses `firstname.lastname` as a scheme with an added number (in case of name duplication) is usually sufficient. The same applies to training providers who have rolling start dates for users.

Some organizations still do not make use of e-mail addresses. As it is a compulsory field in Moodle, it is necessary to work around this issue. You will have to come up with a unique dummy e-mail address scheme or void e-mail addresses that have to be used for identification purposes. In order to avoid the usage of the actual e-mail address, it is necessary that you deactivate it in the user's profile.

Summary

Phew! That was a lot to take in for one chapter. This chapter demonstrated the different ways Moodle provides to manage users. We first looked at what information is stored for each user and how their profiles can be extended. We then performed a number of standard manual and bulk user actions.

We finally dealt with a wide range of user authentication types before concluding the chapter with a best practice section. The next step is to grant user roles, that is, the rights as to what they are allowed to do and what they are not. This will be dealt with in the next chapter.

6

Managing Permissions – Roles and Capabilities

We already touched upon permissions in *Chapter 3, Courses, Users, and Roles*. Now we want to cover roles and capabilities fully, which is a complex but powerful subject. Roles define what users can and cannot see and do in your Moodle system.

In this chapter, we will:

- Understand how permissions work and how they fit into different contexts
- Assign roles to different users in different contexts
- Modify roles and create new ones, including a role for parents or mentors
- Manage a range of administrative role-related settings

Let's start with a short definition that should be borne in mind when managing permissions.

 A role is a collection of capabilities with corresponding permissions.

Moodle predefined roles

Moodle comes with a number of predefined roles. These standard roles are suitable for most educational setups, but some institutions require modifications to the roles system to tailor Moodle to their specific needs.

Each role has capabilities for a number of actions that can be carried out. For example, an administrator and a course creator are allowed to create new courses, whereas all the other roles are denied this right. Likewise, a teacher is allowed to moderate forums, whereas students are only allowed to contribute to them.

The description of each standard role and the short names that are used, internally and in operations, such as user batch upload, given by Moodle, are listed in the following table:

Role	Description	Short Name
Administrator	Administrators have full access to the entire site and to all the courses	`admin`
Course creator	Course creators can create new courses, but not participate or teach in them	`course creator`
Manager	Managers can access courses and modify them, without participation	`manager`
Teacher	Editing teachers can do anything within a course, including changing activities and grading students	`editing teacher`
Non-editing teacher	Non-editing teachers can teach in courses and grade students, but not alter any activities	`teacher`
Student	Students can participate in courses	`student`
Guest	Guests have minimal privileges and usually cannot enter any content	`guest`
Authenticated user	All logged-in users	`user`
Authenticated user on frontpage	All users logged in to the frontpage course	`frontpage`

Before we can actually do anything with roles, we need to understand the concept of contexts, which is dealt with next.

Contexts

Contexts are the areas in Moodle where roles can be assigned to users. A role (remember, a collection of capabilities with corresponding permissions) can be assigned within different contexts. A user has a role in any given context; a context can be a course, a course category, an activity module, a user, a block, or Moodle itself. Moodle comes with seven contexts that you will come across a lot in this chapter:

Context	Scope
System	The entire Moodle system (also known as core or global context)
Course category	A category and sub-category organizing courses
Course	A single course
Activity module	A course activity and resource
Block	A Moodle block
User	A user
Front page	The front page and files that can be accessed outside courses

Each context is like a ring-fenced area or boundary in which certain actions can be carried out. It is also sometimes referred to as a **scope**. You can compare this to a large company with multiple divisions and departments. A manager of the finance division has certain rights and responsibilities for every department in his division, but these do not apply to departments in other divisions of the organization.

To implement such a structure, it is important that role assignments to users should be made at the correct context level. For example, a teacher role should be assigned at the **Course** context level, a moderator for a particular forum should be assigned at the **Activity** context level, an administrator should be assigned at the **System** context level, and so on. While it is technically possible to assign any role in any context, some roles just don't make any sense. Unfortunately, Moodle doesn't warn you about this, since it cannot distinguish between intentional and unintentional assignments.

Contexts are hierarchical, that is, permissions are inherited from higher to lower contexts. Rights in a higher context are more general, whereas the ones at a lower context are more specific. The same applies in the company structure mentioned earlier—a sales manager at country level would have the same rights at regional level, whereas the opposite is not true.

The following diagram shows the contexts that exist in Moodle and how they are arranged hierarchically:

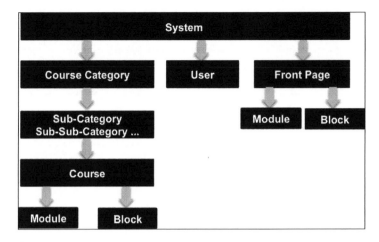

The **System** context is the root node of the hierarchy, that is, every role assigned in this context will apply to any other context below it. The **Course Category** context on the next level acts as a parent to the **Course** context. If **Sub-Category** and **Sub-Sub-Category**, and so on, have been created, respective contexts will exist. On the lowest level, you can see the **Module** and **Block** contexts, respectively. Like the **Course** context, the **Front Page** context has a **Module** and **Block** sub-context (the front page is internally treated as a course). The **User** context is a standalone entity that does not have any children in the hierarchy.

For example, Jim is a teacher for a course. He is assigned a **Teacher** role in the relevant context (that is, the class he is teaching). He will have this role in all the areas of the course, including blocks and activity modules (that is, activities and resources). If however, Jim had been assigned the **Teacher** role in the **Course Category** context instead, he would have the same rights in all the courses in this category and all its sub-categories. This also means that he will receive e-mails about all the assignments, in all the courses, even if he doesn't teach in them.

Organizing contexts hierarchically has a number of advantages that will sound familiar to readers who have knowledge of object-oriented technologies:

- **Inheritance**: The rights and permissions set at one level are passed down to lower levels, which simplifies maintenance
- **Overriding**: The rights and permissions can be changed at lower levels, which we will deal with later on
- **Extensibility**: The new contexts might be added in future versions of Moodle, when and if required, without changing any of the existing roles system

Assigning roles

As mentioned before, assigning roles to users is done for and in a particular context. The process of the actual role assignment (except for courses) is similar for each context. What is different is the location of each context and the method of its access. The process of assigning roles to users is described first, before outlining how and where to assign them in individual contexts:

1. Navigate to any **Assign roles** screen for the required context, for example, **Front page settings | Users | Permissions | Assigned roles** (I will explain how to find the **Assign roles** screen for each context later). You will see this:

Front page roles ⊙

Please choose a role to assign

Role	Description	Users with role	
Manager		0	
Teacher		2	Matthew Bates Mary Fawcett
Non-editing teacher		0	
Student		18	More than 10

Back to Front page

2. In the preceding screenshot, you can see that there are currently two teachers assigned (**Matthew Bates** and **Mary Fawcett**) and **18** students (only up to 10 names are displayed).

3. Select the role to which you wish to assign a user by clicking on the role name or, if there are more than 10 assignees, click on the **More than 10** link. For example, if you wish to allocate more **Student** roles, you will be directed to the following screen:

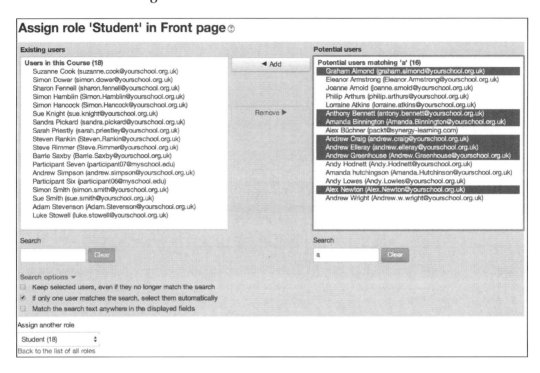

4. Assign the role to users by selecting their names from the **Potential users** list and moving them to the category using the **Add** button. Hold down the *Shift* key to select a range of users and the *Ctrl* key (Apple or *Command* key on a Mac OS) to select multiple users. To revoke users' role assignments, select the person in the **Existing users** list, and move them back to the **Potential users** group by clicking on the **Remove** button.

> Once a user has been assigned a role, permissions will be granted immediately. There is no need to save any changes.

If your list of potential users contains more than 100 entries, no user names are shown, and you will have to use the **Search** box to filter the list of accounts. Moodle uses a live search, that is, as soon as you start typing, the list of users is updated immediately. There are a number of self-explanatory **Search options** underneath the left **Search** box. You might have to expand the area if it is collapsed:

- **Keep selected users, even if they no longer match the search**
- **If only one user matches the search, select them automatically**
- **Match the search text anywhere in the user's name**

So far, we have dealt with the general concept of contexts, and looked at how to assign roles to users within a context. We now deal with each individual context, as shown in the diagram at the beginning of the chapter that depicts Moodle's context hierarchy.

Assigning roles in the incorrect context is a common source of problems. It is highly recommended to check the current context regularly to make sure no unintended rights are granted. In other words, test your role assignments thoroughly.

The System context

The **System** context covers the entire Moodle system. Assignment takes place from **Users | Permissions | Assign system roles**. In our system, only two roles appear that can be assigned. We already mentioned that it doesn't make sense to assign certain roles in certain contexts. Inside a role, it is possible to specify in which context types may be assigned. Only these two roles have been selected, which is the reason for the limited choice.

Assign roles in System ⓘ

WARNING! Any roles you assign from this page will apply to the assigned users throughout the entire system, including the front page and all the courses.

Please choose a role to assign

Role	Description	Users with role	
Manager		1	Sue Smith
Course creator		0	

You will see the familiar screen that allows the assignment of roles to users. The only difference from the generic screen outlined earlier is the **WARNING! Any roles you assign from this page will apply to the assigned users throughout the entire system, including the front page and all the courses.** warning.

In most Moodle systems with predefined roles, it only makes sense to assign the **Manager** role if you wish to allow read-only access to a user for all the courses, for example, an inspector, business manager, or school principal. Assigning the **Course creator** role to a user allows him/her to create new courses in any category. If, for example, a **Teacher** role is assigned in the **System** context, it means that the user would not only be allowed access to every single existing course in the site, but also to all the courses created in the future.

There are scenarios when global roles are justified, for instance, in very small organizations, or if Moodle hosts only a very small number of courses that are attended by all users. Also, some new user-defined roles, such as a school inspector, are designed to be assigned at a global level.

One role that can only be assigned at a system level is the **Administrator** role. This task has been given a dedicated area under **Users | Permissions | Site administrators**. When you installed Moodle, a primary administrator was created, which cannot be modified or deleted. You can, however, create additional administrator accounts. The procedure is identical to assigning users in any other context, with the exception that you have to confirm the assignment.

> Make sure you keep the number of Moodle administrators to a minimum! This will improve consistency of your system, increase security, and avoid potential mismanagement of the site.

The Course Category context

The **Course Category** context covers all the courses within a category and all of its sub-categories. The role assignment takes place under **Courses | Manage courses and categories**, where you have to select **Assign roles** in the respective course drop-down menu. The same mechanism applies to sub-categories, sub-sub-categories, and so on.

A typical role that is assigned in the **Course Category** context is the **Course creator** role. It will allow a dedicated user to create new courses within the specified category, which is very often a department or division. The standard **Course creator** role does not include teacher capabilities, that is, a course creator cannot edit course content. In smaller organizations, it may be required to grant the **Teacher** role access to all the courses within the category.

The Course context

As the name suggests, in this context, all role assignments that cover a course are granted. The assignment takes place in the actual course. We have already come across this in *Chapter 4, Course Management*, when we dealt with enrolments. In fact, enrolments in courses are treated as roles in the **Course** context. As enrolments contain some unique options (start date, end date, and a suspension option) and due to the fact that these enrolments are often carried out by (non-technical) teaching staff, a different user interface has been implemented. However, within a course, when you go to **Users | Enrolment methods** in the **Settings** block and then click on the **Enrol users** icon in the **Edit** column of the **Manual enrolments** method, you will see a familiar-looking screen. We have already dealt with the additional expiry options in the center of the screen when we covered enrolments.

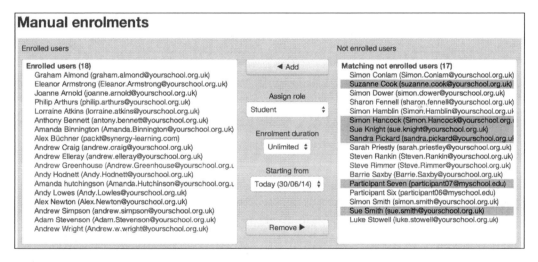

When a student is enrolled in a course, either by self-enrolment or any other enrolment mechanism, Moodle will automatically assign the **Student** role in the relevant **Course** context. This also applies if you upload users in batch mode and specify a course to which a user has to be enrolled.

If you have to assign roles to users who are not enrolled, but have a role in the course, go to **Users** | **Other users** in the **Settings** block and click on the **Assign roles** button. This applies to the **Manager** role, for instance, or a newly-created role, such as supervisor teacher. The user interface is in line with the enrolment interface, not the general roles interface:

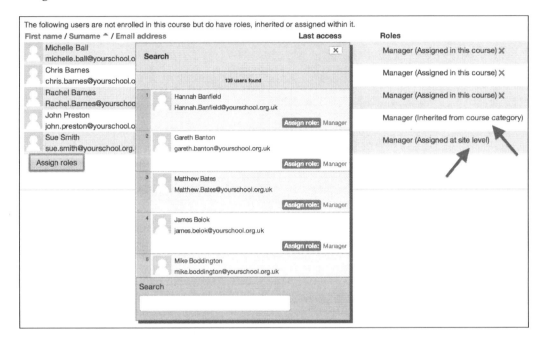

The preceding screenshot also displays any users who have inherited a role in this course, for instance, one user has been assigned in the **Course category** context and one at the **System** level (see arrows in the preceding screenshot).

The Module context

Once you are inside a course, it is possible to assign roles to users for individual modules, such as resources and activities. While editing the module properties, you will see three role-related links in the activity-specific **Administration** block. The one labeled **Locally assigned roles** will lead to the familiar screen to **Assign roles**. The **Permissions** and **Check permissions** links let you change the inherited roles and verify the roles of the individual users. We will deal with this later in the chapter.

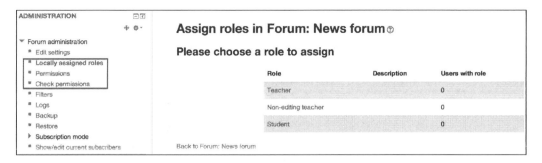

The **Module** context is often used by teachers to grant additional rights to their students. A regularly-cited example is that of a forum moderator. If you wish to put a student in charge of a forum so that he/she learns how to moderate discussions, he/she requires the rights to edit and delete posts (among others). These rights are provided by the **Teacher** role and it is perfectly feasible to assign a **Teacher** role to a student in a single activity.

By default, users with a **Teacher** role have the rights to assign roles in the **Module** context. However, it is often up to the Moodle administrator to carry out the task on their behalf due to the complexity of the roles system. The same applies to the **Block** context, which is covered next.

The Block context

Similar to the **Module** context, the **Block** context allows the assignment of rights on block level within a course. You will see an **Assign roles** link in the drop-down menu when selecting the **Actions** icon (editing has to be turned on).

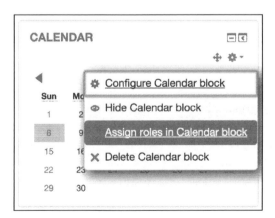

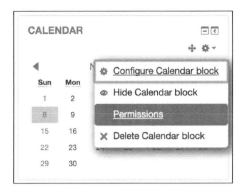

If your system doesn't contain a role that has been granted rights to be assigned in the **Block** context, you will see a menu item, **Permissions**, instead. This is the case, by default. We will deal with modifying roles later on.

It is possible to control the users who can view blocks. For example, you might have a block that you don't want guest users to see. To hide that block from guests on the front page, access the roles page of the block by clicking on the **Assign roles** icon and then the **Permissions** link in the **Administration** block (or use the direct **Permissions** link if applicable). Select the **Guest** role from the **Advanced role override** drop-down list, set the **moodle/block:view** capability to **Prevent**, and click on **Save changes**. We will deal with capabilities further down.

The same mechanism also applies to blocks outside courses, whether on the front page, in My Moodle, on the default profile page, or inside activities.

The User context

The **User** context is a standalone context, which has only the **System** context as parent. It deals with all the issues relating to a user outside a course. They include the user's profile, forum posts, blog entries, notes and reports, logs, and grades.

The assignment of roles takes place in the profile of the user where you need to select **Preferences** in the **Administration** pane. The **Assign roles relative to this user** link *does not appear, by default!* You need to have a role that can be assigned in the **User** context. None of the predefined roles make sense to be applied in such a way, which is why this only applies to user-defined roles. An often-cited example of a custom role to be applied in the **User** context is the **Parent/Mentor** role, which we will deal with in the *Creating custom roles* section.

Preferences

User account

- Edit profile
- Preferred language
- Forum preferences
- Editor preferences
- Messaging

Roles

- This user's role assignments
- Assign roles relative to this user
- Permissions
- Check permissions

Roles assigned in the **User** context will only have access to information accessible from the user screen. They will not have access to any courses.

The Front page context

In Moodle, the front page is a course and, at the same time, not like a course. In other words, it is a special course! The **Front page** context has the **System** context as parent and, like the **Course** context, **Module** and **Block** as the sub-contexts. It is accessed via **Front page settings | Users | Permissions | Assigned roles**. We already looked at the familiar interface at the beginning of the section when explaining how to assign roles in general.

A typical user in the **Front page** context is a designer who is responsible for the layout and content of the front page of the Moodle system. When assigned, only the **Front page** menu and its submenus are accessible. Most sites apply either the **Teacher** role or create a dedicated designer role.

Multiple roles

It is common for a user to be assigned to more than a single role. For example, a class teacher is also made course creator for the year group he is responsible for (**Category** context), or he is in charge of the Moodle administration (**Site**), or he acts as a support teacher in a different class (**Course**), or he is the parent of a child (**User**). In fact, every logged-in user is automatically assigned the **Authenticated user** role in the **System** context. We will deal with this later in the chapter.

A significant part of the roles infrastructure in Moodle is the ability to assign multiple roles to a user at the same time. The equivalent in our initial company example is a member of staff who is in charge of the marketing department, but is also temporarily assisting in the sales division where he/she is acting as a trainer.

To specify an additional role, the actual context has to be selected, as discussed earlier. You will then be able to assign additional roles as necessary.

The problem is the potential for conflicts, which Moodle has to resolve. For example, if one role has the ability to delete a forum post and another one does not, but a user has been assigned both roles in the same context, which right applies? While Moodle has a built-in resolution mechanism for these scenarios, it is best to completely avoid such scenarios.

In fact, it is technically possible to assign two or more roles to the same user in the same context. Having said this, it is hard to think of situations where such a setup would actually make sense.

> If you are desperate to know about the built-in resolution mechanism mentioned earlier, see the section on **Conflict resolution of permissions** at https://docs.moodle.org/en/Override_permissions.

Capabilities

So far, we have given users the existing roles in different Moodle contexts. In the following few pages, we want to have a look inside a role where capabilities dictate what functionality is allowed. Remember, a role is a collection of capabilities with corresponding permissions. Once we have understood capabilities, we will modify the existing roles and create entirely new, custom ones.

Role definitions

The existing roles are accessed via **Users** | **Permissions** | **Define roles**. The screen that will be shown is similar to the familiar **Assign roles** screen, but has a very different purpose:

Manage roles	Allow role assignments	Allow role overrides	Allow role switches		

Role ⑦	Description	Short name	Edit
Manager	Managers can access course and modify them, they usually do not participate in courses.	manager	↓ ⚙ ✕
Course creator	Course creators can create new courses.	coursecreator	↑ ↓ ⚙ ✕
Teacher	Teachers can do anything within a course, including changing the activities and grading students.	editingteacher	↑ ↓ ⚙ ✕
Non-editing teacher	Non-editing teachers can teach in courses and grade students, but may not alter activities.	teacher	↑ ↓ ⚙ ✕
Student	Students generally have fewer privileges within a course.	student	↑ ↓ ⚙ ✕
Guest	Guests have minimal privileges and usually can not enter text anywhere.	guest	↑ ↓ ⚙
Authenticated user	All logged in users.	user	↑ ↓ ⚙
Authenticated user on frontpage	All logged in users in the frontpage course.	frontpage	↑ ↓ ⚙ ✕

When you click on a role name, its composition is shown. Each role contains unique **Short name** (used when uploading users), **Custom full name**, and optional **Custom description**:

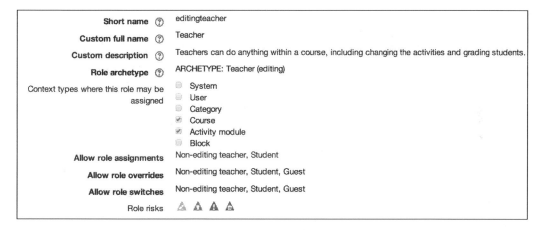

The **Role archetype** field specifies which permissions are set if the role is reset to its default value. The setting further determines what values any new permissions will have, when introduced in future versions of Moodle. These settings will then be applied during the update process.

The **Context types where this role may be assigned** field is set to the context in which the role will be allowed as an option. This reduces the risk that roles are assigned in contexts where they shouldn't. We have already come across this when we tried to assign roles in the **Block** or **User** context, and Moodle prevented us from doing so.

The next three fields (**Allow role assignments**, **Allow role overrides**, and **Allow role switches**) show which roles users who are assigned the current role are allowed to assign, override, and switch, respectively. The **Role risks** field indicates which of the four available risks the current role has. All this information will make more sense once we have dealt with it in more detail.

In addition to these parameters, each role consists of a large number of capabilities. Currently, Moodle's role system has more than 400 of them. If you have installed plugins, this number might even be higher.

 A capability is a description of a particular Moodle feature.

Examples are grading an assignment or editing a Wiki page. Each capability represents a permissible Moodle action and is displayed as a single row in the list of all the capabilities.

To simplify searching for capabilities, use the provided **Filter** mechanism. It only shows the capabilities (with both—the name as well as the description) that match the filter criterion:

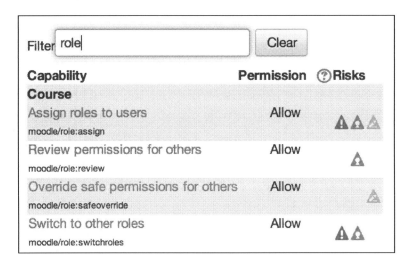

Each capability has the following components:

- **Description**: The description, for example, **Upload new users from file**, provides a short explanation of the capability. On clicking a capability, the online Moodle documentation for that capability is opened in a separate browser window.

- **Name**: The name, for instance **moodle/site:upload users**, follows a strict naming convention—`level/type:function`—which identifies the capability in the overall role system. The level states to which part of Moodle the capability belongs (such as `moodle`, `mod`, `block`, `gradereport`, or `enrol`). The type is the class of the capability, and the function identifies the actual action.

- **Permission**: The permission of each capability has to have one of the four values, explained in the following table:

Permission	Description
Not set	By default, all the permissions for a new role are set to this value. The value in the context where it will be assigned is inherited from the parent context. To determine this value, Moodle searches upward through each context, until it finds an explicit value (**Allow**, **Prevent**, or **Prohibit**) for this capability, that is, the search terminates when an explicit permission is found.
	For example, if a role is assigned to a user in a **Course** context and a capability has a **Not set** value, then the actual permission will be whatever the user has at the category level, or, failing to find an explicit permission, at the site level. If no explicit permission is found, then the value in the current context is set to **Prevent**.
Allow	To grant permission for a capability, set the permission to **Allow**. It applies in the context in which the role will be assigned and all contexts which are below it (children, grand-children, and so forth).
	For example, when assigned in the **Course** context, students will be able to start new discussions in all forums in that course unless some forum contains an override or a new assignment with a **Prevent** or **Prohibit** value for this capability.
Prevent	To remove permission for a capability, set the permission to **Prevent**. If it has been granted in a higher context (no matter at what level), it will be overridden. The value can be overridden again at a lower context.
Prohibit	This is the same as the **Prevent** permission, but the value cannot be overridden again at a lower context. The value is rarely needed, but useful when an administrator wants to prohibit a type of user from certain functionality throughout the site, in which case the capability is set to **Prohibit** and then assigned in the site context. A situation where this applies is when a user is a bad student who is not allowed to post to the forums.

Principally, permissions at lower contexts override permissions at higher contexts. The exception is **Prohibit**, which, by definition, cannot be overridden at lower levels.

- **Risks**: Moodle displays the risks associated with each capability, that is, the risks that each capability can potentially raise. They can be any combination of the following four risk types:

Risk	Icon	Description
XSS		Users can add files and texts that allow cross-site scripting (potentially malicious scripts which are embedded in web pages and executed on the user's computer)
Privacy		Users can gain access to private information of other users
Spam		Users can send spam to site users or others
Data loss		Users can destroy a large amount of content or information

 Risks are only displayed; it is not possible to change these settings since they are only acting as warnings. When you click on a Risk icon, the **Risks** documentation page is opened in a separate browser window.

Moodle's default roles have been designed with the following capability risks in mind:

Role	Allowed risks
Administrator	All capabilities, with a few exceptions
Teacher	Certain capabilities with XSS and privacy risks, mainly adding and updating content
Student	Certain capabilities with spam risks
Guest	Only capabilities with no risks

Modifying roles

To edit a role, either click on the **Edit** button at the top of the **View role details** screen or select the appropriate icon in the **Edit** column on the main roles screen.

When editing a role, you can change the standard fields as well as its permissions. For example, some schools change the role name student to pupil, while some training organizations change the role name teacher to instructor. Bear in mind that this only changes the name of the role, not the corresponding labels used throughout Moodle. You will learn how to do this in the *Localization* section in *Chapter 9, Moodle Configuration*.

When you change capabilities in a role that has been derived from a **Role archetype,**, its original values are highlighted when you click on the **Show advanced** button. For example, in the following screenshot, **Manage templates** has been set to **Not set**, but the **Allow** value remains highlighted; do not forget to save your role changes, once applied:

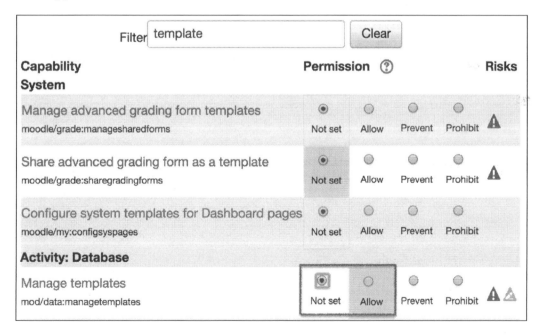

Unless you are confident with role modifications, it is recommended to duplicate a role first (via the **Export** functionality on the top of this screen and the creation of a new role described further down) and then edit it. Keeping the default roles untouched also makes maintenance easier in case multiple administrators work on the same system or a third party is providing support.

For example, if, due to privacy or other reasons, your organization decides not to allow users to see the profiles of other users, you would edit the **Student** role, search for the **moodle/user:viewdetails** capability, and change it from **Allow** to **Not set**.

 It is not possible to modify the **Administrator** role via the Moodle interface.

Overriding roles

It is possible to override permissions of a role in a given context using the **Permissions** link in the role assignment screen. You are shown a screen that describes which role has been given or has inherited permission for any of the capabilities of the current module activity (here, an assignment):

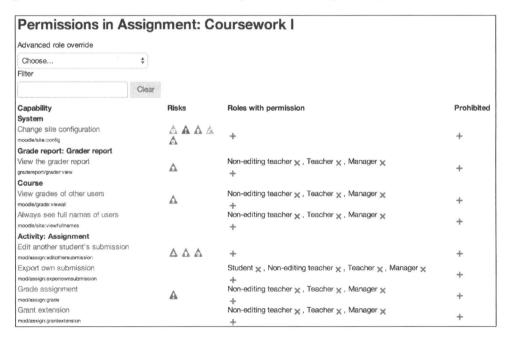

Overrides are specific permissions designed to change a role in a specific context, allowing you to tweak your permissions as required. Tweaking involves granting additional rights or revoking the existing rights. Once you select a role from the **Advanced role override** drop-down menu, you will see a familiar screen that shows the details of each capability of the activity for this particular role.

For example, while learners with the role of student in a course are usually allowed to start new discussions in forums, there is one particular forum for which you want to restrict that capability; you can set an override that prevents the capability for students to start new threads in this forum (namely, **mod/forum:startdiscussion**).

Overrides can also be used to open up areas of your site and courses to grant extra permissions to the users. For instance, you may want to experiment giving students the ability to grade some assignments (see the following screenshot) or to peer rate forum posts.

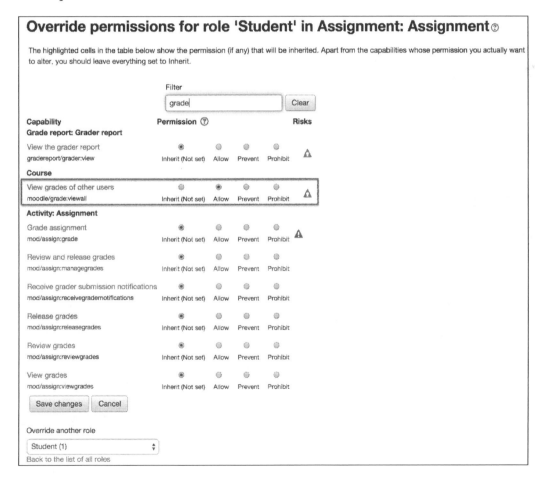

Creating custom roles

Moodle allows the creation of new roles. The examples of such custom roles are parent, teaching assistant, secretary, inspector, and librarian in an educational setting and training coordinator, assessor, mentor, or staff manager in a business context. The new roles are defined at **Users | Permissions | Define roles** using the **Add a new role** button.

Before you get to the familiar role-editing screen, you have the option to select an existing role or archetype from the drop-down menu, or to import a role (in XML format) that has been exported either in your Moodle instance or in another system (using the **Export** button when viewing role details).

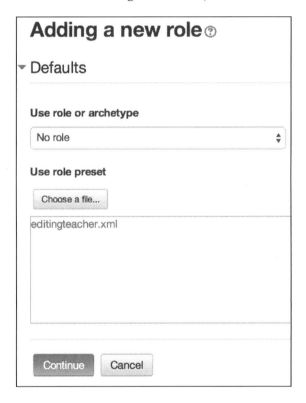

Using the existing roles as a basis is a commonly-used way of creating a new role. It not only minimizes the amount of work required, but also reduces errors in creating new roles. If you wish to create a role from scratch, that is, without any presets or inherited archetypes, leave both settings empty and continue to the next screen.

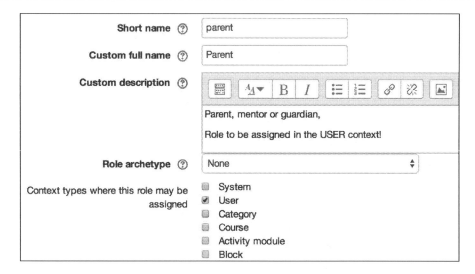

Make sure that you specify **Context types where this role may be assigned**. If you miss out a context, it will not be possible to assign the role. If you allow a context that is not suitable for the role, you run the risk that it will potentially cause problems.

Example roles

Moodle Docs has provided a number of sample roles that might be relevant to your organization (for example, refer to the custom roles section at `https://docs.moodle.org/en/Creating_custom_roles`). If not, they offer a good starting point to create other roles. Some useful samples are as follows:

- **Demo teacher**: This role is used to provide a demonstration teacher an account that has a password and profile that cannot be changed (for more details on this role, visit `https://docs.moodle.org/en/Demo_teacher_role`)

- **Forum moderator**: This role is used in a particular forum and provides a user with the ability to edit or delete forum posts, split discussions, and move discussions to other forums (for more details on this role, refer to `https://docs.moodle.org/en/Forum_moderator_role`)

- **Calendar editor**: This role is used to enable a user to add site events to the calendar (for more details on this role, refer to `https://docs.moodle.org/en/Calendar_editor_role`)

- **Question creator**: This role is used to enable students to create questions for use in quizzes (for more details on this role, refer to `https://docs.moodle.org/en/Question_creator_role`)

- **Blogger**: This role is used to limit blogging to specific users (for more details on this role, refer to `https://docs.moodle.org/en/Blogger_role`)

The parent/mentor role

One of the most popular and sought-after custom roles in Moodle is the one of a parent, guardian, or mentor. The idea is to grant permission to users to view certain profile information, such as activity reports, grades, blog entries, and forum posts of their children, wards, or mentees. This can be achieved with the creation of a new role. Furthermore, the specially-introduced **Mentees** block has to be placed on the front page to give users, who have been assigned the role, access to the **User** context.

For creating a new role, follow these steps:

1. Go to **Users | Permissions | Define roles**.

2. Add a new role, continue on the **Defaults** screen, and name it **Parent** or **Mentor**. Provide an appropriate **Shortname** and **Description**.

3. Leave the **Role archetype** type set to **None**.

4. Check the **User** checkbox for the **Context types where this role may be assigned** field.

5. Change the capabilities **moodle/user:viewdetails** and **moodle/user:viewalldetails** to **Allow**. This grants access to the user profile page.

6. Change the following capabilities in the **Users** section to **Allow**, which grants access to individual areas on the user profile page:

   ° **moodle/user:readuserposts**: To read the child's forum posts

   ° **moodle/user:readuserblogs**: To read the child's blog entries

   ° **moodle/user:viewuseractivitiesreport**: To view the child's activity reports and grades

7. Save the role using the **Create this role** button.

8. Create a user account for parent. Each parent requires a separate user account, which is set up as explained in the previous chapter (go to **Users | Accounts | Add a new user** and add details for the parent or use Moodle's bulk upload facility). In our example, the father is **Roy Harris** and his children are **Frank Harris** and **Paul Harris**, as shown in the following screenshot:

First name / Surname	Email address	City/town	Country	Last access	Edit
Frank Harris	Frank.Harris@yourschool.org.uk	Holywood	United Kingdom	Never	✕ 👁 ⚙
Paul Harris	paul.harris@yourschool.org.uk	Holywood	United Kingdom	Never	✕ 👁 ⚙
Roy Harris	roy.harris@ext.yourschool.org.uk	Holywood	United Kingdom	Never	✕ 👁 ⚙

9. Link parent to pupil. Each parent has to be linked to each respective child. Unlike the creation of users, this process cannot be automated via batch files yet and is a potentially time-consuming process. It is expected that this feature will be added to user batch creation in the near future. There exists a contributed plugin (`https://tracker.moodle.org/browse/CONTRIB-3938`), which supports automatic role assignment of several parents/mentors from LDAP or a database.

10. Access the first child's profile page, select the **Preferences** link in the **Administration** pane and click on **Assign roles relative to this user**.

11. Choose **Parent** as the role to assign.

12. Select the parent (**Roy Harris**) from the **Potential users** list and add him to the **Existing users** list.

13. Repeat the first three steps for the second child, **Paul Harris**.

14. A special **Mentees** block has been introduced to facilitate access to user information. Follow these steps to add it:

    1. Go to your front page and click on the **Turn editing on** link.

    2. Add the **Mentees** block to the front page (it can also be added on the default dashboard) and change its title to **Parent access** via the **Configuration** icon.

    3. Login as **Roy Harris**, and you should see the following block:

When a name is clicked upon, the respective user profile will be shown, which includes any posts sent to forums, blog entries, and activity reports, including logs and grades.

Testing new roles

After creating a new role, it is recommended to test it thoroughly before it is assigned to any users. To do this, create a test account and assign the new role to it. Log out as administrator and log in as the newly-created user to test the new role or use the **Login as** function to masquerade as the test user. Alternatively, use a different browser to test out the role without logging out as administrator.

If you have modified a predefined role and would like to roll back to its factory settings, go to **Users | Permissions | Define roles**, select (do not edit) a role, and click on the **Reset** button. This will replace its existing values with the one from the built-in capabilities.

The complexity of the roles system and the ability to assign multiple roles to multiple users in multiple contexts calls for a mechanism to verify the correctness of the permissions set. This problem is amplified by the fact that permissions can be inherited and then overridden at lower levels again.

Moodle has a built-in permission checker that displays the values of any capabilities in the context in which the checker has been called. The facility is called via the **Check permissions** link in a specific context. For example, in the following screenshot, we have called the permission checker in the **User** context of **Paul Harris** and showed the permissions of user **Roy Harris**. It confirms the settings of the earlier created **Parent** role.

Check permissions in User: Paul Harris

Roles for user Roy Harris

- parent in User: Paul Harris
- Authenticated user in System

Permissions for user Roy Harris

Capability	Allowed
Users	
View and manage own earned badges moodle/badges:manageownbadges	Yes
View public badges in other users' profiles moodle/badges:viewotherbadges	Yes
Edit user messaging profile moodle/user:editmessageprofile	No
Edit user profile moodle/user:editprofile	No
Manage blocks on user profile of other users moodle/user:manageblocks	No
View all user blogs moodle/user:readuserblogs	Yes
View all user forum posts moodle/user:readuserposts	Yes
View user full information moodle/user:viewalldetails	Yes
View user last ip address moodle/user:viewlastip	No
See user activity reports moodle/user:viewuseractivitiesreport	Yes
User sessions report	
Manage own browser sessions report/usersessions:manageownsessions	Yes
Course	
View grades of other users moodle/grade:viewall	No

At site level, there are two additional mechanisms that help to identify any potential issues with roles. The capability report (**Users | Permissions | Capability overview**) shows, for a selected capability, what permission it has in the definition of one or many selected roles. It also shows if the capability has been overridden anywhere in the system, which is a great help when you try to locate any local modifications.

In the example screenshot, I have selected the capability **mod/forum:rate: Rateposts** and **All** roles. The report that follows shows the values of the capability in all the roles. Of particular interest is the **Student** role, which is shown *all the way down* to the forum in a course, where it has been overridden:

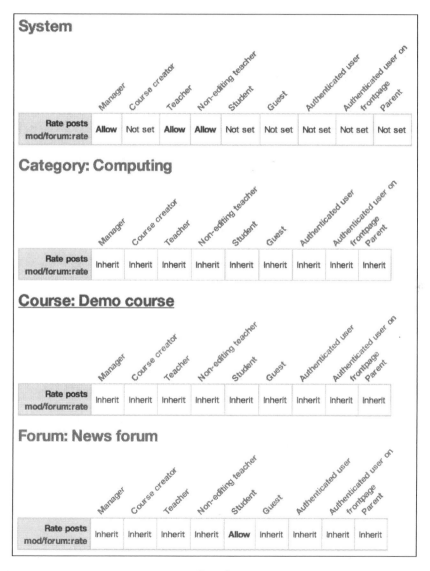

System

	Manager	Course creator	Teacher	Non-editing teacher	Student	Guest	Authenticated user	Authenticated user on frontpage	Parent
Rate posts mod/forum:rate	Allow	Not set	Allow	Allow	Not set	Not set	Not set	Not set	Not set

Category: Computing

	Manager	Course creator	Teacher	Non-editing teacher	Student	Guest	Authenticated user	Authenticated user on frontpage	Parent
Rate posts mod/forum:rate	Inherit	Inherit	Inherit	Inherit	Inherit	Inherit	Inherit	Inherit	Inherit

Course: Demo course

	Manager	Course creator	Teacher	Non-editing teacher	Student	Guest	Authenticated user	Authenticated user on frontpage	Parent
Rate posts mod/forum:rate	Inherit	Inherit	Inherit	Inherit	Inherit	Inherit	Inherit	Inherit	Inherit

Forum: News forum

	Manager	Course creator	Teacher	Non-editing teacher	Student	Guest	Authenticated user	Authenticated user on frontpage	Parent
Rate posts mod/forum:rate	Inherit	Inherit	Inherit	Inherit	**Allow**	Inherit	Inherit	Inherit	Inherit

The second tool can be found at **Users | Permissions | Unsupported role assignments**. As the name suggests, it lists any role assignments that are not valid. This usually happens when you upgrade from a previous version of Moodle. If any assignments are listed, you will have to manually modify or remove them.

Roles management

We have now dealt with the most important tools to use, modify, and create roles. Moodle offers a number of additional features that are important when working extensively with roles.

Allowing roles assignments and overrides

By default, some roles have the right to allow other roles to assign roles. For instance, a teacher is only allowed to assign **Non-editing teacher** and **Student** roles, whereas the manager is allowed to assign all the roles except the **Guest**, **Authenticated user**, and **Authenticated user on frontpage** roles (because these are automatically assigned when a user signs in for the first time). There are instances when you either wish to change the default settings, for example, when a teacher assigns roles to other teachers, or when the newly-created roles have to be managed. To achieve this, select the **Allow role assignments** tab by navigating to **Users | Permissions | Define Roles**:

Manage roles	Allow role assignments	Allow role overrides	Allow role switches						

You can allow people who have the roles on the left side to assign some of the column roles to other people

	Manager	Course creator	Teacher	Non-editing teacher	Student	Guest	Authenticated user	Authenticated user on frontpage	Parent
Manager	☑	☑	☑	☑	☑	☐	☐	☐	☐
Course creator	☐	☐	☐	☐	☐	☐	☐	☐	☑
Teacher	☐	☐	☑	☑	☑	☐	☐	☐	☑
Non-editing teacher	☐	☐	☐	☐	☐	☐	☐	☐	☐
Student	☐	☐	☐	☐	☐	☐	☐	☐	☐
Guest	☐	☐	☐	☐	☐	☐	☐	☐	☐
Authenticated user	☐	☐	☐	☐	☐	☐	☐	☐	☐
Authenticated user on frontpage	☐	☐	☐	☐	☐	☐	☐	☐	☐
Parent	☐	☐	☐	☐	☐	☐	☐	☐	☐

In the preceding screenshot, the modified allowances have been highlighted. The teachers are allowed to assign the **Teacher** role and both the course creators and the teachers are allowed to assign the new **Parent** role.

The identical mechanism exists for role overrides and role switches. They are accessed via the **Allow role overrides** and **Allow role switches** tabs, respectively, on the same screen.

Assigning of default roles

In certain situations, standard roles are assigned. These can be specified in the **User policies** section under **Users | Permissions**:

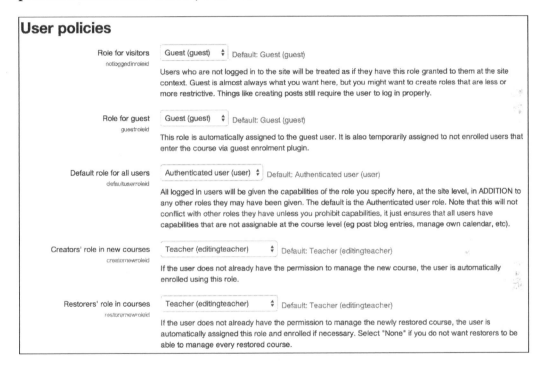

The preceding screenshot shows the assignment of the default role for visitors (users who are not logged in) and the role for guest.

Moodle comes with a predefined role called **Authenticated user**, which is the default role for all logged-in users. It is assigned to *every* logged-in user, in addition to any other roles. The role has been created to grant users access to certain functionality, for example, posting blog entries, managing personal calendar entries, changing profile fields, and so on, even if they are not enrolled in a course.

You can further specify what role is given automatically (via the **Creator's role in new courses** drop-down list) to users who have created a course, but don't have any permissions yet in the course. An equivalent setting exists for users restoring courses from backups called **Restorers' role in courses** (see *Chapter13, Backup and Restore*).

> Changing settings in **User policies** can have major impact on what new users are allowed to do on your Moodle system, so double-check the default roles before they are applied!

In addition to the default roles in the **User policies** section, it is also possible to specify a default front page role. This can be accessed in **Front page | Front page settings**. To enable logged-in users to participate in activities positioned on the front page, the **Default frontpage role** field can be set, usually to **Student** or **Teacher**. It is also possible to allow the logged-in users to participate in these activities by setting an authenticated user role override.

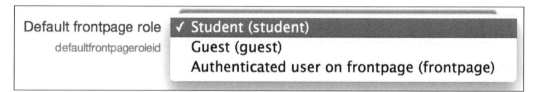

Default frontpage role | ✓ Student (student)
defaultfrontpageroleid | Guest (guest)
 | Authenticated user on frontpage (frontpage)

Moodle role assignment – best practice

Roles sometimes cause problems in Moodle sites, and it is therefore advised to follow some recommendations regarding roles:

- Only touch the roles once you have understood them thoroughly
- Never grant a user a role that is beyond his/her competence
- Avoid assigning multiple predefined roles to users when possible
- Avoid system roles as much as possible
- Avoid role assignments that don't make sense
- Keep track of role assignments to ensure maintainability in the future
- Do not change the permissions of predefined roles

Summary

In this chapter, you learned what roles are and how they are applied in different contexts. We then covered the modification of existing roles before creating our own custom roles such as parent, inspector, or librarian. Finally, we looked at the management of administrative role-related settings.

Getting your head round the roles concept in Moodle is vital if you wish to add, modify, or remove functionality for a distinct group of users. As always, there is a trade-off between the complexity of such a system and its flexibility. While you can argue about the user-friendliness of the roles system, it has certainly proven to be one of the most powerful concepts in Moodle.

The interconnectedness between courses, users, and roles is crucial. Once this has been set up and configured properly, your Moodle is technically ready to go. However, before that, you probably want to change the look and feel first. This is what the next chapter is all about.

7
Moodle Look and Feel

Your system is now fully operational with users, courses, and roles in place. It is now time to change its look and feel. Out goes the Moodle default theme and in comes a site that is in line with the corporate branding of your organization!

After providing a general overview of Moodle's look and feel elements, we will cover the following subjects:

- **Front page customization**: This includes front page settings, block arrangements, front page roles, backup, restore, and questions. You will also learn how to support personalization through the Dashboard feature, make blocks sticky, and how to streamline the navigation on your site.

- **Moodle themes**: This includes theme selection, theme types, and theme settings. We will also cover the support for mobile devices, that is, cell phones and tablets.

- **Editor configuration**: This includes the configuration of the Atto HTML editor.

- **Accessibility**: Here, we will cover support for Moodle users with different types of accessibility problems, such as visual impairment and motor difficulties.

 Theme creation is not covered in this book as it is not the task of an administrator but of a designer with good CSS skills. *Designing Moodle Themes, Susan Smith Nash, Packt Publishing* is a good video to familiarize yourself with the basics of Moodle's themes and designs.

An overview of the look and feel

Moodle can be fully customized in terms of layout, branding, and device support. It has to be stressed that certain aspects of changing the look and feel require advanced design skills. While you, as an administrator, will be able to make some adjustments, it will be necessary to get a professional frontend designer involved, especially when it comes to styling.

The two relevant components for customization are the Moodle front page and Moodle themes. Before we cover both areas, let's try to understand which part is responsible for which element of the look and feel of your site.

In the upcoming screenshot, have a look at the front page of the Moodle site after we have logged in as the administrator. It is not obvious which parts are driven by the Moodle theme and which ones by front page settings. The following table, which looks at the page's elements from the top to the bottom when the core **Clean** or **More** theme has been applied, sheds some light on this:

Element	Setting	Theme	Other
Site title	X		
Pull-down menu	X		
Username, profile picture, and personal menu	X	X	
Logo		X	
Language dropdown		X	X
Dockable sidebar	X	X	
The Navigation and Administration blocks (position)	X		
The Available courses block (position)	X		
The Available courses block (content)			X
The Course categories and Calendar blocks (position)	X		
The All courses link in the Course categories block	X		
Icons, font colors, headers, borders, and so on of all blocks		X	
Show icons to collapse blocks	X		
Show icons to dock blocks	X	X	
Footer text		X	
Copyright statement		X	
Number of columns		X	

While this list is by no means complete, it hopefully gives you an idea that the look and feel of your site is driven by a number of different elements. It should also give you an idea about the types of elements that can be modified.

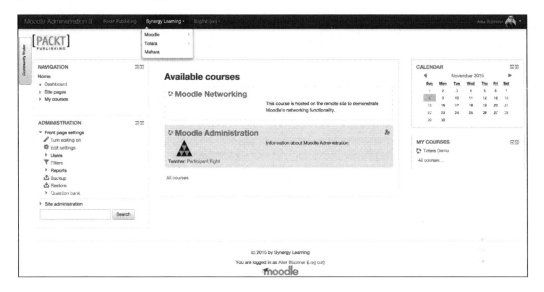

In short, the settings (mostly front page settings as well as a few related parameters) dictate what content users will see before and after they log on. The theme is responsible for the design scheme or branding, that is, the header and footer as well as the colors, fonts, icons, and so on, used throughout the site.

Site versus Dashboard

Moodle contains two types of pages that can be used for the home page:

- **Site pages**: This is a home page that is identical for all users. Well, sort of: its structure is static, whereas its content is likely to change depending on the user who is logged in. For example, every Site page might contain a block that displays the courses a user is enrolled into. This page is also known as Site home.

- **Dashboard**: This personal home page can be customized for each user. For legacy reasons, this top-level page is often referred to as My Moodle or My home.

By default, authenticated users will see **Dashboard** as their home page. You can change this by navigating to **Appearance | Navigation**, where you have the option to specify **Default home page for users**. The options are **Site**, **Dashboard** (default), and **User preference**. If latter is chosen, the user can make this choice by going to **Front page settings | Make this my default home page** in the **Administration** block.

In the following screenshot, you can see the impact on the breadcrumb trail and **Navigation** block for the **Site** (on the left-hand side) settings and **Dashboard** (on the right-hand side):

We will first look at how to customize the **Site** front page before modifying the default layout for **Dashboard** and streamlining the navigation of your site.

Customizing your front page

Moodle's front page changes after a user has logged in. The content and layout of the page before and after login can be customized. Look at the following screenshot. It is the same site that the preceding screenshot was taken from but before a user had logged in:

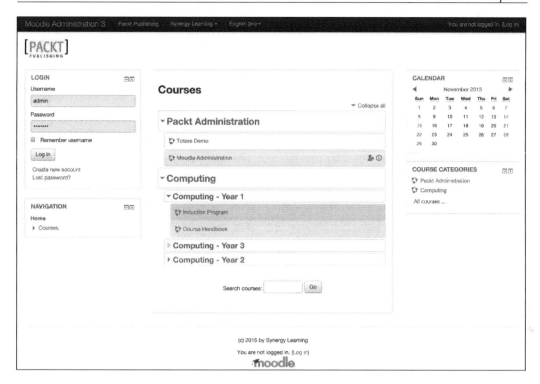

In this particular example, the **Login** block is shown on the left-hand side and the **Course categories** and **Courses** as well as a course search box are displayed in the center, as opposed to the list of available courses. Additionally, the **Administration** block is not displayed.

Bear in mind that some implementations may not have an unauthenticated view. This is the case if a single sign-on mechanism has been implemented.

The front page settings

In order to customize the front page (go to **Front page | Front page settings**), you either have to be logged in as the Moodle administrator, or you have been granted front page-related permissions in the **Front page** context:

The following parameters are available on the Front Page settings page:

Setting	Description
Full site name	This is the name that appears in the browser's title bar. It is usually the full name of your organization or the name of the dedicated course or qualification that the site is used for.
Short name for site	This is the internal name of your site that is used at various places, for instance, as part of the backup name or when networking the site.
Front page summary	This description of the site will be displayed on the front page, through the Site description block. The description text is also picked up by the Google search engine spider, if allowed.
Front page	Moodle can display up to five elements in the center column of the front page when not logged in: News items, List of courses, List of categories, Combo list (this displays categories and courses), and Course search box. The order of the elements is the same as the one chosen in the pull-down menus.

Setting	Description
Front page items when logged in	This is the same as Front page but it's used when a user is logged in. A sixth item is provided to be displayed, namely, Enrolled courses, which shows a list of courses that the user is enrolled into. That view does not make any sense before the user has been authenticated with Moodle.
Maximum category depth	When course categories are shown, this setting specifies how many levels of the hierarchy are displayed. It is useful to limit this if your category hierarchy's depth is greater than three or four.
Maximum number of courses	This shows the number of courses that are shown on the front page. If more courses are available, a link to More courses is shown.
Include a topic section	If ticked, an additional topic section (just like the topic block in the center column of a course) appears on top of the front page's center column. It can contain any mix of resources or activities that are available in Moodle. It is very often used to provide information about the site or to include an image or video.
News items to show	This includes a number of news items that are displayed.
Comments displayed per page	This setting dictates how many entries are shown if the Comments block is used on the front page. This setting really belongs to the Comments block and might be moved in the near future.
Default front page role	If logged-in users need to be allowed to participate in front page activities, a default front page role should be set. The default is Authenticated user on the front page.

Front page settings mainly dictate what is displayed in the center of the page. Now, let's have a look at the blocks on the left-hand side and the right-hand side of the page.

Arranging front page blocks

To configure the left-hand side and right-hand side column areas with blocks, you have to turn on editing in the **Front page settings** area of the **Administration** block. Once turned on, you will see the **Add a block** block, which contains all the available blocks that can be added to the front page (except the ones that have already been added and only allow a single instance):

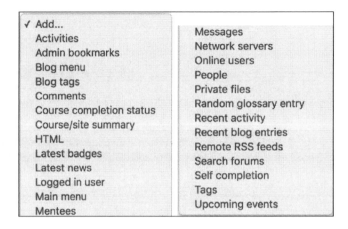

Blocks are added to the front page in exactly the same way as courses. To change their position, use the Move icon. Some blocks have settings that are unique to that block and which can be accessed through the Configuration icon. For example, the **Navigation block** allows you to specify whether the block can be docked and how certain types of content are displayed:

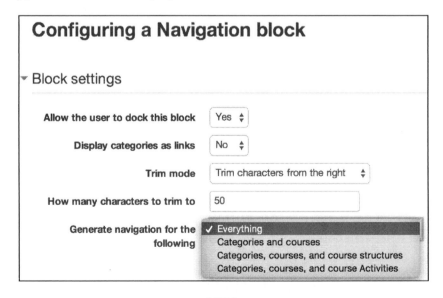

In addition to block-specific settings, every block contains two sets of parameters that control its behavior. The two sections, **Where this block appears** and **On this page**, will be shown for every block:

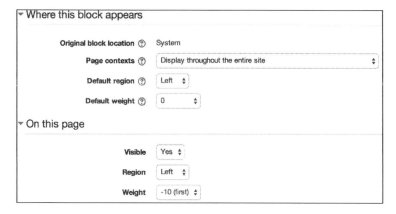

A block, like a role, can be assigned in a context (here, **Front page**) and its properties are inherited and overridden in subcontexts. The first set of settings specify where the block will be displayed and what the default properties are. The second set of settings specify the properties in the current context. The following parameters are available:

Setting	Description
Original block location	This shows the context in which the block has been created. This is sometimes referred to as the home context. As with roles, pages may inherit blocks from a parent context.
Page contexts (not in all contexts)	This setting dictates on which pages the block will be shown; the options that are available are: • **Display on front page only** • **Display on the front page and any pages added to the front page** • **Display throughout the site** In other contexts, such as **Courses**, other (context-sensitive) options will be shown, depending on the original block location and your current location.
Display on page types (unavailable on the front page)	The options that are available depend on the context that the block is shown in, for example, **Only user profile pages** and **My home page** in the **User** context, or **Any page**, **Any course page**, and **Any type of course main page** in **Courses**.

Setting	Description
Default region (Left, Right)	This determines whether the block's position is on the left-hand side or on the right-hand side.
Default weight (-10...10)	Think of a block as a balloon: the lighter the weight of the block, the higher up its position, and the heavier the weight, the further down it will be placed.
Visible (Yes, No)	This determines whether the block is shown or hidden.
Region (Left, Right)	This is the same as **Default region**. On **My Home** and other profile pages, content is offered as a third option (refer to the default Dashboard and Profile pages section further along).
Weight (-10...10)	This is the same principle as **Default weight**.

In the preceding screenshot, the block is shown in the right-hand column in the first position. However, when it is displayed on any other page, the block is initially shown on the left-hand side and has a weight of -5.

The **Main menu** block allows the addition of any installed Moodle resource or activity inside the block. For example, using labels and links to (internal or external) websites, you are able to create a menu-like structure. Another block that has proven popular on the front page is **Online users**, which displays a list of everybody who's currently logged in to your Moodle site. The **HTML** block lets you add any HTML code, which is useful for any type of content that cannot be displayed using standard Moodle blocks.

> The **Navigation** and **Administration** blocks cannot be deleted via the standard menu. If you need to hide them on the front page, set **Visible** to **No** in the **Configuration** settings.

If the **Include a topic section** parameter has been selected in **Front page settings**, you have to edit the area and add any installed Moodle activity or resource. This topic section is usually used by organizations to add a welcome message for visitors, which is often accompanied by a picture or other multimedia content.

> Double-check what your site looks like when you are not logged in. Make sure no information is visible that should only be accessible to logged-in users.

Logging in from a different website

The purpose of the **Login** block is for users to authenticate themselves by entering their credentials in the form of a username and password. It is possible to log in to Moodle from a different website, maybe your organization's home page, effectively avoiding Moodle's front page and the **Login** block. To implement this, you will have to add some HTML code on the remote page from which you wish the user to log in:

```
<form class="loginform" name="login" method="post"
action="http://www.mysite.com/login/index.php">
<p>Username :
<input size="10" name="username" />
</p>
<p>Password :
<input size="10" name="password" type="password" />
</p>
<p>
<input name="Submit" value="Login" type="submit" />
</p>
</form>
```

The form will pass the username and password to your Moodle system. You will have to replace www.mysite.com with your URL; this address has to be entered in the **Alternate Login URL** field by navigating to **Plugins | Authentication | Manage authentication**.

Other front page items

The Moodle front page is being treated as a standalone component in Moodle and has, therefore, been given a top-level menu with a number of features that can all be accessed through **Front page settings** in the **Administration** block:

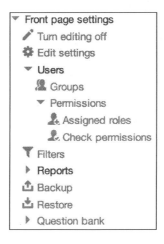

We have already looked at **Front page settings**; now, let's take a brief look at the other available options. Since the front page is treated like a course (internally, it has course ID of 1), a number of settings are available, which are identical to their course counterparts.

Front page users

The front page has its own context in which groups can be created and roles can be assigned to users. This allows a separate user to develop and maintain the front page without having access to any other elements in Moodle. Since the front page is treated as a course, a **Teacher** role is usually sufficient for this. It is possible to upload users as teachers in the front page with a CSV file using the site's short name as the course1 field, teacher in the role1 field and, if required, the chosen group name in the group1 field).

We discussed this feature in detail in the previous chapter, which dealt with the management of roles.

Front page filters

Any filters that have been activated can be configured at the course level. The same applies to the front page. We will discuss filters in detail in *Chapter 9, Moodle Configuration*, when we look at different configuration settings.

Front page reports

These are identical to course reports. We will be looking at these options in *Chapter 10, Moodle Logging and Reporting*.

The front page backup and restore

The front page has its own backup and restore facilities to back up and restore any elements of the front page, including any content. The mechanism of performing a backup and restore is the same as course backups, which is dealt with in *Chapter 13, Backup and Restore*.

Like all other course backups, front page backups are stored in the User backup folder of your user file (System/<your name>/Userbackup).

Front page questions

Since the Moodle front page is treated in the same way as a course, it also has its own question bank, which is used to store any questions used in front page quizzes. For more information on quizzes, question types, and the question bank, go to Moodle Docs at `https://docs.moodle.org/en/Quiz_activity`.

The default Dashboard and Profile pages

There are two special pages that users are able to customize themselves. These are the **Dashboard** page—we came across this in the introduction—and the **Profile** page.

Once logged in, users will have the ability to edit these pages by adding blocks to the respective areas and changing any blocks that have already been added by default. They also have the ability to reposition certain elements. You, as the administrator, have the ability to specify what these default blocks are, where they are positioned, and control how much customization can be carried out. When users customize their **Dashboard** or **Profile** page, they also have the ability to reset the respective pages to these defaults.

The two default settings can be found by navigating to **Appearance | Default Dashboard page** and **Appearance | Default profile page**, respectively. Once on the page, you have to click on the **Blocks editing on** button. Any blocks that you place on the default pages will appear on the users' pages. Interestingly, using the standard **Move** icon, you can place blocks in the center column! It is a shame that the same functionality does not (yet) exist on the front page or even in courses, by default, as shown in the following screenshot:

Not only that, you can also make blocks sticky. These are blocks that you wish to display on every page, effectively making them compulsory blocks that cannot be modified or deleted. To facilitate this, the block settings have to be extended with the **Select pages** setting, which is shown in the properties of any block in **Default Dashboard page** (take a look at the block settings, which were discussed earlier). If set to **Any page matching the above**, the block will appear on all those subpages and cannot be modified, effectively making the block sticky. The same mechanism applies to the default profile page.

To prevent users from editing their **Dashboard** and **Profile** pages, change the **moodle/my:manageblocks** and **moodle/user:manageownblocks** capabilities in the Authenticated user role, respectively.

Customizing navigation

There are a number of settings that impact how your users will navigate your site, regardless of whether they are on the **Site** home page, their **Dashboard**, or inside a course. This takes place when you navigate to **Appearance** | **Navigation**:

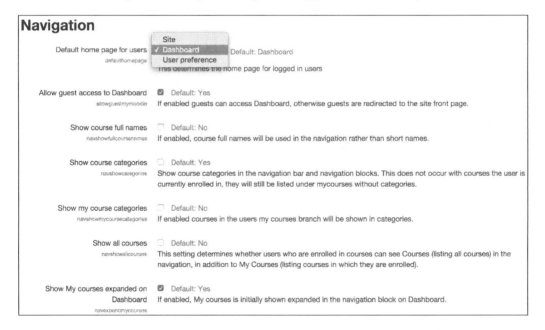

The vast majority of these mostly self-explanatory settings deal with the level of detail that is shown in courses and categories in the **Navigation** block as well as some related blocks.

The subject of displaying courses and categories comes up regularly when customizing Moodle sites. The common cause for concern is that the list of courses seen on the screen is overwhelming, and it will be difficult for users to navigate through the entire category hierarchy.

> Only you, as the administrator, can see the long list of all the courses and categories. Users will only see the courses they are enrolled in.

Bearing this in mind, there are a number of ways that the entire category structure can be exposed to users:

- Through the **All courses** link in the **Courses** block, unless the **Hide all courses link** option has been checked by navigating to **Plugins | Blocks | Courses**. Here, you can also specify that the admin will only see their own courses.
- By selecting **List of categories** or **Combo list** in the front page settings.
- Through the **Courses** listing in the **Navigation** block. This is controlled by the settings seen in the preceding screenshot.

The users that are shown alongside the course description. This is related to the way in which courses and categories are presented to the user. By default, this is only users with the **Teacher** role. You can change this via **Course contacts** by navigating to **Appearance | Courses**. Here, you can also specify a further number of useful settings:

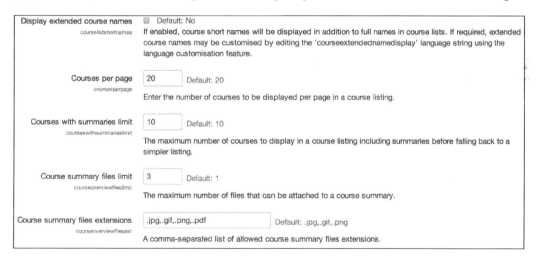

Courses per page is a threshold setting that is used when displaying courses within categories. If there are more courses in a category than specified, the page navigation will be displayed at the top of the page. Also, when a combo list is used, course names are only displayed if the number is less than the specified threshold. For all the other categories, only the number of courses is shown after the category name.

Course authors have the ability to enter a course summary. This usually contains a textual description, but it can also contain files, for example, the curriculum as a PDF. You limit the number of courses with the summary shown on the front page via the **Courses with summaries limit** setting. By default, only one file can be attached; you might need to increase this **Course summary files limit**. In the preceding screenshot, we have also added the PDF format as a valid **Course summary files extensions**.

Replacing the front page

As we have seen so far, Moodle provides us with a great set of tools to customize the front page. Sometimes, though, you might want to replace this with a custom front page. The home page of `https://moodle.org/` is a good example of where this has been implemented successfully.

Moodle lets you add a custom script to the front page. To implement this feature, you will have to add the following line to your `config.php` file:

```
$CFG->customfrontpageinclude="<dirroot>/local/<yourfrontpage>";
```

Bear in mind that this will display the output of the `<yourfrontpage>` PHP file at the top of the content area, in addition to any elements of the front page. This way, you have the best of both worlds: the Moodle elements (disable the ones you don't require) and your custom elements.

Moodle themes

Moodle provides a flexible skinning mechanism to brand your site according to existing guidelines. As mentioned in the introduction, we will only cover the theme settings that can be accessed from the Moodle administration menu. For details on how to create Moodle themes, refer to the *Designing Moodle Themes, Susan Smith Nash, Packt Publishing* video by Packt Publishing, or contact your Moodle Partner who will be able to offer you professional theme design services. There are also some good pointers that you can find at `https://docs.moodle.org/dev/Themes`, which assume that you have a good understanding of HTML and CSS.

Fixed width versus fluid versus responsive themes

There are three types of Moodle themes that are supported by Moodle. They are as follows:

- **Fixed width themes**: These are themes where the width of the canvas is fixed, for example, to 1,024 points. The advantage of this is the simplicity of development but the downsides are a high degree of inflexibility. Fixed width themes can only be justified if all your users use exactly the same screen resolution and no mobile devices have to be supported.

- **Fluid themes**: Fluid or dynamic width themes use up a certain percentage of a user's screen estate. This can be limited by minimum and maximum widths, for example, a theme uses up 100% of the screen width but not more than 1,600 pixels. More flexible than fixed width themes, but there is a requirement to have a dedicated theme for different types of devices.

- **Responsive themes**: Responsive themes adapt to the device, its screen resolution, and the screen orientation automatically. Not only this, they also change due to the content that is displayed, navigation that is used, and the orientation of the screen elements. Responsive Moodle themes are based on Bootstrap 3.

 The future of e-learning is in mobiles, and this is reflected by Moodle, which only ships two responsive themes called **Clean** and **More**.

Selecting a Moodle theme

Themes, standard or custom, can be selected by going to **Appearance** | **Themes** | **Theme Selector**:

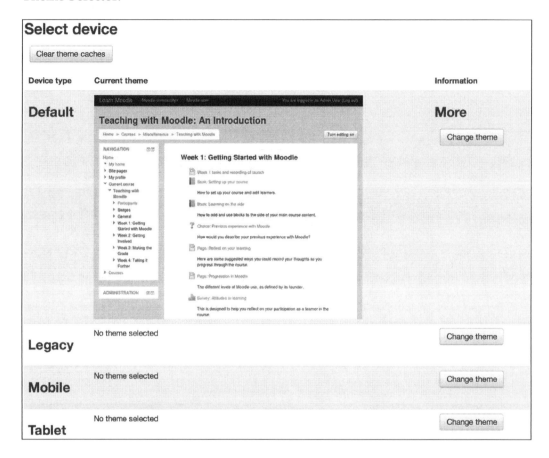

You can select up to four themes for your site that support different device types, which are as follows:

- **Default**: This is the theme that is normally used unless any of the other types are detected. Device detection has to be enabled in the theme settings.

- **Legacy**: If you have users in your system who are stuck in the previous millennium, that is, still using Internet Explorer 6, this theme will be used instead of the default one. Moodle does not ship with a theme that supports legacy browsers, but you can install one from `https://moodle.org/plugins/` called **Standard** (legacy).

- **Mobile**: This theme is used when a smartphone is detected.
- **Tablet**: This theme is used when a tablet is detected.

 All modern browsers (the latest versions of Firefox, Internet Explorer, Chrome, and Safari) are fully supported by Moodle. Internet Explorer 8 and other old browsers are not supported! IE 10 is required for the drag and drop upload of content from outside the browser into Moodle.

If you use a responsive theme, which is highly recommended, there is usually no need to select a theme for legacy, mobiles, and tablets.

The **Clear theme caches** button at the top of the screen is relevant if changes have been made to the themes and updates have not been propagated yet.

 Make sure that the selected theme is compatible with you version of Moodle. Older themes will not work in Moodle 3+. You must only use themes that support the Moodle 3 theme engine.

Theme types

To understand most theme settings, we require a little bit of background. Like roles, themes are assigned in different contexts, namely, **Site** (system), **User**, **Course**, and **Category**. However, two additional areas, that is, Session and Page, are supported by Moodle. These so-called theme types are explained in the following list:

- **Site theme**: If no other theme is selected, this theme is applied throughout the site. This is the default when you first install Moodle.
- **User theme**: If enabled, users are allowed to select their personal theme as part of their profile.
- **Course theme**: If enabled, each editing teacher can specify a course theme in the course settings (**Force** theme parameter in course settings).
- **Category theme**: This theme can be set for each course category (this is the **Force** theme parameter in the category settings).

- **Session theme**: If you need to apply a theme temporarily (that is, until you log out), you can add the theme parameter to the URL of a course. For example, on our site, we would replace `http://.../course/view.php?id=5` with `http://.../course/view.php?id=5&theme=packttheme`.

    ○ There are a number of scenarios where this feature is useful. Theme testing provides themes through links instead of Moodle settings (theme gallery or theme switching)

    ○ Provision of themes for different devices, for example, for mobile phones or game consoles.

- **Page theme**: Page themes are set in code and have only been added for completeness.

The following table shows theme priority: where it is displayed and where the setting is changed. To change the precedence order, modify the `$CFG->themeorder` parameter in `config.php`. The default is set to `array('page', 'course', 'category', 'session', 'user', 'site');`:

Type	Overrides	Displays	Setting location
Site	None	This displays all the pages, except the course and category, if set.	Theme selector
User	Site	This displays all the pages, except course and category, if set.	User profile
Course	Site/user/category/session	Course	Course settings
Category	Site/user/session	This displays all the courses in the category, except the course, if set.	Category editing
Session	Site/user	This displays all the pages, except the course and category, if set.	`config.php`
Page	All	This depends on code	In code

There is some trade-off when allowing theme types other than the site theme: while allowing User, Course, Category, and other such themes, additional processing is required that will add overhead to your system and place an increased demand on your server. However, not allowing these themes limits the level of customization that can be carried out in your site (uniformity versus personalization).

Theme settings

Armed with all the information to this point, the theme settings (go to **Appearance |
Themes | Theme settings**) are almost self-explanatory:

Theme settings

Theme list themelist	Default: Empty Leave this blank to allow any valid theme to be used. If you want to shorten the theme menu, you can specify a comma-separated list of names here (Don't use spaces!). For example: standard,orangewhite.
Theme designer mode themedesignermode	☐ Default: No Normally all theme images and style sheets are cached in browsers and on the server for a very long time, for performance. If you are designing themes or developing code then you probably want to turn this mode on so that you are not served cached versions. Warning: this will make your site slower for all users! Alternatively, you can also reset the theme caches manually from the Theme selection page.
Allow user themes allowusethemes	☑ Default: No If you enable this, then users will be allowed to set their own themes. User themes override site themes (but not course themes)
Allow course themes allowcoursethemes	☑ Default: No If you enable this, then courses will be allowed to set their own themes. Course themes override all other theme choices (site, user, or session themes)
Allow category themes allowcategorythemes	☑ Default: No If you enable this, then themes can be set at the category level. This will affect all child categories and courses unless they have specifically set their own theme. WARNING: Enabling category themes may affect performance.

Setting	Description
Theme list	To limit the number of available themes, name them in the text box, separated by commas and with no spaces!
Theme designer mode	This is only for theme designers or developers. It effectively turns off theme caching. Do not use this on a production site as it will slow down your system significantly!
Allow user themes	Users will be able to set their own themes.
Allow course themes	Editing teachers can set course themes.
Allow category themes	This enables category themes.
Allow theme changes in the URL	This enables session themes.
Allow users to hide blocks	By default, users are allowed to show and hide blocks through the icon present at the top-right of each block, which toggles between a plus and minus symbol. This can be turned off if the functionality is not wanted.
Allow blocks to use the dock	By default, all blocks can be docked in the sidebar through the dock icon. This can be turned off if the functionality is not required.

Setting	Description
Custom menu items	Here, you can add a pull-down menu underneath the header of your page. Each entry represents a menu item in the form of `<Indent><Text>[|<URL>] [|<Tooltip>] [|<Language>]`.
	`<Indent>` is a series of hyphens: no hyphens indicate a top-level menu; one hyphen, a sub-menu; two hyphens, a sub-sub-menu; and so on. `<Text>` is the label of the menu item, the optional `<URL>` is the internal or external link, and `<Tooltip>` is the optional balloon help.
	For example, the following **Custom menu items** entry will generate the menu shown in the theme in the first screenshot of the chapter:
	``` Packt Publishing|http://www.packtpub.com Synergy Learning -Moodle --Hosting|http://www.synergy-learning.com/moodle/moodle-hosting --Support|http://www.synergy-learning.com/moodle/moodle-support --Themes|http://www.synergy-learning.com/moodle/moodle-theme-design -Totara --Hosting|http://www.synergy-learning.com/totara/totara-hosting --Support|http://www.synergy-learning.com/totara/totara-support --Development|http://www.synergy-learning.com/totara/totara-development --Consultancy|http://www.synergy-learning.com/totara/totara-consultancy --Themes|http://www.synergy-learning.com/totara/totara-theme-design -Mahara|http://www.synergy-learning.com/mahara ```
	You can add a language code or a separated list of codes as the last item, which will only be shown if the user has currently selected the listed language, for example `English|http://www.synergy-learning.com||en` and `German|http://www.synergy-learning.de||de,de_du, de_kids`.
User menu items	This is similar to the previous menu but only customizes the user menu at the top-right corner. You can specify which menu items will appear between **Profile** and **Logout** as these two items cannot be removed.
	``` User menu items grades,grades|/grade/report/mygrades.php|grades customusermenuitems messages,message|/message/index.php|message preferences,moodle|/user/preferences.php|preferences Moodle Homepage|http://moodle.org" target="_blank ```
	The syntax for each entry is as follows:
	`<Item><URL>[|<Icon>]`
	`<Item>`is either a text entry (in our example Moodle home page) or a pair`<langstringname><componentname>`. The former is an entry from the language pack, the latter is the name of the Moodle component. An example of this is `editmyprofile,core|/user/edit.php|edit`.

Setting	Description
Enable device detection	Moodle can distinguish between the **default** and **legacy** browsers as well as the **mobile** and **tablet** devices. If enabled, different themes can be selected for each device type.
Device detection regular expressions	Unsupported device types can be added if you know the regular expression (also known as the mobile browser ID or user agent string) that will be sent by the device.

Now that we have the skill set to work with themes, it is time to customize the existing themes.

Customizing themes

As an administrator, you are unlikely to be involved in the creation of a full-blown custom theme as this task requires strong designing skills and a deep knowledge of CSS and HTML. However, you will be able to make basic modifications to existing themes.

Theme customization basics

Moodle uses **Cascading Style Sheets** (CSS) to describe the presentation of each element that is displayed. CSS is used to define different aspects of the HTML and XHTML presentation, including colors, fonts, layouts, and so on.

To learn more about theme basics, go to `https://docs.moodle.org/dev/Themes_overview`, where you will find a very well-documented and detailed help section. You might also want to install a number of useful tools when customizing themes such as the popular Firebug.

At the heart of CSS are so-called styles; Moodle uses consistently plain English for the naming of styles. For the forum elements that are displayed in the following screenshot, a few sample styles have been labeled:

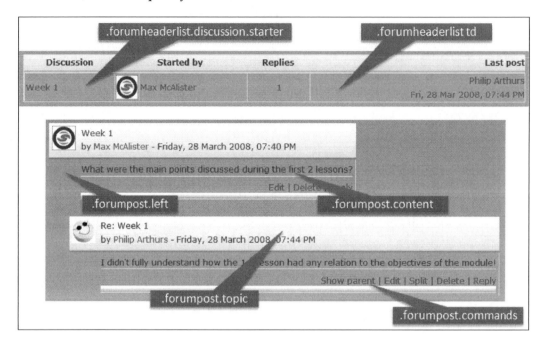

You can see that each element of Moodle is represented by a style. In total, there are well over 2,000 (!) styles in Moodle, which give a designer a high degree of freedom.

Moodle themes can be customized through their respective settings by going to **Appearance | Themes | <Theme name>**. Different themes provide different settings. Here is a screenshot of the different types of parameters in the **More** theme:

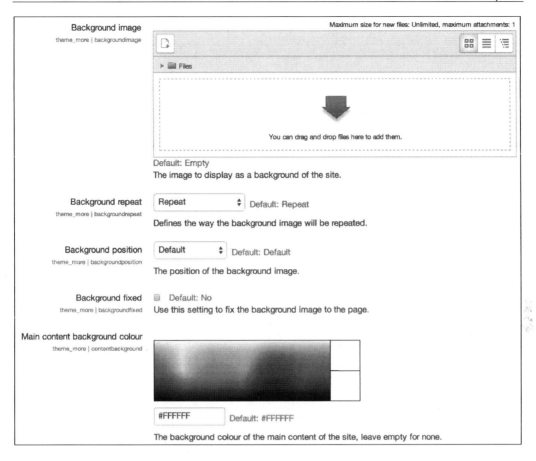

Typical theme settings include the following elements:

- **Font size**: This is the default font size that's used in a theme.

- **Color picker**: This refers to the selection of foreground and background colors, link colors, or the header color. The color picker offers a preview, which is quite helpful.

- **Image**: A URL can be specified to replace the one shown in the header or background.

- **Column width**: You can choose the width of the center column in terms of pixels. Other (usually fixed width) themes let you specify the width of the left-hand side and right-hand side column, separately.

- **Languages menu**: This is a checkbox that indicates whether the languages menu is shown.

- **Footnote**: The footnote text can be fully customized through the standard Moodle editor, that is, images or the HTML code can be also added.

- **Custom CSS**: This text box, which has been added to all the themes that ship with the core Moodle, lets you change any style in the theme. In the following example, the background of the body has been changed to black with yellow text. Additionally, `font-size` has been increased to `16px`. These settings are useful for learners who are visually impaired:

```
Custom CSS                    body {
theme_formal_white | customcss    background-color: #000000;
                                  background-image: none;
                                  color=#FFFF00;
                              }

                              p {
                                  font-size: 16px;
                              }

                              Default: Empty
```

The **Clean** and **More** themes that ship with Moodle let you customize your site to a certain degree via the Moodle frontend without needing to edit CSS files in the server. For example, the site that has been used to take screenshots for this book has been themed using the **More** theme.

A popular theme that you will find in the themes section on `https://moodle.org/` is called **Essential**. Once installed (refer to *Chapter 8, Moodle Plugins*), it provides a wide range of customization options, ranging from custom menus, front page slide shows, and marketing spots to social networking icons and links to mobile apps. Here is a sample customization of the **Essential** theme:

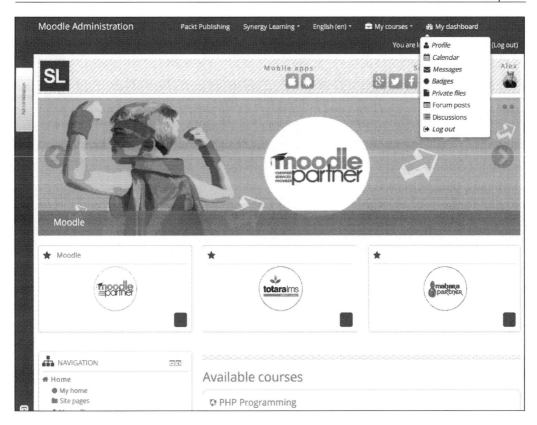

The Moodle editor

The editor is central to any user experience in Moodle since it is used throughout the site for a wide range of operations. This includes posting in forums (learner), providing feedback to submissions (teacher), and editing content (editing teacher). You, as the administrator, should ensure that the editor is configured in a way that facilitates your users' requirements.

Moodle's default editor is called Atto, which has been developed by Moodle for Moodle. Atto has been designed to work with responsible themes, support left-to-right as well as right-to-left strings, provide accessibility support, and is fully configurable.

Prior to Moodle 2.7. the TinyMCE editor was used, which is still supported. We will not deal with TinyMCE since it is expected that this editor will be phased out over future releases. Additionally, Moodle contains a built-in plain text editor that has been implemented to enter any text that does not require formatting, for instance, source code.

To get access to the available editors and their settings, go to **Plugins | Text editors | Manage editors**:

Manage editors

Available text editors

Name	Enable	Up/Down	Settings	Uninstall
Atto HTML editor	👁	↓	Settings	Uninstall
TinyMCE HTML editor	👁	↑ ↓	Settings	Uninstall
Plain text area	👁	↑		

Please choose the editor plugins you wish to use and arrange them in recommended order.
Changes in table above are saved automatically.

The idea of the **Text editors** plugin area is that additional editors can be installed and utilized throughout Moodle (refer to *Chapter 8, Moodle Plugins*). These can either be replacements for default editors or editors that enter specialized content. Furthermore, each button in Atto is implemented as a Moodle sub-plugin, which allows for flexible extension of the editor.

> It is recommended that you use Atto as the default editor as this is the one that will be maintained in the future and also fully supports mobile devices.

You can enable/disable each editor, change the order (in which they will be displayed when choosing an editor), and adjust the editor's settings through the **Settings** link.

Configuring the Atto editor

By default, the editor is configured to look like this (when expanded):

This is specified in the **Toolbar config** setting under the list of editor plugins:

```
Toolbar config              collapse = collapse
editor_atto | toolbar       style1 = title, bold, italic
                            list = unorderedlist, orderedlist
                            links = link
                            files = image, media, managefiles
                            style2 = underline, strike, subscript, superscript
                            align = align
                            indent = indent
                            insert = equation, charmap, table, clear
                            undo = undo
                            accessibility = accessibilitychecker, accessibilityhelper
                            other = html
```

Toolbar buttons are organized in groups, for example, collapse, style1, and list. Group names have to be unique, and the order dictates in which order groups of buttons are displayed.

Two tools that are regularly requested by users to be added to the toolbar are to change the foreground and background color of the selected font, respectively. To do this, add the following line in the **Toolbar config**, where appropriate:

```
color = fontcolor, backcolor
```

When you navigate to **Plugins | Text editors | Atto HTML editor | Collapse toolbar settings**, you can specify via the **Show (n) first groups when collapsed** option which buttons are shown when the editor toolbar is not expanded.

You have the ability to install Atto's editor plugins, which add additional buttons to your editor. Examples of `https://moodle.org/plugins/` are audio recording, word counter, and MS Word import.

The Atto editor autosaves its content in predefined intervals. This is helpful if users close their page by accident since the content will be restored the next time they return to the same form. You have the ability to adjust this **Autosave frequency** setting by navigating to **Plugins | Text editors | Atto toolbar settings**. Beware, a very high frequency, such as a second, will have a negative impact on performance.

Extending the functionality of tables

The Atto editor contains a powerful table mode, which supports the formatting and customization of tables. To equip your users with the full functionality, you might turn on the features by going to **Plugins | Text editors | Atto HTML editor | Table settings**:

Supporting mathematical equations

If you have users who make regular use of mathematical equations, you have two options:

- **Equations via TeX**: TeX is a typesetting language that supports a wide range of mathematical operations. You will need to enable the TeX filter by navigating to **Plugins | Filters | Manage filters**.

- **Equations via MathJax**: MathJax is a JavaScript library that displays a mathematical notation in web browsers using various markups including TeX. You will need to enable the MathJax filter by going to **Plugins | Filters | Manage filters**.

Once you have activated either or both filters, you can specify their details in the respective filter settings as well as the toolbar options by navigating to **Plugins | Text editors | Atto HTML editor | Equation editor settings**.

Alternatively, you can install the WIRIS plugin for Atto, which is an advanced editor for mathematical formulae (`https://moodle.org/plugins/atto_wiris`).

Adding some awesomeness

FontAwesome is a font icon toolkit which, at the time of writing, contains almost 600 fully scalable vector icons. In order to support this great set of features, you will have to go through the following steps:

1. Install the Font Awesome Icon Filter plugin from `https://moodle.org/ plugins/filter_fontawesome`. **Refer to** *Chapter 8, Moodle Plugins,* on how to do this.

2. Activate the filter by navigating to **Plugins | Filters | Manage filters**.

3. Add the following line to the within HEAD section by going to **Appearance | Additional HTML**:

   ```
   <link href="//netdna.bootstrapcdn.com/font-awesome/4.4.0/css/font-
   awesome.min.css" rel="stylesheet">
   ```

Once this has been successful, your users will be able to add icons via a text input like this:

```
[fa-quote-left fa-4x pull-left fa-muted]This is only a simple example
of a pull quote. You can also add spinning icons, fun big icons or
even Bootstrap components.
```

This will result in the following output:

> This is only a simple example of a pull quote. You can also add spinning icons, fun big icons or even Bootstrap components.

How awesome is this?! For the full documentation of the Font Awesome filter, check out `docs.moodle.org/en/FontAwesome_filter`. For a list of all the icons, actions, as well as good examples, refer to the main Font Awesome site at `fontawesome.io`.

Accessibility

In most educational settings, accessibility (the ability for users with certain disabilities to access Moodle's functionality) is now a legal requirement. So, it is important to make sure that your system complies with the respective standards. An area has been dedicated to Moodle accessibility in Moodle Docs, which you can access at `https:// docs.moodle.org/en/Accessibility`. It provides useful links to standards, guidelines, legislations, and also subject-related tools and resources.

Guaranteeing accessibility through Moodle themes

CSS is Moodle's representation layer that is independent from the content layer, which is represented in XHTML 1.0 Strict. Thus, accessibility can be achieved through the theme itself.

Once you have implemented your accessibility styles, either directly in the theme or through **Custom CSS**, as shown earlier on, Moodle provides links to three external sites, which check the current page for standard compliance. To activate these, go to **Development | Debugging** and check the **Show validator links** box. After saving the changes, links to **Validate HTML**, **Section 508 Check**, and **WCAG 1 (2, 3) Check** will be displayed at the bottom of your page (if they're supported by your theme).

One popular option is to incorporate accessibility options and offer them in the theme as options. Have a look at the header of the following custom bespoke theme (courtesy of, and designed by, Synergy Learning). It contains a color switcher in the top-right corner to cater to different visual impairments. Additionally, three different font sizes can be selected:

There is also a useful third-party **Accessibility** block, which lets the user change the font size and background color of their Moodle site. It further supports text-to-speech functionality. You can find it in the **Modules and Plugins** section at https://moodle.org/. The installation of third-party modules is covered in detail in *Chapter 8, Moodle Plugins*.

Accessibility support through the Moodle editor

Moodle is fully compliant with all major accessibility standards. This has been achieved by implementing XHTML 1.0 Strict, which only allows the usage of compliant HTML constructs and the implementation of the Moodle forms library. This guarantees consistency across forms and also supports standard screen readers.

The compliance is only guaranteed for Moodle pages (assuming that the theme follows all the standards) but not for newly created and uploaded content or any third-party learning resources. Moodle comes with a text filter called **HTML tidy**, which checks whether the HTML code is XHTML compliant, tidying it up wherever necessary. You will have to activate the filter by navigating to **Plugins | Filters | Manage filters**. You also have to make sure that the PHP has been compiled with the **LibTidy** option.

The Atto editor contains an Accessibility checker, which checks that the entered HTML code conforms to accessibility guidelines.

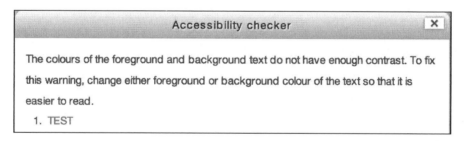

Support for a screen reader

A **screenreader** is a form of assistive technology that's used by blind and partially sighted users to interpret what is displayed on the screen. Once the information has been located, it can be vocalized using speech synthesis software and audio hardware.

Moodle supports screen-reading devices, such as Jaws and NVDA. Special configuration is not required.

Screen readers can only read text and the ALT tag in images. It is, therefore, highly recommended that you provide these tags in any images that are used. The Atto editor comes with a plugin, called the **Screenreader helper**, which checks the entered code for screenreader compatibility.

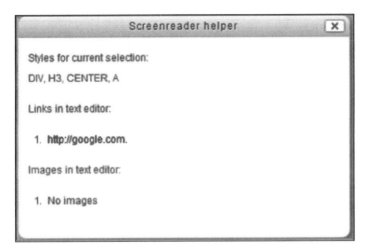

Summary

After providing a general overview of the elements involved in the look and feel of Moodle, this chapter covered the front page and theme customizations of Moodle as well as editor configuration and accessibility. We also dealt with supporting mobile devices. Read more about all of these in *Chapter 16, Moodle Networking*, when we cover web services, which allow the usage of your site with the help of dedicated mobile apps.

As mentioned earlier, the front page in Moodle is a course. This has advantages (you can do everything that you can do in a course and a little bit more), but it also has drawbacks (you can only do the same things that you do in a course and might feel limited by this). However, some organizations are now using Moodle's front page as their main home page. Again, this might or might not work for you.

Now that your Moodle looks (hopefully) the way you want it to, it is time to enable all the functionalities that you wish to offer your users. Plugins and configuration settings are dealt with in the next two chapters.

8
Moodle Plugins

Your system is now fully operational and has the look and feel to reflect the branding of your organization. As with all the complex web-based applications, there are a significant number of configuration activities that can be carried out to bring Moodle in line with your organization's needs and requirements.

One of the many strengths of Moodle is its pluggable architecture. Moodle supports a wide range of plugins, which will be covered in this chapter.

- **Module plugins**: These cover the core functionality available in a course, a front page, dashboard, and user profile pages. These include **Activity modules**, **Blocks**, and **Filters**.
- **Repositories**: Repositories allow the incorporating of data into Moodle, either from internal sources or external sites.
- **Portfolios**: These are the opposite of repositories. Portfolios allow the exporting of content from Moodle to other applications or data storage.
- **Miscellaneous plugins**: These include **Course formats**, **Question types and behaviors**, **Plagiarism prevention**, **Licenses**, and **Availability restrictions**.

There are a number of additional plugin types that have been covered in other chapters, namely, **Enrolments** (*Chapter 4, Course Management*), **Authentication** (*Chapter 5, User Management*), **Message outputs** (*Chapter 9, Moodle Configuration*), **logging** and **reports** (*Chapter 10, Moodle Logging and Reporting*), **Cache** (*Chapter 12, Moodle Performance and Optimization*), **Admin tools** (*Chapter 14, Moodle Admin Tools*), and **web services** (*Chapter 15, Moodle Integration*).

The second part of this chapter deals with the management of plugins. You will learn the following essentials about installing third-party add-ons:

- **Good, bad, and ugly third-party add-ons**: As externally developed software is not scrutinized by Moodle's quality assurance process, you will have to judge the trustworthiness of non-core add-ons. A checklist of criteria is provided to make this decision a bit easier.

- **Popular third-party add-ons**: There are well over 1,000 titles to choose from. We will discuss the most popular ones that will be relatively useful to you before outlining a couple of organizational decisions regarding plugins.

- **Installing third-party add-ons**: We will describe the installation of the **Collapsed Topics** format plugin via the admin interface, the manual installation process for the popular **Configurable Reports** and custom reports builder, and the installation of the **Certificate** module via Git and the command line.

- **Upgrading and uninstalling third-party add-ons**: Here, we will describe how to keep installed plugins up to date and how to remove them from your Moodle instance.

Let's start with an overview of plugins.

Plugins – an overview

Moodle plugins are modules that provide some specific, usually ring-fenced functionality. You can access the plugins area via the **Plugins** menu that is shown in the following screenshot:

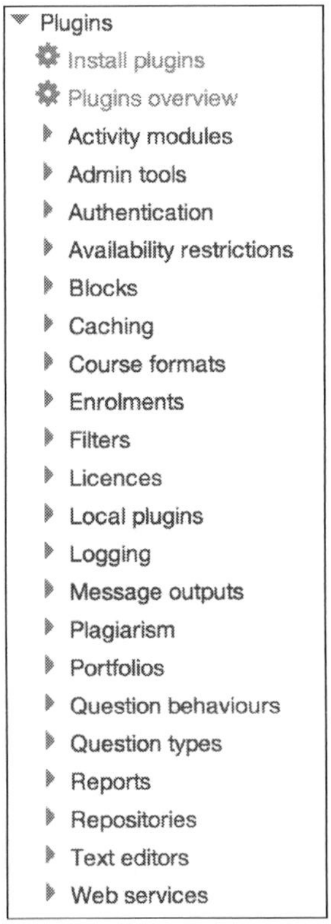

Install plugins lets you add third-party add-ons to your Moodle system. This is dealt with in the second part of this chapter. **Plugins overview** displays a list of all the installed plugins. The information shown for each plugin includes **Plugin name**, an internal **Identifier**, its **Source** (standard or extension), its **Version** (in the date format), its **Availability** (enabled or disabled), a link to the **Settings** plugin, an option to **Uninstall** the plugin, and some **Notes** (usually in the form of dependencies or errors). This table is useful to get a quick overview of what has been installed on your system and what functionality is available. You can also perform **Check for available updates** via the button at the top of the screen.

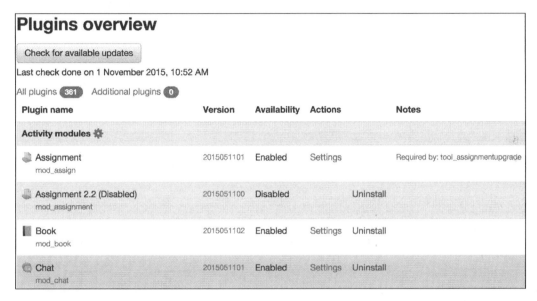

Some areas contain a significant number of plugins, for instance, authentication method and question type. Other categories only contain one or two plugins. The expectation is that more plugins will be developed in the future, either as part of the Moodle core or by third-party developers. This guarantees the extensibility of Moodle without the need to change the system itself. We will be dealing with third-party add-ons in detail in the second part of this chapter.

 Be careful when modifying settings in any of the plugins. Inappropriate values can cause problems throughout the system.

One type of plugin that we haven't mentioned yet is called **local** plugins. This is the recommended place for any customizations that do not fit in any of the plugin types that have already been mentioned. These customizations can be changed according to the existing functionalities or the introduction of new features. For more information on local plugins, check out the `readme.txt` file in the `local` directory. This is in the root directory of your Moodle installation (`dirroot`).

Now that we have dealt with the commonalities among plugins, let's have a look at the different types of plugins available in your Moodle platform, grouped according to module plugins, repositories, portfolios, and miscellaneous plugins.

Module plugins

Moodle distinguishes between three types of module plugins that are used in courses, the front page, and on the dashboard:

- **Activity modules** (these also include resources)
- **Blocks**
- **Filters**

Activity modules

Navigating to **Plugins** | **Activity modules** | **Manage activities** displays the following screen:

Activity module	Activities	Version	Hide/Show	Settings	Uninstall
Assignment	1	2014051201	👁	Settings	
Assignment 2.2 (Disabled)	0	2014051200	👁̸		Uninstall
Book	0	2014051200	👁	Settings	Uninstall
Chat	0	2014051200	👁	Settings	Uninstall
Choice	0	2014051200	👁		Uninstall
Database	0	2014051200	👁	Settings	
Feedback	0	2014051200	👁̸	Settings	
Folder	0	2014051200	👁	Settings	Uninstall
Forum	3	2014051201		Settings	
Glossary	0	2014051200	👁	Settings	
IMS content package	0	2014051200	👁	Settings	Uninstall
Label	0	2014051200	👁	Settings	Uninstall
Lesson	0	2014051200	👁	Settings	Uninstall
External Tool	0	2014051200	👁	Settings	Uninstall
Page	0	2014051200	👁	Settings	Uninstall
Quiz	0	2014051200	👁	Settings	
File	0	2014051200	👁	Settings	Uninstall
SCORM package	0	2014051200	👁	Settings	Uninstall
Survey	0	2014051200	👁		Uninstall
URL	0	2014051200	👁	Settings	Uninstall
Wiki	0	2014051200	👁		Uninstall
Workshop	0	2014051200	👁	Settings	Uninstall

The table displays the following information:

Column	Description
Activity module	Icon and name of the activity/resource as they appear in courses and elsewhere.
Activities	The number of times the activity module is used in Moodle. When you click on the number, a table, displays the courses in which the activity module has been used.
Version	Version of the activity module (this is in the YYYYMMDDHH format).
Hide/Show	The open eye indicates that the activity module is available for use, while the closed eye indicates that it is hidden (unavailable).
Settings	Link to activity module settings (this is not available for all items).
Uninstall	Performs the delete action. Some of the activities, for instance, Forum, cannot be deleted as they are required by some core functionality.

Clicking on the **Hide/Show** icon toggles its state; if it is hidden, it will be changed to be shown and vice versa. If an activity module is hidden, it will not appear in the **Add an activity** or **Add a resource** drop-down menu in any Moodle course. Hidden activities and resources that are already present in courses are hidden but are still in the system. This means that once the activity module is visible again, the items will also reappear in the courses.

If you delete an activity or resource that has been used anywhere in Moodle, all the already created activity modules will also be deleted and so will any associated user data! Deleting an activity module cannot be undone; it has to be installed from scratch.

 It is highly recommended that you do not delete any activity modules unless you are 100% sure that you will never need them again. If you wish to prevent the usage of an activity or resource type, it is better to hide it instead of deleting it.

The **Feedback** activity has been around for some time as a third-party add-on. It is hidden by default because it has been newly introduced in the core of Moodle 2 due to its popularity. You will probably want to make this available to your teachers.

Settings are different for each activity module. For example, the settings for the **Folder** module only contains a single parameter, whereas the settings for the **Quiz** module allows the modification of a wide range of parameters.

The settings for Moodle **Activity modules** are not covered here as they are mostly self-explanatory and also dealt with in great detail in the Moodle Docs of the respective modules. It is further expected that some of the activity modules will undergo a major overhaul in the 3.x versions to come, making any current explanations obsolete.

There is, however, one parameter that is shared across all Moodle activities, which can be found by going to **Plugins | Activity modules | Common activity settings**. By default, the **Require activity description** option is turned off. Make sure that this setting remains that way unless you want to become unpopular with your course authoring colleagues. Otherwise, for every activity and resource that is added to a course, a meaningful description has to be added. While this is a good practice, reality has shown that this is commonly bypassed by adding some dummy text or simply a dot.

The strategic direction of Moodle in future versions is to make activities as pluggable as possible. An example of this is the **Assignment** module, where you can see **Submissions plugins** and **Feedback plugins**. For instance, there is an expectation that the **Feedback** and **Survey** modules will be replaced by a new activity to deal with questionnaires, which will support plugins for different fields and question types.

Configuring blocks

Navigating to **Plugins | Blocks | Manage blocks** displays a table, as shown in the screenshot that follows. It displays the same type of information as for **Activity modules**. Additionally, you have the ability to **Protect instances**. This is intended to protect blocks, such as **Navigation** and **Settings**, which are difficult to get back if deleted accidentally.

You can delete any Moodle block except **Administration** and **Navigation**. If you delete a block that is used anywhere in Moodle, all the already created content will also be deleted. Deleting a block cannot be undone; it has to be installed from scratch.

 Do not hide the **Administration** block as you will not be able to access any system settings anymore.

Most blocks are shown by default (except the **Feedback** and **Global search** blocks). Some blocks require additional settings to be set elsewhere for the block to function. For example, RSS feeds and tags are to be enabled in **Advanced features** or the **Feedback** activity modules are to be shown.

Name	Instances	Version	Hide/Show	Protect instances ⑦	Settings	Uninstall
Activities	0	2015051100	👁	🔓		Uninstall
Activity results	0	2015051100	👁	🔓		Uninstall
Admin bookmarks	1	2015051100	👁	🔓		Uninstall
Administration	1	2015051100	👁	🔒		
Blog menu	0	2015051100	👁	🔓		Uninstall
Blog tags	0	2015051100	👁	🔓		Uninstall
Calendar	3	2015051100	👁	🔓		Uninstall
Comments	2	2015051100	👁	🔓		Uninstall

The parameters of all standard Moodle blocks are explained in the respective Moodle Docs pages.

Configuring filters

Filters scan any text that has been entered via the Moodle HTML editor and automatically transform it into different, and often more complex, forms. For example, entries or concepts in glossaries are automatically hyperlinked in text, URLs pointing to MP3 or other audio files that become embedded, flash-based controls that offer pause and rewind functionality, uploaded videos are given play controls, and so on.

Moodle ships a number of filters, which are accessed by navigating to **Plugins | Filters | Manage filters**:

Filter	Active?	Order	Apply to	Settings	Uninstall
Multimedia plugins	On	↓	Content		Uninstall
TeX notation	Off, but available	↑ ↓	Content	Settings	Uninstall
Glossary auto-linking	Off, but available	↑ ↓	Content		Uninstall
Display emoticons as images	On	↑	Content	Settings	Uninstall
Activity names auto-linking	Disabled		Content		Uninstall
Algebra notation	Disabled		Content		Uninstall
Word censorship	Disabled		Content	Settings	Uninstall
Database auto-linking	Disabled		Content		Uninstall
Email protection	Disabled		Content		Uninstall
MathJax	Disabled		Content	Settings	Uninstall
Multi-Language Content	Disabled		Content	Settings	Uninstall
HTML tidy	Disabled		Content		Uninstall
Convert URLs into links and images	Disabled		Content	Settings	Uninstall

By default, all the filters are disabled. You can enable them by changing the **Active?** status to **On** or **Off, but available**. If the status is set to **On**, it means that the filter is activated throughout the system but can be deactivated locally. If the status is set to **Off, but available**, it means that the filter is not activated but can be enabled locally.

In the preceding screenshot, the **Multimedia plugins** and **Display emoticons as images** (smileys) filters have been turned **On** and will be used throughout the system as they are very popular. The **TeX notation** and **Glossary auto-linking** filters are available but have to be activated locally. The former is only of use to users who deal with mathematical or scientific notation and will trigger the **Insert equation** button in the Moodle editor. The **Glossary auto-linking** filter might be used in some courses. It can then be switched off temporarily at the activity module level when learners have to appear for an exam.

Additionally, you can change the order in which the filters are applied to text using the up and down arrows. The filtering mechanism operates on a first come first served basis, that is, if a filter detects a text element that has to be transformed, it will do this before the next filter is applied.

Each filter can be configured to be applied to **Content and headings** or **Content** only, that is, filters will be ignored in the names of activity modules. The settings of some filters are described in detail in the Moodle Docs. As with activities and blocks, it is recommended that you hide filters if you don't require them on your site.

In addition to filter-specific settings, Moodle provides a number of settings that are shared among all filters. These settings are accessed by going to the **Filters | Common filter settings** menu and are shown in the following screenshot:

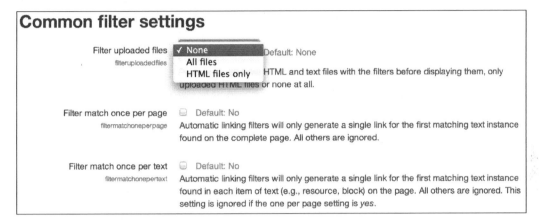

The three settings are as follows:

Setting	Description
Filter uploaded files	By default, only text entered via the Moodle editor is filtered. If you wish to include uploaded files, you can choose any of them from the HTML files only and All files options.
Filter match once per page	Enable this setting if the filter stops analyzing text after it finds a match, that is, only the first occurrence will be transformed.
Filter match once per text	Enable this setting if the filter only generates a single link for the first matching text instance found in each item of text on a page. This setting is ignored if the Filter match once per page parameter is enabled.

Moodle repositories

File picker is central to almost all file operations in Moodle. Files can be selected from a wide range of sources known in Moodle as **repositories**. Moodle repositories are accessed by navigating to **Plugins** | **Repositories** | **Manage repositories**:

Name	Active?	Order	Settings
Embedded files	Enabled and visible ⬍	⬇	Settings
Server files	Enabled but hidden ⬍	⬆⬇	Settings
Recent files	Enabled and visible ⬍	⬆⬇	Settings
Upload a file	Enabled and visible ⬍	⬆⬇	Settings
Private files	Enabled and visible ⬍	⬆⬇	Settings
Youtube videos	Enabled and visible ⬍	⬆	Settings
Alfresco repository	Disabled ⬍		
Box	Disabled ⬍		

Each repository has one of the following three states:

- **Enabled and visible**: The repository will be available throughout the system.

- **Enabled but hidden**: Already set up repositories will be available, but no new instances can be created. This only applies to repositories that allow multiple instances (discussed later in this section).

- **Disabled**: The repository is not available in your Moodle system.

The order in which the repositories are listed reflects the order in which the repositories appear in **File picker**. This can be changed using the up and down arrows. As soon as a repository has been enabled, a **Settings** link will be displayed for almost all the repositories. Every repository has a `repository plugin name` parameter that lets you override its default name. Some repositories also have additional settings, which will be discussed throughout this chapter.

 When you disable a repository plugin, its settings and all of its instances will be removed. You have the option to download any content or references there to Moodle.

Some repository types support multiple instances. The number of existing site-wide, course-wide, and private user instances are displayed under the **Settings** link. These can then be configured in the relevant context, that is, by going to **Course administration | Repositories** in the course settings and also by navigating to **Preferences | Manage instances** in the **Repositories** section of a user:

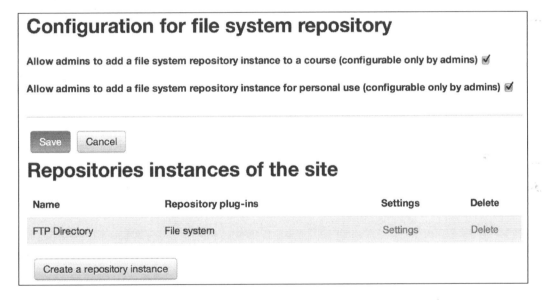

Site-wide instances are created as part of **Settings** when managing the plugins, for example, the **File system** repository:

For the sake of simplicity, we distinguish between internal and external repositories. An **internal repository** is one that accesses internal Moodle files. An **external repository** is located outside Moodle, either on some local media, in another application's data storage, or in the cloud.

Internal repository plugins

There are a number of internal repository plugins to choose from, as follows:

Name	Description	Settings
Server files	These are files on your Moodle system to which a user has access. Files are arranged in a hierarchy reflecting Moodle contexts (refer to *Chapter 2, The Moodle System*).	
Recent files	Recently used and uploaded files.	**Number of recent files**
Private files	Personal files of a user, which can be accessed throughout Moodle.	
File system	Allows access to subdirectories in the $CFG->dataroot/repository. A readable directory has to be selected for each instance. Setup and access have been covered in *Chapter 2, The Moodle System*.	**Allow users to add a repository instance into the course (can be configured only by admins)** **Allow users to add a repository instance into the user context (can be configured only by admins)**
Embedded files	Allows users to reuse the files embedded in the current text area.	
Legacy course files	Access to files after migrating from Moodle 1.9	

Server files, **Recent files**, and **Private files** are managed by Moodle. The **User quota** parameter can be specified for private files by going to **Security | Site policies**. The default value is 100 MB. The **File system** plugin has already been described in detail in *Chapter 2, The Moodle System*, where external access to the Moodle filesystem was required, for example, to upload files via FTP.

One area that requires some attention is the **Legacy course files** plugin. In Moodle 1.x, all the files were stored in a course files area. They were not linked to a specific activity, resource, or any personal files, which can be accessed across courses, that exist. This caused problems with backups, data security, and data integrity. A new File API has been introduced in Moodle 2, which rectifies these shortcomings. An issue arises when updating from Moodle 1.9 to Moodle 2 (you cannot upgrade straight to Moodle 3.x). During the migration process, Moodle is able to allot files to activities and resources, but it does not know what to do with unused files or files that have been linked from within certain resources. It stores these in the **Legacy course files** area. Users will have to move these files to the appropriate place manually, that is, their personal files area as well as resources and activities.

Two settings related to legacy files can be found in **Common repository settings**, which will be dealt with at the end of the **Repository** section.

 Legacy course files are intended to be a temporary measure. The objective is to discontinue their use once all the files have been migrated.

External repository plugins

External repository plugins will add, that is, copy, stream, or link, new files or content to your Moodle system. They may be uploaded from your local computer, a USB pen drive, network drive, or a cloud storage, such as Google Drive, Dropbox, Microsoft OneDrive, Box, and Amazon S3. Additionally, external applications, such as Alfresco, EQUELLA, Flickr, Picasa, and YouTube, are supported as sources.

It is expected that the number of repository plugins will grow in the near future to access other storage types and applications. Repository API of Moodle makes the development of these add-ons relatively painless for a programmer.

Data storage repositories

The following repository plugins form a part of the core of Moodle and act as file or data storages. They are described in detail in the following table:

Name	Description	Settings
Upload a file	Manually uploading a file that can be accessed from your local PC or Mac. This will be used a lot by all users.	
WebDAV repository	Access to a WebDAV server. A repository instance has to be created in the course or user context where a number of parameters have to be specified, such as Name, WebDAV type, WebDAV server, WebDAV path, Authentication, and the optional WebDAV server port, WebDAV server user, and WebDAV server password parameters.	Allow users to add a repository instance into the course (can be configured only by admins) Allow users to add a repository instance into the user context (can be configured only by admins)
Google Drive	Access to users' documents in Google Drive. Access has to be granted by each user when the plugin is used for the first time. It requires OAuth2.0.	CLIENT ID and CLIENT SECRET

Name	Description	Settings
Microsoft OneDrive	Access to users' documents in MS OneDrive. Access has to be granted by each user when the plugin is used for the first time.	Client ID Secret
Dropbox	Access to a single Dropbox folder, not one for each. Click and follow the Dropbox developers link under the Settings link, and click on the Create an App button to get access to the two required parameters (App key and App secret).	Dropbox API Key Dropbox Secret Cache Limit
Box	Similar to the Dropbox repository. Follow the link on the Settings page and log on for an API key.	Client ID Secret
Amazon S3	Access to the Amazon S3 storage service, including the ability to select in which geographical region your data will be stored.	Access key Secret key Amazon S3 endpoint
URL Downloader	Importing a file via a URL link. This can be an internal or external web address.	

Application repositories

The application repository plugins connect to applications and are part of the Moodle core. They are described in detail in the following table:

Name	Description	Settings
Alfresco repository	Access to Alfresco, a commercial, open source content management system. Both copying and linking are supported.	Allow users to add a repository instance into the course Allow users to add a repository instance into the user context
Flickr	Access to the personal accounts of Flickr, a photo sharing site. A login required when accessing it the first time.	API key Secret
Flickr public	Access to the public area of photo sharing site, Flickr.	API key Allow users to add a repository instance into the course Allow users to add a repository instance into the user context

Name	Description	Settings
Picasa web album	Access to Picasa web albums. A login is required. It requires OAuth2.0.	Client ID Secret
Youtube videos	Access to the YouTube video platform. Videos will be streamed to Moodle, not copied.	API key
Merlot.org	Access to MERLOT (Multimedia Education Resource for Learning and Online Teaching).	License key
Wikimedia	Access to the Wikimedia Commons platform.	
EQUELLA	Access to the EQUELLA repository	Allow users to add a repository instance into the course Allow users to add a repository instance into the user context

A number of shared settings can be found by navigating to **Plugins | Repositories | Common repository settings**. They are explained in detail in the following table:

Setting	Description
Cache expire	This setting specifies the number of listings that are stored locally. The default value of 120 seconds is sufficient unless you have users with erroneous connections.
Get file timeout	Timeout needed to download external files.
Sync file timeout	Timeout needed to synchronize external files.
Sync image timeout	Timeout needed to synchronize images.
Allow external links	By default, this setting is enabled. External links are supported by some repositories, for instance, File system or Alfresco.
Legacy course files in new courses	Legacy course files have been discussed earlier; unless really necessary, it is recommended that you leave this option unchecked.
Allow adding to legacy course files	If legacy course files exist in a course, this setting allows the adding of new files to it. This should be avoided if possible.

Once the repository setup has been completed, it is best to test the access from a number of contexts (users, sites, and courses) and also make sure that no users have access to sources that they shouldn't have and vice versa.

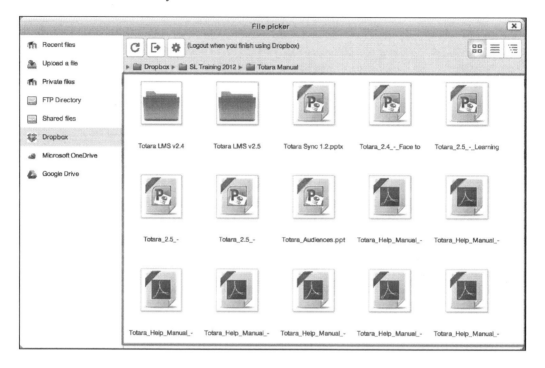

Now that our **File picker** is fully populated and your users are able to get content into Moodle, let's have a look at how they can achieve the opposite and get content out of Moodle.

 Additional information on all the mentioned Moodle repositories can be found at `https://docs.moodle.org/en/ Repositories`.

Moodle portfolios

According to Moodle Docs, Moodle portfolios enable data, such as forum posts or assignment submissions, to be exported to external systems.

Moodle portfolios have to be enabled by selecting the **Enable portfolios** parameter in **Advanced features**. Once this has been done, you have access to all the available portfolio plugins by going to **Plugins** | **Portfolios** | **Manage portfolios**.

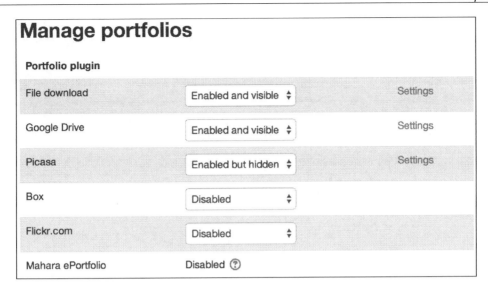

Each portfolio has one of the following three states:

- **Enabled and visible**: The portfolio will be available throughout the system
- **Enabled but hidden**: Portfolios have to be activated to be used
- **Disabled**: The portfolio is not available in your Moodle system

Once a portfolio has been set up, users will see an **Export to portfolio** link or icon at various places in their courses (for instance, assignment submissions, forum posts, and glossary entries). When this link is clicked, they will have to select one of the existing destinations from the **Select destination** drop-down menu. Depending on the chosen portfolio type, additional actions have to be taken, for example, log in to the site, confirm the file type, or grant access to the external application.

Export formats that are currently supported are HTML, LEAP2A, images, and text. It is expected that additional formats, such as PDF, will be added in future.

Like repositories, each portfolio plugin has a **Name** setting, where the default plugin label can be changed. Unlike repositories, multiple instances do not exist, nor is it possible to change the order of the plugins.

The following portfolio plugins are a part of the Moodle core:

Name	Description	Settings
Box	Follow the on-screen instructions to obtain **API key**. A login to Box.net is required. If successful, users will have to specify whether the created HTML file will be shared and in which folder it has to be placed.	**Client ID** **Client Secret**
Google Drive	Permission has to be granted at first use. An HTML file will be created automatically in the users' **Documents** area. OAuth 2.0 required.	**Client ID** **Client Secret**
File download	The export formats that are supported are HTML and LEAP2A (a popular e-portfolio format).	
Flickr.com	Follow the on-screen instructions to obtain **API key**. Authorization is required at first use.	**API key** **Secret string**
Mahara ePortfolio	This is disabled by default. It's only available if a valid network connection to Mahara or the Totara Social system has been established and the **MNet authentication** plugin has been enabled. *Chapter 16, Moodle Networking*, has been dedicated to networking.	**MNet host** **Enable LEAP2A portfolio support**
Picasa	Access has to be granted when used for the first time. A picture will be placed in the **Drop Box** area of the users' Picasa albums. OAuth 2.0 is required as well.	**Client ID** **Secret**

Users have the ability to select which available portfolios are presented in their **Export to portfolio** list. Once you go to **Preferences** | **Configure** in the **Portfolios** pane, you have the option to hide any configured portfolio plugin.

Manage your portfolios

Content which you have created, such as assignment submissions, forum posts and blog entries, can be exported to a portfolio or downloaded. Any portfolio that you do not wish to use may be hidden so that it is not listed as an option to export content to.

Name	Portfolio plugin	Show / hide
File download	download	👁
Google Drive	googledocs	👁
Mahara ePortfolio	mahara	👁

Furthermore, when you navigate to **Preferences | Transfer logs** in the **Portfolios** pane, you will be shown a list of any **Currently queued transfers** and **Previous successful transfers**. The former lists all the pending exports, which can either be continued (the green button) or cancelled (the red button). The latter displays details on all the recent transfers that have been made:

Currently queued transfers

Export area	Portfolio plugin	Export info	Transfer expiry time	
Forum	Mahara ePortfolio	Exporting content from Forum: News forum	Sunday, 13 July 2014, 5:22 PM	● ●
Forum	Not yet selected	Exporting content from Forum: News forum	Sunday, 13 July 2014, 5:10 PM	● ●

Previous successful transfers

Portfolio plugin	Export area	Transfer time
File download	Forum	Saturday, 12 July 2014, 5:23 PM
File download	Assignment	Saturday, 12 July 2014, 5:21 PM

There are a number of settings that apply to all portfolios, which can be accessed by going to **Plugins | Portfolios | Common portfolio settings**. They include two thresholds for file sizes (**Moderate transfer filesize** and **High transfer filesize**) and two for the number of database records (**Moderate transfer dbsize** and **High transfer dbsize**). If the actual values exceed the threshold values, users will be warned that the export might take some time.

 Additional information on all the mentioned Moodle portfolios can be found at docs.moodle.org/en/Portfolios.

Miscellaneous plugins

There are a number of additional plugin types that are used less frequently than the ones already covered. It is expected that more will be added to these categories in the future, either as part of the Moodle core or third-party add-ons.

Course formats

Course formats drive the way learning content is displayed in courses. Moodle drives four course formats; additional formats can either be downloaded from `https://moodle.org/` or be custom developed. Three popular third-party course formats are the **Grid format** (`https://moodle.org/plugins/format_grid`), **Collapsed Topics** format (see installation later in the chapter), and the **Socialwall** format, which mimics a Facebook-like course layout (`https://moodle.org/plugins/format_socialwall`).

Course formats

Name	Enable	Up/Down	Uninstall	Settings
Single activity format	👁	⬇	Uninstall	Settings
Social format	👁	⬆ ⬇	Uninstall	
Topics format	👁	⬆ ⬇	Uninstall	
Weekly format	Default	⬆		

Default format can be changed in Course default settings

You can **Enable** and disable course formats and change the order of their appearance via the **Up/Down** arrows. Once uninstalled, the source of the format has to be removed at the system level to avoid reinstallation. Some course formats have settings that are usually **Default** values.

You can specify the default course format for new courses by going to **Courses | Course default settings**.

Question types and behaviors

Moodle's **Quiz** activity module includes a number of question types, such as **Multiple choice**, **Short answer**, and **Drag and drop onto image**. Moodle has a powerful question engine that supports a range of question behaviors. These are the methods through which submitted questions are dealt with. In true Moodle style, both constructs are handled as plugins, and it is possible to add additional **Question types** and **Question behaviors** to the system.

To take a look at the available question types, go to **Plugins | Question types | Manage question types**.

Question type	No. questions	Version	Requires	Available?	Settings	Uninstall
Calculated	0	2015051100	Numerical	👁 ↑ ↓		
Calculated multichoice	0	2015051100	Numerical, Calculated, Multiple choice	👁 ↑ ↓		Uninstall
Calculated simple	0	2015051100	Numerical, Calculated	👁 ↑ ↓		Uninstall
Description	0	2015051100		👁 ↑ ↓		Uninstall
Drag and drop into text	1	2015091100	Select missing words	👁 ↑ ↓		
Drag and drop markers	1	2015091100	Select missing words, Drag and drop onto image	👁 ↑ ↓		
Drag and drop onto image	1	2015091100	Select missing words	👁 ↑ ↓		
Embedded answers (Cloze)	0	2015100201	Multiple choice, Numerical, Short answer	👁 ↑ ↓		Uninstall
Essay	0	2015051100		👁 ↑ ↓		Uninstall
Matching	0	2015051100		👁 ↑ ↓		
Missing type	0	2015051100		↑ ↓		
Multiple choice	0	2015051100		👁 ↑ ↓		

You can only enable/disable each question type, change the order in which it is displayed when choosing a question, and then delete it. The **Settings** column is reserved for third-party types and more sophisticated question types are introduced in future versions of Moodle. When clicking on the number of questions, you will be shown a screen that shows all the courses that contain questions of the respective type.

Closely related to question types are question preview defaults. The settings you see when going to **Plugins | Question types | Question preview defaults** are used when a user previews questions in the question bank for the first time.

To take a look at the available question behavior, go to **Plugins | Question behaviors | Manage question behaviors**. For each behavior under the **Behavior** column, **No. question** attempts and its **Version** are listed. If a type has one or more prerequisites that have to be installed, they will be displayed in the **Requires** column. The **Available?** and **Uninstall** columns have the same functionality as the settings for question types.

Availability restrictions

Inside Moodle courses, a course author has the ability to restrict access to individual activities or resources. The types of available restrictions can be configured by navigating to **Plugins | Availability restrictions**.

Plugin	Version	Hide/Show
Restriction by activity completion	2014051200	👁
Restriction by date	2014051200	👁
Restriction by grades	2014051200	👁
Restriction by group	2014051200	👁
Restriction by grouping	2014051200	👁
Restriction by profile	2014051200	👁

You only have the option to show and hide each restriction; by default, all the plugins are enabled. Some restrictions require other elements to be present or configured, respectively. For example, groups and groupings only appear in a course's **Access restriction** when these exist in a particular course.

A popular third-party availability restriction, called **Restriction by language** (https://moodle.org/plugins/availability_language), has been described in a little bit more detail in the **Localization** section in *Chapter 9, Moodle Configuration*.

Licences

A license can be selected when adding a file via **File picker**. This information will then be attached to the metadata of the file. To configure the licenses available to your users, go to **Plugins | Licences**.

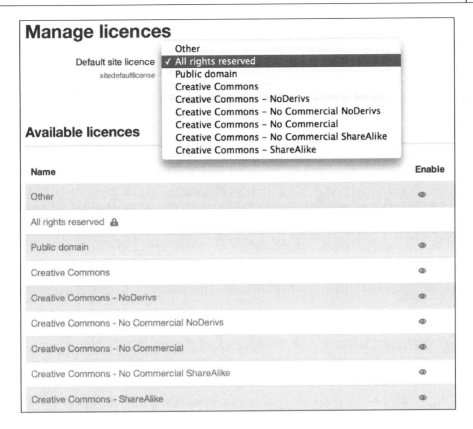

As seen in the preceding restrictions, you only have the option to show and hide each license; by default, all the entries are enabled.

Plagiarism prevention

The idea behind plagiarism prevention is to check the submitted content of students against the work of others—the higher the overlap, the more likely that the content has been plagiarized. This can either be done by users in the same Moodle instance or through public resources.

Plagiarism prevention has to be enabled by selecting the **Enable plagiarism plugins** parameter in **Advanced features**. Once this takes place, you have access to any installed plagiarism prevention plugins when you navigate to **Plugins** | **Plagiarism prevention** | **Manage plagiarism plugins**.

At the time of writing this, there are about a dozen plugins available at `https://moodle.org/` that cater to plagiarism prevention. However, only about half of these are kept up to date by their developers, so you'd better check their current state. The two most popular are **Turnitin** and **Urkund**. Some of the plugins are explained here:

- **Turnitin**: This appears to be the most popular option among educational organizations, which is why it has been described in more detail later in this section.

- **Crot**: This is an appealing open source alternative (`www.crotsoftware.com`) that does not rely on external mechanisms, and no documents will be transferred to an external server. However, the Moodle plugin has not been updated for a while, and it remains to be seen whether this will happen soon. The Docs page is located at `https://docs.moodle.org/en/Plagiarism_Prevention_Crot_2.0`.

- **Urkund**: It is another commercial plagiarism prevention tool. You will find details about the Moodle plugin at `https://docs.moodle.org/en/Plagiarism_Prevention_URKUND`.

The add-ons have to be downloaded from the **Modules and plugins** area at `https://moodle.org/` and installed on your Moodle server (refer to next section in this chapter).

A paid subscription is required when you visit `http://www.turnitin.com/`. Once installed and configured, the Turnitin plagiarism prevention functionality will be available as part of the **Assignment** module inside courses.

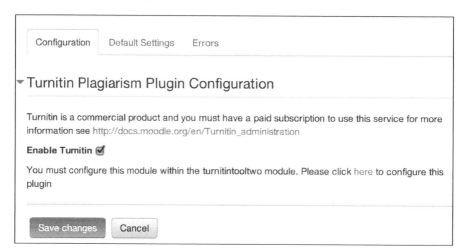

Once you have entered **Turnitin Account ID** and **Turnitin Secret Key**, you are ready
to configure the plugin on the screen shown and the **Turnitin Defaults** tab. Given
the vast number of settings, it might be best to involve someone who deals with
educational and curriculum matters in your organization. More details and further
information on these settings can be found at `https://docs.moodle.org/en/
Plagiarism_Prevention_Turnitin`.

Installing third-party plugins

There exists a plethora of third-party Moodle software that add new functionalities,
fix problems, or integrate Moodle with external systems and cloud services. Let's
start with an overview of third-party software.

Third-party software – an overview

Moodle comes with a number of core modules that include **Activity modules** (for
example, **Quiz** and **Assignment**), **Filters** (**Multimedia plugin** or **Algebra notation**),
Blocks (**Calendar**). It also contains a number of other components, such as **Enrolments**
and **Authentication** plugins, course and grade reports, **Repositories** and **Portfolios**,
Question types, and so on. While the provided functionalities sufficiently satisfy
a majority of users, there is a growing demand for additional software. Also,
requirements change over time and new functionalities, for instance, those that provide
support for certain social networking activities, are needed in your Moodle system.

Due to Moodle's open source nature and modularity (that's what the *M* in Moodle
stands for, after all), it is relatively straightforward for developers to add new
functionalities or modify existing features. These can range from minor modifications
(patches) or hacks to full-blown modules. You can get access to the **Plugin directory**
page by visiting `https://moodle.org/plugins/`, which contains all the approved
non-core modules and themes.

You have a number of options to navigate through the plugin directory:

- Using **Search** with the help of a keyword
- Using **Categories** that are shown on the front page of plugins
- Using **Navigation** in the side block where you can also register new plugins

Either way, you should always end up with a list of add-ons. Once you click on
the name of a plugin, you will be provided with details, such as its description,
installation instructions, statistics, and so on.

At the time of writing this, there are over 1,100 third-party Moodle software titles, and the number is growing continuously. You will find all kinds of add-ons, ranging from the weird and wonderful to the very powerful.

Good add-ons and bad add-ons

Every module that is part of the core of Moodle has gone through a thorough quality assurance process. The potential problem with third-party add-ons is that you don't know anything about the quality of the software.

While it is possible to uninstall modules if they don't fit your purpose, you will have to make sure that you don't put barriers in place for future updates. If an add-on is not maintained, it is unlikely that it'll be able to support any upcoming versions of Moodle, and you will either have to delete the module that's already in use or you won't be able to upgrade your system. Also, a module might cater to some required functionality but can also compromise the security of your system.

There are a number of criteria that indicate whether an add-on is trustworthy or not. They are as follows:

- **Popularity**: Moodle maintains statistics on its downloads, which can be found at `https://moodle.org/plugins/stats.php`. You will see all the plugins that have been downloaded in the previous year and the last two months, respectively. While there is no guarantee, the more popular a module, the more likely it is to be of a high standard.

- **Ratings**: Each add-on page allows users to mark a plugin as their favorite. Again, there's no guarantee here, but the more admins who have favored an add-on, the more likely that this is indicative of a good add-on.

- **Level of active support**: Some of the most valuable third-party add-ons have vanished because they are unsupported. Your best bet is if the add-on is supported by a major stakeholder in Moodle, such as the Open University or a Moodle Partner. The maintainer should have been active in the community for the past 60 days.

- **Forum posts and comments**: Users are encouraged to post comments, problems, and praise about each module. Read through the posts to get an idea about what other users have experienced. Be suspicious about modules that are not talked about at all. Also, check whether there are any reviews in the **Reviews** section.

- **Documentation**: Each add-on should have a dedicated page in Moodle Docs. It is usually not a good sign if the page does not exist or is only a wiki stub. Also, it is a good practice if a change log is kept for the developed software.

- **Standalone**: It is imperative that third-party add-ons do not modify any core code (known as patches that are supplied in the form of patch files). This is important as the changes will be overridden with every Moodle update and the modifications will have to be reapplied.

- **Supported versions**: Support for current versions and one or more previous versions of Moodle is a sign that the software is being actively maintained. You can take a look at any of the existing versions in the **Versions** tab.

- **Backup and restore support**: If applicable, the add-on should be supported by the course backup and restore facility. Otherwise, what good is an activity if it is not included in your archives?

- **Code**: If you can read PHP code, have a look at the actual source code of the add-on. Try to find answers to the following questions:
  - Is the code well structured, and can it be easily followed?
  - Is the source code well commented?
  - Does the module follow the Moodle coding guidelines (https://docs.moodle.org/dev/Coding)?

- **Official approval**: Moodle has recently tightened the process of accepting third-party plugins to its database. While this process does not guarantee the functionality, security, or the integrity of the add-on, it evaluates the code at a high level. Once this stage has been passed, it will be accepted in the plugins' database. Add-ons stored elsewhere, for example, on a developer's home page, should only be trusted if they come from a well-known source.

- **Developer**: Some developers are known to produce very well-written Moodle add-ons. Programmers that are affiliated with a Moodle Partner are usually a good bet, as are core developers, Moodle documenters, and particularly helpful Moodlers.

Popular add-ons

The following is a list of some popular third-party Moodle add-ons (in alphabetic order), available through **Plugins directory** at https://moodle.org/plugins/, as well as a brief description for each plugin:

- **Adminer**: This module is a repackaged version of Adminer. Once installed, you will see a new **Moodle Adminer** item in the **Server** menu in the **Site administration** section. This is useful to create database backup dumps among other database-related operations.

- **Certificate**: This fully-customizable activity generates PDF certificates for students once they have fulfilled certain conditions. We will use this module to demonstrate how to install plugins via Git later on.

- **Checklist**: This Moodle package, comprising of an activity module and a block, allows teachers to create a checklist for the benefit of their students. The teacher can monitor all the students' progress as they tick off each of the items in the list. Items can be indented and marked as optional. Students are presented with a progress bar, and they can add their private items to the list.

- **Collapsed Topics**: This course format lets users expand and collapse individual topics, tackling the issue of the infamous scroll of death. We use the course format as an example to show how to install a plugin via the admin interface.

- **Configurable reports**: This is a powerful report generator that lets you create various types of custom reports, including filters, groupings, and visual representation. We will cover its functionality in *Chapter 10, Moodle Logging and Reporting* and will discuss the installation of the module later in the chapter.

- **Essential**: This is a very powerful theme with tons of configuration options, such as front page sliders, marketing spots, and social networking icons. We came across this theme in the previous chapter that dealt with the look and feel of your site.

- **Google OAuth2**: This authentication plugin lets users authenticate via their Google, Facebook, Windows, Linkedin, or any other login.

- **Grid format**: This represents each topic in a course as an icon and shows activities inside the topic in a lightbox style display.

- **HotPot**: The HotPot activity module allows teachers to administer Hot Potatoes and TexToys quizzes via Moodle.

- **Progress Bar**: This block is a time management tool for students that visually shows what activities and resources a student is supposed to interact with in a course.

- **Questionnaire**: This provides an alternative to feedback activity.

Keep monitoring the list of recently released plugins at `https://moodle.org/plugins/` (go to **Plugins administration** | **Reports** | **Recently approved plugins**) via the provided RSS feed or **@moodleplugins**. There are always great new add-ons being launched, which might be useful for your site.

Organizational decisions around plugins

Before you go wild and bombard your Moodle system with dozens of plugins, sit back and reflect on the following questions:

- Who is the plugin for?

  Does the plugin cater for the needs of a wide range of users or only a handful of trainers with very specific needs? Is it a nice-to-have gimmick or a must-have feature? Neither is a problem, just be aware of this.

- What are the requirements of your users?

  It has proven very useful to gather your staff's requirements from a representative group of users. Math teachers have other needs that are different from language coaches, novices need tools that are separate from experts, and course authors request features that are dissimilar to those required by course coordinators. Gather all the requirements first, and then make an informed decision on which plugins are needed to cater to the majority.

- What is the impact on your users?

  Adding new activities, questions types, and course formats is a great way to equip your teachers with new tools to build engaging learning content. However, take into account the skills of your staff and the time they would have to invest to master these add-ons.

- What is the impact on your infrastructure?

  Some plugins require access to other systems, for instance, authentication plugins or cloud services. Other plugins rely on a commercial service, for example, video conference tools or plagiarism detection systems. Make sure that the plugin suits your infrastructure and there is a sustained budget in case regular fees have to be paid.

- Is there an alternative?

  Make sure that the requirements cannot be catered to by on-board tools. If this is not the case, trawl Moodle's plugin directory for alternative options.

Be very selective with the plugins you add to your system – the less add-ons you have to maintain, the less maintenance work and potential hassle you are facing long-term.

Installing third-party add-ons

A good piece of advice is to avoid experimenting with new add-ons on a production site. Most organizations set up a shadow site of their live server to be used as a sandbox. Once the installation has been successful, the procedure is reapplied on the production site.

Additionally, it is recommended that you make a complete site backup before installing any third-party software. This way, you can roll it back in case of a disaster.

Most add-ons are structured in a very similar way. However, some modules either don't follow this standardized approach or require other steps, especially when the module communicates with other software systems. Each plugin should contain a file (usually called README) with installation instructions. It is important that you read these first before installing a module.

Installing the Collapsed Topics format plugin via the web interface

The easiest way to install a plugin is by going to **Plugins | Install Plugins**. However, you will have to make sure that the target directory on your server is writable, which is not recommended on production sites for security reasons but is usually acceptable on test sites. There are two options that show you how to use a plugin installer:

When you click on the **Install plugins from the Moodle plugins** directory button, you will be directed to the familiar plugins section on `https://moodle.org/`. You will have to log into the site in order to perform installations. Also, bear in mind that your site's full name, URL, and Moodle version will be sent as well in order to ensure a smooth installation process. Once you have located the plugin you wish to install (here, it's in the Collapsed Topic format), you will see an additional **Install now** button appear:

Once selected, a list of your sites will be shown and you need to select **Install now** again. You will be redirected back to your Moodle site where a message will indicate whether the plugin can be installed or a problem has arisen, for instance, that the target directory is not writable. Once this has been confirmed, the plugin validation will be carried out, and the already familiar **Plugins check** screen has to be confirmed before the installation is carried out:

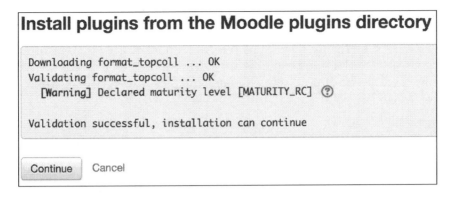

Once **Upgrade Moodle database now** has been clicked, the standard installation process kicks off.

Alternatively, you can download the plugin and upload it by navigating to the **Plugins | Install Plugins** interface. You will have to confirm the validation screen before the installation is performed. Once successful, you will be confronted with a number of default settings for the course format.

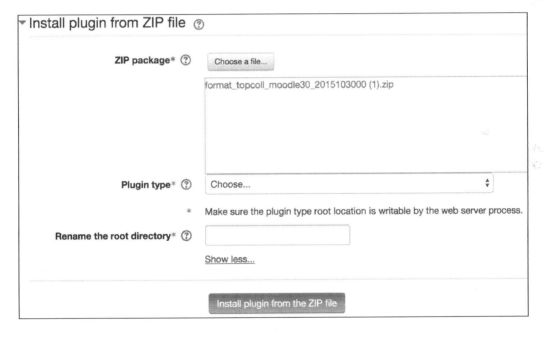

For plugins that correctly declare their component's name, the installer is automatically able to detect the type of plugin. If auto detection fails, choose the correct **Plugin type** manually. The installation procedure can fail if an incorrect plugin type is specified! If you need to change the root directory for the plugin installation, you'll see an option called **Rename the root directory** once **Show more...** is selected.

Installing the Configurable Reports plugin manually

As an alternative to installing plugins via the admin interface, you can perform these tasks manually. For the purpose of demonstrating these steps, we have chosen the **Configurable Reports** module for a number of reasons. It satisfies all the criteria outlined earlier, it is a very useful and popular activity, and it is packaged in the standard format.

After locating the add-on in the plugins repository (`https://moodle.org/plugins/block_configurable_reports`), download the version of the software that fits the version of your Moodle system (here 3.0). Next, put Moodle in maintenance mode (**Server | Maintenance mode**). While it is possible to add most modules while Moodle is in use, it is not recommended that you do this as this can lead to some unforeseen problems.

The module follows the standardized structure of add-ons, that is, it includes the same directory hierarchy as Moodle. It is best to copy the ZIP file to the `$CFG->dirroot/blocks` directory and unpack the file via `unzip configurable_reports.zip`. You might have to change the user and group to the same as the folders in those directories.

Now, go to your **Notifications** page in the **Site administration** section. The module behind this page will recognize that a new module has to be installed and kick off the installer:

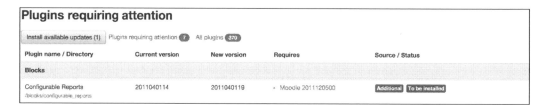

You will see a new entry in the **Blocks** table called **/blocks/configurable_reports** with the status **To be installed**. Once you confirm this via the **Upgrade Moodle database now** button, a number of database tables with fields are created and populated with values. The overall success of the installation will be displayed.

That's it! All you have to do now is make sure that the module works properly in Moodle. In case of the **Configurable Reports** module, go to **Plugins | Blocks | Manage blocks**, and you will see an entry for the newly installed add-on.

It is important that you check that the block is working as intended. In case of the **Configurable Report** add-on, you can find detailed information in the Moodle Docs at https://docs.moodle.org/en/blocks/configurable_reports. We also have a dedicated *Report generation* section in *Chapter 10, Moodle Logging and Reporting*.

> Finally, don't forget to disable Moodle's maintenance mode and let your users know that the new functionality is available!

Installing the Certificate module via Git

An alternative to installing and updating plugins is via Git. Developers are encouraged to maintain their personal Git repository, which might contain multiple Moodle extensions. We are going to use the popular Certificate module as an example to demonstrate how to install a contributed extension from its Git repository.

When you browse to the plugin page of the **Certificate** module, you will see a link to **Source control URL**, which will direct you to the github entry of the plugin. Github is the de facto standard site to manage Git repositories.

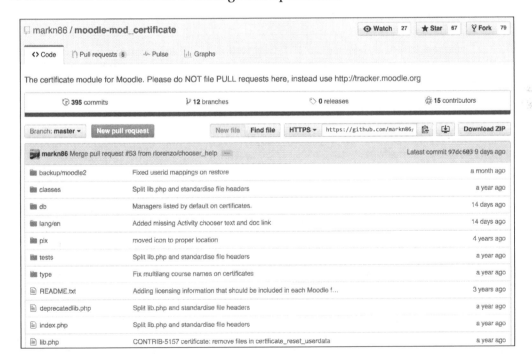

To install the module, you have to execute the following steps:

1. Change to the `$CFG->dirroot/mod` directory (this is where all the modules are stored).

2. Execute the following `git` command:

    git clone https://github.com/markn86/moodle-mod_certificate.git certificate

    This creates a new subdirectory certificate and makes a local copy of the `Certficate` code repository. The path is the same as the one you saw in the previous screenshot.

```
root@debian:/var/www/packt/mod# git clone https://github.com/markn86/moodle-mod_certificate.git certificate
Cloning into certificate...
remote: Reusing existing pack: 1979, done.
remote: Total 1979 (delta 0), reused 0 (delta 0)
Receiving objects: 100% (1979/1979), 3.46 MiB | 811 KiB/s, done.
Resolving deltas: 100% (1009/1009), done.
```

3. Go to the **Notifications** page in your Moodle system and run through the upgrade screens. The **mod_certificate** module will be added. Once these have been saved, the module will be available by navigating to **Plugins | Activity modules | Manage activities**.

Installing plugins via the command line

Moodle itself does not support the installation of plugins via its CLI, but there is a utility called Moosh that does exactly this. You will find the tool in the Moodle plugins database (`https://moodle.org/plugins/view.php?id=522`). To install Moosh, extract the downloaded package and set a symbolic link to your programs folder:

```
sudo ln -s $PWD/moosh.php /usr/local/bin/moosh
```

You should now be able to execute Moosh from the command line. For further installation options, have a look at `http://moosh-online.com/`.

Moosh is a bit different in that it is not a plugin as such but a command-line tool that supports over 80 commands, two of which are relevant in the context of installing plugins:

- `moosh plugin-list`: This command lists all the plugins (the full name, short name, available Moodle versions, and a short description) that are available at `https://moodle.org/plugins/`; it makes sense to apply some filters, such as the module name, since the list is huge.

- `moosh plugin-install mod_certificate 1`: This command downloads and installs the current version of the **Certificate** module. It doesn't get any easier than this! To obtain the version number, use the aforementioned `plugin-list` command (`moosh plugin-list | grep "Certificate"`).

There is also a command to uninstall a plugin; for instance, take a look at this one:

```
moosh plugin-uninstall mod_certificate
```

To get an overview of all the plugins installed on your Moodle instance: use this command

```
moosh info-plugins
```

You will come across MOOSH at various places in this book, and an entire section has been dedicated to the tool in *Chapter 14, Moodle Admin Tools*.

Keeping plugins up to date

One main challenge that Moodle administrators face is to keep plugins up to date. The preceding installation steps are sufficient for a one-off installation, but do not cater to situations that call for maintaining the plugins.

How do you know that new plugins are available? You can either be notified automatically by e-mail (go to **Server | Update notifications**, as covered in *Chapter 1, Moodle Installation*), or you can check manually (**Notifications**).

There is a newer version for some of your plugins available!

See plugins overview page for more details.

Check for available updates

Keeping plugins up to date depends on the installation method you chose initially:

- **Web interface**: Go to the **Plugins | Plugins overview** where the **Install available updates** button will initiate the update process of any available plugins (download and installation).

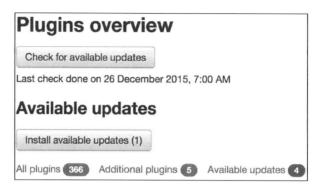

- **Manually**: You will have to download the latest version at `https://download.moodle.org/` and reinstall, as described previously.

- **Git**: To keep the module up to date over time, you will have to create a local branch of the module that is synchronized with the remote branch on github. You will find detailed instructions on how to do this at `https://docs. moodle.org/en/Git_for_Administrators`.

- **Command line**: All you need to do is to rerun the same command as you did during installation, that is, `moosh plugin-install <plugin> <moodle_version>`.

Uninstalling third-party add-ons

If you decide to uninstall a third-party add-on and the module is listed in the **Activities**, **Blocks** or **Filters** section in the **Plugins** menu, you have to use the provided **Uninstall** option.

Deleting an add-on will also delete all the user data that's associated with the module, irreversibly!

The delete operation will remove all the data associated with the module and display a message, as shown in the following screenshot, to confirm the success of doing this. To complete the deletion and prevent the block from reinstalling itself the next time you go to the **Notifications** page, you will have to delete the directory from your server.

Uninstalling Certificate

You are about to uninstall the plugin *Certificate*. This will completely delete everything in the database associated with this plugin, including its configuration, log records, user files managed by the plugin etc. There is no way back and Moodle itself does not create any recovery backup. Are you SURE you want to continue?

Continue   Cancel

You will also have to remove the installed files from `$CFG->dirroot/mod` or any other location where the files have been stored. If you don't perform this step, the add-on will be reinstalled next time you go to the **Notifications** page. Other types of add-ons that cannot be deleted from within Moodle, for example, the **Assignment** type, will also have to be removed manually.

Summary

In this chapter, you learned how to configure different types of plugins in Moodle. We covered four main types of plugins, namely, module plugins, repositories, portfolios, and miscellaneous plugins. We then covered the essentials of managing third-party Moodle add-ons.

You've hopefully experienced a flavor of the breadth and depth of additional functionalities that are available for VLE. It not only demonstrates the extensibility and popularity of Moodle but also shows the significant benefit of open source software, namely, the ability to programmatically enhance a program to a user's requirements.

As Moodle becomes more popular, large commercial providers are dedicating resources to develop plugins that connect with their software or service. Examples of this are web conference suites from WebEx and Adobe or an entire suite of plugins that provide integration with Office 365 (`https://moodle.org/plugins/browse.php?list=set&id=72`).

The consistent manner in which plugins have been implemented demonstrates the modular architecture of Moodle and flattens the learning curve when additional modules are added in the future and have to be administered.

Now, let's move on to the last part of the Moodle configuration.

9

Moodle Configuration

Moodle comes with a multitude of configuration options. In this chapter, we will cover the most important settings, most of which are likely to be relevant to your organization. We will distinguish between educational and technical configurations:

- **Educational configuration**: These settings are likely to require input from other stakeholders in the organization as they cover areas that are of a pedagogical (not technical) nature. The areas that are covered are collaboration (blogs, comments, and tags), badges, LTI, localization, grades and gradebooks, and a number of miscellaneous settings.

- **Technical configuration**: These are settings that require some technical knowledge about your infrastructure. The topics that are dealt with are synchronous communication (instant messaging and video conferencing), asynchronous communication (inbound and outbound messaging as well as RSS feeds), and a number of experimental settings.

There are a number of additional configuration topics that are covered in dedicated chapters. These topics include plugins (*Chapter8, Moodle Plugins*), security (*Chapter11, Moodle Security and Privacy*), optimization (*Chapter12, Moodle Performance and Optimization*), and networking (*Chapter16, Moodle Networking*).

Collaboration

One of Moodle's many advantages is its built-in support for collaboration among learners and instructors. This ranges from a number of collaborative course activities, such as, **Forum**, **Wiki**, **Glossary**, and **Database**, the ability to run activities in a group mode, and support for groupings. Additionally, there are three social activities in Moodle that have to be configured by the administrator. These include blogs, comments, and tags, as discussed in the following sections.

Configuring blogs

Blogs are a means for users to express themselves either in the form of a learning journal or as a personal account of events. The blogging mechanism provided to users allows the creation of personal as well as public entries and also posts relating to a course.

As an administrator, you will have to **Enable blogs** in the **Advanced features** menu. Once the blogs are enabled, there are a number of settings that are available when you navigate to **Appearance | Blog**:

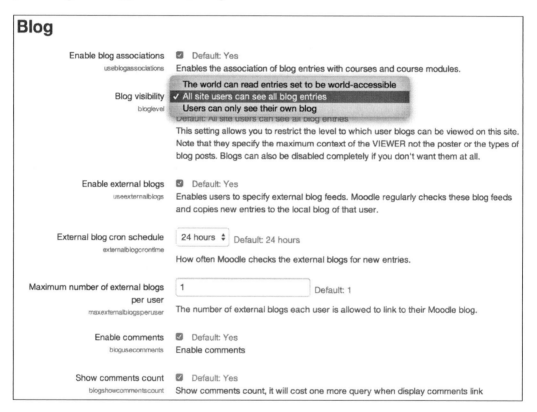

Settings	Description
Enable blog associations	If the **Enable blog associations** checkbox is checked, course and activity blogs are available, which allow learners to choose link entries to a course or course module. If it is unchecked, all the blog posts will be converted to user blog posts. The setting can be overridden locally via the **moodle/blog:associatecourse** and **moodle/blog:associatemodule** role capabilities.

Settings	Description
Blog visibility	The self-explanatory options are: • **The world can read entries set to be world-accessible** • **All site users can see all blog entries** (default) • **Users can see only their own blog** The choice of option depends on the policy of your organization and how blogs are used as part of the learning process.
Enable external blogs	Moodle supports external blogs, for example, from WordPress or Google's Blogger. If enabled, users will have the ability to link their blogs by navigating to **My profile settings** | **Blogs** | **Register an external blog** in the **Settings** block. The entries will be shown as if they have been entered in the Moodle blog but cannot be modified.
External blog cron schedule	How often the update is carried out is set here. The options are **12 hours**, **24 hours**, **2 days**, or **7 days**.
Maximum number of external blogs per user	This indicates the number of external blogs each user is allowed to link to their Moodle blog.
Enable comments	A key feature of blogs is the ability for others to provide comments on blog posts; for instance, a teacher can leave private or public feedback on a journal entry.
Show comments count	This shows the number of comments that are received.

Supporting comments

We have just come across comments in blogs. Moodle comes with a generic comments functionality that is independent of the one in the blogging module. It allows the placement of the **Comments** block in any context of the system, for instance, in a course or an individual activity.

This feature is enabled by default but can be disabled via the **Enable comments** parameter in the **Advanced features** link.

There are a number of areas where additional comment-related settings can be set, for instance, when they are included in backups or supported by certain activities. There is also a report that you can take a look at by going to **Reports** \| **Comments**, where you can see all the comments that are given throughout the system. You might want to check this every so often in case anything offensive or inappropriate has been entered.

You can search for comments using the **Search** box to see all of these settings. As always, these settings can be overridden locally via the respective role capabilities.

Managing tags

Tagging is the process of describing artefacts or users using keywords. These tags are then harnessed to search, share, and perform other collaborative activities in order to match interests.

As with blogs and comments, tags can be enabled (this is the default setting) and disabled for the entire site. This can be done via the **Enable tags functionality** parameter in **Advanced features**.

Users create their own tags that represent their private or educational interests and, depending on the size of their social network (in our case, Moodle and any Internet services that can be incorporated), matching will take place. However, as an educational institution, you might want to create a number of site-wide tags that can be used in addition to the user-defined tags. Examples of these global tags are organization-related keywords, topics that your entity specializes in, campaigns that your company runs, or newsworthy topics that are relevant to your institution. To set these tags, go to **Appearance | Manage tags**.

You can add a site-wide tag by entering its name in the textbox at the top and clicking on the **Add official tags** button. All the global tags are shown in this list, where, for each tag, the following information is displayed:

Field	Description
Tag name	This is the name of the tag. When you select the tag, you see which users have been tagged with this tag. Furthermore, you have the option to add/remove the tag to suit your own interests and also flag the tag as inappropriate (refer to **Flag**).
First name/Surname	This is the creator of the tag, which links to the user profile.

Field	Description
Count	This is the number of times the tag has been used throughout the site. These will be used as a basis for the Tag block that is shown on the left-hand side.
Flag	This shows whether the flag has been flagged as inappropriate and the number of times in brackets.
Modified	This shows the last time the tag was edited.
Official	When a tag is official, it will show up globally.
Actions	Editing the tag allows you to add a description and also enter related tags. These will then show up when a user has selected the tag.
	Deleting will remove the tag from the system.

If you need to block users from tagging you will need to create a separate role and adjust the two relevant capabilities **moodle/tag:create** and **moodle/tag:edit**.

Moodle also supports course tags, allowing students to tag courses. This has to be enabled via the **Show course tags** parameter in **Plugins | Blocks | Tags**. Bear in mind that this will change the look of the **Tags** block.

Configuring and managing badges

According to `http://openbadges.org/`, a badge is *an online representation of a skill you've earned*. Moodle can act as a badge consumer and a badge producer or issuer. As a consumer, a user has the ability to display badges earned elsewhere; as an issuer, badges can be earned in Moodle and displayed or collected elsewhere. Moodle distinguishes between two types of badges:

- **Course badges**: These are badges that are awarded at the course level, for example, for completing certain activities
- **Site badges**: These are badges that are related to site-wide activities, such as successfully completing a set of courses

First, badges have to be enabled in **Advanced features**. As an administrator you will then have to configure the usage of badges by going to **Badges | Badges settings**:

Badges settings

Default badge issuer name badges_defaultissuername	Packt Default: Packt Name of the issuing agent or authority.
Default badge issuer contact details badges_defaultissuercontact	packt@synergy-learning.com Default: ▓▓▓▓▓▓@synergy-learning.com An email address associated with the badge issuer.
Salt for hashing the recepient's email address badges_badgesalt	badges1398797015 Default: badges1398797015 Using a hash allows backpack services to confirm the badge earner without having to expose their email address. This setting should only use numbers and letters. Note: For recipient verification purposes, please avoid changing this setting once you start issuing badges.
Enable connection to external backpacks badges_allowexternalbackpack	☑ Default: Yes Allow users to set up connections and display badges from their external backpack providers. Note: It is recommended to leave this option disabled if the website cannot be accessed from the Internet (e.g. because of the firewall).
Enable course badges badges_allowcoursebadges	☑ Default: Yes Allow badges to be created and awarded in the course context.

The **Default badge issuer name** and **Default badge issuer contact details** settings set the name and e-mail address of your organization, which is displayed with the badges that are being issued. Make sure these have been approved internally; if set incorrectly, achievements from your site will potentially not be credible.

Salt for hashing the recipient's email address, also known as the badge salt, allows other badge consumers to verify badge earners without exposing their e-mail address. Once set, it should not be altered.

The two remaining settings allow users to display badges from `https://backpack.openbadges.org/backpack/login` (**Enable connection to external backpacks**) and to **Enable course badges**.

Adding badges

Site-wide badges have to be added by navigating to **Badges | Add a new badge**. This task can be delegated via the **moodle/badges:manageglobalsettings** capability. In order to create a new badge, you will have to add the following information:

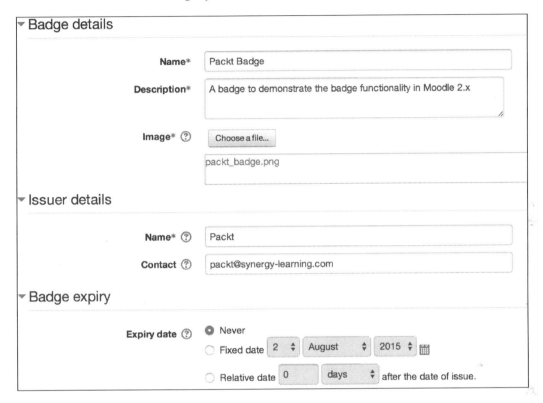

Badge details comprises of **Name**, **Description**, and **Image**. You can either use one of the many online badge creation tools (for instance, https://www.openbadges.me/) or get a professional to design the badge images.

Issuer details have been set automatically using the values provided in **Badge settings**.

As the name suggests, **Badge expiry** specifies when the validity of a badge lapses. This is, for instance, relevant in compliance settings. There are three settings. They are as follows:

- **Never** (default)
- **Fixed date** (specific date)
- **Relative date** (specifies the number of `<time frame>` after the issuing date)

Once a badge has been created, you need to add badge criteria, which specifies when the badge will be awarded to a user:

- **Manual issue by role**: Select any role (usually **Teacher**) which is allowed to manually award the badge. This is based on the **moodle/badges:awardbadge** capability. If more than one role has been selected, you need to specify **This criterion is complete when ...** as **All of the selected criteria are completed** (for example, when a teacher and manager have to award the badge) or **Any of the selected criteria are completed** (either of the two user roles is sufficient).

- **Completing a set of courses**: You have to select at least one course from the list of courses. The courses that are listed are the ones that have course completion activated. For each course, you have the option to specify a minimum grade and by when this has to be achieved. If more than one course is chosen, you will again specify the **This criterion is complete when ...**option.

- **Profile completion**: You can select one or many user profile fields, which also include user-defined profile fields. This is usually only used in conjunction with any of the other two settings, for example, the badge can only be issued to any learner from a specific country.

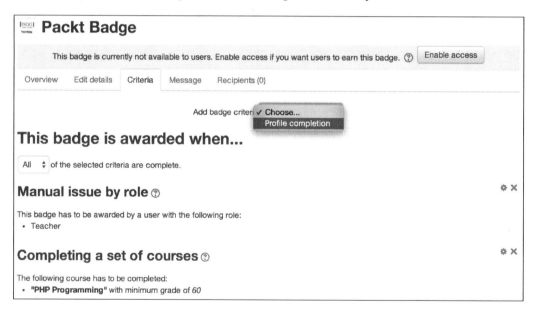

In the **Message** tab, you should specify **Badge message** that is being sent out to users on awarding a badge. Inside **Message body**, you can use three self-explanatory place holders, such as %badgename%, %username%, and %badgelink%. It is recommended that you **Attach the badge to message**.

Make sure you **Enable access** to the badge, which effectively activates the usage of the badge. You can manage all your site-wide badges by navigating to **Badges | Manage badges**.

Supporting the LTI consumers and producers

According to IMS, **Learning Tools Interoperability (LTI)** is a *standard for learning tool interoperability to allow remote tools and content to be integrated into a Learning Management System*. In Moodle, it is often referred to as an external tool, which supports LTI 2.0. Moodle and can act as an LTI consumer (external content can be used in Moodle) and LTI provider (Moodle content can be used in other LTI consumers):

- **Moodle as an LTI consumer**: You have the option to configure external tools, which will then appear in the **External Tool Types** activity inside a course (go to **Plugins | Activity modules | Manage external tool types**. Each tool comprises a name and a base URL, which have to be provided by the provider. Additionally, **Consumer key** and **Shared secret** are needed. Here, a number of LTI tools have been created:

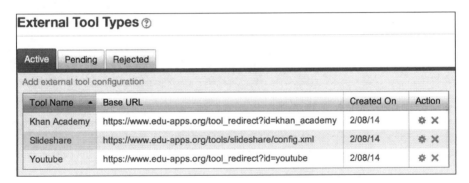

- **Moodle as an LTI producer**: For Moodle to operate as an LTI consumer, a plugin has to be installed, which you can find at `https://moodle.org/plugins/view.php?plugin=local_ltiprovider`. We do not want to provide more details on this as they are explained very well as a part of the provided documentation.

 You can find more information on Moodle acting as an LTI consumer and producer, respectively, at `https://docs.moodle.org/en/External_tool`.

Localization

Localization is concerned with the adaptation of software so that it can be used in different locales. A locale is linked to a region where certain cultural aspects apply, such as, language, formatting of dates and times, calendric representation, and so on.

As Moodle is used throughout the world, and given the fact that many educational establishments span across continents, it is important that localization is fully supported. The key areas in which Moodle can be configured are language-related settings and calendric information.

> If your main language is something other than (UK or USA) English, make sure you select this during installation. This way, locale settings as well as role names and descriptions will be localized properly.

Languages, idiomas, 语言, and اللغات

Moodle supports over 75 languages, including Latin! To represent the character sets of multiple languages, a standard called **Unicode** has been adopted; it covers the most modern scripts that are used throughout the world. Moodle also fully supports right-to-left writing systems such as Arabic.

Language packs

Locales are characterized by standardized two-letter region codes representing a language and optional letters. For example, **pt** represents Portuguese as spoken in Portugal, whereas, **pt_br** represents Brazilian Portuguese. Moodle uses the same representation for its more than 100 available language packs. Some packs of nonstandardized languages have made their way into Moodle, such as Deutsch Kids, an adopted version that's targeted at young learners. For these specialized packs, new codes have been made up by their creators, for example, **de_kids**.

In order to support a language, you have to install its language pack, which contains all the terms used in Moodle. Moodle will download any requested language packs from `https://download.moodle.org/`. Go to **Language | Language packs** to include new packs:

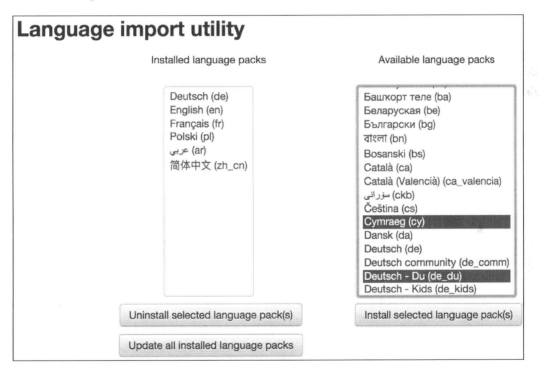

In the preceding screenshot, six language packs, consisting of Arabic, German, English, French, Polish, and simplified Chinese, have been installed (you can see them in the list on the left-hand side). To add more language packs, select one or many locales on the right-hand side and click on the **Install selected language pack(s)** button. To reverse this operation, select a single or multiple language packs in the list on the left-hand side and click on the **Uninstall selected language pack(s)** button.

The **English(en)** language pack cannot be uninstalled. It is used as a reference language in cases where strings in other languages are not translated. Some language packs are not complete, and sometimes, only non-admin features have been translated.

Once installed, the user can choose a language (if configured) from the language menu, which is usually located in the header or from within their profile. Bear in mind that only terms and phrases that are part of Moodle will change. Any content created will not be translated unless the content is configured to make use of the multilingual feature (refer to the *Language customization* section). We've already looked at multilingual menu items, which were covered in *Chapter 7, Moodle Look and Feel*.

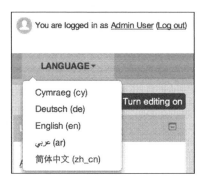

Language packs are kept and maintained at `download.moodle.org/langpack/3.x` (where, x is the current release version number). Some packs are updated more frequently than others; clicking on the **Update all installed language packs** button copies the latest versions to your server.

Language settings

Moodle offers a number of language settings that you can find by going to **Language | Language settings**. These settings are listed in the following table:

Settings	Description
Language auto detect	By default, Moodle detects the language from the used web browser locale. If you wish to override this and use the default site language instead, uncheck the checkbox.
Default language	This allows you to select the language that will be used throughout the site, unless it's overridden by individual users via the language menu or from their profile. Only those languages appear for which a language pack has been installed and is shown in the language menu.

Settings	Description
Display language menu	If enabled, the language menu will be displayed on the front page header. The user will always have the ability to change the language in their profile, no matter what the setting is. Some themes do not support this feature.
Languages on language menu	If left empty, all the installed languages will appear in the language menu. To narrow down this list, specify a comma-separated list of locale codes.
Cache language menu	Unless you add or remove language packs, it is recommended that you leave this setting enabled. It caches the language menu on the front page.
Cache all language strings	Unless you modify a language pack, it is recommended that you leave this setting enabled. It caches all the language strings rather than loading them dynamically.
Site wide locale	The localization operations are internally driven by system locales, which are selected on the basis of the chosen language pack. If you wish to change this (which is hardly ever required), select the site-wide locale in its operating system format such as en_US.UTF-8. The file has to be installed as part of the operating system.
Excel encoding	When downloading data in the Microsoft Excel format (such as in gradebook reports or log files), Moodle uses the Unicode format. Older versions of Excel only support Latin encoding.

There are three additional language-related settings that are placed elsewhere:

- The **Full name format** option, which you can see by going to **Users | Permissions | User policies**, allows you to choose the format of the full name. There are a number of placeholders that can be used in the field, for example, **first name** and **first name phonetic**. If the **language** placeholder (default) is entered, the format of the full name is decided by the current language pack. This way, you can cater to local sensitivities with regard to first names.

- The **Alternative fullname format** option, which you can see by navigating to **Users | Permissions | User policies**, is the same as **Full name format**, but it defines how names are shown to users with the **moodle/site:viewfullnames** capability

- The **Allow extended characters in usernames** parameter, which you can see by going to **Security | Site policies**, removes the limitation of only using alphanumeric characters in usernames.

Language customization

Each phrase, term, and string used in Moodle is represented in language files, which are tied to certain modules in Moodle (these are located in the `lang` directory). There are almost 20,000 (!) language strings in Moodle, which demonstrate the scale of the system. You have the ability to change any language string in Moodle. You might want to change words or phrases, for example, you may want to change *Grades* to *Marks*, *Outcomes* to *Work indicators*, *Teacher* to *Instructor*, and so on.

To customize a language file, go to **Language | Language customization**, where you will first have to choose a language to be customized. Clicking on the **Open language pack for editing** button will lead to the checkout step; this might take a few seconds. Once this has been done, you can click on the **Continue** button.

 Moodle creates a `local` directory, located inside `$CFG->dataroot`, where it stores your edited phrases. Make sure that you have write access to the `lang` directory to avoid any error messages.

Moodle keeps a separate language file for each module. This separation is beneficial as it frees the underlying code (developed by programmers) from the localization (worked on by translators). However, the disadvantage is that you need to know where (that is, in which PHP module) the respective strings are located. However, Moodle offers a good filtering mechanism to simplify the search for strings that are to be modified.

Let's say you wish to change the term *Guest* to *Visitor*. As it is likely that the term *Guest* appears in a number of different modules, it is safe to select all the items in the **Show strings of these components** list.

You further have filter criteria to choose from. The options include **Customised only** for strings that have been changed in previous sessions, **Help only** for balloon help tool tips, and **Modified only** for phrases that are changed in the current session. The **Only strings containing** parameter requires the word or phrase you are looking for (in our case, **guest**). Internally, Moodle uses string identifiers, which can also be used to search content. To do this, just enter the string identifier in the **String identifier** textbox:

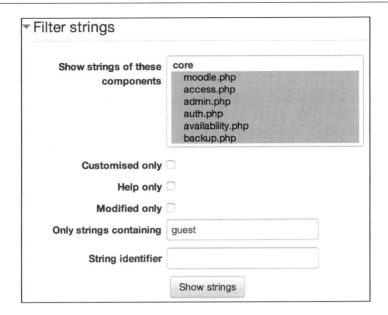

Once the search has been successful, the following information is shown for each string that matches the filter:

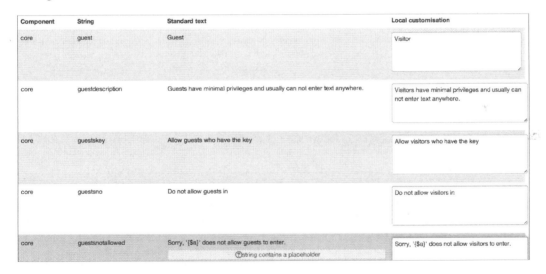

Item	Description
Component	This is the system component to which the string belongs. This also includes third-party add-ons.
String	This is the string identifier (mainly used by programmers).

Item	Description
Standard text	This consists of the string text or phrases in English. If the language that's been chosen is other than English, the translated version is displayed underneath.
Local customisation	This is where you can override the current text.

You might have spotted the **$a** parameter in the fifth phrase from the top. This is a so-called placeholder, which is substituted on the fly; in this instance, it is substituted with the name of a course. These have to be included in the local customization. Some placeholders will contain a parameter, such as $a->id or $a->query. You should keep them as they are used to avoid any problems.

Make sure that you click on the **Save changes to the language pack** button to reflect the changes on your Moodle site. These changes will be maintained when your site is updated.

You can grant users access to the **Language customization** menu via the **report/customlang:edit** and **report/customlang:view** role capabilities.

There is also a setting called **Show origin of languages strings**, which you can see by going to **Development | Debugging,** that is useful when you customize a language pack. If this setting is enabled, it shows the file and string identifier besides each string as the output on the screen.

If you wish to contribute to a language pack or want to create a new one, go to the Moodle languages portal at https://lang.moodle.org/. On this site, you will find information on how to utilize the AMOS tool and the AMOS Moodle block (for more details, take a look at https://docs.moodle.org/dev/AMOS_manual).

Multilingual content

If you have users who deal with multilanguage content, it is recommended that you turn on the **Multi-Language Content** filter by going to **Plugins | Filters | Manage filters**. The **Multi-Language Content** filter supports the <span lang="xx"class="multilang"> tag by default; the older <lang> tag can be enabled as well in the settings of the filter. Your designers and content creators might want to make use of this feature, especially when dealing with language-related content.

An additional plugin has already been mentioned in the previous chapter when we dealt with availability restrictions (https://moodle.org/plugins/availability_language). Once the add-on has been installed, your users will have the ability to restrict individual activities and resources that are based on the selected language. In addition to the available standard restrictions, such as activity completion and user profile, course authors will also be able to specify a language as the criteria.

Calendaric information

Different cultures represent calendric information—date, times, and time zones—in different formats.

 Locales have to be installed for non-English calendars to work properly. On Unix systems, check with the `locale-a` locale. Otherwise, your days in the calendar will be displayed in English.

Calendars

By default, Moodle formats date and time according to the set locale for Gregorian calendars. Other calendars are supported but they have to be installed as a plugin. To do so, follow the instructions in *Chapter 8, Moodle Plugins* and browse in the **Calendars** section in the plugins database.

A few additional settings are changeable by going to **Appearance | Calendar**. The fields that are relevant to localization are shown in the following screenshot (I have installed the Japanese calendar plugin):

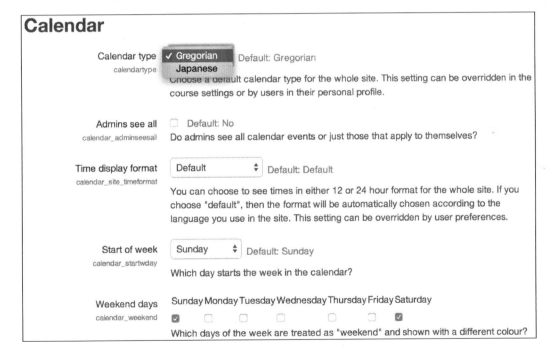

Calendar type is the default setting for the site and all its users, which can be overridden in the user profile via **Preferred calendar**. If you need to see all the calendar events, turn on **Admins see all**; otherwise, you will only see your own events. Times are displayed according to the selected locale; **Time display format** can be overridden by a 12-hour or a 24-hour clock. Different countries have a different start day for the week, for instance, in North America, the week starts from **Sunday**, whereas in Europe, it starts from Monday (**Start of week**). Not all countries use the default values of **Saturday** and **Sunday** as the weekend days. For example, in Islamic countries, the weekend is on Friday and Saturday, whereas Sunday is a normal working day. This can be specified in the **Weekend days** parameter.

Time zones

Moodle supports systems that span across time zones. This happens in three scenarios:

- In countries that cover more than a single time zone
- Sites that have learners from multiple countries/time zones
- In a situation where the server is hosted outside the time zone of the organization, for example, with an Internet Service Provider

To modify the default time zone parameters, go to **Location | Location settings**:

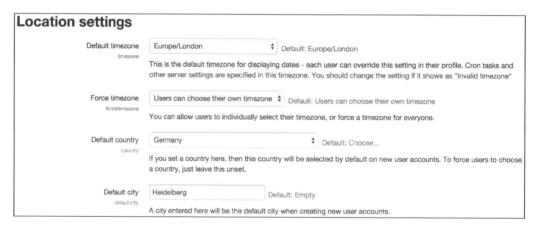

The value selected in the **Default timezone** parameter is used throughout the system. The default value is set during installation, but this might not reflect your local time. Each learner can change this setting in their user profile, unless it is forced to a particular time. Displayed times, for example, for an assignment deadline, are adjusted to the selected time zone. If specified, **Default country** and **Default city** are used for new user accounts.

Every so often, rules in certain time zones (there are almost 2,300 separate ones!) change, for instance, the adjustment of daylight savings time. In this case, you should update these settings by navigating to **Location** | **Update timezones**. New versions of Moodle always contain the latest version of the time zone rules.

Grades and gradebook settings

The gradebook is one of the most important constructs of any virtual-learning environment. If it's formal, any form of assessment (formative, interim, or summative) is supported and Moodle is no exception. A **gradebook** is a container that holds grades for all the learners in Moodle. The flexibility and customizability of the Moodle gradebook results in a very high degree of complexity. As a consequence, there are a huge number of administrator settings at your disposal that affect the way teachers, trainers, and assessors use grades throughout the system.

The majority of settings are tightly linked to the gradebook and the related reports are dealt with by teachers at course level. A site-wide agreement on default values and global settings for grades should be in place for your organization.

Additionally, the inline help for each setting is very comprehensive, as is the accompanying area in the Moodle Docs at `https://docs.moodle.org/en/Grader_ report`, which contains a number of pages that are dedicated to administrators. We only briefly describe each section (submenu) in the **Grades** area in the **Site administration** section and highlight some key parameters, which are listed as follows:

- **General settings**: These are parameters that influence the gradebook and grades in general. A setting that is turned off by default and is required regularly is **Enable publishing** (the ability to publish results via external URLs). Another setting that is changed frequently is **Navigation method**, in which most users prefer the **Tabs** option as it is consistent with the rest of Moodle.

- **Grade category settings**: Grades are organized into categories and, here, you can set the relevant settings.

- **Grade item settings**: These are settings that impact individual grades and grade items.

- **Scales**: Here, you can specify site-wide scales that are used for the purpose of grading and rating. The global scales are often linked to qualifications that are offered by your organization. Most sites remove the provided **Separate and Connected ways of knowing** scale as it doesn't map to their learning environment.

    ° Each scale comprises a name, the scale itself (a list of comma-separated items), and an optional description. Scales can be uploaded indirectly via the Outcome menu at the course level.

- **Outcomes**: Outcomes are used by most vocational and some academic curricula to specify the expected competencies or goals of a subject that is being taught. Outcomes have to be enabled in the **Advanced features** link.
    - ° You can either add global (standard) outcomes one by one, or create a CSV file and upload it in the batch mode from the **Outcome** menu at the course level (select the **Import as standard outcome** option).
    - ° Each outcome comprises a full name, short name, scale, and an optional description. The import file supports certain values in its header, such as `outcome_name`, `outcome_shortname`, `outcome_description`, `scale_name`, `scale_items`, and `scale_description`.
    - ° There are plans to improve outcomes and competencies in the near future, so keep an eye on the release notes of future versions.

- **Letters**: A lot of education systems use a system of letters (A, A-, B+, …, and F) to grade items. Here, you specify which percentage range corresponds to which grading letter.

- **Report settings**: Moodle comes with a number of predefined gradebook reports. The respective settings determine the appearance and content of the reports. If additional user-defined reports (plugins) are installed in your system, this list is likely to have a separate configuration page for each report type (a good tutorial on how to create your own custom reports can be found at `https://docs.moodle.org/dev/Gradebook_reports`). The different types of reports are:
    - ° **Grader report**: This setting includes whether to show calculations, show or hide icons, column averages, and so on. Teachers can override most of the settings in the **My report preferences** tab.
    - ° **Grade history**: The gradebook keeps track of all the changes that are made to the gradebook entries. Here, you can specify how many entries will be displayed on the page. You can **Disable grade history** by going to **Server | Cleanup**. On the same page, you can also specify the length of time that the grade history should be kept (**Grade history lifetime**).
    - ° **Overview report**: This consists of two settings that determine whether the ranking information is shown and how to deal with totals that contain hidden grades, respectively.
    - ° **User report**: This shows the settings that determines whether the ranking information is shown and how to deal with hidden items.

We have only touched on the customization options of the gradebook. Some Moodle Partners run courses that are dedicated to the management of the usage of the gradebook and any of its related functionalities.

Miscellaneous educational settings

There are a number of remaining settings and parameters that might have to be configured on your system, depending on whether the functionalities will be used by your teachers and learners. These settings are:

- **Restricted access**: This is a feature that's often required by course authors and teachers to set conditions to control whether an activity or resource can be accessed. By default, this is not activated; it has to be turned on by navigating to **Advanced features | Enable restricted access**.

- **Completion tracking**: This is needed in courses if the progress of learners has to be tracked. Again, this feature is disabled by default and has to be turned on by navigating to **Advanced features | Enable completion tracking**.

- **Annotate PDF**: Teachers have the ability to annotate PDF submissions directly in Moodle. If this is required, make sure that Ghostscript is installed on your server and the correct path is specified by going to **Plugins | Activity modules | Assignment | Feedback plugins | PDF annotation**.

- **Other settings**: Other course-related settings can be seen by going to **Courses | Course default settings**, as discussed in *Chapter 4, Course Management* and *Chapter 8, Moodle Plugins*.

Communication

Communication is a key feature in Moodle as it enhances the learning experience of all the users that are involved. Moodle supports synchronous and asynchronous communication, which have to be configured by the administrator.

Synchronous communication

We cover two types of synchronous communication in Moodle: instant messaging and video conferencing, both of which are discussed in the following sections.

Instant messaging

Moodle's inbuilt facility for instant messaging is the **Chat** activity that is used in courses or the front page. The module works out of the box and without any configuration using **Ajax method** (default) or **Normal method**. However, it creates a significant load on the server in large installations or when chat rooms are used intensively.

To rectify this, the activity supports a chat server daemon, which has to be configured. You can set up of the daemon by navigating to **Plugins | Activity modules | Chat**.

To make use of a chat server daemon, you will have to change **Chat method** to—you guessed it—**Chat server daemon**. The daemon, usually called `chatd`, has to run in the background on your Unix system (it does not work on Windows servers). This might either be a PHP script or an executable. The **Refresh userlist** (the interval that's used to update a user list) and **Disconnect timeout** (the time without connection after which a user is treated as disconnected) parameters are common for all chat methods and might have to be adjusted if you experience connection issues.

The chat server daemon-specific settings require **Server name**, the **Server IP** address, and **Server port** that is used by `chatd`. These can be on the same system as Moodle (as shown in an earlier screenshot) or, for better performance, on a separate or dedicated server. The **Max users** parameter specifies the maximum number of users who can use a chat simultaneously.

An alternative method to the chat daemon is the use of a stream to update conversations in the normal chat method. However, Apache has to be configured to support this update method.

Video conferencing

One often requested synchronous feature that is absent from the Moodle core is video conferencing. However, there are a number of external systems for which Moodle plugins have been developed. The most popular ones are:

- **Adobe Connect**: This is an enterprise web conferencing solution for online meetings, e-learning, and webinars
- **Big Blue Button**: This is an open source web conferencing system
- **Open Meetings**: This is an open source, browser-based software that allows you to instantly set up a conference
- **WebEx Meeting**: This is Cisco's popular video conferencing and collaboration tool

Providing video conferencing to your teachers and learners has one major technical drawback—depending on the types of tools that are used (audio, whiteboard sharing, recording, video) and the quality that is chosen (sampling rate and resolution), the facility can be very bandwidth-hungry. This is why most providers offer dedicated hosting services in addition to local installation options.

The installation of third-party plugins is covered in detail in *Chapter 8, Moodle Plugins*. All the video conferencing systems that have been mentioned also come with comprehensive configuration and usage instructions. The following screenshot is of the configuration screen of the **WebEx Meeting settings** plugin for Moodle:

WebEx Meeting settings

API Settings

Site Name webexactivity | sitename	packt	Default: Empty

The url part before .webex.com. If your site url was "https://example.webex.com", you would enter "example" above.

WebEx Admin username webexactivity | apiusername	packtadmin	Default: Empty

The username for an admin account on your site. This should be an accounted dedicated for Moodle for security reasons.

WebEx Admin password webexactivity | apipassword	••••••••••••••	Unmask

The password for an admin account on your site.

Username Prefix webexactivity | prefix	mdl_	Default: mdl_

This string will be prefixed to all usernames created by this module.

Asynchronous communication

There are two types of asynchronous communication options available in Moodle—messaging and RSS feeds.

Messaging configuration

Moodle comes with a flexible messaging facility that can be seen as a basic multichannel communication system. It does not only support *messages* from users to other users but also *notifications* between Moodle and its users. You, as an administrator, might be notified when updates are available, and a learner might get notified when an assignment is due. Not only this, users can also reply to forum posts via e-mail or even send attachments to their private files.

Sender	Receiver	Type	Direction
User	User	Message	Outbound
Activity	User	Notification	Outbound

Sender	Receiver	Type	Direction
System	User	Notification	Outbound
External	Activity	e-mail	Inbound
External	Private files	e-mail	Inbound

We can distinguish between inbound and outbound messages, as seen from the perspective of Moodle. For instance, a message sent from one (Moodle) user to another (Moodle) user is seen as outbound, as the sending takes place within Moodle. A file that's sent via e-mail by a learner to his private files is seen as inbound, as Moodle is receiving the attachment. We will be dealing with both types of directions in the remainder of this section.

Outbound messaging

Messaging has to be turned on by checking the **Enable messaging system** checkbox in **Advanced features**.

Each user has the ability (via **Messaging** in the **User account** section in their **Preferences**) to configure how to receive messages, depending on whether they are online or offline. For each notification type (such as subscribed forums, posts, or feedback notifications), the following so-called message outputs can be selected once they have been enabled and configured:

- **Popup notification**: This uses the built-in messages tool and does not require any customization.
- **Email**: The message will be forwarded to an e-mail address.
- **Jabber message**: Jabber is an instant messaging protocol, which is used by a number of popular clients, such as Google Talk and Apple's iChat. Other applications (for example, Facebook) provide an interface to Jabber.
- **Mobile notifications**: Messages will be sent to the mobile Moodle app. This is described in more detail in *Chapter 16, Moodle Networking*.
- **Other**: It is expected that additional channels, for example, Twitter, Google+, or SMS, will be added in the future, most likely as third-party plugins.

Email, **Mobile notification**, and **Jabber message** (and any additionally installed notification methods) have to be configured before they are available to users in your Moodle system. This configuration takes place by going to **Plugins | Message outputs | Manage message outputs**:

Manage message outputs

Name	Enable	Settings
Popup notification	👁	
Jabber message	Not configured	Settings
Email	👁	Settings
Mobile notifications	Not configured	Settings

From this screen, you can also launch the configuration screen for each message output via the respective **Settings** link:

E-mail configuration

Like instant messaging, Moodle's e-mail works without any configuration using its internal PHP-based method. To improve its performance and make use of your existing e-mail infrastructure, you have to configure an SMTP host:

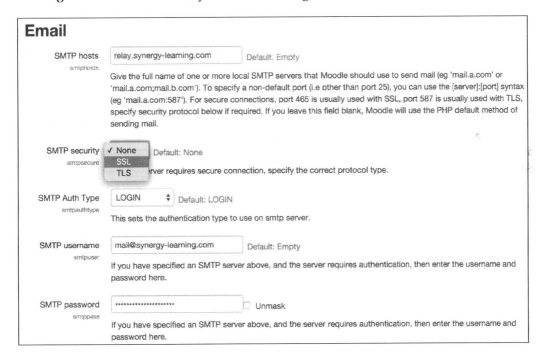

Email

SMTP hosts
smtphosts
relay.synergy-learning.com   Default: Empty

Give the full name of one or more local SMTP servers that Moodle should use to send mail (eg 'mail.a.com' or 'mail.a.com;mail.b.com'). To specify a non-default port (i.e other than port 25), you can use the [server]:[port] syntax (eg 'mail.a.com:587'). For secure connections, port 465 is usually used with SSL, port 587 is usually used with TLS, specify security protocol below if required. If you leave this field blank, Moodle will use the PHP default method of sending mail.

SMTP security
smtpsecure
✓ None   Default: None
SSL
TLS   rver requires secure connection, specify the correct protocol type.

SMTP Auth Type
smtpauthtype
LOGIN ⬍   Default: LOGIN

This sets the authentication type to use on smtp server.

SMTP username
smtpuser
mail@synergy-learning.com   Default: Empty

If you have specified an SMTP server above, and the server requires authentication, then enter the username and password here.

SMTP password
smtppass
••••••••••••••••••••   ☐ Unmask

If you have specified an SMTP server above, and the server requires authentication, then enter the username and password here.

Setting	Description
SMTP hosts	This is the name or IP address of the SMTP server. If multiple servers exist, they have to be separated by a semicolon(;). The standard port syntax is supported.
SMTP security	This is the protocol to be used if a secure connection is required.
SMTP Auth Type	This is the authentication type to be used when connecting to an SMTP server.
SMTP username	This is self-explanatory.
SMTP password	This is self-explanatory.
SMTP session limit	These are the number of messages (groups) that are sent per SMTP session.
No-reply address	This is the *From* address for a user when a notification is sent from an activity; for example, the notification for a forum.
Always send email from the no-reply address	Use this setting if anti-spoofing controls are blocking your users' e-mails.
Characterset	This is the character set to be used to send e-mails.
Allow user to select characterset	This specifies whether users are allowed to override the default setting in their user profiles.
Allow attachments	This specifies whether e-mails can have attachments, for instance, forum posts or badges.
Newline character in mail	Different mail servers treat and convert newline characters differently. Change this only if you experience problems with line spacing.

If you experience issues sending e-mails, check the **Debug email sending** checkbox by going to **Development | Debugging**. This will display detailed information when sending e-mails via SMTP.

The Jabber configuration

You require access to a Jabber host to be able to use this feature. You can either set up your own XMPP server or use a commercial host, for example, Google Talk. Jabber's configuration settings are shown in the following screenshot:

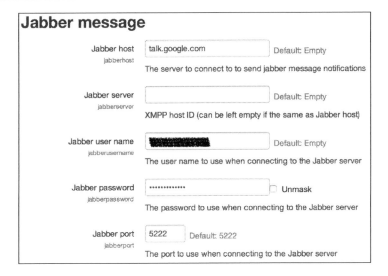

Once the self-explanatory fields in Jabber's configuration screen have been set up, each user will have the ability to specify their Jabber ID by navigating to **My profile settings | Messaging**.

Mobile notifications

In order for Moodle to send push notifications to its mobile app, you need to configure the setting by going to **Plugins | Message outputs | Mobile notifications**. You will need to request an access key in order to make use of the public Air notifier instance (refer to the link at the bottom of the screen).

Mobile notifications

Airnotifier URL airnotifierurl	https://messages.moodle.net Default: https://messages.moodle.net The server url to connect to to send push notifications.
Airnotifier port airnotifierport	443 Default: 443 The port to use when connecting to the airnotifier server.
Mobile app name airnotifiermobileappname	com.moodle.moodlemobile Default: com.moodle.moodlemobile The Mobile app unique identifier (usually something like com.moodle.moodlemobile).
Airnotifier app name airnotifierappname	commoodlemoodlemobile Default: commoodlemoodlemobile The app name identifier in Airnotifier.
Airnotifier access key airnotifieraccesskey	2394cb72634c0cb934785674ebd5 Default: Empty The access key to use when connecting to the airnotifier server.

Request access key

Details on the mobile app and its settings are described in *Chapter 16, Moodle Networking*.

Default message output

Once your message outputs have been configured, each user has the ability to set preferences for any notification types that they have permissions to receive as well as each configured message output. This takes place in **Messaging** in the **User account** section of their **Preferences**. As the administrator, you should specify the default values for these settings. Additionally, you can decide which settings non-administrator users cannot change by going to **Plugins | Message outputs | Default message outputs**:

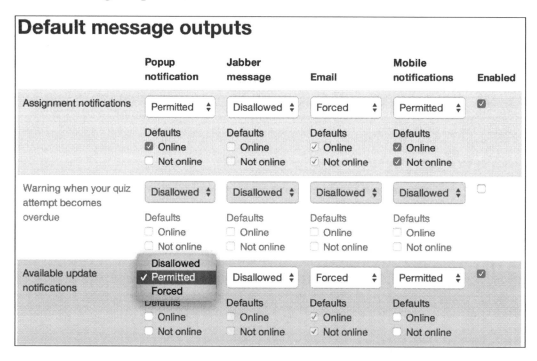

For each notification type you, can individually specify for every message output (**Popup notification, Jabber message, Email**, and **Mobile notifications**) whether the default settings are as follows:

- **Disallowed**: If this is selected, the functionality is deactivated

- **Permitted** (default): If this is selected, users can change settings in their profile

- **Forced**: If this is selected, values are frozen and cannot be modified locally

The values under **Defaults** are **Online** (when logged in to Moodle) and **Not online** (when not logged in).

In the preceding screenshot, users will receive an e-mail about **Assignment notifications**, whether or not they are online. They cannot change this setting so as to avoid claims that they were unaware of any deadlines. When they are online, they will receive a pop-up message. This setting can be overridden in their profile message settings. Jabber has been disallowed for this notification type. If the user has the mobile app installed on their smartphone, they will receive a notification, regardless of whether they are online or not.

Additionally, you have the option to disable notifications of a particular type for all messaging channels. This was done for **Warning when you quiz attempt becomes overdue**.

Inbound messaging

Moodle allows users to reply to forum posts via e-mail and send attachments to their private files. In order to allow this to happen, **Enabled incoming mail processing** has to be activated by going to **Server | Incoming mail configuration | Mail settings**.

You further have to configure a mailbox and incoming mail server settings:

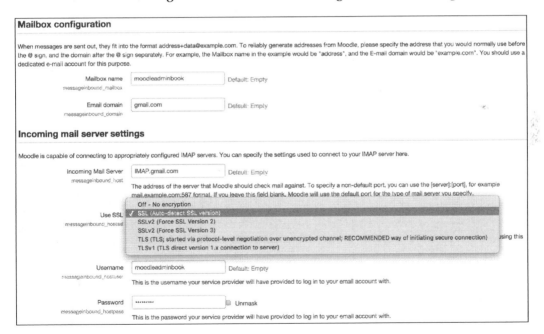

It is highly recommended that you use a dedicated e-mail address for this. Don't use your day-to-day e-mail address! The following settings have to be configured (we use the fictive `moodleadminbook@gmail.com` e-mail address):

Setting	Description
Mailbox name	This is an e-mail account (`moodleadminbook`).
Email domain	This is the domain name of the e-mail provider (`gmail.com`).
Incoming Mail Server	This is the URL of the IMAP server (`IMAP.gmail.com`). IMAP has to be enabled for your e-mail account.
Use SSL	This consists of the types of e-mail encryptions that are used. It is recommended that you make use of this if they are supported by your e-mail server. Check the security settings of the mail server.
Username	This is self-explanatory. It is the same as the mailbox name.
Password	This is self-explanatory.

Once this has been configured, you have to specify which types of e-mails will be processed by Moodle. These are called message handlers and can be accessed by navigating to **Server** | **Incoming mail configuration** | **Message handlers**. These have been implemented as plugins to allow further message handlers in the future.

Name Class name	Description	Enabled	Edit
Reply to forum posts \mod_forum\message\inbound\reply_handler	Reply to forum posts via email	Yes	⚙
Invalid recipient handler \tool_messageinbound\message\inbound\invalid_recipient_handler	If a valid message is received but the sender cannot be authenticated, the message is stored on the email server and the user is contacted using the email address in their user profile. The user is given the chance to reply to confirm the authenticity of the original message. This handler processes those replies. It is not possible to disable sender verification of this handler because the user may reply from an incorrect email address if their email client configuration is incorrect.	Yes	⚙
Email to Private files \core\message\inbound\private_files_handler	Store attachments to an e-mail in the user's private files storage space.	No	⚙

There are three message handlers that come with Moodle:

- **Email to Private files**
- **Reply to forum posts**
- **Invalid recipient handler**

The first two have already been mentioned and should be self-explanatory. The invalid recipient handler deals with messages from senders that do not match the e-mail address of the user. It is recommended that you do not disable this message handler for security reasons.

To enable any of the other two handlers, select the Configuration icon in the Edit column and tick the **Enabled** setting. It is recommended that you leave the expiry setting as is.

A good explanation of an incoming e-mail configuration with hints for other e-mail servers can be found at `https://docs.moodle.org/en/Incoming_mail_configuration`.

Support contact

A topic related to asynchronous communication is users of your Moodle system seeking assistance. When you go to **Server | Support contact**, Moodle lets you specify **Support name**, an **Support email** address, and **Support page**.

Your contact details are displayed at various places throughout Moodle, for instance, during self-registration. There is no support block you can put on the front page but you can easily mimic this using a (sticky) **HTML** block.

Support contact		
Support name supportname	Alex Büchner	Default: Alex Büchner
	This is the name of a person or other entity offering general help via the support email or web address.	
Support email supportemail	packt@synergy-learning.com	Default: packt@synergy-learning.com
	This email address will be published to users of this site as the one to email when they need general help (for example, when new users create their own accounts). If this email is left blank then no such helpful email address is supplied.	
Support page supportpage	packt.synergy-learning.com	Default: Empty
	This web address will be published to users of this site as the one to go to when they need general help (for example, when new users create their own accounts). If this address is left blank then no link will be supplied.	

Configuration RSS feeds

Really Simple Syndication (RSS) feeds have to be enabled via the **Enable RSS feeds** setting in **Advanced features**. Moodle supports the consumption as well as the production of RSS feeds!

The RSS consumption takes place in the **Remote RSS Feeds** block and can be configured by navigating to **Plugins | Blocks | Remote RSS feeds**. The parameters available are **Entries per feed** (the number of atoms that are loaded and displayed) and **Timeout** (the amount of time before the feed expires in the cache).

The RSS production can take place within a number of activities, namely, **Blog, Database, Forum**, and **Glossary**. Each module has a **Enable RSS feeds** setting in its respective plugin settings. For security and privacy, each RSS feed URL contains an automatically created token for the user. If there is an suspicion that this has been compromised, users can reset this via the **Security keys** link in the **User account** section of their preferences.

Experimental settings

Moodle is a very dynamic software that evolves and improves constantly. Some functionality is still in the experimental stage but is sufficiently mature to be included in a shipped version. These features can be seen by going to **Development | Experimental | Experimental settings**.

The list changes over time. Some features have passed quality assurance and moved to the set of core features (for instance, the AJAX support resided in the experimental section for almost two full versions), while others will be included over time. Other features, such as global search, have been removed since they were not technically feasible. At present, the following three settings are available:

Experimental settings

Enable Safe Exam Browser integration enablesafebrowserintegration	☐ Default: No This adds the choice 'Require Safe Exam Browser' to the 'Browser security' field on the quiz settings form. See http://www.safeexambrowser.org/ for more information.
Drag and drop upload of text/links dndallowtextandlinks	☐ Default: No Enable or disable the dragging and dropping of text and links onto a course page, alongside the dragging and dropping of files. Note that the dragging of text into Firefox or between different browsers is unreliable and may result in no data being uploaded, or corrupted text being uploaded.
Enable CSS optimiser enablecssoptimiser	☐ Default: No When enabled CSS will be run through an optimisation process before being cached. The optimiser processes the CSS removing duplicate rules and styles, as well as white space removable and reformatting. Please note turning this on at the same time as theme designer mode is awful for performance but will help theme designers create optimised CSS.

Setting	Description
Enable Safe Exam Browser integration	This will be dealt with in *Chapter 11, Moodle Security and Privacy*.
Drag and drop of text/links	Currently, Moodle supports the dragging of files into course pages. Enabling this link also supports the dragging and dropping of text.
Enable CSS optimiser	When enabled, the theme code will be optimized. Refer to *Chapter 7, Moodle Look and Feel*.

It is needless to say that any functionality in the experimental section should be used with caution and that potential problems are possible to be encountered.

Summary

In this chapter, you learned how to configure relevant system settings that were not dealt with in a dedicated chapter. We covered educational configurations dealing with collaboration, badges, LTI, localization, grades and the gradebook, and a number of miscellaneous settings. We then moved on to the more technical configurations, which mainly focused on synchronous and asynchronous communication as well as some experimental settings.

The abundance of features available via the *Site administration* section can initially be overwhelming, but you will get to terms with them relatively quickly. Also, expect this increase in features with every new version of Moodle.

This concludes part 2 of this book that dealt with Moodle's configuration. We are now ready to move on to all the aspects of Moodle's maintenance.

10
Moodle Logging and Reporting

Moodle collects usage data from all sorts of activities that take place from the time a user logs in until he or she logs out. This data can be utilized for a range of reporting and analytics activities that will be dealt with in this chapter. After a detailed overview of the underlying **Moodle logging framework** with its components events and log stores, you will learn about four types of techniques:

- **Moodle's reporting facilities**: This includes activity reporting and user tracking as well some basic statistics

- **Report generation**: This covers some powerful add-ons to create user-defined reports

- **Data analysis**: This includes web log analyzers and live data trackers, such as Google Analytics and Piwik

- **Miscellaneous reports**: This covers a number of additional reports that are provided by Moodle

Moodle's logging framework

Moodle has a built-in powerful logging framework that is, as expected, fully customizable and extensible. The idea behind the logging mechanism is as follows:

- A user performs an action that triggers an event. An example of this is a student who posts a reply on a forum.

- The log manager monitors the event and then decides whether it will be logged or ignored. This is dictated by site-wide log manager settings.

For example, by default, there is no setting for not storing forum-related information, so data about who posted what in which forum thread is passed on.

- The log manager sends the data to the log store plugin, which filters or enriches the information.

  The passed on data might be enriched with the IP address and a timestamp.

- The data is then written to the actual **Log Store**.

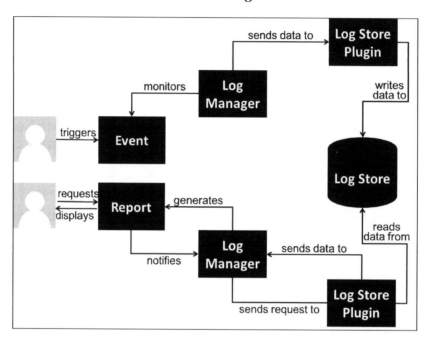

Now, let's take a look at what happens when a user requests a report. An example of this is a report on student participation in course forums. This can be explained as follows:

- The reporting module notifies the log manager, who passes on the request to the log storage plugin.

- If more than one log storage has been set up, the user will need to select one.

- The log storage plugins read the relevant data from the log store and passes it back to the log manager.

- The log manager generates the report, which is then displayed to the user.

Before we deal with specific reports, let's take a look at the individual components of Moodle's logging framework in more detail:

Events

There are related elements that deal with events in Moodle, such as event lists and event monitoring rules. Both will be covered in the subsections that follow.

Event lists

Most actions in Moodle have the ability to trigger an event. You can take a look at the list of all the available events by going to **Reports | Events list**. This list will grow over time with internal and external events being added.

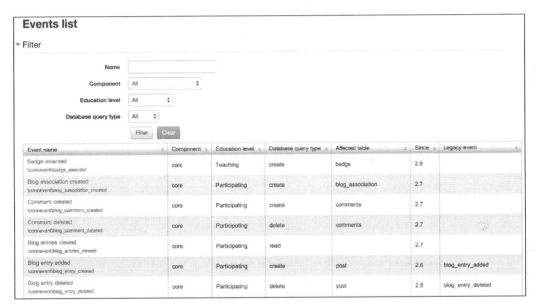

Each event comprises the following elements:

Element	Description
Event name	Name of the event and internal unique identifier.
Component	The Moodle component that the event belongs to. This is usually core, a course module, or some other part, such as statistics or logs.
Education level	There are three levels: Participating, **Teaching**, and **Other**.
Database query type	There are four query types that can occur: **read**, **update**, **create**, and **delete**.

Element	Description
Affected table	Database table being affected.
Since	Moodle version when the event has been introduced.
Legacy event	Event triggered in the legacy log store (this only contains events from version 2.6).

You have the ability to filter the list by **Name, Component, Education level**, and **Database query type.** By clicking on an event name, you will be able to see a more detailed presentation of the same information. Here, we have selected the **User added to cohort** event:

User added to a cohort

Explanation of the event	User added to a cohort event class.
Database query type	create
Education level	Other
Affected table	cohort
Legacy event	cohort_member_added
Parent Event	\core\event\base
Plugins observing this event	Log store manager (tool_log)
	Event monitor (tool_monitor)
	Cohort sync (enrol_cohort)

In addition to **Explanation of the event**, the screen shows **Parent Event** and a list of **Plugins observing this event**. While the explanation is self-explanatory, the latter two pieces of information require some explanation:

- **Parent Event**: Internally, events are organized in a hierarchy. For an administrator, this is done only for information.

- **Plugins observing this event**: These are the plugins that monitor the event. Here, we have a log store manager (called `tool_log`), the event monitor itself, and the Cohort sync module, which ensures that every time a user is added to a cohort they will also be enrolled in linked courses.

Event monitoring rules

Administrators and teachers have the ability to define events to which one can subscribe. These patterns of activities are represented as rules that contain an event as well as a frequency. Once such a pattern has been detected, an event will be triggered, which then sends a message to all subscribers.

While users with editing teacher rights have the ability to set up their own rules at the course level, you, as the administrator, are more likely to define a set of required rules to which teachers will subscribe. Learners can also subscribe to rules once they are granted the **tool/monitor:subscribe** capability.

First of all, you will have to enable event monitoring by navigating **Reports | Event monitoring rules**. Once you've done this, you have the ability to add new rules on the same page and subscribe to those rules via the **Event monitoring** link that now appears on the **Preferences** page.

Let's add our first event rule via the **Add a new rule** button by going to **Reports | Event monitoring rules**. Once you have entered **Rule name**, you have to select **Area to monitor**. The values in the list are identical to the ones you came across in the **Component** dropdown, as seen in the preceding events report. Once chosen, the **Event** list will be populated with all the available events that the component supports. The description is optional, but it is recommended that you provide this for potential subscribers. **Notification threshold in minutes** specifies the number of events within a specified time period that are required for **Notification message** to be sent. The body of this message can include any or all of the following placeholders:

- {link}: Link to the location of the event
- {modulelink}: Link to the area monitored
- {rulename}: Rule name
- {description}: Description
- {eventname}: Event

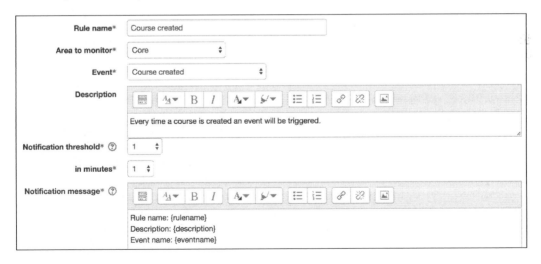

Any user with the **tool/monitor:subscribe** capability now has the ability to subscribe to events via the **Event monitoring** link in the **Miscellaneous** section in their **Preferences**.

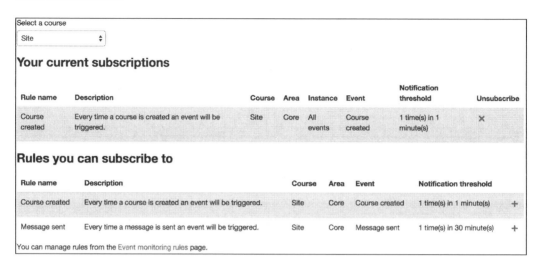

Before subscribing to a course, you will have to **Select a course** that is monitored (**Site** covers all the courses). From now on, a notification message will be sent when the subscribed rule is triggered.

The log manager

The log manager is an internal component that monitors events and passes data to all enabled log store plugins. Moodle comes with a predefined log manager; however, it is possible that this will be replaced by other log manager plugins. For now, as an administrator, you have no means of configuring the log manager.

The log store

A log store plugin is associated with a physical log store and dictates what data is stored and read in the log store, respectively. Moodle ships with three log store plugins, namely **Standard log**, **External database log**, and **Legacy log** (**Plugins | Logging | Manage log stores**). We are going ignore the legacy log as this will be discontinued over time. The standard log is the replacement for the legacy log, which supports all new logging concepts and also provides better performance. In its **Settings**, you can specify whether to **Log guest access**, how long to **Keep logs for**, and **Write buffer size**.

You can configure an external database log store if you wish to write logging information to a database that's separate from Moodle. This is useful if you wish to improve performance and/or if you wish to collect data for more detailed analysis or learning analytics. This is shown in the following screenshot:

External database log

Database settings

Connection details for the external log database: Test connection

Choose database driver logstore_database | dbdriver	Improved MySQL (native/mysqli) ▲▼	Default: Choose...
Database host logstore_database | dbhost	127.0.0.1	Default: Empty
Database user logstore_database | dbuser	packt	Default: Empty
Database password logstore_database | dbpass	••••••••	☐ Unmask
Database name logstore_database | dbname	packt_log	Default: Empty
Database table logstore_database | dbtable	packt_log	Default: Empty

Name of the table where logs will be stored. This table should have a structure identical to the one used by logstore_standard (mdl_logstore_standard_log).

By default, the same databases are supported as when we installed Moodle. Also, the database host, user, password, and name settings are identical to the ones we covered in *Chapter 1, Moodle Installation*. Additionally, you have to specify **Database table**, the structure of which has to be identical to the one stored in `mdl_logstore_standard_log`. Make sure that you test the connection (the link is at top of screen); if successful, the check will display the columns that the external table contains.

You also have the ability to specify a number of settings for a persistent database connection. This is useful if you have a lot of logging traffic on your site and performance is an issue.

Now comes the interesting part of the external log store plugin. You have the ability to specify a number of filters, which will then be applied when storing the data:

- **Log guest actions**: This tells you whether guest actions are stored or not. Usually, this is not required unless you wish to log all users' traffic.

- **Educational levels**: These are the three types that we came across in the events sections, namely **Teaching**, **Participating**, and **Other**.

- **Database query types**: These are the four types we came across in the events sections, namely, **Create**, **Read**, **Update**, and **Delete**.

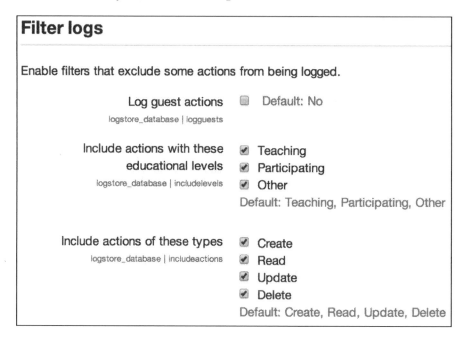

There are two types of scenarios that tell you when filtering logs is useful: when privacy regulations do not allow the storing of actions of certain users or types (refer to *Chapter 11, Moodle Security and Privacy*) and when reporting from the log store does not require certain actions; this will also have a beneficial impact on performance.

At the time of writing this, there is only a single log storage plugin that's available in the **Admin tools** section of `https://download.moodle.org/` (this is **xAPI**; it emits events from the Moodle Log store as xAPI or the TinCan statements). However, it is expected that this number will increase in the near future. The support of NOSQL databases will be particularly interesting, and these have proven beneficial for a wide range of learning analytics reports and analyses.

Reports

A report is pretty much what you expect it to be: a module that generates a view of data. There are two types of reports in Moodle: ones that are supplied with data from a log store and others that are being generated on the fly without log store input. You can view a list of reports by going to **Plugins** | **Reports** | **Manage reports**:

Reports

Plugin	Log stores that support this report	Version	Uninstall
Activity completion	Log store not required	2015111600	Uninstall
Activity report	Legacy log, Standard log	2015111600	Uninstall
Backups report	Log store not required	2015111600	Uninstall
Config changes	Log store not required	2015111600	Uninstall
Course completion	Log store not required	2015111600	
Course overview	Log store not required	2015111600	Uninstall
Course participation	Legacy log, Standard log	2015111600	Uninstall
Events list	Log store not required	2015111600	Uninstall
Live logs	External database log, Legacy log, Standard log	2015111600	Uninstall
Logs	External database log, Legacy log, Standard log	2015111600	Uninstall
Performance overview	Log store not required	2015111600	Uninstall
Question instances	Log store not required	2015111600	Uninstall
Security overview	Log store not required	2015111600	Uninstall
Statistics	Legacy log, Standard log	2015111600	Uninstall
User sessions report	Log store not required	2015111600	Uninstall

You can see when a report requires a log store and, if so, which ones are supported. Initially, we will focus on reports that are based on log stores.

An overview of reporting

Depending on your setup and configuration, Moodle records a detailed log of each action that is performed by a user. By default, each record (or hit) contains data about the following:

- Who (user)
- What (action)
- When (date and time)
- Where (IP address)

Given this trail of information, it is possible to perform two reporting tasks using Moodle's on-board facilities, namely reporting and statistics.

Reporting is mainly concerned with the summary information of users' activities, say, the number of views of a learning resource in a particular course. Ideally, reports allow some interaction to drill down to more specific information, usually via filters. This is useful if you need to locate data about an individual, activity, or a course. For example, a pupil insists that he or she has submitted an assignment, which cannot be located; the tracking log will be able to shed light on this.

Moodle offers a **Statistics** mode, which provides a graphical summary of the number of hits in courses and the entire site.

Bear in mind that most information you retrieve as part of data reporting is also available to teachers at the course level. While teachers use this information mainly in a pedagogical context (to monitor progress and measure performance), your role as an administrator requires you to view this data in a site-wide context. Furthermore, you are the one who is likely to be approached if any problems occur, for example, if a student claims to have submitted an assignment that is not on the system or a teacher is not able to log in from home. Additionally, the local course view provides activity reports that are more targeted at a teacher's perspective and, if activated, also some basic statistics.

Moodle's reporting facilities

A report presents the content of the Moodle log in a sort of uniform format. Different reports make use of the same log. The site-wide logs can be accessed by going to **Reports | Logs**. At the top of the page, you have the ability to drill down to the data via filters:

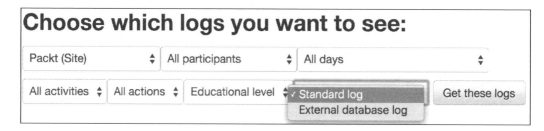

The following filters are available:

Field	Description
Courses	Select a specific course or the entire Moodle site (Site logs).
Groups	Select a specific group or **All groups**. This is only displayed if the group mode is enabled in the selected (filtered) course.
Participants	Select a specific user or **All participants**.
Date	Specify a particular day or all days of activity. Unfortunately, it is not (yet) possible to specify date ranges.
Activities	Select whether you wish to run a report of **All activities** or **Site errors**. This list changes when a course has been selected.
Actions	You can choose among **All actions**, **Create**, **View**, **Update**, and **Delete**. These are the four options we came across when taking a look at events.
Educational levels	You can choose from **Teaching**, **Participating**, **Other**, and **Educational Level**, which is identical to all levels. These are the three options we came across when taking a look at events.
Log store	If more than one log store has been set up, you have to select the one from which the data is being read.

Once you have selected a course and clicked on the **Get these logs** button, the content in each drop-down menu changes in a context-sensitive manner. For example, the participants menu contains all the names of users who have a role in the course, and the activities menu is populated with activities and resources. If you watch the breadcrumb trail, you will see what happens internally. Moodle temporarily redirects the reporting tool inside the selected course where the course log viewer is called, which is identical in appearance.

Once you have selected your filtering criteria, a report is displayed, as follows:

Time	User full name	Affected user	Event context	Component	Event name	Description	Origin	IP address
27 Dec, 07:40	Alex Büchner	Web Service	User: Web Service	System	User updated	The user with id '2' updated the profile for the user with id '325'.	web	192.168.56.1
27 Dec, 07:31	Alex Büchner	Alex Büchner	User: Alex Büchner	System	User profile viewed	The user with id '2' viewed the profile for the user with id '2'.	web	192.168.56.1
27 Dec, 06:50	Alex Büchner	-	System	Event monitor	Subscription created	The user with id '2' created the event monitor subscription with id '3'.	web	192.168.56.1
27 Dec, 06:50	Alex Büchner	-	Front page	Event monitor	Subscription deleted	The user with id '2' deleted the event monitor subscription with id '2'.	web	192.168.56.1
27 Dec, 06:50	Alex Büchner	-	Course: Totara Demo	System	Course viewed	The user with id '2' viewed the course with id '24'.	web	192.168.56.1
27 Dec, 06:50	Alex Büchner	-	System	System	User has logged in	The user with id '2' has logged in.	web	192.168.56.1
27 Dec, 06:50	Joanne Arnold	-	System	System	User logged out	The user with id '160' has logged out.	web	192.168.56.1

This tabular information is displayed in the reverse order of a user's access date and time, that is, the last hit is displayed first. The columns of the table represent the following information:

Field	Description
Time	Date and time of the hit.
User full name	Name of the user — if a particular user is selected, the same value will be displayed in each row.
Affected user	If the action has an impact on another user, it will be displayed.
Event context	The context in which the event has been triggered. A link directs you to the context, for instance, a course.
Component	The event component (refer to the *Events* section that you took a look at earlier in this chapter).
Event name	The event that has been triggered. When selected, a pop-up window with the event will open.
Description	A short description of what the user has been doing — this is very useful to see what resources are being accessed or check whether an individual has viewed the resource that they claim to have read. An example might read like this: The user with ID 123 has posted content in the forum post with ID 2. This is done in discussion 2 that's located in the forum with the course module ID 8.
Origin	Indicates whether the hit came from Moodle itself (**web**) or a web service (**ws**).
IP address	The (unresolved) IP address; this is useful in order to take a look at where the user accessed the page (for example, from home or within the organization).

At the bottom of the results page, you have the option to **Download table data as** a number of formats (Excel, ODF, tab-separated, CSV, or XHTML).

When you click on the IP address in the log, a new page will open that displays the registered location of the user's IP as a pin on the world map (this is not the case for local or private IP addresses), as shown in the following screenshot. The default lookup tool being used is called **NetGeo** (http://www.geoplugin.com/). For more accurate results, you will need to install a local copy of the MaxMind GeoLite database (http://dev.maxmind.com/) or specify a Google Maps API key. Both settings are found in the **IP address lookup** section by going to **Location | Location settings**.

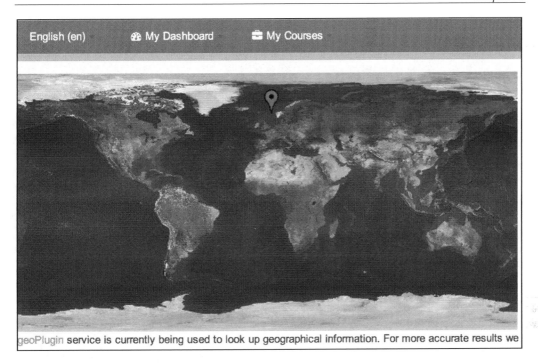

geoPlugin service is currently being used to look up geographical information. For more accurate results we

Live logs

Moodle provides a live view of activities in the last hour. It is a prepared report that shows activities that took place in the previous 60 minutes and is updated automatically every 60 seconds. It can be accessed by navigating to **Reports** | **Live logs**. You have the option to **Pause live updates** via the button besides the log reader selector.

This is useful if you have changed the configuration, for instance, for a supported authentication or enrolment mechanism, and want to ensure that it is working properly. Alternatively, you can just sit back and watch what is happening on your site.

The format of the screen is identical to the preceding standard log. Note that the first entry in the live log is you looking at the live log!

Error reports

When selecting **Site errors** from the activities drop-down menu, all the errors (mainly failed logins that have occurred) are displayed. For example, the report that is shown in the following screenshot displays invalid logins as well as some failed attempts to send an e-mail to users:

Time	User full name	Affected user	Event context	Component	Event name	Description	Origin	IP address
24 Dec, 07:48	-	Pupil Four	System	System	Email failed to send	Failed to send an email from the user with id '-20' to the user with id '305' due to the following error: "You must provide at least one recipient email address.".	cli	192.168.56.1
24 Dec. 07:48	-	Pupil Three	System	System	Email failed to send	Failed to send an email from the user with id '-20' to the user with id '304' due to the following error: "You must provide at least one recipient email address.".	cli	192.168.56.1
8 Oct, 10:19	Alex Büchner	-	System	System	User login failed	Login failed for the username 'admin' for the reason with id '3'.	web	192.168.56.1
8 Oct, 10:19	Alex Büchner	-	System	System	User login failed	Login failed for the username 'admin' for the reason with id '3'.	web	192.168.56.1
8 Oct, 10:19	Alex Büchner	-	System	System	User login failed	Login failed for the username 'admin' for the reason with id '3'.	web	192.168.56.1
9 Aug. 14:19	Alex Büchner	-	System	System	User login failed	Login failed for the username 'admin' for the reason with id '3'.	web	192.168.56.1

It is a good practice to check the error logs on a regular basis to identify problems on your site and potential unauthorized access attempts. These reports can also be set up to be sent by e-mail to the site administrator (refer to *Chapter11, Moodle Security and Privacy*).

Course and user reports

Moodle supports reporting at the course and user level. This feature can be utilized by teachers to monitor the progress of students for particular activities, or it could be used by managers to view the access patterns of their staff. Given the sensitivity of such data and the policies of your organization, access to some operations has to be deactivated via roles and capabilities.

The reports that Moodle provides when you navigate to **Courses** | **Reports** in the **Navigation** block are as follows:

Report	Description	Capability
Activity completion	A matrix showing users versus activities and their completion status.	**report/progress:view**
Activity report	Shows the number of views, related blog entries, and the last access for each activity and resource in the current course.	**report/outline:view**

Report	Description	Capability
Course completion	Progress report listing students versus a criteria matrix (course completion has to be enabled).	**report/completion:view**
Course participation	For a selected activity module or resource and time period, all the actions performed by a user are shown.	**report/ participation:view**
Logs	Same as site-wide logs, but with the courses menu, this is frozen to the current course.	**report/log:view**
Statistics	View the course statistics report (refer to the *Statistics* section).	**report/stats:view**

The types of reports that Moodle provides via the **Activity reports** section in the user profile are shown in the following table. Access to the menu can be controlled via the **moodle/user:viewuseractivitiesreport** capability, but you cannot access individual reports.

Report	Description
Today's logs	Same as site logs but only for today's data of the current user; this is supplemented by an hour-by-hour graph.
All logs	Same as site logs but only for the current user; this is supplemented by a day-by-day graph.
Outline report	Lists each topic or week and displays a summary of activity modules for each item. It displays the title of the resource (hyperlinked), number of views, last access, and the time since the last access.
Complete report	Displays the same information as showed in **Outline report**, just in a different format.
Statistics	Views the course statistics report for a particular user (refer to the *Statistics* section).
Browser sessions	Displays all the active sessions, including the IP address. You can log out of each session, except the current session.
Grade	User report of the gradebook for the current user.

An example report of **All logs** is shown in the following screenshot:

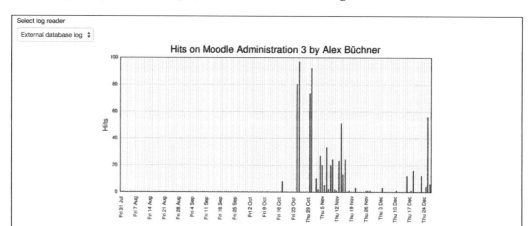

As mentioned earlier, teachers in a course have full access to the same information to monitor progress and track performance. However, you, as the administrator, are often approached with claims, problems, or other anomalies. To shed light on these, you will have to look into the log data.

Information on statistics has been mentioned a few times in course reports, which we will cover next.

Statistics

Moodle has a built-in statistics module, which you can reach by going to **Reports | Statistics**. By default, the component is disabled; this has to be changed first (**Enable statistics** in **Advanced features**) along with some settings.

Statistics settings

The **Statistics** module is deactivated by default due to the fact that the component is very resource-hungry both in terms of disk space usage and, more importantly, memory usage.

Use the **Statistics** module only if you really require the information and can accept some potentially significant performance reduction.

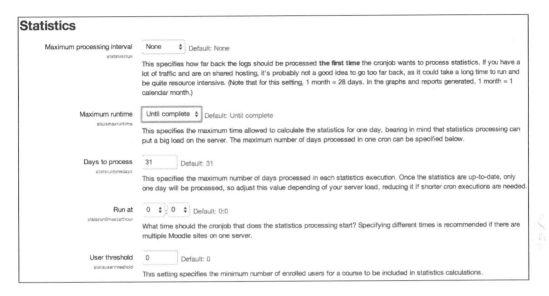

You can locate the statistics settings by navigating to **Server | Statistics**. The following parameters are available:

Setting	Description
Maximum processing interval	After enabling the **Statistics** module, Moodle utilizes the logs that are described here to derive statistical information. Here, you need to specify the time that Moodle should go back by in order to gather the stats. Be aware that this is quite a resource-intensive operation.
Maximum runtime	You can limit the time for which the statistics gathering process is allowed to run; this is another mechanism to avoid too much burden on the system.
Days to process	Number of days that will be processed in each statistics execution.
Run at	Time at which the statistics processing should start. It is highly recommended that you ensure that this does not clash with the site backup as both operations are potentially very resource-intensive.
User threshold	Here, the **Statistics** module can be instructed to ignore courses with less than a certain number of enrolled users.

Now, let's have a look what statistics actually look like.

Statistics view

Once you have selected **Course**, **Report type** (views, posts, logins, or all of these), and **Time period**, a graph and some tabular information will be displayed. Basically, the data that's shown represents the number of *hits* on a certain day, broken down by roles:

If no data is displayed, you might have to readjust the settings of your statistics. Also, while the statistics gathering is in progress, a message might be displayed, stating that the module is in the catch-up mode. If this is the case, you have to wait until the processing has been completed.

I don't know about you, but I find this information unsatisfactory. Given the burden that the module places on our system and the amount of available data, this seems like a very simplistic—some would say useless—way to display statistics.

An extension to the Statistics module is a plugin called **Overview Statistics** (`https://moodle.org/plugins/report_overviewstats`). This provides you with some more analyses on users who are logging in, user countries, preferred languages, and some course stats.

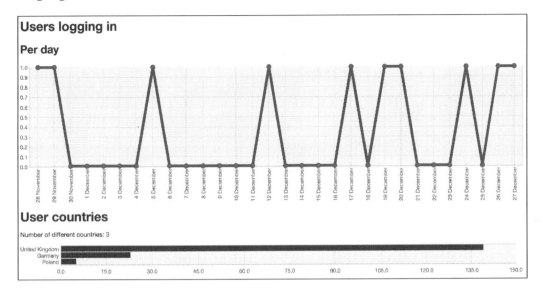

While this is an improvement over the Statistics facility, it is still far from ideal. To rectify the situation, let's take a look at report generation and alternative techniques that make use of external data analysis tools.

Report generation

Moodle comes with a number of predefined reports that are based on stored log information. While this is sufficient for certain activities, there are two drawbacks to this approach:

- It is not possible to create user-defined reports
- Additional data stored in the database or summary information is not taken into account

The following two tools rectify this situation.

Configurable reports

Configurable reports is a third-party plugin for Moodle, which will appear as a block once it has been installed. The installation of the add-ons has been described in detail in *Chapter 8, Moodle Plugins*.

Anyone who has been given permission can create new reports at the site or course level. Configurable reports supports five types of reports:

- **Courses report**: Reports using course data
- **Categories report**: Reports using category data plus optional embedded course reports
- **Users report**: Reports using user data and their course activities
- **Timeline report**: Reports across time for courses, users, and their activities
- **SQL report**: Any valid SQL statement can be used to query the Moodle database

Depending on what type of report has been chosen, different selection criteria (fields, conditions, ordering, and calculations) are offered. Additionally, filters for a drill-down can be specified, the layout can be created, and permissions for who are allowed to run the report can be set. Furthermore, the report builder has the ability to plot different types of graphs.

The unique feature of Configurable reports is the ability to create reports that are based on **Custom SQL**. If you are familiar with the SQL language and the underlying Moodle database schema, you have the ability to add queries, such as the one shown in the following screenshot (taken from `https://docs.moodle.org/en/ad-hoc_contributed_reports`):

| View report | Custom SQL | Filters | Template | Permissions | Calculations | Plot - Graphs | Report | Manage reports |

```
SQL Query*
 1  SELECT
 2  user2.firstname AS Firstname,
 3  user2.lastname AS Lastname,
 4  user2.email AS Email,
 5  user2.city AS City,
 6  course.fullname AS Course
 7  ,(SELECT shortname FROM prefix_role WHERE id=en.roleid) AS ROLE
 8  ,(SELECT name FROM prefix_role WHERE id=en.roleid) AS RoleName
 9
10  FROM prefix_course AS course
11  JOIN prefix_enrol AS en ON en.courseid = course.id
12  JOIN prefix_user_enrolments AS ue ON ue.enrolid = en.id
13  JOIN prefix_user AS user2 ON ue.userid = user2.id
```

[Save changes] [Cancel]

Press F11 when cursor is in the editor to toggle full screen editing. Esc can also be used to exit full screen editing.

List of SQL Contributed reports

1) Choose a remote report categories   course ▼

2) Choose a report form the list   most_active_courses.sql ▼

```
SQL query
 1
 2  SELECT COUNT(l.id) hits, l.course courseId, c.fullname coursename
 3  FROM prefix_log l INNER JOIN prefix_course c ON l.course = c.id
 4  GROUP BY courseId
 5  ORDER BY hits DESC
```

Further information on the Configurable reports plugin can be found on its Moodle Docs page at `https://docs.moodle.org/en/Configurable_reports`. In the preceding screenshot, you can also see a link to **List of SQL Contributed reports**, which is a very good starting point to create you own reports.

The Totara report builder

Totara LMS contains a powerful report builder. It has been planned that parts of the tool will be added to the Moodle core in the near future. Totara LMS is an open source Moodle distribution that's targeted at commercial and public sector organizations as well as NGOs (`https://www.totaralms.com/`).

The upcoming screenshot shows you a user-defined report that takes Moodle's site data as its source. Based on the selected data, columns and filters will be predefined, which can be changed. Additionally, a search and filter criteria have been configured to add some interactivity to the report.

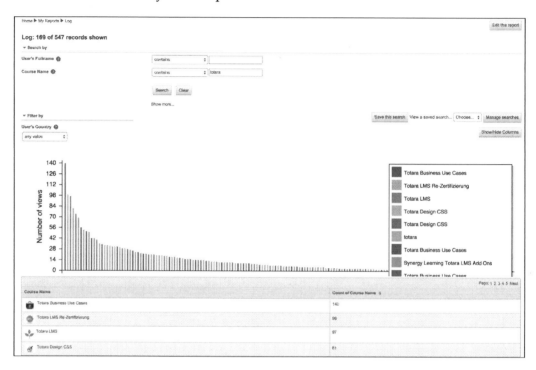

In addition to the expected features of a report generator (columns, including summary information and sorting, search, filters, pagination, and so on), the Totara report builder contains a number of interesting features:

- **Interactivity**: Once a report has been shown, a user can apply drill-down operations.

- **Content control**: Restriction of records and information that are available when a report is viewed.

- **Graphs**: Various graph types are supported to aid visual representations, which can be fully customized via the SVG settings.

- **Access control**: A restriction through which users and roles are allowed to view a report.

- **Performance settings**: Prefetching (caching) of reports is supported.

- **Scheduling**: Reports can be scheduled for execution by each user who will the receive a report by e-mail. Additionally, exporting (CSV, Excel, ODF, and Google Fusion tables) to a filesystem is supported, which allows for integration with other systems.

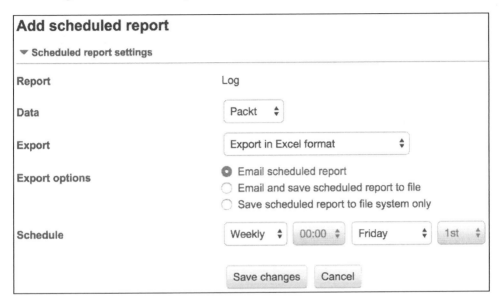

The screenshots in this section have been taken from a Totara system. At the time of writing this, it is not certain which features will make it into the Moodle core, but the general approach should come across to you. The report builder is an ideal tool to interactively create a wide range of user-defined reports that are based on supported sources.

Data analysis

If these described reporting facilities do not satisfy your hunger for usage data, you might consider using external web analysis tools, such as web log analyzers. You can also utilize a *live data tracking system*, such as Piwik and Google Analytics, that can be embedded in your Moodle site.

Web log analyzers

Web servers, such as Apache and Microsoft IIS, keep textual log files that keep track of every hit on a website. The fields and their formats can be customized so that each log file will look potentially different from the other. The following two lines are from our Moodle test site (IP addresses have been replaced and server directories are shortened):

```
123.45.67.89 - - [26/Feb/2015:08:15:30 +0000] "GET .../synergy-
learning/packt/httpdocs/course/view.php?id=3 HTTP/1.0" 404 1045 "-""-"
123.45.67.89 - - [26/Feb/2015:08:15:30 +0000] "GET .../synergy-
learning/packt/httpdocs/mod/quiz/view.php?id=12 HTTP/1.0" 404 2180"-
""-"
```

As you can see, these files are not meant to be read by human beings. Instead, a web log analysis software exists, which can read and interpret these files. Open source examples are AWStats, Webalizer, and munin; a popular commercial product is WebTrends.

These tools produce detailed statistics that look at the log files from every possible angle. The problem when using web log analyzers with Moodle is that they are database-driven, which requires parameterized URLs (the `?id=12` part). You will have to configure the software you use to reflect these parameters, for example, at the course level.

Google Analytics and Piwik

Google Analytics and Piwik are two feature-rich services that track any traffic to your Moodle site and offer an abundance of statistics on visitors, traffic sources, content, user-defined goals, and much more.

In order to support either of the two systems, you will need to install the **Analytics plugin** (`https://moodle.org/plugins/local_analytics`), which lets you configure the connection between your Moodle system and the tracker. It provides a means of sending **Clean URLs**, which overcome the issue of the parameterized URLs that we came across when looking at web log analyzers.

Analytics

Enabled local_analytics | enabled	☑ Default: Yes Enable Analytics for Moodle
Analytics local_analytics | analytics	Piwik ◆ Default: Piwik Choose the type of Analytics you want to insert
Site ID local_analytics | siteid	1 Default: 1 Enter your Site ID or Google Analytics
Image Tracking local_analytics | imagetrack	☑ Default: Yes Enable Image Tracking for Moodle for browsers with JavaScript disabled (only for Piwik)
Analytics URL local_analytics | siteurl	packt.synergy-learning.com Default: Empty Enter your Piwik Analytics URL without http(s) or a trailing slash (for both Google Analytics types leave empty)
Tracking Admins local_analytics | trackadmin	◯ Default: No Enable tracking of Admin users (not recommended)
Clean URLs local_analytics | cleanurl	☑ Default: Yes Generate clean URL for in advanced tracking
Tracking code location local_analytics | location	Header ✓ Top of body Default: Header Footer The place on the page where you want to place the code, header will yield the most reliable results, but footer gives the best performance. If you do not get correct results in Google/Piwik set this to "Header"

Google Analytics is a free service (`https://www.google.com/analytics`) that tracks any traffic to your site, but you will have to sign up for an account first.

An elegant way to incorporate Google Analytics is via the **Essential Theme**, which we briefly covered in *Chapter 7, Moodle Look and Feel*. It not only supports the enabling of Google Analytics on your site but also lets you specify your tracking ID.

If you do not have access to a theme that has been built-in Google Analytics support, you will have to add the following piece of code to the `footer.html` file of your theme before the `</body>`tag (this will be generated by Google Analytics for you):

```
<script>
(function(i,s,o,g,r,a,m){i['GoogleAnalyticsObject']=r;i[r]=i[r]||function(){
  (i[r].q=i[r].q||[]).push(arguments)},i[r].l=1*new
  Date();a=s.createElement(o),
```

```
    m=s.getElementsByTagName(o)[0];a.async=1;a.src=g;m.parentNode.
    insertBefore(a,m)
})(window,document,'script','//www.google-analytics.com/analytics.
js','ga');

ga('create', 'UA-XXXXXXXX-X', 'auto');
ga('send', 'pageview');

</script>
```

You need to update xxxxxxxx-x in the preceding sample with your own Google Analytics account number. While it is possible to add the code in the header.html file, it is not recommended that you do this as it has an impact on the perceived performance of your system.

Once setup, you will be able to see the powerful analytics of your Moodle site, as shown in the following screenshot:

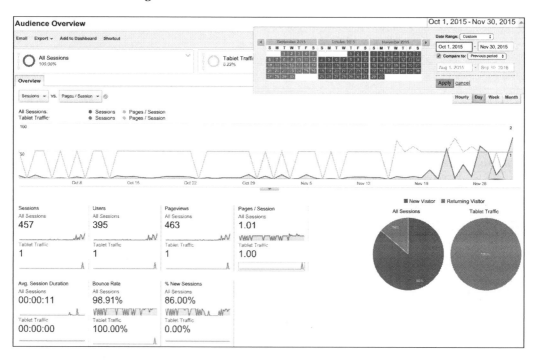

If Google Analytics appeals to you, but you need to store your data locally, Piwik is a very good alternative. Piwik (http://piwik.org/) is an open source alternative to Google Analytics, which can be installed on a local server and used for other websites as well.

Miscellaneous reports

Moodle ships with a number of additional reports that assist the administrator in monitoring certain activities that take place. Some are only described briefly; for others, references to dedicated chapters are given. All the reports are accessible via the **Reports** menu. These reports are listed as follows:

- **Comments**: A table is shown containing **Author** and **Content** of any comment that's left on the system. You have the ability to delete any of the comments. For more information on this topic, refer to the *Collaboration* section in *Chapter 9, Moodle Configuration*.

- **Backups**: For each automated backup, **Course, Time taken, Status** (OK, **Skipped, Unfinished,** or **Error**), and the time of **Next backup** are listed. For more information on backups, refer to *Chapter 13, Backup and Restore*.

- **Config changes**: The table shows any changes that are made to settings in the **Site administration** section. For each modification, **Date, Firstname/ Surname, Plugin, Setting, New value,** and **Original value** are shown.

  This is a great tool to use when something has gone wrong on your site as you can go back and check what has been changed recently. This report is also useful when you have to support a site that's administered by another user.

  Additional information on these config values is provided in *Appendix, Configuration Settings*.

Config changes

Page: 1 2 3 4 5 6 7 8 9 10 11 12 13 14 15 16 17 18 ...43 (Next)

Date ↑	First name / Surname	Plugin	Setting	New value	Original value
Monday, 25 August 2014, 1:41 PM	Alex Büchner	logstore_database	dbtable	mdl_log	packt_log
Monday, 25 August 2014, 1:40 PM	Alex Büchner	core	maxcategorydepth	3	2
Monday, 25 August 2014, 1:39 PM	Alex Büchner	core	statsfirstrun	all	none
Monday, 25 August 2014, 1:39 PM	Alex Büchner	core	statsruntimestarthour	6	5

- **Course overview**: The report shows some basic statistics on courses. The options for a period to be selected are:
    - **Most active courses**: Number of hits per course
    - **Most active courses(weighted)**: Based on activities per user

     ○   **Most participatory courses(enrolments)**

     ○   **Most participatory courses(views/posts)**

In each report, a table is shown and a graph visualizes the course data. Make sure that **Statistics** is enabled in **Advanced features**.

- **Performance overview**: Some basic performance checks. We will deal with these in *Chapter 12, Moodle Performance and Optimization*.

- **Question instances**: The report shows the **Context** (usually course) and **Total**, **Visible**, and **Hidden** instances in which questions of a selected type or all types are used.

- **Security overview**: A list of some key issues that can compromise the security of your system, as listed in the **Issue** column, with links to the relevant settings, **Status (OK, Information, Warning,** and **Critical**), and a **Description**. We will cover this report in *Chapter11, Moodle Security and Privacy*.

- **Spam cleaner**: If your system has self-registration activated and user profiles have been created by spammers, this report will list and clean all compromised profiles according to the provided key words. We will cover this in *Chapter11, Moodle Security and Privacy*.

Summary

Moodle reporting has recently undergone a significant makeover. The newly introduced logging framework, which we covered in detail, provides a foundation for flexible reporting and learning analytics. Additionally, a new report generator is currently under development, which will replace a lot of the mechanisms described in this chapter. However, the underlying principles of reporting on the course, user, and site-level will remain intact.

In this chapter, you learned how to report user activities using Moodle's internal reporting facilities, report generation alternatives, as well as external web analytics tools. We also dealt with a number of miscellaneous reports that are provided by Moodle.

One concern about the introduction of more flexible and powerful reports and metrics is the preservation of users' privacy and the protection of associated data that's been stored. The next chapter will cover these aspects.

11

Moodle Security and Privacy

Moodle, like any other web application, has the potential to be misused. Moodle has dedicated an entire section to security settings which administrators can use to fine-tune its safety. After an overview of Moodle's security, you will learn about the following topics:

- **Security notifications**: You will learn how to set up a number of notification mechanisms that warn you about potential security issues and look at the built-in security report.

- **User security**: We will look at access to Moodle (self-registration, guest access, protection of user details, and course contacts), Moodle passwords, security in roles, and spam prevention.

- **Data and content security**: We will deal with potential issues in content created within Moodle and the visibility of this content. You will learn how to set up a site policy and configure the antivirus scanner.

- **System security**: We will discuss configuration settings (location of the data root directory and the cron process), HTTPS, and IP blocker.

We'll conclude the chapter with information on privacy and data protection concerns.

Packt Publishing has a dedicated title on *Moodle Security* in its portfolio at `https://www.packtpub.com/hardware-and-creative/moodle-security`. While it covers Moodle 1.9, the majority of the topics are relevant to Moodle 3.x, too.

Security – an overview

Moodle takes security extremely seriously, and any potential issues are given the highest priority. Fixed vulnerabilities of serious issues usually trigger the release of minor versions, which emphasize the importance of the subject.

The security of a system is as good as its weakest link. Moodle relies on underlying software, hardware, and network infrastructure; security can potentially be compromised in a number of areas. As the focus of this book is on Moodle and its administration thereof, we only cover the security elements of Moodle per se. The following areas are not dealt with, and it is necessary to consult the respective documentation on security issues:

- **Software**: As described in *Chapter 2, The Moodle System*, Moodle's key components comprise a web server (usually Apache or Microsoft IIS), database server (MySQL, MS SQL Server, PostgreSQL, MariaDB, or Oracle), and a programming language (PHP). Additional PHP and operating system extensions are required, for instance, to support the aforementioned database systems. We will be only touching on some Moodle-specific PHP and Apache settings.

- **Hardware**: Moodle runs on (physical or virtual) servers that have to be physically hosted. There is ongoing debate about the safety and security of such systems, which is reflected by ever-extending precautions by data centers.

- **Network**: Any system that is part of a network is potentially vulnerable. Configuration of firewalls, proxy servers, and routers as well as general network security are key aspects in protecting your system from any attacks.

A number of these topics are covered at `https://docs.moodle.org/en/ Security`.

One rule that applies to all elements is that the latest software updates should be installed regularly. Updating Moodle was covered in *Chapter 1, Moodle Installation*.

With the increasing complexity and growing popularity of Moodle, it is imperative that you make sure that all possible measures are taken to prevent any security issues. Let's get started.

Security notifications

Moodle has set up a dedicated site, which you can find at `https://moodle.org/ security/`, that deals with security issues. If you register your Moodle site, which is highly recommended, your e-mail address will automatically be added to the security alerts mailing list, which gives you advanced notice of vulnerabilities and updates a couple of days prior to public release. To set this up, go to **Registration**, fill in the required information, and click on the **Register with Moodle.org** button.

Moodle notifications

When you click on the **Notifications** link in the **Site administration** section, Moodle will display any potential issues with your site. This link is also used to initiate the installed Moodle updates and plugins (refer to *Chapter 8, Moodle Plugins*).

Three messages are displayed in the following screenshot; the first two issues would clearly fall into the security category:

Your site configuration might not be secure. Please make sure that your dataroot directory (/var/www/packt/packtdata) is not directly accessible via web.

Enabling the PHP setting *display_errors* is not recommended on production sites because some error messages may reveal sensitive information about your server.

The cron.php maintenance script has not been run for at least 24 hours. ⑦

Moodle monitors failed login attempts in its log file, as described in *Chapter 10, Moodle Logging and Reporting*. Repeated login failures can indicate that unauthorized users are trying to get access to your system. In addition to checking your log files regularly, you should consider monitoring these activities by configuring the settings when you navigate to **Security | Notifications**:

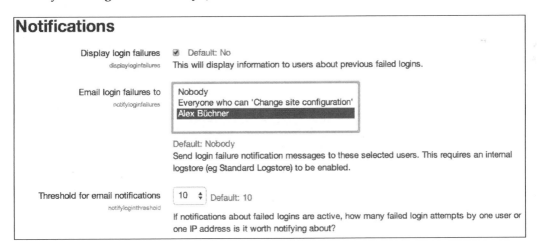

You can specify whether users will see a message displayed on their screens about previous failed logins and who will be e-mailed about login failures. You can further set the number of failed logins from the same IP address that will trigger these notifications.

While this is not foolproof, it can potentially highlight some problems within your system, and it is recommended that you activate it. Another benefit of getting these notifications e-mailed to you is the customer care aspect of being able to get back to legitimate users who have felt frustrated when trying to get access to your site.

Security report

Another mechanism that we have already touched on in *Chapter 10*, *Moodle Logging and Reporting*, is the security report (go to **Reports | Security overview**):

Security overview

Issue	Status	Description
Insecure dataroot	OK	Dataroot directory must not be accessible via the web.
Displaying of PHP errors	Warning	The PHP setting to display errors is enabled. It is recommended that this is disabled.
No authentication	OK	No authentication plugin is disabled.
Allow EMBED and OBJECT	Critical	Unlimited object embedding enabled - this is very dangerous for the majority of servers.
Enabled .swf media filter	OK	Flash media filter is not enabled.
Open user profiles	OK	Login is required before viewing user profiles.
Open to Google	OK	Search engine access is not enabled.
Password policy	OK	Password policy enabled.
Email change confirmation	OK	Confirmation of change of email address in user profile.
Writable config.php	OK	config.php can not be modified by PHP scripts.
XSS trusted users	Warning	RISK_XSS - found 5 users that have to be trusted.
Administrators	OK	Found 1 server administrator(s).
Backup of user data	Warning	Found 1 roles, 0 overrides and 2 users with the ability to backup user data.
Default role for all users	OK	Default role for all users definition is OK.
Guest role	OK	Guest role definition is OK.
Frontpage role	OK	Frontpage role definition is OK.
Web cron	Warning	Anonymous users can access cron.

The report shows a number of potential key security issues, their status (**OK**, **Information**, **Warning**, and **Critical**), and a short description (as shown in the preceding screenshot). When you click on the issue name, you will be redirected to a page that provides more information about the problem and, if available, also a further link to the settings page where you can rectify the situation (here, it's **Site policies**):

The **Security overview** report is a good starting point to identify some potential issues. However, it does not replace a full security audit, penetration test, or health check as offered by some Moodle Partners.

User security

The key to the security of your system lies in making sure that users only have access to their privileged areas in Moodle. In this section, we will be dealing with access to Moodle, passwords, security in roles, and spam prevention.

Access to Moodle

Users can access Moodle in different ways, and it is important to configure access mechanisms correctly. Some of those potential access risks are applicable in **non-SSO settings**.

Self-registration

Self-registration is a great feature, which, once set up, reduces the workload of the administrator significantly. However, it poses a potential risk that unwanted users are creating an account either manually or automatically. To reduce this risk, a number of settings are located in the **Common settings** section by going to **Plugins | Authentication | Manage authentication**:

Allowed email domains allowemailaddresses	.edu, synergy-learning.com Default: Empty
	If you want to restrict all new email addresses to particular domains, then list them here separated by spaces. All other domains will be rejected. To allow subdomains add the domain with a preceding '.'. eg **ourcollege.edu.au .gov.au**
Denied email domains denyemailaddresses	Default: Empty
	To deny email addresses from particular domains list them here in the same way. All other domains will be accepted. To deny subdomains add the domain with a preceding '.'. eg **hotmail.com yahoo.co.uk .live.com**
Restrict domains when changing email verifychangedemail	☑ Default: Yes
	Enables verification of changed email addresses using allowed and denied email domains settings. If this setting is disabled the domains are enforced only when creating new users.
ReCAPTCHA public key recaptchapublickey	6LeD9MQSAAAAAHi2FvLDUnEGX Default: Empty
	String of characters used to display the reCAPTCHA element in the signup form. Generated by http://www.google.com/recaptcha
ReCAPTCHA private key recaptchaprivatekey	6LeD9MQSAAAAAEzeXFzPdsjWln Default: Empty
	String of characters used to communicate between your Moodle server and the recaptcha server. Obtain one for this site by visiting http://www.google.com/recaptcha

These five settings have been described in detail in *Chapter 5, User Management*.

Guest access

Moodle provides a feature, called **guest access**, to users who do not wish to register with a site (not to be confused with a guest user in a course). While this is very useful for some public sites (such as https://moodle.org/), it is unwanted in most educational and commercial settings. To deactivate guest access, go to the **Common settings** section and navigate to **Plugins | Authentication | Manage authentication**. Once there, change the **Guest login button** setting from **Show** to **Hide**.

A second setting that relates to guest access is can be seen by going to **Users | Permissions | User Policies**, where you will find the **Auto-login guests** checkbox. Turn this on only if you want visitors to log in automatically when they enter a course with guest access.

If you allow guest access as an authentication method, you can specify inside courses whether guest access is available as an enrolment mechanism, and you can also specify a guest access password. We dealt with this in *Chapter 4, Course Management*.

Protection of user details

Identity theft is a common problem on the Internet, and Moodle is no exception. To avoid the possibility of fraudsters gathering details about authenticated users, a number of settings can be seen by navigating to **Security | Site Policies**:

Site policies

Protect usernames *protectusernames*	☑ Default: Yes By default forget_password.php does not display any hints that would allow guessing of usernames or email addresses.
Force users to log in *forcelogin*	☐ Default: No Normally, the front page of the site and the course listings (but not courses) can be read by people without logging in to the site. If you want to force people to log in before they do ANYTHING on the site, then you should enable this setting.
Force users to log in for profiles *forceloginforprofiles*	☑ Default: Yes This setting forces people to login as a real (non-guest) account before viewing any user's profile. If you disabled this setting, you may find that some users post advertising (spam) or other inappropriate content in their profiles, which is then visible to the whole world.
Force users to log in to view user pictures *forceloginforprofileimage*	☐ Default: No If enabled, users must login in order to view user profile pictures and the default user picture will be used in all notification emails.
Open to Google *opentogoogle*	☐ Default: No If you enable this setting, then Google will be allowed to enter your site as a Guest. In addition, people coming in to your site via a Google search will automatically be logged in as a Guest. Note that this only provides transparent access to courses that already allow guest access.
Profile visible roles *profileroles*	☐ Manager ☐ Course creator ☑ Teacher ☑ Non-editing teacher ☑ Student ☐ Guest ☐ Authenticated user ☐ Authenticated user on frontpage Default: Teacher, Non-editing teacher, Student List of roles that are visible on user profiles and participation page.

Setting	Description
Protect usernames	If a user cannot remember their username or password, Moodle provides a **Forgotten password** screen. By default, the message displayed reads: **If you supplied a correct username or email address then an email should have been sent to you**. If the protection is turned off, however, the message reads as **An email should have been sent to your address at ******@<domain name>**, which could allow the guessing of the username.
Force users to login	By default, the front page of Moodle is visible to everyone, even if they are not logged in to the site. If you wish to force users to log in before they see the front page, change this parameter. As a result, your users will only see the login screen when they enter your site.

Setting	Description
Force users to login for profiles	When set to **Yes** (default setting), users will have to log in with an authentic account before they can access the profile pages of other users.
Force users to login to view user pictures	If disabled (default setting), guests will be able to see pictures of other users in their profile. Otherwise, the default user image will be shown.
Open to Google	Moodle can be configured to allow Google to crawl through courses with guest access and add the content to its search engine database. This functionality is turned off by default.
Profile visible roles	Any role that is selected will be visible on user profiles and participation pages.

Further down in the **Site policies** screen, you have the ability to activate **Email change confirmation**. If it's set to **Yes**, users will be sent an e-mail to confirm that their change of e-mail address in their profile is genuine.

Course contacts

When courses are displayed on the front page, users who are not logged on to the system will see a description and the names of the course managers of each course by clicking on it. By default, these are the teachers of the course. To change the names that are displayed for each course, go to **Appearance | Courses**, and select the roles to be displayed in **Course contacts**:

Courses

Course contacts
coursecontact

- ☐ Manager
- ☐ Course creator
- ☑ Teacher
- ☐ Non-editing teacher
- ☐ Student
- ☐ Guest
- ☐ Authenticated user
- ☐ Authenticated user on frontpage

Default: Teacher

This setting allows you to control who appears on the course description. Users need to have at least one of these roles in a course to be shown on the course description for that course.

To hide the names completely, deselect all the roles. As a result, no names will appear when the course descriptions are shown.

Moodle passwords

Moodle offers a password policy feature that applies to manual accounts and which can be configured by going to **Security | Site policies**, as shown in the following screenshot:

The following self-explanatory constraints for passwords are available (default values are recommended as a minimum):

- **Password length** (≥0)
- **Digits** (0...9)
- **Lowercase letters** (a...z)
- **Uppercase letters** (A...Z)
- **Non-alphanumeric characters** (such as $%&*)
- **Consecutive identical characters** (≥0)

- **Password rotation limit** (the number of times before a user can reuse a password)

- **Maximum time to validate password reset request** (when password recovery is being triggered)

- **Log out after password change** (all browser sessions except the current one)

- **Group enrolment key policy** (this specifies whether the specified password policy rules should apply to a group enrolment key or not)

Password expiry can be specified for manual accounts (go to **Plugins | Authentication | Manual accounts**). We've already dealt with the three **Enable password expiry**, **Password duration**, and **Notification threshold** settings in *Chapter 5, User Management*. If you use an external authentication, for instance, an LDAP server, you will have to specify the expiry duration within the particular LDAP server(s).

You also have the option to lock out user accounts after too many failed logins. You can find the relevant settings by going to **Security | Site policies**. **Account lockout threshold** lets you specify the number of failed logins required to trigger a reactivation e-mail to the user. The **Account lockout observation window** setting lets you specify the period during which further failed logins will be included in the current suspension. **Account lockout duration** lets you specify the time after which the account will be unlocked automatically. Again, if you use an LDAP server for authentication, the lockout thresholds will be defined within the LDAP instance.

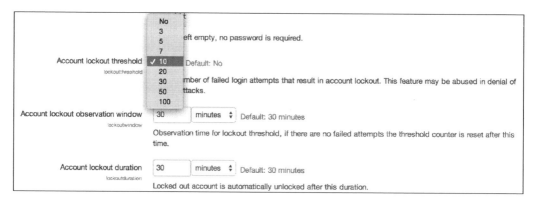

Most web browsers now offer a means to autocomplete passwords in a browser vault. While this is convenient for the end user, it also poses a security risk. If you wish to prevent browsers from autocompleting account passwords, select **Prevent password autocompletion on login form** by navigating to **Security | HTTP security**. Related to this setting is the option to remember usernames via cookies, which will then be entered in the login form when opened. You can configure the **Remember username** parameter by going to **Security | Site policies**.

It is highly recommended that you use a strong password (long, complex, and random) for the Moodle administrator account(s) even if the password policy is deactivated.

Moodle stores passwords in an encrypted form using a so-called md5 hash. To improve the security of the passwords further, Moodle supports **password salting**, which adds a separate random string to the md5 hash of each user password.

Moodle used to apply a single site-wide salt to passwords, which was stored in the config.php file as $CFG->passwordsaltmain. If your site has been updated from an earlier version of Moodle (2.4 or lower), this salt will still exist and should be kept until you can ensure that every user is logged in to the site only once, which triggers a conversion to the safer scheme. You might consider forcing this via the **Force password change** option in **Bulk user actions**.

If you ever lose your admin password and have no means of recovering it, you are able to manually override the password field in the mdl_user table in the SQL database. Because the passwords stored are md5 hash encrypted, you will have to replace the current value with an encrypted password. For example, to set the password to newpassword, you need to use the following SQL statement:

```
UPDATE mdl_user
    SET password = md5('newpassword')
WHERE username = 'admin';
```

If your database does not support the md5 function, you will have to set password to the actual md5 hash tag. For example, this would be 5e9d11a14ad1c8dd77e98ef9b53fd1ba for newpassword. Use one of many available online generators to find out the tag.

The first time you log in to Moodle, the salt will be added and the new encrypted password will be stored in the database. More information on password salting in Moodle can be found at https://docs.moodle.org/en/Password_salting.

Security in roles

Moodle allows the creation of custom roles, such as Parent, Teaching Assistant, Secretary, Inspector, and Translator. However, the flexibility of this powerful mechanism comes with a price in the form of a potential security risk. On the other hand, one could argue that it also solves a potential security risk, for instance, by limiting the access of a teaching assistant, there is no need to not grant full teaching access.

Moodle displays the risks associated with each capability, that is, the risks that each capability can potentially raise. To recapitulate from *Chapter 6, Managing Permissions – Roles and Capabilities*, the five risk types are explained in the table that follows:

Risk	Icon	Description
Configuration		Users can change the site configuration and behavior
XSS		Users can add files and texts that allow cross-site scripting (potentially malicious scripts that are embedded in web pages and executed on the user's computer)
Personal		Users can gain access to the private information of other users
Spam		Users can send spam to site users or others
Data loss		Users can destroy large amounts of content or information

Because risks are only displayed to indicate what potential damage a capability can cause, you are responsible for the role definitions and contexts in which the roles are applied. Make use of the capability report and system permission checker, as we discussed in *Chapter 6, Managing Permissions – Roles and Capabilities*.

 It is highly recommended that you minimize the number of global role assignments in custom roles as they are applicable throughout the entire site, including the front page and all the courses.

The **Authenticated user** role is assigned to everybody who is logged in to your site. It does not conflict with any other role and guarantees that certain operations can be carried out outside courses. Make sure that you don't change the scope of this role unless you really have to as any changes to this role will apply to every authenticated user on the system.

Default roles for different user types are assigned by navigating to **Users | Permissions | User Policies**. We dealt with these settings in detail in *Chapter 6, Managing Permissions – Roles and Capabilities*. Make sure that these settings are set correctly, especially for the guest and visitor-related roles.

Spam prevention

If Moodle is not configured correctly, it allows spammers to insert content into user profiles of accounts that are created via self-registration. This type of attack is known as **profile spam**. To prevent this, make sure that the following settings are set correctly (which they are, by default):

- Only use e-mail-based self-registration if it is really necessary. No self-registration, no spam!

- Keep the **Force users to login for profiles** parameter enabled in your site policies (refer to the *Protection of user details* section). This way, you can prevent anonymous visitors and search engines from seeing user profiles.

- Make sure that the **Profiles for enrolled user only** parameter remains enabled.

Also, be aware that legit users can be the cause of spam. Make sure that no user has any unnecessary capabilities in their roles that allow for this (refer to spam risk in the *Security in roles* section). You might even consider the creation of a spammer role that allows access to activities, such as forums, but prevents content from being posted. You further have the option to limit access to changing profiles to only those users who are enrolled in a course via the **Profiles for enrolled users only** setting, which can be seen when you navigate to **Security | Site policies**.

If your site has been victim to spam, go to **Reports | Spam cleaner**. You can either let Moodle **Autodetect common spam patterns** (the list makes for some interesting reading!) or search for your own keywords:

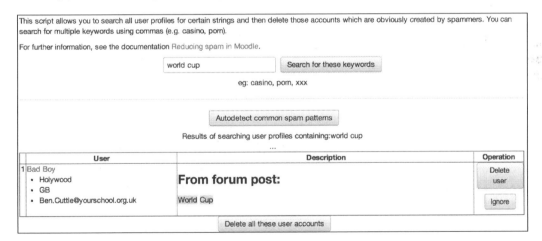

Any user profiles where the **Description** field contains any of the listed keywords, are shown. You then have the option to delete the user account(s). For more information on spam prevention in Moodle, check out `https://docs.moodle.org/en/Reducing_spam_in_Moodle`.

Data and content security

Content can potentially contain malicious elements. It further needs to be protected from unauthorized access. In this section, we shall deal with the security of data and content.

Content created within Moodle

Users are able to create content in Moodle by either using the resource editor or uploading files. A number of settings are available to partly prevent the misuse of these.

HTML allows the embedding of code that uses the explicit `<EMBED>` and `<OBJECT>` tags. This mechanism has recently gained popularity with sites, such as YouTube, Prezi, Voki, and Google Maps, providing code to be embedded for their users. Potentially, malicious code can be put in the embedded script, which is why its support is deactivated by default. To activate it, go to **Security | Site policies** and locate the **Allow EMBED and OBJECT tags** parameter:

Allow EMBED and OBJECT tags *allowobjectembed*	☑ Default: No As a default security measure, normal users are not allowed to embed multimedia (like Flash) within texts using explicit EMBED and OBJECT tags in their HTML (although it can still be done safely using the mediaplugins filter). If you wish to allow these tags then enable this option.
Enable trusted content *enabletrusttext*	☑ Default: No By default Moodle will always thoroughly clean text that comes from users to remove any possible bad scripts, media etc that could be a security risk. The Trusted Content system is a way of giving particular users that you trust the ability to include these advanced features in their content without interference. To enable this system, you need to first enable this setting, and then grant the Trusted Content permission to a specific Moodle role. Texts created or uploaded by such users will be marked as trusted and will not be cleaned before display.

Moodle's editors automatically remove any unwanted HTML elements and attributes via a so-called HTML purifier. Moodle supports a more secure version called **HTML Purifier**. You have the ability to bypass this mechanism for individual users. Firstly, you have to set the **Enable trusted content** parameter, as shown in the preceding screenshot. Secondly, you will have to allow the **moodle/site:trustcontent** capability for each user who you trust to submit JavaScript and other potentially malicious code.

The multimedia plugin supports a number of audio and video formats. **Shockwave Flash (SWF)** files can contain code that could cause problems on users' local machines. SWF files will only be embedded if the **Flash animation** parameter, which you can see by going to **Appearance | Media embedding**, is turned on and trusted content is enabled.

It is possible to embed Moodle (content) in frames of web applications for content management systems such as Joomla. Potentially, this can cause security problems, which is why the **Allow frame embedding** parameter, which can be seen by going to **Security | HTTP security**, is disabled.

Moodle also comes with a **Word censorship** filter (go to **Plugins | Filters | Manage filters**). However, it also picks up words within words, which doesn't make it that useful as it would mark valid terms, such as sextant, sparse, and altitude. You can either enter additional words and phrases in **Settings** of the filter or edit the `badwords` language string in `filter_censor.php` (careful, this list is far from G-rated).

Visibility of content

Blogging, tagging, and commenting are social networking tools that are popular in Web 2.0 environments. Blog entries, tags, and comments are harnessed for the purpose of searching, sharing, and performing other collaborative activities in order to match interests. The potential issue is that the content is visible to users who should not be able to share or view entries. Moodle has catered for this by providing a number of settings, which we have already dealt with in the *Collaboration* section in *Chapter 9, Moodle Configuration*. Here is a list of areas where the respective functionalities need to be turned on and off:

* **Appearance | Blog | Blog visibility**
* **Appearance | Blog | Enable comments**
* **Advanced features | Enable tags functionality**

If you deactivate any of the mechanisms, tags, comments, and blog entries that are already on the system or kept hidden, they will reappear when the functionality is turned on again. In other words, there is no risk of data loss when turning the functionality off and then back on.

You might also consider creating a dedicated role on your system, for example, a Blogger role utilizing the **moodle/blog:create** capability. This will limit blogging to specific users only—those who have been assigned the new role. You can find more details on the Blogger role in the Moodle Docs at `https://docs.moodle.org/en/Blogger_role`.

Site policy

Users who have access to Moodle are sometimes as much a threat as unauthorized users. If you have a site policy that all users (not just learners) must see and agree to when logging in to Moodle for the first time, you will have some ammunition when taking action against a user who has misused your system. The document, often referred to as an Acceptable Use Policy, should aim to adhere to the **LARK principle—Legal, Appropriate, Responsible, and Kind**.

You can specify the URL address of the text by going to **Security | Site policies**, which includes **Site policy URL** and a **Site policy URL for guests** entry. You will have to specify a URL that contains the policy text, which should be an HTML document. The file is often a publicly accessible URL, for example, a policy that is already available on your main website.

Once the site policy address has been specified, it has to be confirmed by each user the first time they log in to Moodle. If the policy is in any other format than HTML or plain text, only a link will be provided to the selected file. It is, therefore, not recommended to use PDFs or Word files.

School Website Policy

The purpose of this policy is to ensure that the school website protects the safety and confidentiality of the pupils of the school. It has regard to the Superhighway Safety advice of the Department for Education & Skills.

On our school website:

- No close up pictures of pupils will be used
- No photographs of individual pupils will be used
- Images of pupils will not be labelled with their names
- Pupils will only be referred to by first names on our webpages
- No personal details of pupils or staff will be featured

You must agree to this policy to continue using this site. Do you agree?

Yes   No

While the site policy does not prevent any misuse, it introduces a psychological barrier and also protects your organization in case further action needs to be taken. Site policies allow users to understand the expectations of how to most effectively and appropriately use a site. While it often has a legal undertone to dealing with bad users, it can also teach new users about the social expectations of those using the site.

Antivirus

Moodle supports the scanning of uploaded files for viruses using **ClamAntiVirus (ClamAV)**, which is an open source antivirus engine for Unix-based systems. Refer to `http://www.clamav.net/` for details, downloads for different operating systems, and how to keep the virus definition database up to date. You need to install ClamAV on your system. Once installed, the scanner can be configured by going to **Security | Anti-Virus**:

Anti-Virus

Use clam AV on uploaded files *runclamonupload*	☑ Default: No When enabled, clam AV will be used to scan all uploaded files.
clam AV path *pathtoclam*	`/usr/bin/clamdscan` Default: Empty Path to clam AV. Probably something like /usr/bin/clamscan or /usr/bin/clamdscan. You need this in order for clam AV to run.
Quarantine directory *quarantinedir*	Default: Empty If you want clam AV to move infected files to a quarantine directory, enter it here. It must be writable by the webserver. If you leave this blank, or if you enter a directory that doesn't exist or isn't writable, infected files will be deleted. Do not include a trailing slash.
On clam AV failure *clamfailureonupload*	✓ Treat files as OK Treat files like viruses Default: Treat files as OK If you have configured clam to scan uploaded files, but it is configured incorrectly or fails to run for some unknown reason, how should it behave? If you choose 'Treat files like viruses', they'll be moved into the quarantine area, or deleted. If you choose 'Treat files as OK', the files will be moved to the destination directory like normal. Either way, admins will be alerted that clam has failed. If you choose 'Treat files like viruses' and for some reason clam fails to run (usually because you have entered an invalid pathtoclam), ALL files that are uploaded will be moved to the given quarantine area, or deleted. Be careful with this setting.

Setting	Description
Use clam AV on uploaded files	Turn ClamAV on or off.
clam AV path	This provides the location of ClamAV on your system. The typical default paths are provided.
Quarantine directory	By default, any infected files are deleted. If you wish to keep them, specify a writeable directory that is then used to quarantine the files instead.
On clam AV failure	If, for whatever reason, ClamAV fails to run or scan files, you, as the administrator, will be alerted. Additionally, you can change the default **Treat files as OK** setting (the scanner is ignored) to **Treat files like viruses** (all the files are deleted or moved to the quarantine directory if the scanner fails).

There are two limitations of ClamAV:

- ClamAV does not exist for Windows servers. You will need to install a Windows-based virus scanner to provide this functionality and monitor any quarantined files separately.

- ClamAV will have an impact on the performance of your system. This only becomes an issue if the file upload facility is used plentifully. You might have to add 10-20% more RAM to your server if this is the case.

System security

In this section, we deal with configuration settings, login via the secure HTTP, the IP blocker, and the Safe Exam Browser integration.

Configuration security

There are a number of general configuration settings that potentially have an impact on the security of your system.

Access to dataroot

In the **Notifications** screenshot at the beginning of the chapter, you would have probably spotted the warning that the `dataroot` directory is directly accessible via the Internet. Moodle requires additional space on a server to store uploaded files, such as course documents and user pictures. The directory is called `dataroot` and must not be accessible via the Web. If this directory is accessible directly, unauthorized users can get access to content.

To prevent this, move your `dataroot` directory outside the web directory (ensure not to mangle permissions) and modify `config.php` accordingly by changing the `$CFG->dataroot` entry.

In externally hosted environments, it is often not possible to locate the directory outside the web directory. If this is the case, create a file called `.htaccess` in the data directory and add a line containing `denyfromall`.

The cron process

We have already described the cron process in *Chapter 1, Moodle Installation*, and will go into more detail about this in *Chapter 12, Moodle Performance and Optimization*. This is a script that runs regularly to perform certain operations, such as sending notifications, processing statistics, cleaning up temporary files, and so on. Scripts that run at the operating system level can potentially contain malicious code.

It is possible to run the script via a web browser by simply typing in the URL, which is `<yourMoodlesite>/admin/cron.php`. To prevent this, two mutually exclusive settings can be seen by navigating to **Security | Site policies**.

If you only allow the cron process to be executed from the command line, running the script via a web browser will be disabled and a message will be displayed saying **Sorry, internet access to this page has been disabled by the administrator**. The cron process can still be executed automatically if it's set up correctly.

If the **Cron password for remote access** parameter is set, Moodle requires that executing the cron script via a web browser requires the provision of a password in the form of a parameter, such as `<yourMoodlesite>/admin/cron.php?password=yourpassword`. If the password is not provided or is incorrect, an error message, which is the same as the one we saw earlier, is displayed.

Cron execution via command line only *cronclionly*	☑ Default: No If this is set, then the cron script can only be run from the command line instead of via the web. This overrides the cron password setting below.
Cron password for remote access *cronremotepassword*	•••••••••••••••••••• ☐ Unmask This means that the cron.php script cannot be run from a web browser without supplying the password using the following form of URL: `http://site.example.com/admin/cron.php?password=opensesame` If this is left empty, no password is required.

HTTP security

Moodle offers HTTPS support, which runs HTTP requests over SSL (a more secure but slower socket layer). The login of every system is a potential vulnerability. To run the authentication via SSL, enable the **Use HTTPS for logins** parameter, which can be activated by going to **Security | HTTP security**:

HTTP security

Use HTTPS for logins *loginhttps*	☑ Default: No Turning this on will make Moodle use a secure https connection just for the login page (providing a secure login), and then afterwards revert back to the normal http URL for general speed. CAUTION: this setting REQUIRES https to be specifically enabled on the web server - if it is not then YOU COULD LOCK YOURSELF OUT OF YOUR SITE.
Secure cookies only *cookiesecure*	☐ Default: No If server is accepting only https connections it is recommended to enable sending of secure cookies. If enabled please make sure that web server is not accepting http:// or set up permanent redirection to https:// address. When *wwwroot* address does not start with https:// this setting is turned off automatically.
Only http cookies *cookiehttponly*	☐ Default: No Enables new PHP 5.2.0 feature - browsers are instructed to send cookie with real http requests only, cookies should not be accessible by scripting languages. This is not supported in all browsers and it may not be fully compatible with current code. It helps to prevent some types of XSS attacks.

If using manual authentication, HTTPS encrypts the username and password before it is transferred from a user's browser to the server that hosts Moodle. HTTPS has to be enabled on your web server, and you will have to purchase or generate an SSL certificate. Every web server has a different method to enable HTTPS, so you will have to consult the documentation of your server. A good starting point of how to set up SSL/TSL for Apache can be found at `http://httpd.apache.org/docs/current/ssl/ssl_howto.html`.

> If you turn on HTTPS for logins without the relevant system components installed, that is, the PHP extension that is added along with the correct web server configuration, you will lock yourself out of your own system!

By default, HTTPS is only used for the login procedure itself; once a user has logged in, Moodle reverts to HTTP. It is possible to run your entire Moodle system via HTTPS by changing the `$CFG->wwwroot` variable in the `config.php` file to the new secure URL. However, be aware that using HTTPS across the whole site will cause an increase in CPU load on your web server. If this becomes an issue, you can get the HTTPS/SSL accelerator cards that offload the encryption from the main CPU.

Web servers can be configured in a way that they only accept HTTPS URLs. If this is the case on your system, it is recommended that you enable the **Secure cookies only** parameter. Moodle already supports a new feature that instructs web browsers to send cookies only with real requests, which prevents some cross-scripting attacks. However, the **Only http cookies** feature is not supported by all web browsers.

The IP blocker

Users will access your system from stationary and mobile devices. The one thing they all have in common is that they will access your site via an IP address. You have the ability to limit this access by specifying a whitelist and a blacklist by going to **Security | IP blocker**:

IP blocker

Allowed list will be processed first allowbeforeblock	☐ Default: No By default, entries in the blocked IPs list are matched first. If this option is enabled, entries in the allowed IPs list are processed before the blocked list.
Allowed IP list allowedip	192.168 123.45.67.89-99 Default: Empty Put every entry on one line. Valid entries are either full IP address (such as **192.168.10.1**) which matches a single host; or partial address (such as **192.168.**) which matches any address starting with those numbers; or CIDR notation (such as **231.54.211.0/20**); or a range of IP addresses (such as **231.3.56.10-20**) where the range applies to the last part of the address. Text domain names (like 'example.com') are not supported. Blank lines are ignored.
Blocked IP List blockedip	111.22.33.44

The whitelist (**Allowed IP list**) can contain IP addresses in a number of formats (the full IP address, partial address, ranges of IPs, and the CDIR notation). The same applies to the blacklist (**Blocked IP list**). By default, the blacklist has priority over the whitelist. If you wish to reverse this, select **Allowed list will be processed first**.

As an example, you might want to add `10.*.*.*` to your whitelist and blacklist for a particular IP, say, `10.123.45.67`, that was trying to guess your admin password multiple times.

Moodle privacy

Some of Moodle's default functionality might infringe with legislative privacy or data protection regulations in either the country you operate Moodle in or with the rules of the organization for which the VLE is run. An example of this is the ability of teachers to store notes about individual users without them able to view these. As different organizations are obliged to follow different guidelines, for example, FERPA in the United States, we are only able to point you in the direction of some of the most common issues and how to resolve them in Moodle.

The key issue is to protect personal information in educational records. Examples of such data are: personal details, grades, usage data (as described in *Chapter 10, Moodle Logging and Reporting*), and the already mentioned notes by teachers about students.

Information stored about users

Some regulations prescribe what information about users is allowed to be stored, with or without their consent:

- **Log files**: In *Chapter 10, Moodle Logging and Reporting*, we covered two types of features that are relevant in the context of privacy. The first is the type of data that is stored in a log store. We described **External database log**, where you can specify what type of educational actions are being tracked (**Teaching**, **Participating**, and **Other**) and what type of database query types are being stored (**Create**, **Read**, **Update**, and **Delete**). Furthermore, you have the ability to prevent the reports from accessing the data. We have listed all the relevant capabilities for the roles in the *Course and user reports* section of the aforementioned logging and reporting chapter.

- **Notes about users**: Moodle contains a tool that allows users with teacher rights to take notes about students. Other users with teaching rights can potentially see these notes. If this facility is not in conformance with your regulations, go to **Advanced features** and uncheck the **Enable notes** parameter.

If there is any other information about users that it is prohibited to store, you are most likely to find a capability in the roles setting to achieve this.

Information available to other users

Moodle is usually very open about what users can see about each other. While this might be in line with the philosophy of social constructivism, it might not conform to the regulations you have to abide by:

- **Online users**: In a site-wide context, the online users block displays the name of all the users who have been active in the system in the last 5 (default setting) minutes. You can disable this block by hiding it when you go to **Plugins | Blocks | Manage blocks**.

- **User profile information**: A user profile is visible to other users on the system. You can limit what information is shown to nonteachers and nonadministrators by selecting **Hide user fields** when you navigate to **Users | Permissions | User policies**. This also includes two fields providing information on **First access** and **Last access**.

- **Courses a user is enrolled to**: This is the same as the preceding point. You can enroll by selecting the **Mycourses** field.

- **Revealing e-mail addresses**: When searching for users or enrolling them to courses, their e-mail address is shown. To replace this, go to **Users | Permissions | User policies** and select **ID number** for the **Show user identity** parameter instead. The field(s) are only shown to users who have the **moodle:site/viewuseridentity** capability (by default, teachers and managers).

- **Grades**: Grades of students in a course can be seen and edited by teachers. Moodle supports the export of grades, which can be prohibited using a number of `gradeexport` capabilities. It is further possible to publish grades so that they can be viewed via a public URL without access to Moodle. This might be useful for external examiners, but it can cause issues with your privacy regulations and is, therefore, turned off by default (refer to **Enable publishing** by navigating to **Grades | General settings** and various `gradeexport` capabilities.

- **Backups**: Teachers have the ability to take course backups, which also contain user information. We are going to deal with limiting backups in *Chapter 13, Backup and Restore*.

If there is any other information that it is prohibited for other users to see, you are most likely to find a capability in the roles setting to achieve this.

Summary

In this chapter, you learned how to protect your Moodle system from misuse and protect users' privacy. However, it is important to stress that Moodle's security is only a single variable in the overall equation. Make sure that all other underlying software, infrastructure, and hardware components are set up correctly as well.

Most Moodle systems run on the LAMP platform, which has proven to be very secure if configured correctly. Moodle's developers are very conscious that security is vital when dealing with personal user data such as grades. Hence, the topic has been given the highest priority. However, there is no guarantee that your system is 100% protected against misuse. New hacking techniques will emerge and users will continue to be careless with their credentials (you have all seen the post-it notes under the keyboard). So, make sure the security patches and updates on your entire system, not just Moodle, are always up to date and keep educating your users about the dangers. Also, consider undergoing a regular security audit or health check as offered by some Moodle Partners.

Now that you system is secure, let's make sure that it performs to its full potential.

12
Moodle Performance and Optimization

The performance of web-based systems is a critical issue, and it is the key responsibility of an administrator to configure, monitor, and fine-tune the virtual learning environment for maximum speed. While Moodle has the potential to scale to thousands of simultaneous users, good performance management is required to guarantee adequate scalability.

After providing an overview of the subject, we will cover the most relevant topics that are related to Moodle's performance and optimization.

- **Moodle content**: We will look into how content creation, content volume, different content types, and various filter settings can impact the performance of your Moodle system.

- **Moodle Universal Cache**: We look at the different elements of the powerful **Moodle Universal Cache (MUC)**, namely cache types, cache stores, and cache definitions. We will then run you through performance testing of the MUC as well different caching options.

- **Moodle system settings**: A range of system-related performance settings are dealt with, namely:
    - Session handling
    - Cron management and scheduled tasks
    - Module settings (gradebook, chat, and forum)
    - Miscellaneous settings (course backups, log files, system paths, front page courses, as well as roles and users)

We will conclude the chapter with a section on Moodle performance profiling and monitoring.

An overview of performance and optimization

Web applications, in general, and Moodle, in particular, have very distinct application layers consisting of an operating system, web server, database server, and an application that's developed in a programming language. Each layer has its own idiosyncrasies when it comes to optimization. We will mainly focus on the *application layer*, which is the focus of this book.

The following areas are *not* dealt with in any detail in the following pages, and it is necessary to refer to the respective documentation with regard to performance and optimization issues:

- **Operating system performance**: The choice of operating system and its configuration will have a major impact on how Moodle performs. In principle, Linux or any other Unix derivative performs better than any other operating system. PHP applications, such as Moodle, run significantly slower in a Windows environment than on Linux. Some aspects of this have been covered in *Chapter 1, Moodle Installation*, when we dealt with the installation of Moodle.

- **Database performance**: The database is the core element of Moodle, but it's also a major bottleneck since it requires disk access, which is slower than memory access. Entire books and conferences have been dedicated to database optimization with indexing, caching, buffering, querying, and connection handling as the main candidates of discussion. The two optimizations that have a significant impact on your database performance are enabling of query caching and an increase in buffer sizes. You might also want to consider running the database on a separate dedicated server or a cluster. The former is relatively straightforward: once set up, all you need to do is to change the $CFG->dbhost entry in config.php from localhost to the IP address of your database. The latter is significantly more complex and requires strong database administration skills.

  There is also much debate about what database is best suited for Moodle. While the open source camp is divided between MySQL, MariaDB, and PostgreSQL, corporates are split between MS SQL Server and Oracle. Whatever your choice of system, a well set up and tuned database will always perform better than one that is used with out-of-the-box settings — "The best database system is the one you know".

- **Web server performance**: Each web server (Apache, IIS, NginX, and so on) offers an array of optimization settings that include memory handling, caching, process management, and other minor tweaks that are made to it.

- **PHP performance**: There are a number of ways in which PHP can be forced to execute code significantly faster. The key to doing this is using a PHP accelerator in combination with good memory management and caching techniques. Moodle supports OPcache from Zend, which has been precompiled from PHP 5.5 onwards. *Zend OPcache speeds up PHP execution by opcode caching and optimization. It stores precompiled script byte code in shared memory.* You can check whether OPcache is working correctly by going to **Server | Environment**:

Name	Information	Report	Status
php_setting	opcache.enable	ⓘ PHP setting should be changed. PHP opcode caching improves performance and lowers memory requirements, OPcache extension is recommended and fully supported.	Check

  ○ Your `php.ini` file will have to contain the following entries (for details, refer to `https://docs.moodle.org/en/OPcache`):

```
[opcache]
opcache.enable = 1
opcache.memory_consumption = 128
opcache.max_accelerated_files = 8000
opcache.revalidate_freq = 60

; Required for Moodle
opcache.use_cwd = 1
opcache.validate_timestamps = 1
opcache.save_comments = 1
opcache.enable_file_override = 0
```

- **Hardware performance**: We already covered some aspects of this in *Chapter 1, Moodle Installation*, where we mentioned that there is no one-size-fits-all approach when it comes to the ideal hardware setup. For single server systems, the key is RAM: the more, the better. It's as simple as that. Once the level of concurrency increases above a certain level, it is inevitable to use multiple web servers in a load-balanced environment.

While all the preceding criteria apply, some elements can be changed on the fly. For example, during exam week, you might consider increasing the memory available for Moodle, while during the summer break, you can reduce the number of servers to carry out maintenance. More sophisticated setups let you specify load and usage thresholds, which trigger the allocation of resources automatically.

For each area that's mentioned, benchmark and stress tests are available, and they will help you to gauge what performance bottlenecks are present and, after optimization has been carried out, if they have been reduced. There are also add-ons available for most web browsers that display information on how long it takes to load pages, thus offering some indicative performance measurements.

An entire area has been dedicated to performance and optimization in the Moodle Docs. You can find most of the relevant information as well as links to related sites at `https://docs.moodle.org/en/Performance`.

One thing that you should bear in mind is that Moodle's performance cannot be viewed without taking its security into account and vice versa. Very often, improving security comes at a price in terms of performance reduction; for example, running your entire site over HTTPS is often required and recommended, but it will slow down certain operations.

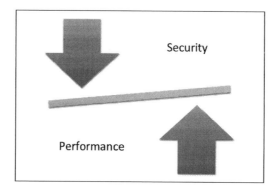

Another trade-off you will face regularly is performance versus functionality. Regularly, certain features, for example, the statistics module, will have a negative impact on how speedily your system performs. Moodle comes with a very basic performance report (**Reports | Performance overview**), which shows some trade-offs.

Performance overview

This report lists issues which may affect performance of the site ⓘ more help

Issue	Value	Comments	Edit
Theme designer mode	Disabled	If enabled, images and style sheets will not be cached, resulting in significant performance degradation.	✿
Cache Javascript	Enabled	If disabled, page might load slow.	✿
Debug messages	MINIMAL: Show only fatal errors	If set to DEVELOPER, performance may be affected slightly.	✿
Automated backup	Enabled	Performance may be affected during the backup process. Backups should be scheduled for off-peak times.	✿
Enable statistics	Enabled	Performance may be affected by statistics processing. Statistics settings should be set with caution.	✿

Let's consider an important issue: **Automatic backup**. This has an obvious impact on performance, but since you are unlikely to turn off backups, we will have to accept the fact that this will decrease the responsiveness of Moodle while backups are running unless you run backups on a dedicated server.

The Moodle content

The content that is created and uploaded by your course creators or front page designers will have an impact on the performance of your system. While you cannot dictate what learning sources are added to Moodle, the following pointers can provide explanations if certain aspects within courses behave sluggishly or users on slower Internet connections experience difficulties accessing learning materials.

Content creation

Moodle is significantly slower when run in the editing mode. Unless you or any other user is not modifying any content, it is recommended that you turn editing off as it puts less strain on the system.

Some content is created quicker in a separate standalone application, such as web development tools, word processors, or SCORM editors, as opposed to the built-in Moodle tools.

Content volume

The amount of content within a course can cause problems for student access, especially when loaded via a mobile device over a cellular connection. While each resource and activity is accessed individually, there are pedagogical limits to the number of learning objects that can be stored in a course. Furthermore, a course with hundreds of large resources is less likely to support a good learning experience than a number of courses broken down in more manageable chunks (content clustering). It will also slow down the backing up and importing of courses.

Content types

Moodle supports a large number of content types, such as office document, graphics, animation, audio, and video. In principal, there exists a trade-off between *size*, *quality*, and *functionality*. There are a number of precautions that can be taken for each type:

- **Office documents**:
    - Save office files as PDF files (which are much smaller in size) unless editing is required

- Encourage the use of online repositories, such as Google Docs and Dropbox, which will put less strain on your server
- Scan text using OCR recognition and not as images

- **Graphics**:
  - Reduce the image resolution, especially when pictures have been taken with digital cameras
  - Reduce the image color depth
  - Use a compression format
  - When using Microsoft Word, insert images in text documents as metafiles (using the **Paste Special** command)
  - Use formats that are supported directly by web browsers (usually JPG and PNG)

- **Audio files**:
  - Reduce the sample rate (especially for spoken content)
  - Mono recording is often sufficient for spoken content
  - Use a compression format such as MP3

- **Animations and video**:
  - Keep animation quality, dimension, and sample rate to a minimum
  - Use Flash or HTML5 for better performance
  - Stream video (from external sources such as `http://www.teachertube.com/`) if possible

These are just a few recommendations that will help reduce the stress on your system. The better your course content creators are informed, the less resources will be taken up by the content per se. While the usage of different types of textual and multimedia resources should be encouraged, it is important to introduce a culture of how these content types are streamlined as much as possible.

Moodle's filter settings

When we looked at filters in *Chapter 8*, *Moodle Plugins*, we laid emphasis on functionality. Now, let's look at them again, highlighting some performance issues. The following is a list ordered by priority when setting up filters by going to **Plugins | Filters | Manage filters**:

1. Activate all the filters that are needed by course creators but not more than those. Having too many Moodle filters active has effects on the server load, especially on lower-end systems. The number of active filters will increase the time it takes to scan each page since filters are applied sequentially, not in parallel.

2. Configure as many active filters as possible using the **Off, but available** setting. They can then be activated locally at any course or activity level.

3. Place the filters that are used most often (usually multimedia plugins) at the top of the list as filters are applied on a first-come-first-serve basis.

Caching is applied to pages that use text filters, that is, copies of text are kept in memory. This is discussed in the caching section later on. Additionally, only turn on **Filter uploaded files** if required by navigating to **Plugins | Filters | Common filter settings**. Also, change **Filter match once per page** and **Filter match once per text** to **On** if this resulting behavior is acceptable.

A bigger problem than content complexity is scalability, which is caused by concurrent users of the system. We will spend the rest of the chapter exploring this issue.

Moodle Universal Cache

Caching stores frequently access data in a temporary storage and expedite its access using a cached copy as opposed to refetched (from disk) or recomputed (in memory) data. This has proven to be one of the most efficient performance optimization techniques and Moodle is no exception.

Moodle contains a powerful caching framework called **Moodle Universal Cache** (**MUC**), which allows certain functions to take advantage of different configured caching services (https://docs.moodle.org/en/Caching). A typical example of a function that makes use of caching is string fetching, especially when multiple languages are supported.

The MUC background

Before we take a look at how MUC works, let's explore some basic concepts first, namely cache types (modes), cache stores, and cache definitions.

Cache types

There are three different cache types in Moodle, often referred to as cache modes:

- **Application cache**: The application cache deals with operations that are Moodle-specific, for example, caching of language strings or configuration settings. This is the most commonly used cache as it has the highest impact on Moodle performance.
- **Session cache**: This is basically the same as your PHP session cache. It is only used in very few scenarios, and we do not need to cover this in further detail.
- **Request cache**: As the name Moodle:request cache suggests, this type of caching is only stored for the lifetime of a request and allows developers to optimize code. Again, this is not a cache type that we, as administrators, have to worry about.

Here's an overview of the different cache types:

Feature	Application	Session	Request
Lifetime	Persistent	Session	Request
Applicable to	All users	User	User
Performance impact	High	Medium	Low
Default cache store	Filesystem	PHP session	Memory

Cache stores

Simply speaking, a cache store is a plugin that connects Moodle to a physical storage where the cached data gets stored; this is also referred to as cache backend. The default cache stores are in the form of a filesystem (for a cache store application), PHP session (session), and memory (request). For most setups, these are sufficient, but for larger sites, it is beneficial to make use of a dedicated application cache store.

Moodle ships with three application cache store plugins, namely **Memcache**, **Memcached**, and **MongoDB**. Other plugins, such as APC, WinCache, and XCache, can be found in the **Cache Stores** section of `https://moodle.org/plugins/`. All the supported cache stores can be found by going to **Plugins | Caching | Configuration**. On our system, only **Memcached** has been installed and configured at the system level, hence the tick in the **Ready** column. The **Supports** column indicates which features are supported by the cache store; the options are **ttl** (time-to-live), **data guarantee**, **key awareness**, and **searching by key**.

Installed cache stores

Plugin	Ready	Stores	Modes	Supports	Actions
File cache	✓	1	Application, Session	data guarantee, ttl, key awareness	Add instance
Memcache		0	Application	ttl	
Memcached	✓	1	Application	ttl	Add instance
MongoDB		0	Application	data guarantee	
Session cache	✓	1	Session	data guarantee, ttl, key awareness	
Static request cache	✓	1	Request	data guarantee, ttl, key awareness	

Configured store instances

Store name	Plugin	Ready	Store mappings	Modes	Supports	Locking mechanism	Actions
mem1	Memcached	✓	16	Application	ttl	Default file locking	Edit store, Delete store, Purge
Default file store for application caches	File cache	✓	0	Application, Session	data guarantee, ttl, key awareness, searching by key	Default file locking	ⓘ Purge
Default static store for request caches	Static request cache	✓	0	Request	data guarantee, ttl, key awareness, searching by key	Default file locking	ⓘ Purge
Default session store for session caches	Session cache	✓	0	Session	data guarantee, ttl, key awareness, searching by key	Default file locking	ⓘ Purge

For each configured cache type, you have the ability to add instances via the respective link in the **Actions** column. Each cache store has different settings, which depend on the supported features in the cache backend. Here are the parameters available in the **Memcached** store:

Once you have set up your cache store and your cache instance, respectively, you will need to add so-called **store mappings**. This is done as part of the cache definitions, which we will cover next.

Cache definitions

Different features in Moodle support caching. In earlier versions, we had a single monolithic cache that was either harnessed by a feature or it wasn't. Now, via the MUC, each feature is represented via so-called cache definitions, which can be configured individually. At the time of writing this, there are over 30 cache definitions available. It is expected that this number will increase with each version. For each definition, the following information is available:

Name	Description
Definition	Name of feature that is being cached
Mode	**Application**, **Session**, or **Request**.
Component	The Moodle component that the definition belongs to (core or module)
Area	The section that the feature belongs to. This is only relevant to developers.
Store mappings	If no customization has taken place, this will be the default cache store of the given cache mode, otherwise, the newly set value (refer to the following point).
Sharing	By default, this will be **Site identifier**. When modified, the possible values can be **Everyone**, **Version**, and **Custom** key (refer to the details further in the later sections).

In the **Actions** column, you have the option to **Edit mappings**, **Edit sharing**, and **Purge** the cache for this specific definition.

Editing mappings lets you specify which cache store is being used as the primary store and, for some definitions, as the final store. This is where you specify which store is being used for a particular feature (cache definition).

By default, each cache definition is shared across the instance of the site. However, there are scenarios where you might want to change this to any of the following options:

Sharing option	Description
Everyone	Every user in the system.
Site with the same ID	If you run a single version of Moodle on a single server, this is identical to the preceding point. If you run Moodle on a multiserver setup, all systems will be included.
Sites running the same version	If you run multiple Moodle instances from one wwwroot, only sites with identical version numbers will be included.
Custom key	If you run multiple Moodle instances from one wwwroot, you can group them via a custom key. For example, you might want to cache all the instances of one country in one store.

In order to clear a cache of a definition, simply select the **Purge** option.

Known cache definitions

Definition	Mode	Component	Area	Store mappings	Sharing	Actions
Accumulated information about modules and sections for each course	Application	core	coursemodinfo	Default file store for application caches	Site identifier	Edit mappings, Edit sharing, Purge
Activity completion status	Application	core	completion	Default file store for application caches	Site identifier	Edit mappings, Edit sharing, Purge
Calendar subscriptions	Application	core	calendar_subscriptions	Default file store for application caches	Site identifier	Edit mappings, Edit sharing, Purge
Concept linking	Application	mod_glossary	concepts	Default file store for application caches	Site identifier	Edit mappings, Edit sharing, Purge
Config settings	Application	core	config	Default file store for application caches	Site identifier	Edit mappings, Edit sharing, Purge

The following diagram visualizes the mapping of cache definitions and also shows the concepts that were previously covered:

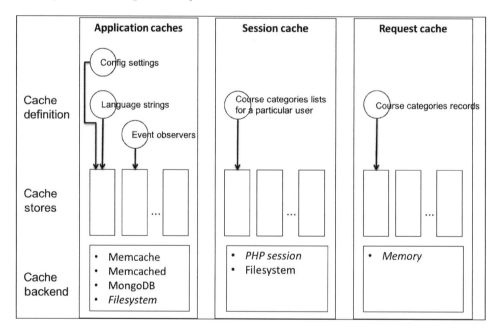

There are two more elements that you can see when you navigate to **Plugins | Caching | Configuration**, which we haven't covered yet:

- **Summary of cache lock instances**: There are different locking mechanisms in shared environments, caches being no exception. By default, Moodle ships with a default file locking mechanism. It is possible to install additional lock instances. However, at the time of print, no such plugins are present at the https://moodle.org/plugins/.

- **Stores used when no mapping is present**: Here, you can specify which default mappings will be used for which cache type.

Now that we have covered all the relevant concepts of MUC, let's have a look at the things to be considered when optimizing your Moodle site.

MUC configuration and testing

We have already explored the complexity of the MUC. While this provides us with enormous flexibility in terms of granular optimization, it makes it impossible to come up with a one-size-fits-all configuration. Somebody in the Moodle community once compared the MUC control panel with a big mixing desk at a concert: it gives you a lot of knobs to play with, but unless you know what each of them does and how they work together, you are unlikely to get good results.

There are a number of factors that impact the configuration of the MUC:

- Usage of the system (volume, diversity, functions, and type)
- Underlying infrastructure (single server, multiple server, virtualization, and so on)
- Types of cache stores used

In particular, when talking about the usage of the system, it is almost impossible to quantify this since it's changing constantly. During the summer break, there will be very little usage; during exam time, the load on the system is likely to rising, and so on.

Performance optimization is an ongoing exercise, which is accompanied by regular performance testing. Moodle provides us with a basic performance test for different cache types (**Plugins | Caches | Test performance**). Here is an example where you can see the results of 10,000 unique requests: the file cache is significantly slower that the sessions cache, a behavior that is not unexpected:

Cache store performance reporting - 10000 unique requests per operation.

Test with 1, 10, 100, 500, 1000, 5000, 10000, 50000, 100000 requests

Store requests when used as a session cache.

Plugin	Result	Set	Get - Hit	Get - Miss	Delete
File cache	Tested	1.5202	0.4715	0.0578	0.2129
Memcache	Untestable	-	-	-	-
Memcached	Invalid plugin	-	-	-	-
MongoDB	Invalid plugin	-	-	-	-
Session cache	Tested	0.0265	0.0160	0.0064	0.0138
Static request cache	Unsupported mode	-	-	-	-

While it is nice to have a built-in performance test tool in Moodle, it has two major shortcomings: first, some plugins are **Untestable**, for instance, **Memcache** and **Memcached**. Second, the test runs only mimics some unique requests but does not mirror their behavior if there are users on your system. To overcome these drawbacks, proper profiling and monitoring is required. This will be dealt with briefly at the end of this chapter.

There are a number of caching-related settings:

- **Language caching**: We dealt with localization in great detail in *Chapter 9, Moodle Configuration*, where we covered the configuration of Moodle. In addition to keeping the number of languages to a minimum, language caching should be utilized.

  Language packs are cached to speed up the retrieval of language strings. You find the **Cache language** menu and **Cache all language strings** parameters by going to **Languages | Language settings**. Unless you are modifying a language pack, it is highly recommended that you leave this setting as **Yes**. It caches all the language strings rather than loading them dynamically.

- **Theme caching**: Moodle caches the images and style sheets of themes either locally in a web browser or on a server. Unless you are designing or modifying a theme, the **Theme designer** mode, which you see when you go to **Appearance | Themes | Theme settings**, should remain off.

  You can clear the theme cache using the **Clear theme caches** button by going to **Appearance | Themes | Theme selector**.

- **Javascript Caching**: Moodle makes use of Javascript and AJAX. The **Cache Javascript** setting that you see when you go to **Appearance | AJAX and Javascript** should be kept on unless you are a developer.

- **RSS caching**: RSS feeds are cached locally. You can modify the time after which the cache is refreshed by changing the **Timeout** parameter by going to **Plugins | Blocks | RSS clients**.

- **Networking caching**: Moodle uses cURL to fetch data from remote sites. The **cURL cache** TTL setting can be modified by going to **Server | Performance.** The larger the time-to-live value is kept in the cache, the better the performance. More on networking in *Chapter 15, Moodle Integration*.

- **Repository caching**: When browsing external repositories, such as Google Docs or system files, the file listing is kept in a local cache. The amount of time that the listing is kept for can be changed via the **Cache expire** parameter by going to **Plugins | Repositories | Common repository settings**.

You can purge all these caches in a single operation by pressing the **Purge all caches** button when you navigate to **Development | Purge all caches**. Effectively, this clears out all the directories in `$CFG->dataroot/cache`. While this feature is more relevant to developers, it is a recommended step after installing updates or when your system is behaving oddly.

Purge all caches

Moodle can cache themes, javascript, language strings, filtered text, rss feeds and many other pieces of calculated data. Purging these caches will delete that data from the server and force browsers to refetch data, so that you can be sure you are seeing the most up-to-date values produced by the current code. There is no danger in purging caches, but your site may appear slower for a while until the server and clients calculate new information and cache it.

Purge all caches

The Moodle system settings

In addition to caching, Moodle offers a wide range of system-related performance settings that are set at various places in the **Site administration** section.

Session handling

A session is initiated for each user who authenticates against Moodle. This also applies to guests. There are a number of relevant settings, which can be found by going to **Server | Session handling**:

Setting	Description
Use the database for session handling	By default, session information is stored in the filesystem. On larger installations or a system that makes use of a clustered environment, it is recommended that you store the information in the Moodle database instead.
Timeout	The period for which a session is kept open when there hasn't been any activity.
Cookie prefix	This setting is only relevant if you run more than a single Moodle instance on the same web server and try to open instances of both in the same web browser. If this is the case, give the cookie a name on each site to avoid any conflicts.
Cookie path	Only change the location of where cookies are stored if there is a requirement for this in your environment.
Cookie domain	If your Moodle system shares its cookie space with another application, you can modify the domain that they both use. Be careful with this setting as it can prevent users from logging in if not specified correctly!

Moodle manages sessions and cookies very well. However, when problems occur, it is sometimes necessary to intervene manually. This should be done locally in the web browser if a specific user experiences issues (clear cache and cookies) or on the server if the problem affects multiple users. The latter is done by clearing the `mdl_sessions` table if sessions are stored in the database or by emptying the `$CFG->dataroot/sessions` directory if sessions are stored in files. Bear in mind that all logged in users will be logged out.

Cron management and scheduled tasks

We have already covered this as part of the installation, but it is worth reiterating that the method of how you call the Moodle cron job can have a significant impact on the performance of the system, especially on larger installations.

If the `cron.php` script is invoked over HTTP (either using `wget` or `curl`), more memory is used than calling directly via the `php -f` command.

Moodle comes with a task scheduler (**Server | Scheduled tasks**) that lets you precisely configure which routine job is running when and how often.

Name	Component	Edit	Last run	Next run	Minute	Hour	Day	Day of week	Month	Fail delay	Default
Legacy log table cleanup \logstore_legacy\task\cleanup_task	Legacy log	⚙	Monday, 25 August 2014, 4:21 PM	Tuesday, 26 August 2014, 7:08 AM	*	6	*	*	*	0	No
Log table cleanup \logstore_standard\task\cleanup_task	Standard log	⚙	Monday, 25 August 2014, 4:21 PM	Tuesday, 26 August 2014, 5:22 AM	*	4	*	*	*	0	Yes
Automated backups \core\task\automated_backup_task	Core	⚙	Never	ASAP	50	*	*	*	*	0	Yes
Clean backup tables and logs \core\task\backup_cleanup_task	Core	⚙	Monday, 25 August 2014, 4:21 PM	Monday, 25 August 2014, 5:10 PM	10	*	*	*	*	0	Yes
Award badges \core\task\badges_cron_task	Core	⚙	Never	ASAP	*/5	*	*	*	*	0	Yes

The following information is provided for each scheduled task:

Field	Description
Name	Name and internal location of the task.
Component	Moodle component that triggers the task.
Last run	Date and timestamp when the task has been run or **Never** (if it has never run).
Next run	Date and timestamp when of when the task has been run or **ASAP** (if it has never run).

Field	Description
Minute, Hour, Day, Day of week, Month	Schedule information in Unix cron format: • `*`: every minute, hour, day, day of week, and month • `*/x`: every *x* minutes, hours, and so on • `x-y`: every minute between *x* and *y* past the hour or every hour between *x* and *y*. • `0` = Sunday, `1` = Monday, and so on
Fail delay	Number of seconds to wait before reattempting a failed task.
Default	Specifies whether the task has been modified (as shown in the following screenshot).

If you wish to change the schedule for any of the tasks, you will need to select the Configuration icon in the **Edit** column. As an example, we have selected the **Check for updates** task:

In addition to the already covered scheduling settings, you also have the option to pause a task (**Disabled**) and revert the original settings (**Reset task schedule to defaults**). The default settings have been set with performance in mind. However, you might want to fine-tune these considering any idiosyncrasies in your setup.

Moodle's memory management has proven to be very efficient. However, there are scenarios when extra memory is required to execute complex PHP scripts. The cron is a candidate of such a complex script as is the course backup. To increase the memory limit, increase the **Extra PHP memory limit** setting by going to **Server | Performance**.

Module settings

A number of Moodle modules offer settings that have an impact on the performance of your Moodle system.

Gradebook optimization

Due to the complexity of the gradebook, there are a number of settings in the **Grades** menu that will have an impact on performance. In general, when more aggregation and other calculations have to be carried out, the population of the gradebook data store becomes slow. For example, the **Aggregate including subcategories** parameter that you see when you navigate to **Grades | Grade category settings** will add some minor overhead to the calculation of grades.

A second gradebook-related area that has an impact on performance is the Gradebook history, which forces Moodle to keep track of any changes in grades. Go to **Server | Cleanup**, and you will see two grade book history settings at the bottom.

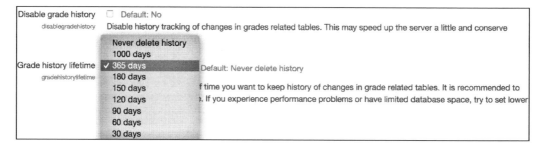

The gradebook history is turned on by default and values are kept forever. You can either turn the facility off completely, or limit the number of days you wish to keep the grade entries.

Chat optimization

By default, Moodle chat uses **AJAX method**, which, like **Normal method**, contacts all participating clients on a regular basis. The upside of both approaches is that they require no configuration and work on any system; the downside is that they have a significant performance impact on the server, especially when the chat activity is used regularly. The solution to this is to use **Chat server daemon**, which ensures a scalable chat environment. However, the daemon, a small system-level program that runs in the background, has to be installed on the operating system level and only works on Unix (check your administration guide for how to do this).

To change the chat method Moodle uses and configure a number of performance parameters, go to **Plugins | Activity modules | Chat**. We dealt with these in the synchronous communication section in *Chapter 9, Moodle Configuration*.

The following table lists the settings that are performance-related and the context (that is, the chat method used) in which they apply.

	AJAX method	Normal method	Server daemon
Refresh user list	√	√	√
Disconnect timeout	√	√	√
Refresh room		√	
Update method		√	
Max users			√

Forums

On systems with very large forums, tracking unread posts can slow down the activity. Though the impact is rather minor, the tracking can be turned off by going to **Plugins | Activity modules | Forum**, where you will find the **Track unread posts** parameter.

Miscellaneous settings

Finally, we deal with a number of performance-related settings that do not belong to any category described so far.

Course backups

As you will learn in the next chapter, course backups have a negative impact on performance during their execution, especially on larger systems. If possible, schedule the backup procedure when the load on the overall system is low. If you turn off site-wide course backups and use system-level backups instead, you avoid performance problems, but you lose the ability to recover individual items. A compromise is to include only important data and leave out less relevant information, such as log files. All this will be dealt with in *Chapter 13, Backup and Restore*.

Log files

In *Chapter 10, Moodle Logging and Reporting*, we looked at Moodle logging, reporting, and analytics. Keeping track of user behavior can potentially have a negative impact on your server.

If you make use of the standard log as a log store (as opposed to an external database), you have the ability via the log store settings to specify the number of days for which user data is kept (the **Keep logs for** parameter). Here, you can also turn off the logging access of guests (**Log guest access**) and specify **Write buffer size**. You can further limit the number of days that the so-called backup log is being kept—you can find the **Keep log for** setting by going to **Courses | Backups | General backup defaults**.

If you have enabled the statistics functionality, be aware that it is likely to have a profound impact on the performance of your system whenever statistical information is updated. Go back to the section on *Statistics settings* in *Chapter 10, Moodle Logging and Reporting*, (**Server | Statistics**), and make sure that the configuration is set to have minimum impact on the server.

System paths

An operation that Moodle performs regularly is the listing of directories. The operation can either be run using Moodle's internal routine coded in PHP or, alternatively, by a native version of the function provided by the host operating system. The latter approach is significantly faster since it reduces the load on your server, but it is only supported in Unix environments.

You can specify the path for the du command by navigating to **Server | System paths**. On most systems, the location of the executable is /usr/bin/du. If this does not work, run the which du command on the Unix shell to find out where the programs are located. Once specified correctly, this will accelerate the displaying of the directory content, especially if they contain a lot of files.

Front page courses

The front page is likely to be accessed frequently by all users. On sites with a large number of courses, displaying all of them every time that the front page is called is unlikely to be a pleasant user experience. You can limit **Maximum number of courses** and **Maximum category depth** by going to **Front page | Front page settings**.

Roles and users

We dedicated an entire chapter to the management of roles. Its powerful flexibility comes at a price, which is a minor drop in performance if a lot of lookups are required in the context hierarchy (avoid global roles) and the override mechanism is applied frequently.

There is also a performance-related setting when it comes to displaying the number of users in the user selector, namely **Maximum number of users per page**, by navigating to **Users | Permissions | User policies**. If you experience speed problems in courses with a large number of users, change this setting and monitor the performance. We will deal with this next.

Moodle performance profiling and monitoring

When you set up your Moodle system, you will be able to take some initial precautions to optimize the performance of your VLE. However, the real test is when Moodle is in full operation, that is, when the system is under load ("there is no test like production!").

Built-in profiling

Moodle provides some basic profiling information that you can turn on in **Development | Debugging**, where you have to enable the **Performance info** option. This will display information about the execution time, RAM usage, number of files in use, CPU usage and load, session size, as well as various filter and caching measures (less information will be shown on a Windows-based installation).

It further displays information on the caches used in the particular page. For each cache, **hits**, **misses**, and **sets** are shown. The caches are highlighted using traffic light colors: red uses up the most, orange some, and green uses up the least amount of resources. This is a rather good indicator to identify performance issues.

The data will be displayed in the footer of Moodle as long as it is supported by the theme in use (for instance, **Clean** and **More**).

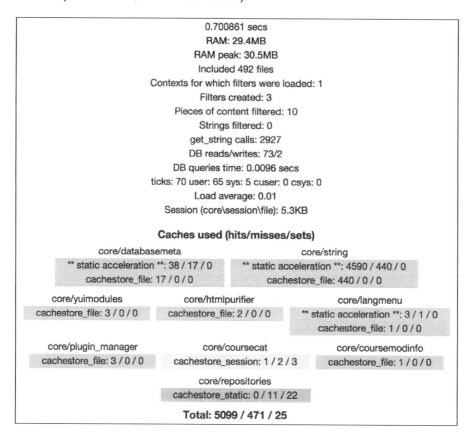

Moodle further supports profiling at the PHP level. While this is mainly targeted at developers, it may be helpful for administrators to identify bottlenecks in their system. Internal profiling is built on top of **XHProf**, which is a hierarchical profiler written by Facebook. It allows the profiling of PHP pages at a relatively low performance cost. First of all, you have to make sure that XHProf works on your server:

1. Install the `php-xhprof` XHProf PHP extension

2. Add the following to your `php.ini` file:

```
[xhprof]
extension=xhprof.so
xhprof.output_dir="/var/tmp/xhprof"
```

3. Restart Apache

Once this is successful (check with `php -m` that the `xhprof` extension is listed), you will see a new menu item when you navigate to **Development | Profiling**.

Enable profiling profilingenabled	☑ Default: No If you enable this setting, then profiling will be available in this site and you will be able to define its behavior by configuring the next options.
Profile these profilingincluded	index.php, /mod/*/view.php Default: Empty List of (comma separated, absolute skipping wwwroot, callable) URLs that will be automatically profiled. Examples: /index.php, /course/view.php. Also accepts the * wildchar at any position. Examples: /mod/forum/*, /mod/*/view.php.
Exclude profiling profilingexcluded	 Default: Empty List of (comma separated, absolute skipping wwwroot, callable) URLs that will be excluded from being profiled from the ones defined by 'Profile these' setting.
Automatic profiling profilingautofrec	0 Default: 0 By configuring this setting, some request (randomly, based on the frequency specified - 1 of N) will be picked and automatically profiled, storing results for further analysis. Note that this way of profiling observes the include/exclude settings. Set it to 0 to disable automatic profiling.
Selective profiling profilingallowme	☐ Default: No If you enable this setting, then, selectively, you can use the PROFILEME parameter anywhere (PGC) and profiling for that script will happen. Analogously, you can use the DONTPROFILEME parameter to prevent profiling to happen
Continuous profiling profilingallowall	☐ Default: No If you enable this setting, then, at any moment, you can use the PROFILEALL parameter anywhere (PGC) to enable profiling for all the executed scripts along the Moodle session life. Analogously, you can use the PROFILEALLSTOP parameter to stop it.
Keep profiling runs profilinglifetime	24 hours ▼ Default: 24 hours Specify the time you want to keep information about old profiling runs. Older ones will be pruned periodically. Note that this excludes any profiling run marked as 'reference run'.
Profiling import prefix profilingimportprefix	(I) Default: (I) For easier detection, all the imported profiling runs will be prefixed with the value specified here.

The profiler can be configured to run automatically (set the **Automatic profiling** frequency to any value except 0, and specify URLs in the **Profile these** field) or manually. The latter can be **Selective** (you have to initiate the profiling) or **Continuous** (once it starts, you have to stop it).

As soon as profiling has been enabled, yet another menu item will appear when you go to **Development | Profiling runs**, which lists summary information on all the profile runs that have been executed:

URL	Date ▾	Execution time	CPU time	Function calls	Memory used	Comment
/index.php →	14 Sep 2014, 19:05	630.200 ms	624.038 ms	44178	11010.406 KB	
/my/index.php →	14 Sep 2014, 19:05	666.049 ms	608.039 ms	35515	14565.789 KB	
/index.php →	14 Sep 2014, 19:05	634.284 ms	628.039 ms	44169	11010.555 KB	
	14 Sep 2014, 19:05	727.964 ms	720.045 ms	46143	14083.781 KB	
/admin/tool/profiling/index.php →	14 Sep 2014, 19:04	3598.208 ms	3588.223 ms	312580	18139.922 KB	
/index.php →	14 Sep 2014, 19:04	642.470 ms	632.039 ms	44797	11065.039 KB	
/admin/tool/profiling/index.php →	14 Sep 2014, 19:04	3170.485 ms	3160.197 ms	304176	17991.770 KB	

When you click on the URL or date of a single run, you can mark the run as a reference and provide a comment for it. You can also view its profiling details, where execution times and memory usage of each function call are shown in tabular form.

From this table, you can view a call graph. However, this requires a dot to be installed (part of the Linux graphviz package) and a path to the dot (usually /usr/bin/dot) to be specified when you go to **Server | System paths**. The result is a scary looking graph showing the order, dependencies, and details of each function call.

The general strategy when dealing with profiling is to identify the functions that take the longest to execute, make tweaks to your setup, and check whether the time has reduced. The difficulty in doing this is to make sure that the test runs take place under the same or, at least, very similar conditions.

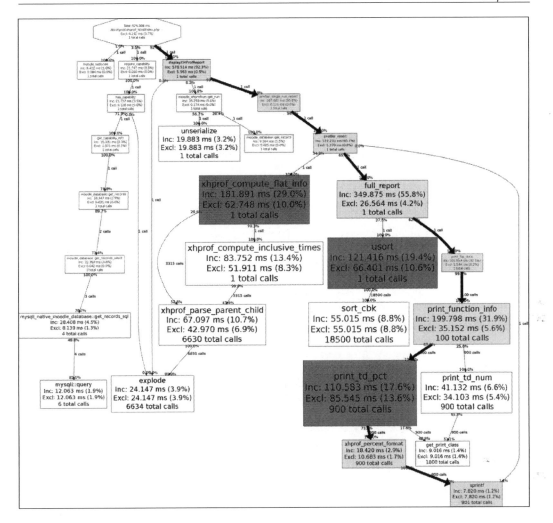

Moodle further comes with a nifty script that lets you generate random course data. This way, you can simulate having hundreds of courses with various levels and types of activities. You have to call the script manually at `<yoursite>/admin/tool/generator`. This is described in more detail in *Chapter 14, Moodle Admin Tools*.

System profiling

In addition to the profiling information that Moodle provides, you can gather more data using a combination of system-level tools:

- Run a monitor to know what your system is doing (for example, use Cacti, an open source graphing tool).

- Run alerts and notification monitors (for instance, Nagios).

- Use a performance measuring suite when you simulate different loads of your system (Apache JMeter is supported by Moodle).

- Install a profile system. Moodle has inbuilt support for XHProf (do a search on it on `moodle.org` for more details).

- Test your network speed (using the `iperf` command).

- Check your disk usage statistics (using the `iostat` command).

- Check what the processes are doing (using `strace`).

All the mentioned systems and tools are for Linux only, and you can find help on how to use them in their respective documentations.

Now that you have been armed with a number of profiling and monitoring tools, you can change the settings as described throughout the chapter. Take a look at what impact, positive or negative, they have on the performance of your Moodle system.

Summary

In this chapter, you learned how to optimize and monitor Moodle's performance.

As you have probably gathered from the content, system, and application, optimization is not always straightforward. It depends on a range of circumstances, such as the system that Moodle is running on, the hardware that it utilizes, the network, the number of concurrent users logged into the system, the types of activities that are carried out, and so on. While basic optimization is usually straightforward, fine-tuning is a bit of an art in itself. A lot of trial and error (that is, profiling) will be required to achieve the ideal setup for your Moodle system.

Some Moodle Partners offer health checks that include performance checkups. It is worth investigating this option if your system runs sluggishly.

Now that your system is ready to perform to its maximum potential, let's make sure that you have a professional backup and recovery strategy in place, which is covered in the next chapter.

13
Backup and Restore

Your hosted Moodle application will contain a lot of very important data such as coursework, assignments, grades, and all administrative data, for example, users, cohorts, and roles. Therefore, it is vital that you have a good backup strategy in place.

Moodle itself supports two types of backups:

- **Course-level backup**: Course backups are usually run on an ad hoc basis and only save the selected course. You will learn how to create course backups, restore courses, and how to copy course content using the related course import facility.

- **Site-level backup**: The site backup option saves all courses and their related data to a specified location at regular intervals. You will learn how to set this up and recover data from it.

Both mechanisms will be covered in detail before we look at **system-level backups**, which include Moodle backups (covering the Moodle software itself as well as the data stored in it) and snapshot creation (full system images).

We will conclude the chapter with two applications that make use of the backup and restore facilities, namely, year-end procedure and course templates.

The course-level backup and restore

We will first have a look at the backup procedure before going into the details of how to recover data during the restore operation. Course backup is a four-step process:

The course backup

To back up an individual course, it is best if you are inside that course, where you have to select the **Backup** link in the **Course administration** section. The backup procedure comprises a number of steps, which are described in the sequel. You can navigate backward to any step via the process links at the top of the screen or using the navigation buttons at the bottom.

Initial settings

There are a number of settings that dictate how the backup will be performed and what type of information will be included.

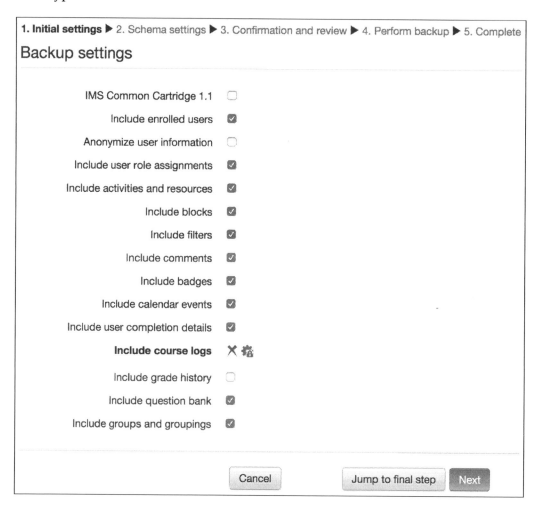

Some settings are only available if other settings have been activated. This is described in the following table:

Setting	Description	Prerequisite
IMS Common Cartridge 1.1	In addition to the Moodle backup format, IMS CC is supported.	None
Include enrolled users	Records can be included in the backup of users who are enrolled in the course.	None
Anonymize user information	User data (username, first name, last name, and e-mail address) will be substituted by aliases. For example, *Jonny Walker* might become `anonfirstname69` `anonlastname69`.	Include enrolled users
Include user role assignments	This specifies whether assigned roles (including locally assigned and overridden roles) should be included.	Include enrolled users
Include activities and resources	This specifies whether course activities are being shown for selection on the next screen.	None
Include blocks	This specifies whether blocks that are placed in the course and their settings (location, weight, and so on) should be included.	None
Include filters	This specifies whether locally used filters should be included.	None
Include comments	This specifies whether user comments should be included.	Enrolled users
Include badges	This specifies whether user badges should be included.	Enrolled users/activities
Include calendar events	This specifies whether calendar events should be included.	Enrolled users
Include user completion details	If set, course completion and progress tracking information will be backed up.	Enrolled users
Include course logs	This specifies whether log files should be included in the archive. Beware that log files can enlarge the backup files significantly.	Enrolled users
Include grade history	Moodle keeps a history of grade changes. Specify whether these should be included in the backup.	Enrolled users
Include question bank	This specifies whether a question bank should be included. If excluded, any quiz activities will also be excluded.	None
Include groups and groupings	This specifies whether information about groups and groupings is included.	None

Backup default values

By default, all options are available for selection to all users who have the appropriate permissions in the course context. If you wish to either change the default values and/or lock certain settings (such as **Include course logs**, as shown in the previous screenshot), go to **Courses | Backups | General backup defaults**:

General backup settings			
Include users backup | backup_general_users	☑ Default: Yes Sets the default for whether to include users in backups.		☐ Locked
Anonymise information backup | backup_general_anonymize	☐ Default: No If enabled all information pertaining to users will be anonymised by default.		☑ Locked
Include role assignments backup | backup_general_role_assignments	☑ Default: Yes If enabled by default roles assignments will also be backed up.		☐ Locked
Include activities and resources backup | backup_general_activities	☑ Default: Yes Sets the default for including activities in a backup.		☐ Locked
Include blocks backup | backup_general_blocks	☑ Default: Yes Sets the default for including blocks in a backup.		☐ Locked

For every single setting, there are two checkboxes. The first represents the default of the setting, whereas, the second value indicates whether it is locked or not. Locking allows you to force certain settings, for instance, the exclusion of users.

Content-only backup versus full-course backup

There are usually two types of course backups that you are likely to perform:

- Content-only backups
- Full-course backups

If you wish to pass a course on to another user or make it available for download, a **content-only backup** is the best option. Another use case is to create a new instance of a course for oneself, for example, taking a course backup from one semester to use in a different semester. As the name suggests, the content-only backup only contains content that can be passed on to another person without transferring any information about its users, roles, grades, and so on. To perform a content-only backup, you have to deselect **Include enrolled users**. You can see from the preceding table that this option is a prerequisite for most other backup options. When you publish courses on a community hub (refer to *Chapter 16, Moodle Networking*), you will also create a content-only backup.

By default, users with teaching rights can only perform content-only backups. This can be changed via the `moodle/backup:userinfo` capability, but it should be done with care.

If you wish to back up a course for potential recovery purposes, you should create a **full-course backup**, which includes user data (for example, forum posts), course data, and user information. To do this, you can leave all the settings in their default values, except **Include grade history**. You can turn off the **Jump to final step** button.

If you wish to back up the log information of the course as well, the **Include course logs** setting has to be enabled. Bear in mind that logs can be very large and often exceed multiple gigabytes when backing up all the courses.

Whether you choose to create a content-only or a full-course backup, Moodle will automatically include the configuration of a course. However, you might experience problems with content that's created by third-party add-ons. If you encounter any issues, you will have to exclude these items from the backup. Ideally, you should report the issue on the tracker (`https://tracker.moodle.org`) so that the maintainer of the module can fix any shortcomings and the contributed module can be included in your backup again.

Schema settings

All learning resources and activities are shown in the order in which they appear in the course. This also includes orphaned content, that is, resources and activities that have been placed in a section that is not shown in the course. If the **Include activities** parameter has been deactivated on the previous screen, only resources are available for inclusion. By default, all the available elements are selected. If you wish to exclude any individual items, you have to deselect them. Additionally, you can exclude/include all the items of a section by selecting/deselecting the section name itself. For instance, in the following screenshot, Topics **2** to **4** and the video resource have been excluded from the backup.

Moodle distinguishes between **course content** and **user data**. For example, in a forum activity, the forum description and all its settings are classified as course content, whereas, all topics, posts, and replies to a forum are classified as user data. If **Include enrolled users** has been left activated on the initial setup screen, user data can be included/excluded for each selected activity and resource. Selecting **Show type options** lets you select the **All** or **none** activities of a particular type.

Select	All / None (Show type options)	
Select	All / None	
General ☑	User data	☑
News forum 📧 ☑	-	☑
Questionnaire 📢 ☑	-	⬜
Topic 1 ☑	User data	☑
A forum 📧 ☑	-	☑
A file 📄 ☑	-	☑
A video 📹 ⬜	-	☑
Assignment 📝 ☑	-	☑
Topic 2 ⬜	User data	☑
Topic 3 ⬜	User data	☑
Topic 4 ⬜	User data	☑
Topic 5 ☑	User data	☑
Hidden file 🧩 ☑	-	☑

Confirmation and review

The third screen lets you choose the backup filename and review the items to be included in the archive.

The default **Filename** is `backup-<type>-<format>-<course name/id>-<year><month><day>-<hour><minute>[-nu].mbz`.

Currently `<type>` is always set to **moodle2**, and the only value supported for `<format>` at the moment is **course**. The optional `-nu` parameter stands for no users.

If you have opted to create **IMS Common Cartridge** as the backup form, the `.imscc` extension will be used instead of `.mbz`.

1. Initial settings ▶ 2. Schema settings ▶ **3. Confirmation and review** ▶ 4. Perform backup ▶ 5. Complete

Filename

Filename*	backup-moodle2-course-6-php-20141101-1127.mbz

The additional **Backup settings** section shows which item has been selected and deselected on the initial settings screen. The **Included items** section indicates with a green tick all resources and activities that will be included as well as any user data that will be part of the course backup. A red cross means that the item has been deselected, whereas, a red cross followed by a lock indicates that it wasn't possible to select the item since a prerequisite has not been fulfilled.

Finalizing a backup

Once you press the **Perform backup** button, the Moodle course archive will be created.

The actual archive file is saved in **Course backup area**. This can take a few minutes depending on the size of the data being backed up. If the **Anonymize user data** setting has been chosen at the beginning, the backup file will be placed in **User private backup area**.

After completion, a brief status message is shown as well as technical information and warnings. You will have to take appropriate actions if this contains any errors or warnings.

Moodle creates a bespoke file format for backups, known as the Moodle Backup Format, using the `.mbz` extension. A Moodle backup file is a compressed file (in the `.tgz` format), consisting of an XML file (which describes the content of the file) and the actual user, course, and log data.

Backups sometimes fail with regard to large courses. The cause is usually that the backup process runs out of time or memory. This usually happens on commercial web hosts that are not dedicated to Moodle. If this happens, increase the `max_execution_time` value in your `php.ini` file.

The course restore

To restore an entire course or parts thereof, use the **Restore** link within a course or in the course category screen. You will be directed to the area where both course backups, private, that is, anonymized, backups and automated backups are stored. Additionally, you can import backup files via the file picker.

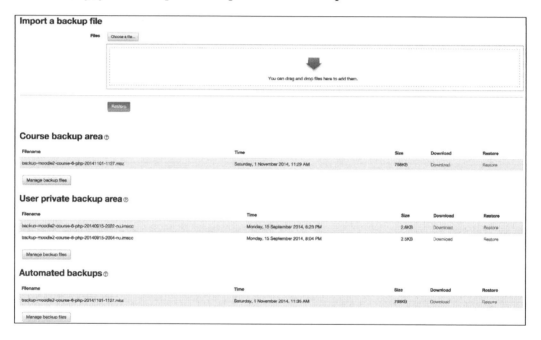

In the preceding example, a single course is present in the course backup area, called `backup-moodle2-course-6-20141101-1127.mbz`. From its name, we already know that the course ID is number 6 and was backed up on November 1, 2014 at 11.27.

Select the **Restore** link besides a backup file to kick off the recovery process. Like the backup, the restore procedure goes through a number of steps. The first screen displays information about the course backup (type, format, mode, backup date/time, Moodle version, backup version, and the URL of the `.mbz` file), backup settings (identical to the initial settings in the backup), and the course details. Once you have confirmed this screen, you have to specify the destination of where to recover the backup.

The restore destination

There are various options to restore a course backup:

1. Restore as a new course.
2. Restore into this course and merge the backup into this course.
3. Restore into this course, delete the contents of this course, and then restore it.
4. Restore into an existing course and merge the backup into the existing course.
5. Restore in an existing course, delete the contents of the existing course, and then restore it.

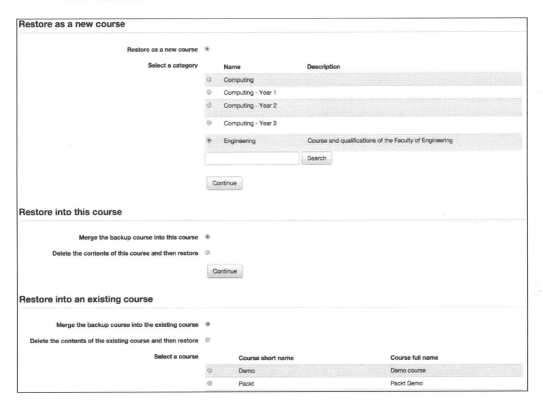

If you wish to **Restore as a new course**, you will have to select a category in which the new course will be created. If the number of categories exceeds 20, you will have to use the provided search facility. Alternatively, you can choose the current course as the destination (**Restore into this course**). You can either combine the current course content with the backup (**Merge the backup course into this existing course**) or replace it (**Delete the contents of this course and then restore**). If you choose the merging option and an activity or resource with the same name exists, both will be kept and not overridden. The third option is to restore the course into another existing course, which you have to select. The same options (merge and replace) exist to restore the backup in the current course. Make sure you click on the correct **Continue** button before you proceed.

Restore settings

The restore settings screen shows all the available options that have been selected during the backup process (refer to the preceding *Initial settings* section). As shown earlier, the choices made here dictate the types of data that will be recovered and which type of content will be offered for further selection. Also, most options have prerequisites that are identical to their backup counterparts.

The backup schema

The backup schema lets you specify a number of course settings. If you restore the backup to an existing course, you have the option to modify the existing settings. These are **Course name**, **Course short name**, and **Course start date**. You can further choose to **Keep current roles and enrolments** (if this is a part of the backup), **Keep current groups and groupings** (if stored in backup), and use the course settings of the backup file instead of the current ones (**Overwrite course configuration**).

Additionally, you have to chose which content and user data has to be included in the recovery procedure. The selection mechanism is very similar to the backup equivalent that was described earlier. By default, all the data that is present is selected. If you wish to narrow down the data to be restored, you have to deselect items manually.

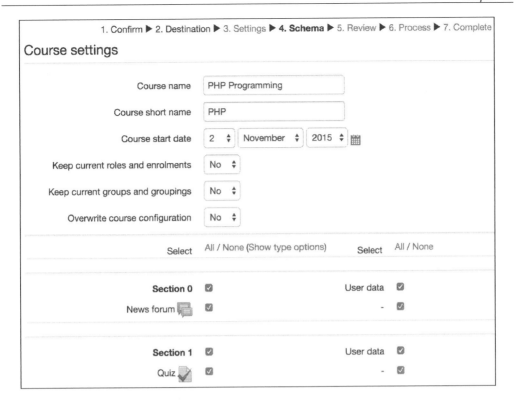

Finalizing a restore

Once you have confirmed the **Schema** screen by clicking on the **Perform restore** button, any selected data will be recovered to the chosen destination. After completion, a brief summary message is shown.

If you see a topic heading labeled **Orphaned activities** in your recovered courses, go to the course settings and increase the number of topics. If you cancel a restore operation halfway, a course called **Course restoration** in progress might be displayed. It is usually safe to delete this course.

The course Import

It is sometimes necessary to copy data from one course to another. To achieve this, Moodle provides the import course data feature. However, unlike the backup function, it will not import user data, such as assignment submissions or forum posts. It will only import the structure of activities, blocks, and filters. For example, you might want to import a single quiz from one course to another.

Teachers are allowed to import content from courses for which they have editing rights; as an administrator, this restriction does not apply. This mechanism bypasses the requirement for a backup and restore procedure if you want to copy course content from one course to another and do not require user data.

First, select the **Import** link from the **Course administration** section. Here, you have to select a course that you wish to import content from. If the list exceeds 10 courses (or whatever has been specified when you go to **Courses | Backups | General import defaults**), you will have to use the provided search facility. You can also select the current course. This way, you can duplicate activities.

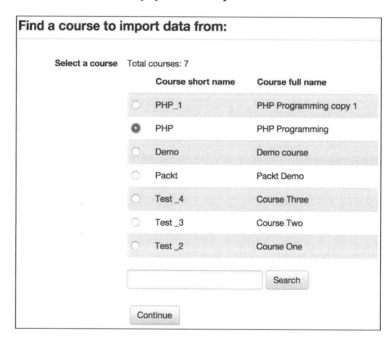

Next, you have to choose whether you wish to import activities and resources, blocks, filters, calendar events, the question bank and/or groups and groupings:

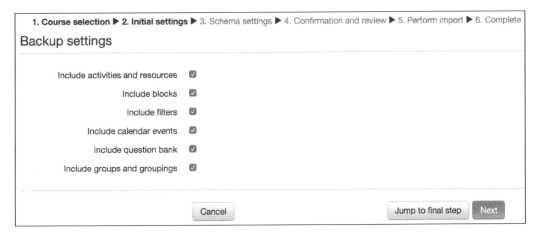

For activities, a familiar selection screen will be shown next. If you choose either filters or blocks, all their content and settings will be copied, that is, no selections will be possible.

As usual, a **Review** screen has to be confirmed with the **Perform import** button before the copying starts, and a concluding summary message will be displayed.

Site-level backups

So far, we have covered how to backup a single course. The site-level backup performs the same operation for every course in the system, including hidden courses and the front page, which is also a course (the name of the front page backup uses the name of the site).

Backup settings

To schedule site backups, go to **Courses | Backups | Automated backup setup**. You will see a number of settings:

Setting	Description
Active	Turns automatic backups on and off (default). Make sure that your backup is activated! You can further set the backup mode to Manual, which allows its execution via the CLI (refer to the command after this table).
Schedule	Specify the days of the week on which the backup has to run.
Execute at	Specify the time of the day that the backup is executed.
Automated backup storage	By default, all backups are stored in Course backup file area of each course. If you wish to keep all the backups in the same location, you have to select the specified directory for automated backups. It is also possible to save the backups in both locations (Course backup file area and specified directory). This will take up twice the storage. For the latter two options, you have to specify the Save to value.
Save to	Specify the full (absolute) path to the directory, and make sure that the access rights are set to writable.
Maximum number of backups kept	Specify the number of backups to be kept. Beware that a large number will have an impact on disk usage. Older versions will be deleted automatically.
Delete backups older than	Backups older than the specified number of days will be deleted automatically.
Minimum number of backups kept	Backups of older or inactive courses will be removed with the previous setting. To avoid this, specify the number of backups you wish to keep.
Use the course name in backup filename	Toggle that switches between the course ID and course name for the default backup filename.
Skip hidden courses	If selected, hidden courses will be excluded from the backup (default).
Skip courses not modified since	Select the number of days to exclude courses that have not be altered since.
Skip courses not modified since previous backup	If selected, only courses that have been changed since the previous backup will be included. This is the most disk space and time-efficient setting. Make sure logging is activated in order to support this mode.

The remainder of the settings page covers **Automated backup settings** that specifies which elements will be included in the backup. These are identical to the initial backup settings, except the anonymize option, which has been excluded.

For the backup to start automatically at the specified time, the cron process has to be set up correctly, which was covered in *Chapter 2, The Moodle System*. Alternatively, you can initiate the backup process via the CLI. The command execution from the shell or for the inclusion in scripts is as follows:

```
sudo -u <apache_user> /usr/bin/php admin/cli/automated_backups.php
```

The script has to be run as an Apache user, usually `www-data`. In the preceding example, it is executed from the main Moodle application directory. The script executes the same script that is called by the cron process.

The recovery of courses is identical to restoring data from course-level backup archives.

Backup reports and notifications

As a Moodle administrator, it is your duty to ensure that the backup execution has been successful. For this purpose, Moodle provides a backup report, which you can find by going to **Reports** | **Backups**.

Last execution log

Course	Time taken			Status	Next backup
Packt	1 Nov, 11:59	-	1 Nov, 11:59	OK	8 Nov, 11:35
Demo course	1 Nov, 11:59	-	1 Nov, 11:59	OK	8 Nov, 11:35
Packt Demo	1 Nov, 11:59	-	1 Nov, 11:59	OK	8 Nov, 11:35
PHP Programming	1 Nov, 11:59	-	1 Nov, 11:59	OK	8 Nov, 11:35
Course One	1 Nov, 11:59	-	1 Nov, 11:59	OK	8 Nov, 11:35
Course Two	1 Nov, 11:59	-	1 Nov, 11:59	OK	8 Nov, 11:35
Course Three	1 Nov, 11:59	-	1 Nov, 11:59	OK	8 Nov, 11:35

The report provides details for each course being backed up, namely, **Time taken** (start and end time), **Status (OK or ERROR)**, and the date and time of **Next Backup**.

Courses in which there hasn't been any activity for 30 days, that is, no changes have been made to the course content and no users have used the course, are excluded from the automated backup, and the status is shown as **SKIPPED**.

As a Moodle administrator, you will receive an e-mail after the execution of the scheduled site-level backup has been completed. It provides details on the total number of courses backed up and a split of how many course backups were okay, had an error, are unfinished, and were skipped. Make sure your e-mail settings have been configured properly (refer to *Chapter 9, Moodle Configuration*). It is highly recommended that you check the content of this e-mail every day.

The backup strategy

There are a number of issues to consider when running automatic site-wide Moodle backups:

- **Backup content**: Make sure that everything included in the archives is needed and anything that is not required is excluded. For instance, do you have to back up the entire log file every night?

- **Backup size**: The size of the backup files can be potentially huge (multiple gigabytes). Ensure that you only keep the number of backups that are required and your setup can cope with.

- **Backup timing**: The backup operation is a CPU and hard disk-intensive operation. Make sure that you schedule it when the load on the site is relatively low. If you run multiple sites on the same server, it is a good idea to time-stagger the backups or create a script that makes of the described CLI. An alternative approach is to set up a separate webserver dedicated just to run the backups.

- **Backup frequency**: Do you need seven daily backups or are weekly backups sufficient? Are there periods (such as weekends) when you can switch off the backup facility altogether?

- **Backup location**: By default, all backup files are saved to the respective courses, which means that the backups are held on the same server as Moodle itself. If you have to recover multiple courses, you will have to locate each archive separately, which is potentially a very time consuming exercise.

You might want to consider backing up on an external device (tape, external disk, NAS drive, SAN, and so on). An alternative to this is to mount a backup device and include its content in the organization-wide backup.

Drawbacks of site-level backups

Site-level backups are a great way to automate course backups and make the lives of individual teachers and instructors easier. However, there are a number of drawbacks that should be stressed on:

- Course backups are potentially very expensive in terms of time and CPU usage.

- It is not uncommon for backups to time out, especially on commercially hosted systems that are not dedicated to Moodle.

- If teachers and instructors run their own backups, there is a likelihood of duplication of archives, which should be avoided if possible.

As the name suggests, you only have to back up courses, not the entire system. While this is sufficient if you have to recover a simple course or a number of activities, it does not provide a solution to the scenario when the entire system has to be restored. You should not use the course backup facility as your sole backup system. Instead, system-level backups should be used as a supplement, which we will look at next.

System-level backups

System-level backups cannot be configured or executed from within Moodle. Instead, they will have to be set up on the system (shell) level. If your system is hosted externally, there is a possibility that you will not have access to the system level, which will prevent you from performing this type of backup. Unless the host already runs system-level backups on your behalf, it is time to change to another provider!

There are two types of system backups that are not mutually exclusive:

- **Moodle backups**: These create an archive of Moodle itself, the course content, and user data.

- **Snapshots**: These create an image of the system, which is used for disaster recovery purposes, that is, if the system has to be rolled back in its totality.

Moodle backups

Moodle distinguishes between the application software itself and the data that is stored in it. The advantage of this separation becomes apparent when creating backups: a software backup is only required when an update has been installed or customization is taking place, whereas, data has to be backed up more frequently.

The Moodle software

Backing up the Moodle software itself is straightforward. All you have to do is to create a copy of the directory and all its subdirectories where the Moodle software is installed (usually called `moodle`). Most administrators would create a single archive of the directory for easier handling (in Unix, use the tar command with the `-cvf` parameter called `tar -cvf <backupfile>`). This step is usually only required before a system upgrade or when you need to archive your entire system.

The Moodle data

Moodle stores its data in two separate locations:

- **Moodle database**: Most content is stored in the Moodle database. You can either use the export feature of `phpMyAdmin` (if installed) or use the following `mysqldump` shell command for MySQL to create a single backup file:

```
mysqldump -u <username> -p [-h <databasehost>] -C -Q -e -a
<database> > <backup-file>.sql
```

  - The `<username>` option has to be replaced with the `-p` database username and will ask you for a password, and `-h <databasehost>` is only required if the database is located on a separate server. The `<database>` option is the name of the database, and `<backup-file>` is the name of the archive to be created. It is common practice to use the `.sql` extension.
  - To recover the database dump, use the following `mysql` shell command:

```
mysql -p <database> < <backup-file>.sql
```

> For more information on `mysql` and `mysqldump`, check out the reference sites at `http://www.mysql.com/`. For other database types, refer to the respective administration guides.

- **Moodle data directory ($CFG->dataroot)**: This is where all the course content resides, for instance, assignments, user profiles pictures, forum posts, and so on. Like the Moodle system, all that has to be done is create a copy of the directory and all its subdirectories. Most administrators would create a single tarball of the directory for simpler handling (in Unix, use the TAR command with the `-cvf` parameters).

> It is important to stop Apache while performing the backup to guarantee that the content is not getting out of sync.

The advantage of this approach is that it is less resource-intensive, can be scripted, and recovery of the full Moodle system is far more straightforward. However, it is impossible to retrieve individual activities without setting up a temporary server, as is possible with course backups.

Snapshot creation

The creation of snapshots is only briefly mentioned for completeness as it is not a Moodle administrator role but a system administrator task. However, you should make sure that such a mechanism is set up in case of any hardware failures or as a way to run a reliable backup of your system.

A snapshot is basically an image of the entire partition on the hard disk that contains the Moodle software itself as well all the data (database and data directory). The advantage of the snapshot is that the entire system can be rolled back to the point when the image was created. However, any data that has been added or modified since this point in time will be overridden. Snapshots cannot be used to recover a single course or parts thereof, but can only be used for a full replacement of the system.

No matter what combination of backups you choose, frequently verify that the backup procedure is actually working. There is nothing worse than a false sense of security, that is, assuming that all your data is backed up when it isn't!

Uses of backup and restore

While the prime purpose of backups is the recovery of data in case of loss, there are a number of applications that can be carried out using some of the techniques covered in this chapter. We are going to briefly describe two of them:

The year-end procedure

Most organizations have some sort of year-end procedure in place. This might be at the end of an academic year, a term, financial year, or in the case of roll-on-roll-off setups, on a monthly basis. Given the nature and importance of the procedure, it is vital that each step is planned well in advance. The key considerations are:

- When do you run the year-end procedure?
- What has to be done?
- Who is involved?
- Where will the archives go?

The following is a list of some typical steps that might or might not apply to your setup. It gives you an idea of how such a procedure may look and demonstrates the importance of the backup facility:

- **Archive**: Create full backups of all courses and even consider including a system backup. Make sure that archives are stored on a separate medium.

- **Grade export**: Export grades course by course. Print, transfer, and store grades on your student management information system.

- **Course reset**: Use the reset feature at the course level to remove any user data (resetting courses can also be done in the batch mode. Refer to the *Managing courses in bulk* section in *Chapter 4, Course Management*).

- **Delete users**: Remove users who have left the organization or disable their accounts.

- **Next year preparation**: Hide or delete obsolete courses and add new courses. Add new users and assign roles to courses.

Course templates

There is often a requirement to create a course template, which is used for the creation of multiple courses. This might be in an organization that puts emphasis on the homogeneity of course structure and layout or an education establishment that wants to simplify the work of their course creators. The steps to achieve this are as follows:

1. Create a course that will become your course template.

2. Add all the elements (activities, resources, filters, blocks, and so on) to the course, change its settings, and arrange the content as required.

3. Create a content-only backup of the course.

4. You can now use the restore mechanism to create as many courses from this template as you wish (this operation can also be done in the batch mode. Refer to the *Managing courses in bulk* section in *Chapter 4, Course Management*).

5. Optionally, you can grant users appropriate rights to the course so that they can use the import facility.

Summary

In this chapter, you learned about the various Moodle backup alternatives. You learned how to create course-level, site-level, and system-level backups as well as data recovery from each type. It is important that your Moodle backup strategy fits in with your organization's overall disaster recovery plan. We also saw some applications that make use of the backup and restore facilities.

Moodle offers a good range of backup and restore options. However, there are sometimes problems with some of the built-in backup and recovery operations. The common causes for problems are timeouts, memory overload, archives that cannot be read, and third-party add-ons. Be aware that these issues exist, and run test recoveries to be on the safer side.

14
Moodle Admin Tools

Moodle ships with a number of administration tools that are not directly accessible via the familiar web interface. There are two types of Moodle "hidden" admin tools that you have at your disposal as part of a standard Moodle installation:

- **Web-based admin tools**: These are tools that can be accessed via the web interface, but you will have to manually enter the URL in order to make use of these unsupported utilities

- **Command Line Interface (CLI)**: The CLI is a built-in mechanism that allows us to automate certain processes via the command line or shell scripts

A powerful alternative to CLI is called **Moosh**, which stands for Moodle Shell. We will explain the way Moosh works and will provide a couple of useful examples. Finally, we will cover another useful external tool called **Adminer**, which lets you manage the underlying database directly from within Moodle.

Web-based admin tools

We have grouped internal web tools into three categories:

- **Upgrade tools**: These include the assignment upgrade helper as well as a multilang upgrade tool

- **Database tools**: These transfer databases from one Moodle server to another, perform search-and-replace operations on text strings in the entire database, and convert MyISAM to InnoDB

- **Other tools**: This category includes a test course generator and a basic health check

Upgrade tools

These tools are usually only applied once. After the upgrade of a particular functionality has been successful, the tool can usually be removed via the **Uninstall** option in **Plugins | Admin tools | Manage admin tools**.

The Assignment Upgrade tool converts assignments from version 2.2 or below to the new assignment activity. It can be accessed in `admin/tool/assignmentupgrade` or directly via **Assignment upgrade helper**. Once called, you will have to select **List assignments that have not been upgraded**. All assignments will be listed and you have the option to upgrade these automatically. Once this has been completed, it is recommended you remove, or at least disable, the **Assignment 2.2** activity in **Plugins | Activity modules | Manage activities**.

Another upgrade tool that is part of your Moodle installation is called **Multilang upgrade**. It can be called via `admin/tool/multilangupgrade`. The multilang HTML syntax was changed a while ago and is not supported anymore (see also the *Localization* section in *Chapter 9, Moodle Configuration*). If any of your users still use the old format, you will need to run this tool once.

Multilang upgrade

The multilang filter syntax was changed in 1.8 and so the <lang> tag is not supported any more.

Example: <span lang="en" class="multilang">Hello!</span><span lang="es" class="multilang">Hola!</span>

Do you want to upgrade the syntax in all existing texts now?

         [Continue]   [Cancel]

Progress:

Rebuilding course cache...

...finished

         [Continue]

Database tools

If you have to move the database of a Moodle instance from one server to another or migrate another Moodle system, you have two broad options. You can either create a database dump manually or via the Adminer tool covered later, or you can use the built-in **database transfer** facility. Your migration tool is available at `admin/tool/ dbtransfer`.

Transfer this Moodle database to another server

This script will transfer the entire contents of this database to another database server. It is often used for migration of data to different database type.

▼ Target database

Type*	Improved MySQL (native/mysqli) ◆
Database host*	127.0.0.1
Database name*	packt2
Database user*	packt2
Database password*	•••••••••• ☐ Unmask
Tables prefix	mdl_
Port	
Unix socket	

▼ Options

Enable maintenance mode ⑦	☑

You will need to provide the details of the database to which the content of the current database will be copied. These settings are identical to the ones applied during installation (see *Chapter 1, Moodle Installation*).

You further have the option to **Enable maintenance mode**, which will turn on maintenance mode during and after the migration. If used, you will have to manually remove the `climaintenance.html` file afterwards.

A tool related to the database migration facility is **DB search and replace**. After you have moved your system to another location, your URL might have changed. Any user who has been using fixed URLs anywhere in their content now faces dead links. As the administrator, you have a script at hand where you can replace any text in the underlying database, except a few tables such as log, session and event tables. You can find the script at `admin/tool/replace`.

Search and replace text throughout the whole database

This script is not supported, always make complete backup before proceeding!
This operation can not be reverted!

Several tables are not updated as part of the text replacement. This include configuration, log, events, and session tables.

▼ Collapse all

▼ DB search and replace

Search whole database for*	http://packt.ab.local
	usually previous server URL
Replace with this string*	http://packt2.ab.local
	usually new server URL
Shorten result if necessary	☐

▼ Confirm

I understand the risks of this operation*	☑

Yes, do it!

The last option, labeled **I understand the risks of this operation**, indicates the potential risk of the execution — unless you are 100% certain that the replacements will not have any impact on the system, you had better stay away from it. Once completed, the script will display all executed SQL queries.

The last database tool only applies to MySQL and is only applicable when you are migrating a system that is still using the legacy MyISAM format. If that is the case, any tables will be converted from MyISAM to InnoDB. This tool can found at `admin/tool/innodb`.

Chapter 10

Other tools

In order to test performance or to find out how your system copes with large courses, you have the ability to use the unsupported course generator, which you will find at `admin/tool/generator`. In order to use it, you will have to make sure debugging is turned on (**Development | Debugging**).

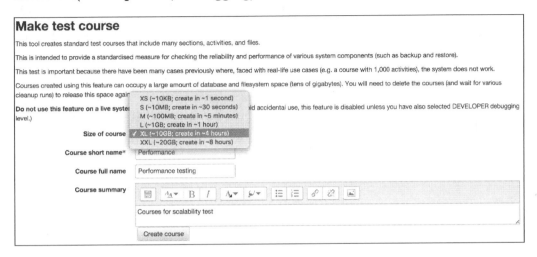

You can select **Size of course** as well as the **Course short name**, **Course full name**, and **Course summary** options. Beware that the generation of large courses may take hours and will have a significant negative impact on your system performance. It is not recommended to perform this operation in production environments.

Another tool, which might come in useful, is called **Health center** and can be accessed at `admin/tool/health`. It shows any potential problems and, if possible, provides advice on how to resolve the issues.

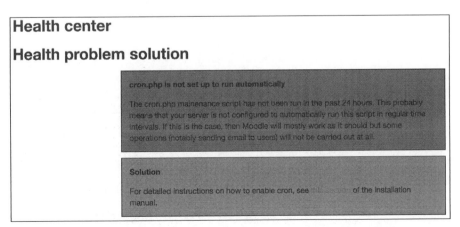

While this does not replace a professional Moodle health check as offered by Moodle partners or a penetration test of your system, it covers a number of typical problems in new setups.

Command Line Interface (CLI)

We have already come across the CLI during the installation chapter when we also dealt with upgrades. However, the CLI has a few more tricks up its sleeve, which we will deal with next.

First of all let us look at the way you call any CLI scripts, which are either located in `admin/cli/*` or in the sub-folder of plugins that offer a CLI option—for example, `auth/ldap/cli`. To call a CLI script, follow the following notation:

```
sudo -u <apache_user> /usr/bin/php admin/cli/<script>.php
```

Your `<apache_user>` is usually `www-data` or `apache`. Every CLI script has a `--help` parameter that offers additional information and also describes calling options. The following is a list of some useful CLI commands. For all others commands, have a look in their respective CLI directories. We do not list any parameters here as these are explained well in the `--help` options.

PHP Script	Purpose
`alternative_component_cache`	Intended for clustered sites that do not want to use a shared cachedir for their component cache.
`automated_backups`	Execute automatic backups ignoring the set schedule.
`backup`	Back up a single course to a named location.
`check_database_schema`	Validation that the current database structure matches the `install.xml` file.
`cron`	Runs the `cron` command (see *Chapter 1, Moodle Installation*).
`fix_course_sequence`	Checks and ensures that course modules and sections reference each other correctly. Only run when you experience inconsistencies.
`fix_deleted_users`	Sometimes users get deleted incorrectly. Only run when you experience inconsistencies.
`fix_orphaned_question_categories`	Script that fixes orphaned question categories.
`install`	Installs Moodle (see *Chapter 1, Moodle Installation*).
`install_database`	Installs Moodle in an empty database. `config.php` must already exist.

PHP Script	Purpose
`maintenance`	Handle maintenance mode. Custom messages are stored in `climaintenance.html`.
`mysql_collation`	MySQL collation conversion.
`mysql_compressed_rows`	Detection of row size problems in MySQL InnoDB tables.
`mysql_engine`	Converts MySQL tables to a different engine.
`purge_caches`	Clears all system caches.
`reset_password`	Resets a user's password, including the admin account.
`upgrade`	Upgrades to a newer version (*Chapter 1, Moodle Installation*).

Additional CLI scripts on `moodle.org` might come in useful. Examples are updating user pictures via the command line or restoring courses.

While useful for the few operations that are supported, the CLI provides a relatively restricted set of commands. Moosh, which we will cover next, overcomes this limitation.

Moosh – the Moodle shell

Before you can make use of Moosh, you will have to install it (see *Chapter 8, Moodle Plugins*). Once it's been installed, you have a vast number of commands (at the time of writing over 80!) at your disposal.

The general syntax of Moosh is as follows:

```
moosh <command> <options>
```

To give you an idea of the types of things you can do with Moosh, we will show you a number of examples.

Tasks	Commands	Description
Clear cache	`moosh cache-clear`	This is the equivalent of `purge_caches` using CLI
Show all plugin types	`moosh info-plugins`	Displays a list of all installed plugins and their installation location.
Create a user	`moosh user-create test`	Create a user with user name test.
Create 10 users	`moosh user-create test{1..10}`	This type of enumeration can be used with a number of Moosh commands.

Tasks	Commands	Description
Create a user with some optional values	`moosh user-create --email mcbuchner@ null.com --city "Heidelberg" --country DE --firstname "Alex" --lastname "Büchner" mcbuchner`	All values are supported; this is just a sample.
Show all files in a course	`moosh file-list course=99`	Outputs information on all files in course with ID 99. There are more file-related commands, such as showing the system path of a file or the ability to upload files directly.

Once you combine Moosh commands with standard shell commands via pipes and streams, you have a powerful arsenal of commands at hand. For example, you might want to find all backups that are larger than 10 MB, archive them, and reclaim the space.

The following example output of Moosh shows the output of the `config-get` command, which lists the value(s) of all configuration settings in Moodle:

```
root@debian:/var/www/packt# moosh config-get
stdClass Object
(
    [rolesactive] => 1
    [auth] => ldap,email,mnet,webservice
    [auth_pop3mailbox] => INBOX
    [enrol_plugins_enabled] => manual,guest,self,cohort,ldap,database,meta,paypal
    [theme] => more
    [filter_multilang_converted] => 1
    [siteidentifier] => wjjgHUmHsz85R0ihiJw2zoB3PIERRhmRpackt.ab.local
    [backup_version] => 2015111600
    [backup_release] => 3.0
    [mnet_dispatcher_mode] => strict
    [sessiontimeout] => 7200
    [stringfilters] =>
    [filterall] => 0
    [texteditors] => atto,tinymce,textarea
    [mnet_localhost_id] => 1
    [mnet_all_hosts_id] => 2
    [siteguest] => 1
    [siteadmins] => 2
    [themerev] => 1451319030
    [jsrev] => 1451319030
    [gdversion] => 2
    [licenses] => unknown,allrightsreserved,public,cc,cc-nd,cc-nc-nd,cc-nc,cc-nc-sa,cc-sa
    [version] => 2015111600
    [enableoutcomes] => 1
    [usecomments] => 1
    [usetags] => 1
    [enablenotes] => 1
    [enableportfolios] => 1
```

For a full list of well over 80 commands and hundreds of options, please refer to the Moosh site at `http://moosh-online.com/commands/`. The list is growing constantly, so make sure you have the latest version installed.

Moodle Adminer

Adminer is an open-source tool to administer different types of SQL databases. A wrapper has been created that lets you access the tool directly from within Moodle. Like Moosh, Moodle Adminer will have to be installed in your Local plugins section (see *Chapter 8*, *Moodle Plugins* for details). You will find the installer at `https://moodle.org/plugins/view.php?plugin=local_adminer`.

Once it's installed, you get access to the database management console via **Server | Moodle Adminer**. As soon as you select the link, the tool will be opened in a modal window and the underlying database used will be opened.

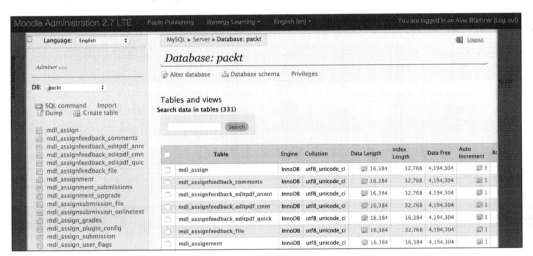

Once you have selected a database, you will be able to perform operations (such as querying, altering data, or creating an SQL dump) without any SQL knowledge. Make sure you only change data if you know what you are doing—otherwise you might introduce an inconsistency to you database and Moodle will not work as expected.

We will not go into using Adminer in detail, since this is beyond the scope of this chapter. You can find all the information you are looking for at `http://www.adminer.org/`.

Summary

In this chapter, we have covered a number of hidden and unsupported admin tools shipped with every Moodle installation. We have further dealt with the Command Line Interface as well as two popular add-ons: Moosh and Moodle Adminer. There are plenty of other tools out there, but the ones selected are by far the most popular ones.

Other ways to extend the reach of Moodle are to network it with other Moodle instances and to integrate it with other systems. We will cover these two approaches in the two remaining chapters.

15
Moodle Integration

We have already taken a look at how Moodle is highly modular, which guarantees extensibility and adaptability. We also mentioned that Moodle can be connected to other Moodle instances or Mahara and Totara Social—we will cover this in *Chapter 16, Moodle Networking*. Now, we are going to look at the integration of Moodle with other external systems via web services.

After providing a brief overview of web services and giving some application examples, you will learn about the following administrative topics:

- **Moodle and web services**: We will provide you with information on the basic concepts of Moodle web services
- **External systems controlling Moodle**: You will learn how to set up the Moodle web service for another application to control Moodle
- **Users controlling Moodle**: You will learn how to set up the Moodle web service for a user as the client
- **Mobile Moodle**: We will explain how to setup Moodle so that it can be used with the official mobile Moodle app

We will not cover any programming aspects of web services as this is not an administrative task. You will find some good documentation for users and developers at `https://docs.moodle.org/en/Web_Services`.

Web services overview

It has always been possible to extend Moodle via code (PHP and JavaScript). Due to Moodle's open source code base, there can be no limitation to what code a developer is able to modify or extend. For you as an administrator, this was not a satisfactory situation, as you have no control over what parts of Moodle are being changed and, equally important, what data is being accessed or altered.

Moodle has a number of APIs that provide an abstract layer for certain functionalities. Examples of this are the Portfolio API, Repository API, and the File API. These are great for programmers as they reduce the amount of code that has to be re-written. In addition to these interfaces, Moodle also provides us with an ever growing number of web services.

> Web services enable other systems to perform operations inside Moodle.

Why would we want this? Well, there are three main scenarios we can think of:

- Other systems in your organization, for instance, the HR system, have to trigger certain actions in your VLE—once a student has been added to the system, an account has to be created in Moodle and enrolment in a number of courses has to take place. Web services simplify this process greatly.

- Mobile apps are gaining enormous popularity with more powerful devices running iOS or Android. Any Moodle app, such as the official one by `http://moodle.org`, should be using web services to communicate with your Moodle instance. We will deal with this a little bit further into the chapter.

- The Community Hub feature requires web services. This will be covered in *Chapter 16, Moodle Networking*.

Why do you as an administrator have to care about web services when they have been designed for developers? Well, that's the other big advantage of web services. The administrator has the ability to control which system is allowed to talk to your Moodle system and which service these systems are allowed to use. This way, you can control who has access to your system and limit what they can do.

Web services in Moodle

First of all, you have to activate web services, which can be accessed by navigating to **Advanced features** | **Enable web services**. Second, you have to enable the **Web services authentication** plugin (**Plugins** | **Authentication** | **Manage authentication**). Once this has been done, go to **Plugins** | **Web services** | **Overview**, which acts as a dashboard to set up Moodle web services.

> A word of warning: Enabling web services comes with a potential security risk as you are granting access to Moodle to outside users and systems. The mantra should always be to open up as few services and functions as possible.

Moodle supports three ways of how external entities can connect via web services:

- **Enable web services for mobile devices** (we will be dealing with this later)
- **Allow an external systems to control Moodle**
- **Users as clients with token**

Two checklists are shown, one for each approach. The following screenshot shows the list for external systems—the one for token-based clients is, with one exception, a subset thereof:

Allow an external system to control Moodle

The following steps help you to set up the Moodle web services to allow an external system to interact with Moodle. This includes setting up a token (security key) authentication method.

Step	Status	Description
1. Enable web services	Yes	Web services must be enabled in Advanced features.
2. Enable protocols	None	At least one protocol should be enabled. For security reasons, only protocols that are to be used should be enabled.
3. Create a specific user		A web services user is required to represent the system controlling Moodle.
4. Check user capability		The user should have appropriate capabilities according to the protocols used, for example webservice/rest:use, webservice/soap:use. To achieve this, create a web services role with protocol capabilities allowed and assign it to the web services user as a system role.
5. Select a service		A service is a set of web service functions. You will allow the user to access to a new service. On the **Add service** page check 'Enable' and 'Authorised users' options. Select 'No required capability'.
6. Add functions		Select required functions for the newly created service.
7. Select a specific user		Add the web services user as an authorised user.
8. Create a token for a user		Create a token for the web services user.
9. Enable developer documentation	No	Detailed web services documentation is available for enabled protocols.
10. Test the service		Simulate external access to the service using the web service test client. Use an enabled protocol with token authentication. **WARNING: The functions that you test WILL BE EXECUTED, so be careful what you choose to test!**

We have already enabled web services and also have to enable protocols. Moodle supports four web services protocols—**SOAP**, **REST**, **XML-RPC**, and **AMF**. We are not going to provide any details on them; for more information, check out `https://docs.moodle.org/dev/Creating_a_web_service_client`. At least one protocol has to be enabled, which one depends entirely on the external application and the protocols supported. Clicking on the **Enabled protocols** link in the overview table when you go to **Plugins | Web services | Manage protocols** will guide you to this screen. Enable a protocol by toggling the show/hide icon in the **Enable** column. Here, **SOAP** protocol has been enabled, which is common in, but not limited to, Microsoft-based environments as shown in the following screenshot:

Manage protocols

Active web service protocols

Protocol	Version	Enable	Settings
AMF protocol	2014051200	⊘	
REST protocol	2014051200	⊘	
SOAP protocol	2014051200	⊙	
XML-RPC protocol	2014051200	⊘	

For security reasons, only protocols that are in use should be enabled.

Web services documentation	☐ Default: No
enablewsdocumentation	Enable auto-generation of web services documentation. A user can access to his own documentation on his security keys page More details. It displays the documentation for the enabled protocols only.

 Depending on the protocol chosen, you might have to install the respective PHP extension, for example, `php-soap`.

It is expected that more web service protocols will be added in the future, in particular, a Java and .Net-compatible WSDL. Now that we have enabled web services and at least one protocol, let's cover the setting up of two types of web service accesses that we have already mentioned.

Enabling web services for external systems

An external system is any application that accesses Moodle and its data in one way or the other. There are eight steps that have to be performed to complete the setup, which follow the workflow described on the web services overview screen:

Create a specific user

Each application should have a separate user account. This way, you can control the capabilities that each external system is going to use. Our user is aptly called web service.

Check user capability

Depending on the protocol you've selected, you have to allow the respective permissions for the user. You achieve this by creating a new role with any of the four capabilities, `webservice/amf:use`, `webservice/rest:use`, `webservice/soap:use`, or `webservice/xmlrpc:use`. This role has to be assigned to the web services user(s) in the **System** context.

Select a service

A service is like a defined interface that an external application can connect to. It is a set of functions, which are covered next. Selecting a service takes place when you go to **Plugins | Web services | External services**. You have to **Add** a **Custom service**:

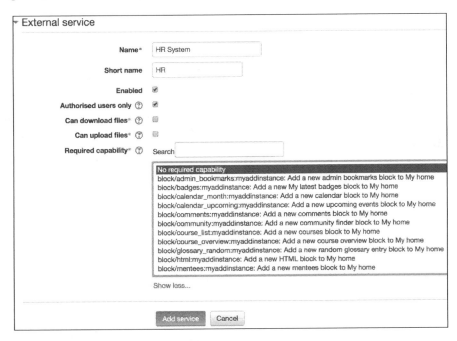

Each external service has to have **Name**, a unique **Short name**, and should be **Enabled**. A service has to be accessed via a token. The **Authorised users only** setting restricts this access to selected users. If it remains unticked, all users with the token permission can access the service.

You can also specify whether the web service **Can download files** or **Can Upload files**. In the context of our HR role, this would be useful if you also manage profile pictures via web services. You can further restrict access by specifying required capabilities that users need to have.

Once you have saved the service, select the shown **Add functions** link.

Add functions

Moodle provides a number of functions that can be accessed via web services. This number will increase in upcoming versions, for example, to support additional features in mobile devices. Each function corresponds to a capability in Moodle roles. The function(s) selected depend(s) on what tasks the external system has to perform and should be set up in liaison with the developer in charge. Since we are connecting to an HR system, we will allow a number of user-related functions:

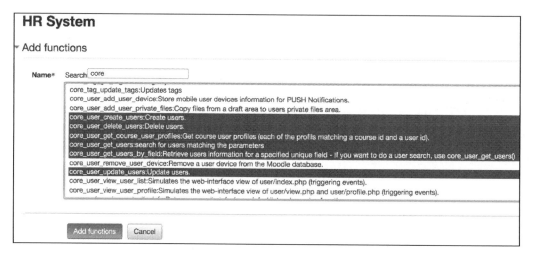

Make sure that you avoid the usage of any deprecated functions, which are labeled as such. These are supported for compatibility with older systems but should not be used as far as possible as these functions will be removed from future versions.

Once you have added the selected functions, you will be shown the required capabilities that a user has to have to access the service. Make sure these have been allowed in the role assigned to the web services user.

Add functions to the service "HR System"

Function	Description	Required capabilities	Edit
core_user_create_users	Create users.	moodle/user:create	Remove
core_user_get_users	search for users matching the parameters	moodle/user:viewdetails, moodle/user:viewhiddendetails, moodle/course:useremail, moodle/user:update	Remove
core_user_get_users_by_field	Retrieve users information for a specified unique field - If you want to do a user search, use core_user_get_users()	moodle/user:viewdetails, moodle/user:viewhiddendetails, moodle/course:useremail, moodle/user:update	Remove
core_user_get_course_user_profiles	Get course user profiles (each of the profils matching a course id and a user id).	moodle/user:viewdetails, moodle/user:viewhiddendetails, moodle/course:useremail, moodle/user:update, moodle/site:accessallgroups	Remove
core_user_delete_users	Delete users.	moodle/user:delete	Remove
core_user_update_users	Update users.	moodle/user:update	Remove

Add functions

Select a specific user

If you selected **Authorised users only** when you created the preceding service, you will have to select these user(s). This takes place when you go to **Plugins | Web services | External services** where you see a list of all the set up services. Select the **Authorised users** link, which will guide you to the familiar user selection screen. Select the web services user you created in step 1.

Once you have selected a user, Moodle will check whether the account has the appropriate settings in order to access the selected functions. If any are missing, they will be displayed under the user selection screen in the **Change settings for the authorised users** section. Clicking on a username will also allow you to restrict access to an IP address and to set an expiry date:

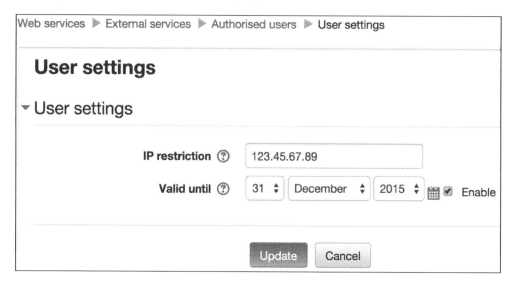

Create a token for a user

Web services use tokens for security. These are created for each user and can be added by going to **Plugins | Web services | Manage tokens**. To add a token, select a user (or multiple users), select the service to be accessed, and optionally specify an IP address (or range) and an expiry date as shown in the following screenshot:

Users will be able to access and reset their web services token by going to **User account | Security keys** in their **Preferences** if they have the `moodle/webservice:createtoken` capability.

Enable developer documentation

Moodle is able to generate documentation for developers for the selected functions in the format of the selected protocol. This is done when you set up the protocols (**Plugins | Web services | Manage protocols**) where you have to tick the **Web services documentation** option. Developers will be able to see the documentation as part of their security keys.

Test the service

Once a web service is setup, functions have been selected, and users have been assigned, it is imperative that you test the service to make sure that it works and, more importantly, that only the required functionality has been opened up that is required by the external system. This is done by navigating to **Development | Web service test client** (select **AMF test client** if you use AMF).

> Be careful with executing functions via the test client as they perform them as though they are executed for real!

First, you have to select **Authentication method** (**simple** for a username and password, **token** for a security key), **Protocol**, and **Function** to test:

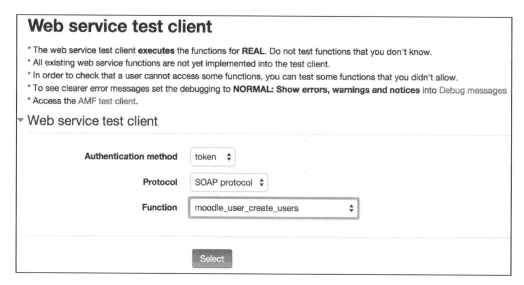

The screen that follows depends on what authentication method has been selected and which function has been chosen. Here, we used **token** and **moodle_user_create_users**:

SOAP protocol: moodle_user_create_users

▾ Web service test client

token	b231c909021b1520f77dcb17c39
username	newuser
password	Password123!
firstname	New
lastname	User
email	newuser@synergy-learning.com
customfieldtype	
customfieldvalue	

WARNING: If you press execute your database will be modified and changes can not be reverted automatically!

[Execute] [Cancel]

Once you have filled in the required values and executed the command (read the WARNING!), you will see a return value in the XML format. To receive a more meaningful message, change the **Debug messages** setting by going to **Development | Debugging** and then to **DEVELOPER**. If the result shown contains a line containing a DEBUGINFO element, an error has occurred. Otherwise, you should check that the function executed actually performed what it was supposed to (in our case, creating a user called new user).

```
URL: http://moodle2.ab.local/webservice/rest/simpleserver.php?wsusername=webservices&wspassword=packt

'<?xml version="1.0" encoding="UTF-8" ?>
<EXCEPTION class="invalid_parameter_exception">
<MESSAGE>Invalid parameter value detected, execution can not continue.</MESSAGE>
<DEBUGINFO>Username already exists: newuser</DEBUGINFO>
</EXCEPTION>
'
```

Enabling web services for users

It is sometimes necessary that users have to access web services directly instead of applications, for example, a developer who needs to execute test runs against the system. The process is a subset of steps already covered in the previous section and follows **Users as clients with token section** on the web services overview screen:

1. Select a service.

2. Add functions.

3. Check the capability of the users. In addition to the protocol use capabilities, the users have to have the `moodle/webservice:createtoken` URL allowed.

4. Test the service.

The Moodle mobile web service

Moodle has released a free app for iOS, Android and Windows Phone that allows users to interact with a Moodle system. At the time of writing this (app version 2.6) of the app supports key functionalities for participants to access certain course content, receive notifications, upload data, view grades, and interact with other users. Additional tools will be added in the very near future.

The Moodle app is an alternative to accessing Moodle via a web browser on a mobile device (a smartphone or tablet). However, it not only supports a subset of learner-centric features, but it also has the advantage that the app has been specifically designed for mobile usage and also supports offline content.

The process of enabling the Moodle app to interact with your Moodle site has been greatly simplified. Once the mobile web service has been enabled by navigating to **Plugins | Web services | Mobile**, a built-in service will be activated (refer to `https://docs.moodle.org/en/Mobile_web_services`).

Mobile

Enable web services for mobile devices enablemobilewebservice	☑ Default: No Enable mobile service for the official Moodle app or other app requesting it. For more information, read the Moodle documentation
CSS mobilecssurl	[ ] Default: Empty A CSS file to customise your mobile app interface.

It is highly recommended that you run your site over HTTPS when allowing mobile devices to access your site. The mobile app will always attempt to use a secure connection first. We covered the setting up of HTTPS in *Chapter 11, Moodle Security and Privacy*.

There is no requirement for the administrator to set up any functions or capabilities as these have already been predefined. To view the functions, check out the **Built-in services** section by going to **Plugins | Web services | External services**. When you click on the **Functions** link, you will be shown a list of all the functions that are used by the mobile web service. However, you cannot modify this list in any way. Additional functions will be added in the near future in sync with the newer versions of mobile apps.

You have also the option to **Edit** the Moodle mobile web service using the same settings as described in this section:

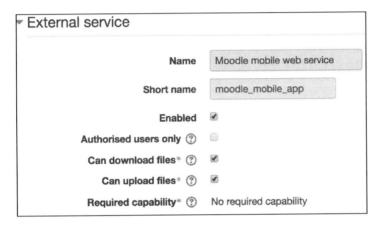

To check whether the Moodle mobile web service is working correctly, go and get your snazzy smartphone, download the Moodle Moodle app from the respective store (`https://download.moodle.org/mobile`), and enter **Site URL**, **Username**, and **Password**. If successful, you will see the landing page of your app:

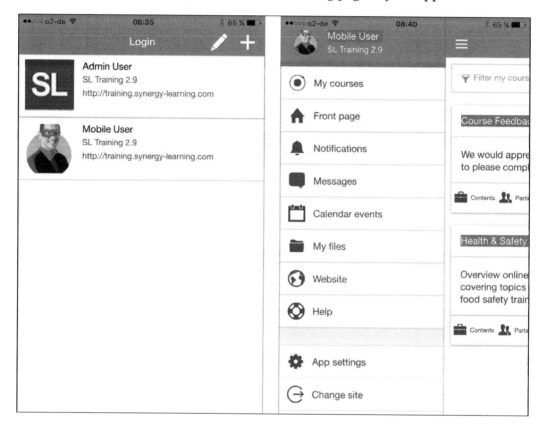

Customizing styles for the Moodle app

Once web services for mobile devices have been enabled correctly, you also have the ability to customize the look and feel of the app (refer to *Chapter 7, Moodle Look and Feel*).

You may have already spotted the **CSS** field when you navigated to **Plugins | Web services | Mobile** earlier. You need to specify the URL of a CSS file (CSS, CSS2, or CSS3). While the file(s) can be stored anywhere accessible, it is recommended that the file is located inside your Moodle installation (usually as a custom theme). Once a style has been applied, the app of the user will change next time a learner opens the app on their mobile device. There is good documentation for mobile themes at `https://docs.moodle.org/dev/Moodle_Mobile_Themes` and `https://docs.moodle.org/dev/Setting_up_your_development_environment_for_Moodle_Mobile_2`.

Mobile app notifications

Moodle Mobile supports push notifications for different mobile platforms. As soon as web services for mobile devices are turned on, a new message output type will be available when you go to **Plugins | Message outputs | Mobile notifications**. The default values connect to the public Moodle messaging server. All you need to do is to request for an access key (via the link at the bottom). This requires that your site be registered with `https://moodle.org/` (refer to the *Finalizing the installation* section in *Chapter 1, Moodle Installation*).

Mobile notifications

Airnotifier URL airnotifierurl	https://messages.moodle.net	Default: https://messages.moodle.net
	The server url to connect to to send push notifications.	
Airnotifier port airnotifierport	443	Default: 443
	The port to use when connecting to the airnotifier server.	
Mobile app name airnotifiermobileappname	com.moodle.moodlemobile	Default: com.moodle.moodlemobile
	The Mobile app unique identifier (usually something like com.moodle.moodlemobile).	
Airnotifier app name airnotifierappname	commoodlemoodlemobile	Default: commoodlemoodlemobile
	The app name identifier in Airnotifier.	
Airnotifier access key airnotifieraccesskey	2394cb72634c0cb934785674ebd577	Default: Empty
	The access key to use when connecting to the airnotifier server.	

Request access key

The public messaging server is a public Airnotifier system and, therefore, carries a degree of risk. It is possible to set up the infrastructure of your own notifications, which involves setting up a local Airnotifier server. You will find instructions and links to resources at https://docs.moodle.org/en/Mobile_app_notifications.

Here is a schematic overview of how push notifications work. APNS, WNS, and Google Cloud Messaging are their respective gateways to relay push notifications.

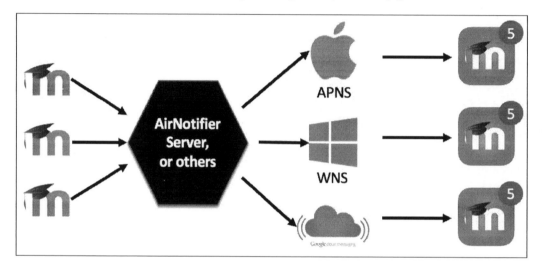

Summary

In this chapter, you learned what web services are and how they can be utilized from within Moodle. We covered the two main administrative tasks, namely setting up web services for external applications and enabling web services for users. We also talked about the enabling process of the Moodle mobile web service.

Keep an eye on the roadmap for web services as some great new features are in the pipeline (https://docs.moodle.org/dev/Web_service_API_functions), for example, web services to support SCORM packages. Also, check out the site for local plugins for the mobile app at https://docs.moodle.org/en/Moodle_Mobile_additional_features.

In the chapter to follow, we will cover another option for Moodle to communicate with other systems, namely via Moodle networking.

16
Moodle Networking

Moodle provides a unique functionality that lets you network multiple Moodle sites. This is useful in a number of contexts—for example, when you want to share resources with other VLEs, partner with another organization, or have a multi-campus setup where each site has its own Moodle setup.

After viewing an overview of Moodle Networking, you will learn about the following topics:

- **Networking prerequisites and security**: You will learn which networking components are required and how security is guaranteed.

- **Peer-to-peer networks**: You will learn how to link two Moodle sites. This feature also works with Totara, a commercial Moodle distribution for enterprise use.

- **Moodle hubs**: You will learn how to connect multiple Moodle sites to a central MNet hub.

- **Mahara or Totara Social integration**: You will learn how to set up Moodle with Mahara, a popular open-source e-portfolio system that makes use of its networking functionality. This feature also works with Totara Social, an enterprise social learning platform based on Mahara.

- **Moodle Community Hub (Moodle.net)**: You will learn how to connect to a Moodle.net (formerly known as MOOCH) and how to set up your own hub. Moodle.net doesn't use MNet per se, but it offers related functionality, which is why it is dealt with in this chapter.

Moodle Docs contain a very well written wiki on Moodle Networking and this chapter follows the document in part: https://docs.moodle.org/30/en/MNet.

Networking overview

Virtual learning environments are usually standalone systems. But learning, in addition to doing, is primarily about communication and collaboration (social constructionist theory). Moodle networking overcomes this limitation and provides a powerful facility to establish logical links among multiple Moodle sites. The following two topologies are supported:

- **Peer-to-Peer**: This layout connects two Moodle systems directly. This topology is favorable if you have two partnering organizations or one site that offers courses in which students from another site wish to enroll.

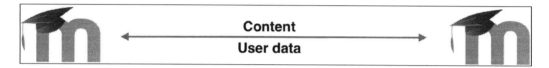

- **Moodle hub**: A hub is a Moodle server (also known as a **MNet hub**) that is configured to accept connections from other Moodle servers, and to provide a set of services to users of these other servers. This topology is favorable if you have a portal that is used for sharing learning resources or courses.

Moodle Networking supports **single sign-on (SSO)**, which provides a seamless integration of multiple Moodle systems. Security is guaranteed by fully encrypting authentication and content exchanges.

 MNet has been designed for Moodle-Moodle pairing. The plan is to replace it in the near future with OAuth2 (for authentication) and web services (for communication and data exchange).

The two topologies are not mutually exclusive and can be mixed in the same network. The following is an example of a large-scale Moodle network (courtesy of Wrexham County Borough Council), where all participating Moodle instances connect to a hub and some schools have established peer-to-peer connections.

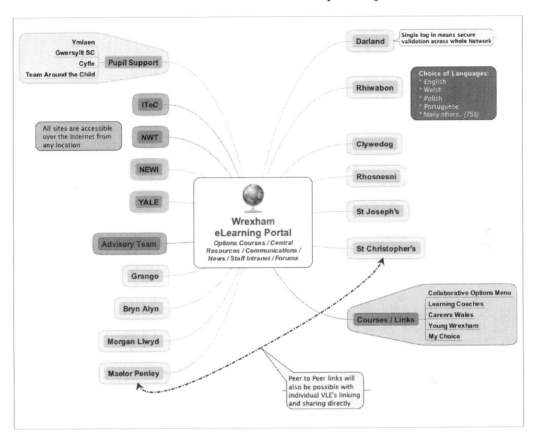

After covering some networking prerequisites and security issues, you will learn how to set up peer-to-peer networks and an MNet hub.

Networking prerequisites and security

Moodle networking requires a number of additional components to be installed on your servers that deal with secure communication and safe data exchange.

Required PHP extensions

The following elements have to be installed on all Moodle servers that are participating in the network:

- `curl`: A PHP library of calls that are specifically designed to safely fetch data from remote sites. If not installed, you have to recompile PHP and add `--with curl` when running `configure`.

- `openssl`: The OpenSSL PHP library provides encryption functionality without the need to purchase an SSL certificate (`--with openssl`).

- `xmlrpc`: A PHP library that supports remote procedure calls via XML (`--with xmlrpc`).

It is possible to add trusted hosts to Moodle, which allows them to execute calls via XML-RPC to any part of the Moodle API (**Networking | XML-RPC hosts**). This is potentially very dangerous and is only meant for developers. We will not be dealing with this functionality in this book.

To make sure whether the required PHP extensions have been installed, go to **Server | Environment** and make sure the status for all three components is **OK**.

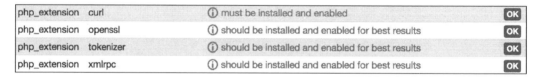

php_extension	curl	ⓘ must be installed and enabled	OK
php_extension	openssl	ⓘ should be installed and enabled for best results	OK
php_extension	tokenizer	ⓘ should be installed and enabled for best results	OK
php_extension	xmlrpc	ⓘ should be installed and enabled for best results	OK

Networking security

The above PHP extensions ensure secure communication and the safe transmission of data between participating sites. Unlike other secure web systems, neither HTTPS nor the purchase of an SSL certificate is required. Moodle will generate a certificate to encrypt the communication, which is done via PHP using the certificate mentioned earlier.

To activate Moodle networking go to **Advanced features** and turn on networking. This step has to be performed on all participating servers in the Moodle network.

Once networking has been enabled, Moodle generates a public/private key pair using OpenSSL. When you later connect to another Moodle site (which also has a set of keys), the public key is exchanged and you will have to confirm that your site will trust this public key. When the two sites exchange data, the sender will sign each request using their private key and encrypt the message with the public key of the receiver. The receiver, holder of the sender's public key and its own private key, will be able to decrypt the message and execute the request. So much for the theory. Now, back to the real world.

Go to **Networking | Settings** where you will see the public key that has been created by OpenSSL. The key has an expiry date that is 28 days from creation; after this, a new key is created (so called **key rotation**). The key can be renewed manually by using the key deletion option on the same screen.

The key expiry duration cannot be changed via a Moodle parameter, but via a configuration setting (see *Appendix, Configuration Settings*). Add `$CFG->mnetkeylifetime=365` to `config.php` to increase the expiry period to a full year to avoid regular renewal of keys.

About your server

Public key:

```
-----BEGIN CERTIFICATE-----
MIIEJDCCA4zgAwIBAgIBADANBgkqhkiG9w0BAQUFADCBwzELMAkGA1UEBhMCREUx
•••
BAoTBVBhY2t0MQ8wDQYDVQQLEwZNb29kbGUxHjAcBgNVBAMTFWh0dHA6Ly9wYWNr
dC5hYi5sb2NhbHhbDEeMBwGA1UdERMVaHR0cDovL3BhY2t0LmFiLmxxvY2FsMSkwJwYJ
c/Zjt15T4c4=
-----END CERTIFICATE-----
```

Valid until: Saturday, 9 August 2014, 5:06 PM

Delete this key

Moodle automatically rotates your keys every 28 days (by default) but you have the option to *manually* expire this key at any time. This will only be useful if you believe this key has been compromised. A replacement will be immediately automatically generated.
Deleting this key will make it impossible for other applications to communicate with you, until you manually contact each administrator and provide them with your new key.

Delete this key   [Delete]

Now that Moodle networking has been enabled and the public key has been generated, it is time to get the servers talking to each other.

Peer-to-peer networks

First, we deal with peer-to-peer networks where two Moodle servers are connected. For demonstration purposes, we have set up two sites (two peers); one is located at `http://training.synergy-learning.com/login/index.php` (Moodle) and the other at `http://totara.synergy-learning.com/login/index.php` (Totara). The two sites do not have to be in the same domain or the same organization. For example, two universities or two high schools might want to offer a collaborative course. They both have their own Moodle system in their own domain and they both control who gets access to which part of their site.

If your two sites are hosted in the same top-level domain and you are accessing both sites from the same web browser simultaneously, change the cookie prefix of one site (**Server | Session handling**) to avoid any conflicts.

Adding a peer

Go to **Networking | Manage peers** and add a new remote host you want to connect to. We are currently working on `http://training.synergy-learning.com/login/index.php` and to establish a link to the remote server we have to enter `http://totara.synergy-learning.com/login/index.php`. Then perform the same step on the other host:

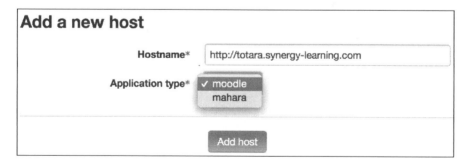

The pull-down menu offers an additional host type: **mahara**. Mahara is an open-source eportfolio system that can be integrated via the Moodle networking mechanism. We will cover this integration later in the chapter. For now, let's leave this setting at **moodle**.

Once the host has been added, enter the name of the **Site**, its **Hostname**, the level of security (**SSL verification**), and the **Public key**. (Optionally, select a **Force theme** that will be used when roaming.) Once the form has been saved, the expiry date (**Valid until**), the **IP address**, and **Cert details** of the remote server are displayed:

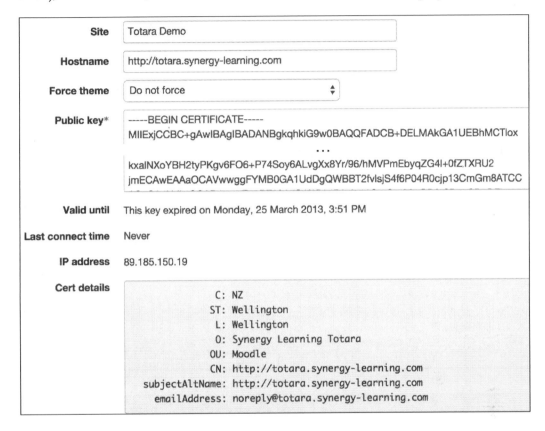

Site	Totara Demo
Hostname	http://totara.synergy-learning.com
Force theme	Do not force
Public key*	-----BEGIN CERTIFICATE----- MIIExjCCBC+gAwIBAgIBADANBgkqhkiG9w0BAQQFADCB+DELMAkGA1UEBhMCTlox ... kxaINXoYBH2tyPKgv6FO6+P74Soy6ALvgXx8Yr/96/hMVPmEbyqZG4I+0fZTXRU2 jmECAwEAAaOCAVwwggFYMB0GA1UdDgQWBBT2fvIsjS4f6P04R0cjp13CmGm8ATCC
Valid until	This key expired on Monday, 25 March 2013, 3:51 PM
Last connect time	Never
IP address	89.185.150.19
Cert details	C: NZ ST: Wellington L: Wellington O: Synergy Learning Totara OU: Moodle CN: http://totara.synergy-learning.com subjectAltName: http://totara.synergy-learning.com emailAddress: noreply@totara.synergy-learning.com

After you have saved the changes you will see three additional tabs at the top of the screen that provide details of the peer connection. You can always come back to this screen by selecting the respective host in **Networking | Peers**.

 Deleted peers are kept on the system and can be reactivated when you attempt to add a new host with the same address.

Peer services

The SSO supported by Moodle avoids the need to log in when roaming to a remote site. The **Services** tab contains four areas. We will currently only focus on the last two, which deal with the SSO. The enrolment and portfolio services will be dealt with later on.

There are two SSO services that represent a two-way process and both services have to be set up on both Moodle sites by the respective administrators.

Peer services can be published and subscribed. It is important to note that publication and subscription are fully controlled by the local administrator. The administrator of the *other* site will never be able to modify any of those settings on *your* site.

Publish the identity provider service to allow your users to roam to the other site without having to re-login there. Subscribe to the identity provider service to allow authenticated users from the other site to access your site without having to re-login.

Publish the service provider service to allow authenticated users from the other site to access your site without having to re-login. Subscribe to the service provider service to allow your users to roam to the other site without having to re-login there.

Take the two collaborating universities we mentioned earlier. University A will publish the identity provider and University B will subscribe to it. Students from University A are now able to access restricted areas at University B's site without having to re-login.

	Local Users	Remote Users
Publish Identity Provider	Allow roaming	
Subscribe Service Provider	Allow roaming	
Subscribe Identity Provider		Grant access
Publish Service Provider		Grant access

Each service has a reciprocal dependency on the other server, as shown in the table. For example, the subscribed SSO (Service Provider) on the local site requires the SSO (Service Provider) to be published on the other site. To allow roaming in both directions, all four boxes on both peers in your Moodle network have to be checked by the respective administrator.

Profile fields

When a user from one site roams to another site for the first time, a local user account is created and certain profile fields will be populated by fetching the data from the remote site. The default fields can be overridden by selecting any of the shown profile fields in the provided list. This setting exists for **Fields to import** (users who roam from another site to the local site) and **Fields to export** (vice versa):

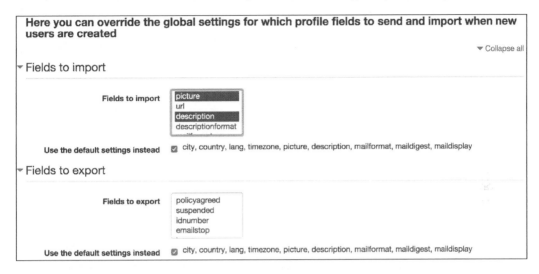

The default fields can be changed in **Networking | Profile fields**. Fields that are included on your import list, but excluded on the remote site's export list, will be ignored.

Bear in mind that no password will be stored on the remote server. As the authentication mechanism will be set to **MNet authentication**, Moodle will check the credentials every time a user logs in. We will deal with authentication next.

Network authentication

To initiate roaming, you have to enable the Moodle network authentication plugin on both sites. Go to **Plugins | Authentication | Manage authentication** and enable the **MNet authentication** option. Every time a new user from a remote site logs in to this site, a user record is created automatically.

MNet authentication

Users are authenticated according to the web of trust defined in your Moodle Network settings.

RPC negotiation timeout: `30`   The timeout in seconds for authentication over the XMLRPC transport.

These host's users can roam in to your site:

     Totara Demo: http://totara.synergy-learning.com

Your users can roam out to these hosts:

     Totara Demo: http://totara.synergy-learning.com

Save changes

In the **Settings** screen, you will see a list of which host's users are allowed to roam in to your site and which local users are allowed to roam out. Only change the **RPC negotiation timeout** parameter if users experience sporadic timeout problems roaming from one site to another.

Allowing roaming

Only users assigned to a role with the `moodle/site:mnetlogintoremote` capability are allowed to roam to other sites. By default, this **Roam to a remote Moodle** capability is turned off and has to be allowed for each role. Go to **Users | Permissions | Define roles**, or revisit *Chapter 6, Managing Permissions – Roles and Capabilities*, for details on how to do this.

To turn on roaming for all users logged in to your site, allow the capability in the **Authenticated user** role. Unless all users are allowed to roam it is worth considering creating a separate roaming role. Alternatively, if you wish to grant (or deny) access to individual users from a remote host, go to **Networking | SSO Access Control**. You have to specify a user name, a remote host (the **All hosts** option is only relevant for the community hub mode, which is discussed later) and the access level (**Allow** or **Deny**).

The newly added user name does not have to exist in either Moodle site! In the list of users, the remote hub ID is displayed and not its name. This is the internal ID, similar to a user ID, group ID, or role ID.

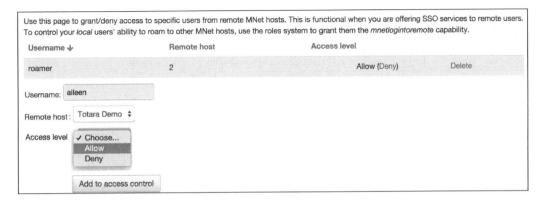

Network users can also be assigned via CSV batch upload. We described the mechanics of the **Users** | **Accounts** | **Upload users** functionality in great detail in *Chapter 5, User Management*. The relevant field in the CVS file is called `mnethostid`.

Network servers block

Moodle provides a **NETWORK SERVERS** block, which has to be added to the front page. The block cannot be configured and is only displayed if the role of the logged-in user has the `moodle/site:mnetlogintoremote` capability mentioned previously set to **Allow**:

The block acts as a launch pad from which to access remote sites. Here, in addition to our Totara Demo peer, we have already set up a link to a Mahara instance, too. Once you click on the remote server, you will be re-directed to the selected site where you can enroll to remote courses. Your first peer-to-peer network is set up!

Moodle displays a different logged in message in the header. Instead of **You are logged in as <user> (Logout)**, the message reads **You are logged in as <user> from <peer> (Logout)**. This is similar to when you masquerade as another user. When you click on your name, you access the profile of the newly created user on the remote server, which cannot be changed. The **Remote Moodle user - profile fetched from <peer>** message is displayed.

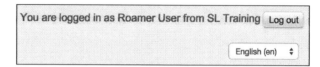

Once roaming has been enabled and configured correctly, users will also see their remote course in the **MY COURSES** section and block, respectively (in our case, only one called **Remote Course**).

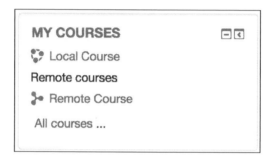

If you want to deny access for a remote user—for example, because of misconduct—go to **Users | Accounts | Browse list of users** and you will see that an additional column has been added to the list of users. Remote users cannot be edited locally, only the site they have logged in from is displayed. In the right-hand column, you select **Deny access** to revoke access to the site. To reverse the operation, select **Allow access**.

First name / Surname	Email address	Department	City/town	Country	Last access ⇧	Edit	
Admin User	admin@synergy-learning.com		Holwood	United Kingdom	53 secs	🖉	
Roamer User	aileen@null.com		Heidelberg	Germany	9 mins 6 secs	(Allow access) 🖉	Deny: SL Training
Admin User	syn-admin@null.com		Holywood	United Kingdom	39 mins 42 secs	(Deny access) 🖉	Allow: SL Training

Network enrolment

This last step is optional and is only required if you wish to grant an administrator in one Moodle system the permission to enroll local users in remote courses, and the other way round. This is useful if you run a shared course that is located on your server, but learners from the remote site should be participants. To minimize the administrative effort at your end, you grant the remote administrator the right to take on this task, which is limited to courses you have specified.

First of all, on the local site (that is, the one that grants the rights to the remote site), go to **Plugins | Enrolments** and enable the **MNet remote enrolments** plugin. This allows the local server to receive enrolments from its remote counterpart. In the **Settings** screen, you have the ability to change the default role (**Student**) for MNet enrolments.

Now, go to **Networking | Peers**, select the remote host, and click on the **Services** tab. Publish and subscribe to the **Remote enrolment service**. This grants remote administrators the right to enroll students on your site and allows local students to enroll in courses on the remote site, respectively. This step has to be repeated on the peer.

Both Moodle sites have now been configured to allow communication between the two servers and courses are set up to enroll remote students. Make sure you activate the **MNet enrolment** method inside your course (see *Chapter 4, Course Management,* for details).

When you go to **Networking | Remote enrolments client**, you will see a list of remote hosts where local users are enrolled. When you click on a host, courses offered for remote enrolment are displayed. You can then edit the enrolments in the same way you would manage users in a local course.

Available courses on Totara Demo

Course short name	Course full name	Role	Action
⚙ **Miscellaneous**			
Remote	Remote Course	Learner	Edit enrolments

Moodle hubs

A Moodle or MNet hub is similar to a peer-to-peer network, the only difference being that it accepts connections from multiple Moodle and Mahara servers. While this could be set up manually using a number of peer-to-peer connections, the hub mode automatically accepts any hosts that try to connect to it. Potentially, this is a big time and maintenance saver, but at the cost of opening up your site to other Moodle instances.

A public learning portal that contains resources to be shared across a number of sites is typically implemented using the hub mode. Each Moodle instance that wishes access to the portal has to be configured to connect to the hub.

Once Networking has been turned on, choose the Moodle site that will act as a hub and go to **Networking | Manage peers** to turn on **Register all hosts**. Effectively, a hub is a regular Moodle site that operates in a special mode.

All hosts are treated like peer-to-peers, with the exception that the **Review host details** tab is empty. All the other settings are identical to the peer-to-peer parameters. You might decide that traffic (that is, authentication and enrolment) should only go one-way: from the different Moodle sites to the hub. You control this by the **SSO-Publish** and **SSO-Subscribe** options under the **Services** tab:

	SSO (IP)	SSO (SP)	Enrolment
Moodle hub	Subscribe	Publish	Publish
Connecting site	Publish Subscribe	Publish Subscribe	Subscribe

Integrating Mahara or Totara Social

According to its website (`https://mahara.org/`), Mahara is an open source eportfolio, weblog, résumé builder, and social networking system, connecting users and creating online learner communities. Mahara is designed to provide users with the tools to demonstrate their life-long learning, skills, and development over time to selected audiences. It has recently become very popular in vocational and academic settings.

Totara Social is an enterprise social learning platform designed to facilitate learning in an online social environment within an organization. Totara Social has been built using Mahara Core and re-uses the networking functionality.

Mahoodle!

Moodle and Mahara (nicknamed Mahoodle) can be easily integrated via the Network function. A very good setup guide can be downloaded from `https://wiki.mahara.org/images/d/d5/Mahoodle.pdf`. We only cover the basic networking-related settings required to establish a link between the two systems. More details can be found in the *Mahara documentation*.

It is assumed that Moodle networking (authentication, role permissions, and so on) has been configured as explained in the previous section. It is further assumed that a recent version of Mahara or Totara Social has been set up and networking components have been installed.

Due to the fact that both Mahara and Moodle use the SSO mechanism of the networking feature, you can configure Moodle so that logged-in Moodle users can navigate to the Mahara site and, without the need to login, start using the e-portfolio system. If users don't have an account on Mahara, their user data will be imported from Moodle and used to populate their Mahara account.

Mahara networking

After logging in to Mahara/TSocial as an administrator, go to **Administration | Configure Site | Networking** and set **Enable networking** and **Auto-register all hosts** to **Yes**. Once this has been confirmed, the screen looks very similar to its counterpart in Moodle, which is not surprising since both modules have been programmed by the same development team:

WWW root	http://social.synergy-learning.com/
	This is the URL at which your users access this Totara Social installation and the URL for which the SSL keys are generated.
Public key	-----BEGIN CERTIFICATE----- MIIEMDCCA5mqAwIBAqIBADANBakqbkiG9w0BAQUFADCBxzEIMAkGA1UEBhMCZ2Tx ... xXxK0Q5fH+AUuFOT+2AVSpNXp8pkYmnEeYnrYTrd2uhcY8DWgRJnyzrPKOpaJJkE JuXfpdqOfDFtu5J0iSHxE7vyhxA= -----END CERTIFICATE-----
	This public key is automatically generated and rotated every 365 days.
SHA1 Fingerprint	00:C6:71:F4:CD:91:28:91:5B:E2:2B:E7:06:0F:09:53:78:0D:28:26
MD5 Fingerprint	71:8E:A7:86:36:50:40:A5:86:9B:93:E9:3D:FE:01:F8
Public key expires	03 January 2016, 9:39 AM
Enable networking	Yes ⬍
	Allow your Totara Social server to communicate with servers running Totara LMS and other applications.
Auto-register all hosts	Yes ⬍
	Create a tenant record for any host that connects to you and allow its users to log on to Totara Social.
	Save changes
Delete this key	Delete

Now that Mahara Networking has been enabled, go to **Admin Home | Institutions** (Mahara) / **Admin Home | Tenants** (TSocial), add a new institution/tenant, and enter its name and display name. At this stage you can leave all other entries, including the hidden locked fields, at their defaults.

Once you have submitted the values, you will be directed to a similar looking screen where you have to select **XMLRPC – Authenticate by SSO from an external application** and **Add** it to the list of supported authentication plugins. This will open a new window, where you have to enter the XML RPC options.

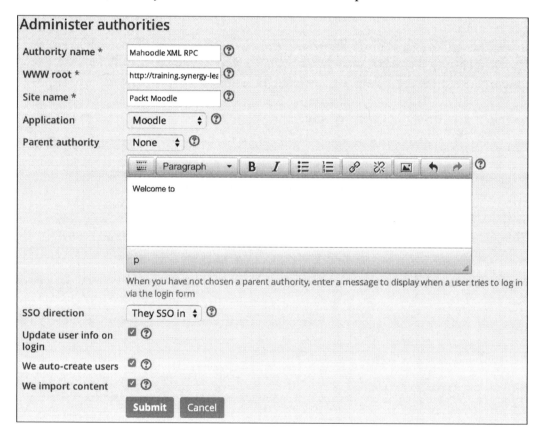

The previous screenshot is the equivalent of the **Peers** and **Services** settings in Moodle.

Option	Description
Authority name	Descriptor of the service
WWW root	URL of your Moodle system

Option	Description
Site name	Description of your Moodle system
Application	Moodle or Mahara/Totara Social
Parent authority	Select another entry if you allow multi-authentication
SSO direction	**They SSO in** (allowing roaming from Moodle to Mahara/TSocial) and **We SSO out** (vice versa)
Update user info on login	Synchronize user data at every login, otherwise only on account creation
We auto-create users	A user record is created when a remote user authenticates for the first time
We import content	Support for the Mahara portfolio plugin (see later)

Adding Mahara to Moodle

Now go back to your Moodle system and add a new host in **Networking | Manage peers**, but this time change the **Application type** from **Moodle** to **Mahara**.

The host details will be displayed and you will have to save them. Then you have to configure the SSO Identity and Service providers as you did earlier.

Once this has been successful, you will see that the Mahara site has been added to the **Network servers** block on your front page (see the block shown earlier). And that is it! Now your users can smoothly move forward and backward between Moodle and Mahara without the need to re-login or multiple browser windows.

The Mahara portfolio

We covered Moodle portfolios in great detail in *Chapter 8, Moodle Plugins*. All available portfolio plugins at **Plugins | Manage portfolios** work out-of-the-box, except the one that allows the exporting of content to Mahara. It is shown as **Disabled** by default until **Portfolio services** have been enabled on the **Services** tab of the Mahara peer (**Publish** and **Subscribe** to both). Once this has been successful you can enable the Mahara portfolio plugin and will be confronted with the following settings:

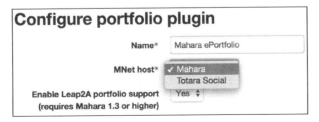

The **Name** is the entry that will appear when exporting content. Select the **MNet host** if you have connected to more than one Mahara/TSocial site. By default all content is transferred as files and stored in a dedicated **Incoming** directory in Mahara. If you use Mahara 1.3 or higher, you can **Enable Leap2A portfolio support**, which transfers content in a context-sensitive way. For example, when a user exports a forum entry in Leap2A format, Mahara will import it as a journal entry instead of a file.

 Make sure the **We import content** setting has been selected in the XMLRPC authentication plugin in Mahara.

Some related functionality that might be of interest is a set of plugins (catering for portfolio assignment submission) that comprises three Moodle add-ons (`https://wiki.mahara.org/index.php/System_Administrator's_Guide/Moodle//Mahara_Integration/View_Submission`). These only work in Mahara and are not supported in Totara Social:

- **Local-Mahara**: This Moodle plugin provides you with the functionality to get listings of a user's Mahara views from within Moodle and submit a Mahara assessment view to Moodle instead of a Mahara group

- **Mahara portfolio assignment**: This Moodle assignment type allows students to select and submit a Mahara view from within Moodle

- **Outcomes artifact**: This Mahara artifact allows the grading of Mahara portfolios using Moodle outcomes

On the same page, you will also find a **Portfolio assignment submission** plugin, which allows the submission of Mahara pages to a Moodle assignment.

The Moodle Community Hub (Moodle.net)

According to Moodle Docs, a *community hub provides a directory of courses for public use or for private communities*. It effectively facilitates the creation of a course portal, where each site can either be a receiver, a sender, or both. The concept has the potential to change the way Moodle courses are advertised and potentially sold by publishers and learning institutions or shared by the community.

Community hubs are not to be confused with Moodle hubs as they are two very distinct concepts. Moodle hubs are for connecting two or more Moodle sites, allowing students to participate in courses outside their institution. Community hubs are like yellow pages where courses are searched, advertised, and shared. An optional payment module has been planned for the future, opening up the facility for commercial course provision.

Users can enroll and import courses from `https://moodle.net/` via the
COMMUNITY FINDER block. We are not dealing with this, as it is not an
administration task. You will find more information about the community hub itself
including a good video at `https://docs.moodle.org/30/en/Community_hubs`.

Instead, we will be looking at the option of creating your own private community
hub, for example for a network of schools or a number of customers. Parts of
this section follow the structure on `https://docs.moodle.org/30/en/Hub_`
`administration`.

A community hub is a standard Moodle site that is run in hub mode. While it is
possible to use an existing Moodle site as a hub or vice versa, it is not recommended
to do so as the front page is being replaced with a search facility, as shown in the
following screenshot:

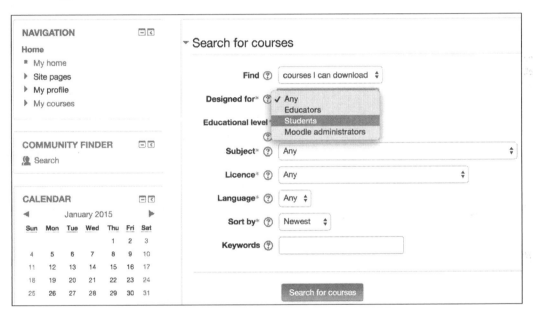

To create a hub server, you will have to go through the following steps:

1. Install a fresh copy of Moodle (see *Chapter 1, Moodle Installation* for instructions)

2. Install the Moodle Hub server plugin directly from `http://github.com/moodlehq/moodle-local_hub` or `https://moodle.org/plugins/local_hub` in your `/local/hub` directory (see *Chapter 8, Moodle Plugins*, for details on installing third-party add-ons)

3. Once this has been successful, you should see a new sub-menu called **Hub** at the bottom of the **Site administration** section:

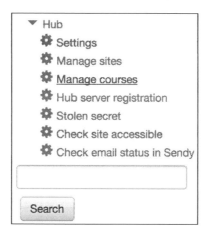

4. Enable web services and enable the XML-RPC protocol in **Plugins | Web services | Manage protocols** (see *Chapter 15, Moodle Integration*, for details of web services)

5. Optionally, configure **ReCAPTCHA** in **Plugins | Authentication | Manage authentication** (see *Chapter 5, User Management*, for details of user management)

6. Set up **SMTP** in **Plugins | Message outputs | Email** (see the *Communication* section in *Chapter 9, Moodle Configuration*)

7. Once you have managed all these steps, go to **Hub | Settings** to provide the following self-explanatory settings of your hub:

Hub version	Tuesday, 7 June 2016 (2014073000)
Name* ⑦	Packt - Moodle Administration 3
Enabled ⑦	☑
Recaptcha ⑦	☐
Privacy ⑦	Don't publish this hub or courses (Private hub) ⬍
Language ⑦	English ⬍
Description* ⑦	This site is accompanying the authoring of Moodle Administration 3 by Packt Publishing (www.packtpub.com)
Contact name* ⑦	Alex Büchner
Contact email* ⑦	packt@synergy-learning.com
Keep current image ⑦	☑

[PACKT
PUBLISHING]

Image ⑦	Choose a file...
	You can drag and drop files here to add them.
Password ⑦	
	Show more...

The next step is for other sites to register to your hub. This takes place in **Server | Hubs**. Either select a public hub or enter the **Private hub URL** and a **Password,** if specified. The information to be provided is identical to when you initially register your site with `https://moodle.org/` (see *Chapter 1, Moodle Installation*, for details). Once you have submitted the details and successfully entered the ReCAPTCHA, your site is registered with the hub. This means that users of this site can publish and share courses with users of other sites also registered with the hub. The external Moodle site and your hub are not connected, nor do users become authenticated with your system. It only allows for exchange and collaborative work on courses published on the hub.

You can see all sites that are registered at your hub at **Hub | Manage sites**:

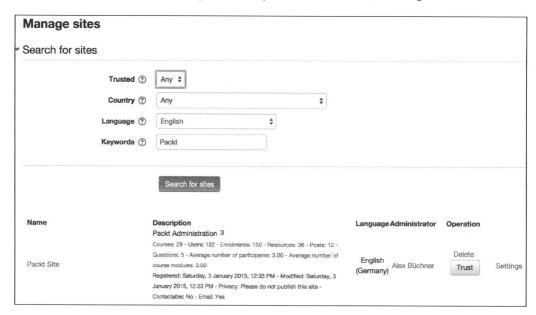

Once you **Trust** a site, it can access your hub via the **Community finder** block.

As soon as courses have been submitted to your hub (via the **Publish** link in the **Course administration** section), you can manage them via **Hub | Manage courses**.

You have the ability to delete courses and change whether they are visible to other users. You can also download or visit the courses, depending how they have been configured by the external party.

The hub server creates a number of roles, users, and web services that must not be modified or deleted!

You can also register your hub with `https://moodle.org/` (**Hub | Hub server registration**). Make sure your hub is not private. Once approved, it will appear in the public list on `https://moodle.net/`.

Internally, each site has been allotted a secret token for identification purposes. If you feel that this has been used maliciously in any way, choose **Hub | Stolen secret**, search for the compromised site, and select **Mark as stolen**. Sites related to this token are going to be removed from the site listing and a message will be sent to the site administrators asking them to re-register. Anybody trying to register with this secret will be asked to generate a new secret for this hub server.

Secret: 35da7d1ee496d88956b4089047238726 Mark as stolen

We only covered how to set up a community hub and how to manage sites and courses that have been registered and published, respectively. Details on tasks that can be performed by non-administrators—such as searching a course on a hub, downloading and restoring a course, as well as enrolling in a remote course—are covered in detail in the Moodle Docs at `http://docs.moodle.org/en/Community_hubs`.

Summary

In this chapter you have learned how to network disparate Moodle (and Totara) systems. After providing an overview of Moodle networking, we covered some prerequisites and security issues. We then dealt with peer-to-peer networks, MNet hubs, and Mahara/Totara Social integration.

The networking facility that is available in Moodle introduces a new dimension to virtual learning environments. Disparate systems can be connected logically and roaming from one Moodle site to another can be facilitated. This opens up entirely new opportunities whether it is among entities within your organization or with external sites.

The covered Moodle Community Hub will allow the creation of communities of practice, provide a facility to enable enrolment in courses on remote sites, and will offer a vehicle for publishers to sell online content. It is still early days, but it can be expected that this novel concept will become highly popular with educators, once it has acquired a certain momentum.

Configuration Settings

The objective of this appendix on configuration settings is to provide you with a list of parameters that can be modified in config.php and the impact that each of the values will have.

We will first examine config.php and explore what types of parameters are supported by Moodle. After providing this overview, we will look at two types of configuration settings:

- **Administration settings**: These are settings that are available via the Site administration menu, but that can be locked with values specified in config.php.
- **System settings**: We distinguish between default and supplementary configuration values. The former will have been created by the installer and are mostly required for Moodle to function; the latter are parameters that change various Moodle behaviors.

Configuration reference: an overview

The configuration file config.php contains a number of settings and variables that heavily influence how Moodle operates. It is located in the main directory of your Moodle system ($CFG->dirroot) and can be edited with any text editor.

 Be careful when modifying config.php! Moodle depends heavily on its content and any faults can cause the software to malfunction.

It is recommended you create a backup of the `config` file before modifying it, so you can roll back to it in case of problems. Also, make sure the file permissions are set properly as the file contains the database username and password. In a Linux environment, the `owner` should be `root`, the `group` also `root`, and the permissions set to `644`.

```php
<?php  // Moodle configuration file

unset($CFG);
global $CFG;
$CFG = new stdClass();

$CFG->dbtype    = 'mysqli';
$CFG->dblibrary = 'native';
$CFG->dbhost    = 'localhost';
$CFG->dbname    = 'packt';
$CFG->dbuser    = 'packt';
$CFG->dbpass    = 'packt';
$CFG->prefix    = 'mdl_';
$CFG->dboptions = array (
   'dbpersist' => 0,
   'dbport' => '',
   'dbsocket' => '',
);

$CFG->wwwroot   = 'http://packt.ab.local';
$CFG->dataroot  = '/var/www/packtdata';
$CFG->admin     = 'admin';
//$CFG->debug    = 5;
$CFG->directorypermissions = 0777;
...
```

The `config.php` values we are interested in are the ones that start with a dollar symbol. Each parameter has the following information format:

`$<object>-><parameter> = <value>;`

The `<object>` parameter is the part of Moodle in which the parameter is used (`$CFG` or `$THEME`). Third-party modules or custom distributions might have introduced their own objects—for example, `$TOTARA`. We will focus on `$CFG` objects as these are most relevant to administrators.

The `<parameter>` is the name of the configuration setting. Each setting has a unique identifier.

The `<value>` parameter is the type of value the parameter accepts. This depends on the type of the setting. The following table provides information for each of the key types:

Type	Moodle Field	Values
Binary	Checkbox	True or 1 and False or 0.
Numeric	Number	The number itself.
String	Text	Text has to be surrounded by single quotes.
Password	Password	Passwords have to be surrounded by single quotes.
List	Pull-down menu	Each value is represented by a number or a string. Unfortunately, there is no consistency for the allocation. For example, while the debug parameter accepts the values 0, 5, 15, 6143, and 38911, the sitemailcharset parameter accepts 0, EUC-JP, and GB18030! The easiest way to find out what values are valid is to change the values in Moodle and check the config change report (see later). Alternatively, you can check the mdl_config table in the database.
Array	Multi-select menu	The comments in the List type apply to this type, too. Values are separated by commas. Again, check the config change report to be on the safe side.

Each parameter has to be terminated by a semi-colon. To comment out a parameter, precede it with two forward slashes.

Before we deal with the different types of setting, we'll discuss a number of tools that might come in useful. As there is no list of available settings, you have to generate your own. To do so, execute the following shell command in your `$CFG->dirroot`:

```
grep -r -h -o '\$CFG->[a-z][[:alnum:]_]*' . | sort -u
```

This will generate a list of all available $CFG variables in alphabetical order. The command moosh config-get (see *Chapter 14, Moodle Admin Tools*) only provides you with a list of all config variables that can be set via Moodle's admin interface and are stored in mdl_config; it excludes the *hidden* variables we are interested in here.

Moodle provides a report that lets you monitor all changes to any config settings via the administration interface. You can find the report at **Reports | Config changes**:

Config changes

Page: (Previous) 1 2 3 4 5 6 7 8 9 10 11 12 13 14 15 16 17 18 ...43 (Next)

Date ↑	First name / Surname	Plugin	Setting	New value	Original value
Monday, 25 August 2014, 9:50 AM	Alex Büchner	theme_essential	analyticsclean	1	
Monday, 25 August 2014, 5:25 AM	Alex Büchner	core	statsruntimestarthour	5	0
Monday, 25 August 2014, 5:25 AM	Alex Büchner	core	statsruntimestartminute	30	0
Thursday, 21 August 2014, 8:12 PM	Alex Büchner	logstore_database	dbuser	root	packt
Thursday, 21 August 2014, 8:12 PM	Alex Büchner	logstore_database	dbpass	********	********
Thursday, 21 August 2014, 8:10 PM	Alex Büchner	logstore_database	dbtable	packt_log	mdl_log

If you are experimenting with configuration variables, you might consider installing the Admin setting presets block, which lets users with the site configuration capability export the site settings to .xml presets, import other sites .xml presets, load (totally or partially) presets settings and rollback the applied changes if necessary.

While its key objective is to package, distribute, and deploy the same settings (presets) to multiple Moodle sites, it can also be used to back up and restore the configuration settings of your Moodle site. You find more information about the tool at https://docs.moodle.org/en/Admin_presets_block. You can download the latest version of the plugin from https://moodle.org/plugins/view.php?plugin=block_admin_presets. Once the block has been installed (see *Chapter 8, Moodle Plugins*), you can select which settings to package up in a preset:

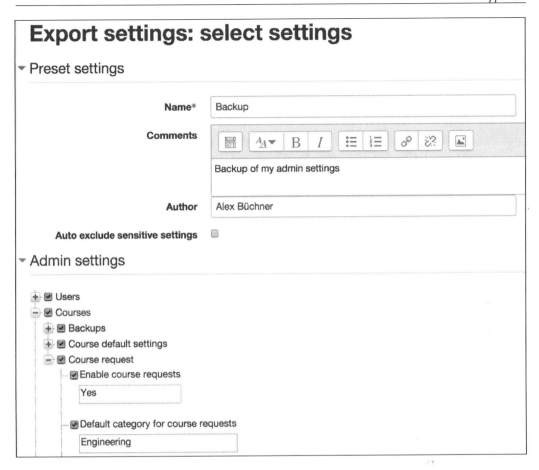

Configuration reference: administration settings

Each parameter in the **Site administration** menus can be configured via `config. php`. If a value has been set via this method, it is effectively hard-coded and cannot be changed via the Moodle interface, not even by the administrator.

For example, you might want to make sure that an administrator does not, even by accident, turn on HTTPS for logins. Activating this would lock everybody out of the site if no SSL certificate is installed. To do this, enter the following line in `config.php`:

```
$CFG->loginhttps=false;
```

How do you know what the parameter is called? Go to the respective setting in Moodle (in this case **Security | HTTP security**) and you will see the name of the parameter underneath the label.

 You can search for any parameter in the search box of the Administration block.

If the value is specified in `config.php`, Moodle will display **Defined in config.php** beside the parameter, which indicates that the setting cannot be changed by the user. Invalid values are also shown for these hard-coded settings. In the following screenshot, the **Debug messages** value is incorrect while the **Display debug messages** value is correct:

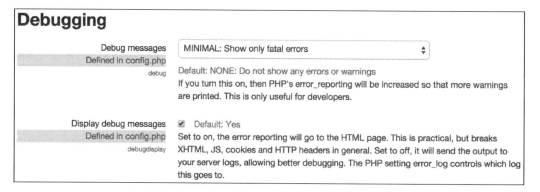

If you wish to force plugin settings, you have to put them in a special array called `forced_plugin_settings` (see the reference to optional parameters later).

Configuration reference: system settings

This is the actual reference for configuration settings. The following explanations have been taken from help pages, forum posts, and comments in source code.

Default parameters

These are settings that have been created by the installer, derived from `config-dist.php`. Most parameters are compulsory in order for Moodle to operate, so be careful when changing any of them. The parameters are listed in the order in which they appear by default in `config.php`:

Parameter	Description
`$CFG->dbtype (String)`	The database system that is used. The four valid values are `mysql` (MySQL), `pgsql` (Postgres), `mssql` (MS SQL Server), `mariadb` (MariaDB), and `oci` (Oracle).
`$CFG->dblibrary (String)`	Currently only `native` is allowed as an entry.
`$CFG->dbhost (String)`	The name of the database host. `localhost` or `127.0.0.1` (if the database is located on the server); as Moodle or any other URL (resolved or unresolved), if located on another server.
`$CFG->dbname (String)`	The name of the database.
`$CFG->dbuser (String)`	The username of the database account.
`$CFG->dbpass (String)`	The password of the database account.
`$CFG->prefix (String)`	By default, all tables in Moodle are prefixed with `mdl_`. This should only be changed if you run multiple Moodle installations using the same database.
`$CFG->dboptions (Array)`	Values that determine database behavior: `dbpersist` (whether an existing database connection can be reused to improve performance, potentially decreasing stability); `dbsocket` (when a UNIX socket is used); and `dbport` (a TCP port if different from default).
`$CFG->wwwroot (String)`	This is the full web address (including `http://`) where Moodle has been installed.
`$CFG->dataroot (String)`	This is the absolute directory name where Moodle's data dictionary is located. The directory has to be readable and writable, but must not be accessible via the Web.
`$CFG->admin (String)`	The admin pages in Moodle are located in the admin directory. If this has to be changed then specify the new directory here as some ISPs don't allow its usage. This approach can also potentially help secure the site from attacks.
`$CFG->directorypermissions (Special)`	These are the permissions (in Unix format) that are applied for directories Moodle is creating. The default is `0777` (`rwx`).

Optional parameters

Almost 400 parameters set in `config.php` are not set by the installer, nor can they be modified via the Moodle administrator interface. These optional parameters allow you to modify the behavior of Moodle without the requirement to change any code.

We only cover a representative list of settings, ignoring those that are only relevant to developers and designers. We have also disregarded obsolete and obscure parameters, as well as ones that have a counterpart in the admin settings. Parameters have been listed in alphabetical order and some have been grouped together for simplicity. Available types are array (*A*), binary (*B*), numeric (*N*), list (*L*), and string (*S*):

Name	Type	Description
`admineditalways`	*B*	Set to `true`; enables admins to edit any post at any time.
`amf_introspection`	*B*	Security setting for the AMF web service protocol.
`apacheloguser`	*N*	Logging Apache: `0=off`, `1=user id`, `2=full name`, `3=username`.
`apachemaxmem`	*N*	Memory threshold over which Apache children will be reaped after they finish serving the request.
`bounceratio`	*N*	Default is `20`. See `$CFG->handlebounces`.

`customfiletype`	*A*	Adding entries to **Server** | **File** types, for instance
		
		 ```$CFG->customfiletypes = array(```
		 ``` (object)array(```
		 ``` 'extension' => 'mobi',```
		 ``` 'icon' => 'document',```
		 ``` 'type' => 'application/```
		 ```x-mobipocket-ebook',```
		 ``` 'customdescription' =>```
		 ```'Kindle ebook'```
		 ```)```
		 ```);```

`customfront pageinclude`	*S*	You can replace the front page with your own version; `https://moodle.org/` uses this approach. Only the center area will be replaced — not the header, footer, or blocks.

Name	Type	Description
customscripts	S	Enabling this will allow custom scripts (to be specified with the full path name) to replace existing Moodle scripts. For example, if `$CFG->customscripts/course/view.php` exists then it will be used instead of `$CFG->wwwroot/course/view.php`. At present this will only work for files that include `config.php` and are called as part of the URL (`index.php` is implied). Custom scripts should not include `config.php`. Warning: Replacing standard Moodle scripts may pose a security risk and/or may not be compatible with upgrades. However, this is useful when having to patch a particular page without actually overwriting the core code.
debugusers	S	Comma-separated list of user IDs that always see debug messages.
defaultblocks	A	Default block variables for new courses—for instance, `participants`, `activity_modules`, `search_forums`, `admin`, `course_list`, `news_items`, `calendar_upcoming`, `recent_activity`. This setting can be overridden for different course types, such as `defaultblocks_social`, `defaultblocks_weeks`, and `defaultblocks_topics`.
dirroot	S	The absolute directory name where Moodle has been installed.
disablemycourses	B	This setting will prevent the `My Courses` page being displayed when a student logs in. The site front page will always show the same (logged-out) view.
disableonclickaddoninstall	B	Disables the on-click plugin installation feature and hides it from the server administration user interface.
disablestatsprocessing	B	Prevents stats processing and hides the GUI.
disableupdateautodeploy	B	Disables update deployment. Useful when deployment is done via Git checkouts.
disableupdatenotifications	B	Disables update notifications. Useful when deployment is done via Git checkouts.

Name	Type	Description
disableusercreationon restore	B	Completely disables user creation when restoring a course. Enabling this setting results in the restore process stopping when a user attempts to restore a course requiring users to be created.
divertallemailsto	S	Divert all outgoing e-mails to this address to test and debug emailing features.
emailconnectionerrorsto	S	E-mail database connection errors to someone. If Moodle cannot connect to the database, then e-mail this address with a notice.
filedir	S	You can specify an alternative to dataroot.
filelifetime	N	Seconds for files to remain in caches (default is 86400 = 24 hours). Decrease this if you are worried about students being served outdated versions of uploaded files.
filepermissions		Same as directorypermissions in the default parameters, but for created files.
forced_plugin_settings	A	Plugin settings have to specified as an array of arrays: array('plugin1' => array('param1' => 'value1', ('param2' => 'value2', ...), ('plugin2' => array('param1' => 'value1', ('param2' => 'value2', ...), ...);
forcedefaultmymoodle	B	If set, the My Moodle page cannot be customized by users.
forcefirstname forcelastname	S	To anonymize user names for all students. If set, then all non-teachers will always see this for every person.
gradeoverhundredprocentmax	N	If unlimitedgrades is set, you can specify a maximum value (1 = 100%, default = 10).
handlebounces	B	This is for handling e-mail bounces. Used in conjunction with minbounces and bounceratio.
httpswwwroot	S	wwwroot for SSL pages.
includeuserpasswordsin backup	B	Allows user passwords to be included in backup files. Use only if you can guarantee that all your backup files remain private as password hashes can be unencrypted.

Name	Type	Description
keeptempdirectorieson backup	B	Keeps the temporary directories used by backup and restores them without being deleted at the end of the process. See also the *Managing courses in bulk* section in *Chapter 4, Course Management*.
langlocalroot	S	Alternative directory to `$CFG->dataroot/lang`.
maildomain	S	Your e-mail domain.
mailprefix	S	md1+ is the separator for Exim and Postfix, md1- is the separator for qmail.
minbounces	N	Default is 10. See `$CFG->handlebounces`.
mnetkeylifetime	N	Number of days when the networking key expires. See *Chapter 16, Moodle Networking*, for details.
noemailever	B	When working with production data on test servers, no e-mail or other messages should ever be sent to real users.
opensslcnf	S	Location of the `openssl.cnf` file.
passwordsaltmain	S	Random string added to the md5 password hash. See *Chapter 11, Moodle Security and Privacy*, for details.
preferlinegraphs	B	This setting will make some graphs (for instance, user logs) use lines instead of bars.
preventscheduledtaskchanges	B	Disables editing of tasks in **Server | Scheduled** tasks.
reverseproxy	B	Enable when setting up advanced reverse proxy load-balancing configurations and port forwarding.
showcrondebugging	B	Adds debug info to cron output.
showcronsql	B	Show executed SQL queries during cron execution
skiplangupgrade	B	Disables automatic language update and lets translators (lang pack maintainers) keep their `moodledata/lang/*` to update manually.
sslproxy	B	Enable when using external SSL appliance for performance reasons.
supportuserid	N	E-mails to supports can be redirected to another user.

Name	Type	Description
tagsort	S	Sorts tags in a tag cloud by a specified field, `default = 'name'`.
themedir	S	Adds an extra theme directory outside `$CFG->dirroot`.
themeorder	A	Priority of themes from highest to lowest. Default is `array('course', 'category', 'session', 'user', 'site')`.
themerev	B	Prevents theme caching.
tracksessionip	B	Moodle will track the IP of the current user to make sure it hasn't changed during a session. This will prevent the possibility of sessions being hijacked via XSS, but it may break things for users using proxies that change all the time (such as AOL).
trashdir	S	Alternative location for `$CFG->dirroot/ trashdir`.
undeletableblocktypes	A	The blocks in this list are protected from deletion—for example, `navigation`, `settings`.
upgradekey	S	Password protection during the upgrade process. See `https://docs.moodle. org/en/Upgrade_key` for details.
upgraderunning	B	Pretends a Moodle update is running.
upgradeshowsql	B	Shows executed SQL queries during upgrades.
usepaypalsandbox	B	For testing PayPal using the PayPal developer sandbox.
usezipbackups	B	Use ZIP compression in backups instead of the default TGZ.

Index

A

B

Thank you for buying
Moodle 3 Administration
Third Edition

About Packt Publishing

Packt, pronounced 'packed', published its first book, *Mastering phpMyAdmin for Effective MySQL Management,* in April 2004, and subsequently continued to specialize in publishing highly focused books on specific technologies and solutions.

Our books and publications share the experiences of your fellow IT professionals in adapting and customizing today's systems, applications, and frameworks. Our solution-based books give you the knowledge and power to customize the software and technologies you're using to get the job done. Packt books are more specific and less general than the IT books you have seen in the past. Our unique business model allows us to bring you more focused information, giving you more of what you need to know, and less of what you don't.

Packt is a modern yet unique publishing company that focuses on producing quality, cutting-edge books for communities of developers, administrators, and newbies alike. For more information, please visit our website at www.packtpub.com.

About Packt Open Source

In 2010, Packt launched two new brands, Packt Open Source and Packt Enterprise, in order to continue its focus on specialization. This book is part of the Packt Open Source brand, home to books published on software built around open source licenses, and offering information to anybody from advanced developers to budding web designers. The Open Source brand also runs Packt's Open Source Royalty Scheme, by which Packt gives a royalty to each open source project about whose software a book is sold.

Writing for Packt

We welcome all inquiries from people who are interested in authoring. Book proposals should be sent to author@packtpub.com. If your book idea is still at an early stage and you would like to discuss it first before writing a formal book proposal, then please contact us; one of our commissioning editors will get in touch with you.

We're not just looking for published authors; if you have strong technical skills but no writing experience, our experienced editors can help you develop a writing career, or simply get some additional reward for your expertise.

Moodle Administration

ISBN: 978-1-84719-562-3   Paperback: 376 pages

An administrator's guide to configuring, securing, customizing, and extending Moodle

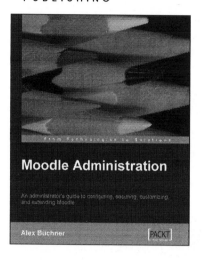

1. Moodle has evolved from an academic project to the world's most popular virtual learning environment. During this evolution, its complexity has risen dramatically and so have the skills that are required to administer the system.

2. While there is plenty of literature for Moodle course creators, there has been, with the exception of some disparate online resources, no Moodle administrator book. Until now!.

Moodle 2 Administration

ISBN: 978-1-84951-604-4   Paperback: 420 pages

An administrator's guide to configuring, securing, customizing, and extending Moodle

1. Moodle has evolved from an academic project to the world's most popular virtual learning environment. During this evolution, its complexity has risen dramatically and so have the skills that are required to administer the system.

2. Moodle 2 Administration is a complete, practical guide to administering Moodle sites. It covers how to set up Moodle in any learning environment, configuration and day-to-day admin tasks, as well as advanced options for customizing and extending Moodle.

3. The author, who has been administering systems for over 20 years, has adopted a problem-solution approach to bring the content in line with your day-to-day operations.

Please check **www.PacktPub.com** for information on our titles

Moodle 2.0 First Look

ISBN: 978-1-84951-194-0   Paperback: 272 pages

Discover what's new in Moodle 2.0, how the new features work, and how it will impact you

1. If you are planning to upgrade your site to Moodle 2.0 and want to be up-to-date with the latest developments, then this book is for you.

2. It highlights changes to the standard installation and explains the new features with clear screenshots, so you can quickly take full advantage of Moodle 2.0.

3. With its step-by-step introduction to the new features of Moodle 2.0, this book will leave you confident and keen to get your own courses up and running on Moodle 2.0.

Moodle 2.0 Multimedia Cookbook

ISBN: 978-1-84951-470-5   Paperback: 256 pages

Add images, videos, music, and much more to make your Moodle course interactive and fun

1. By including multimedia, such as animated graphics, bitmaps, photographs, and videos in your Moodle site, you can enhance the enjoyment of your site's users and sustain their attention.

2. Moodle 2.0 Multimedia Cookbook provides a plethora of recipes showing you how to manage, link, and embed different multimedia resources into your Moodle course – ideal if you don't have the time to read a long tutorial and want quick ways to enhance your Moodle course.

3. This cookbook will give you inspiration and teach you to do things you never knew were possible. Link, edit, and embed bitmaps and photographs to illustrate your lessons.

Made in the USA
Lexington, KY
24 March 2017